To Martin —
donum auctoris,
12 July 1998

ROME AND PERSIA AT WAR, 502–532

ARCA
Classical and Medieval Texts, Papers and Monographs

37

ROME AND PERSIA AT WAR, 502–532

GEOFFREY GREATREX

FRANCIS CAIRNS

Published by Francis Cairns (Publications) Ltd
c/o The University, Leeds, LS2 9JT, Great Britain

First published 1998

British Library Cataloguing in Publication
A catalogue record for this book is available from the British
Library

ISBN 0 905205 93 6

Printed in Great Britain by
Antony Rowe Limited, Chippenham, Wiltshire

parentibus optimis

Contents

Maps

Battle Plans

(All Maps and Battle Plans drawn by Maurice Clayton)

Chronological Tables

Preface

This book contains the first detailed modern account of the war fought between Rome and Persia at the opening of the sixth century A.D. Its origin lies in my doctoral thesis, *Procopius and the Persian Wars* (Oxford, 1994), which dealt not just with the events of the war but also with Procopius' treatment of them. In formulating the present monograph, however, I have concentrated on the events themselves, giving equal consideration to the various available sources. The work aims to serve a useful purpose by providing a basic, accessible narrative of the war, and by setting it in the broader context of Roman-Persian relations in late antiquity; for the cursory nature of the accounts hitherto offered by larger-scale works has inevitably led to inaccuracies, and, on occasion, actual errors.

Those to whose erudite advice and patient encouragement this work is indebted of necessity make up a long list; it is a pleasure to acknowledge their help.

In the first place my thanks go to the supervisor of my thesis, James Howard-Johnston, who has continued to take an interest in it even after its submission. I am grateful also to John Matthews and Cyril Mango, who helped to supervise the thesis. Its transformation into the present work was begun during tenure of a research fellowship at the Department of Classical Studies at the Open University, to which I am also grateful for a visiting research fellowship in 1996. My colleagues there, especially Chris Emlyn-Jones, Lorna Hardwick and Janet Huskinson, were supportive and understanding towards one whose research interests diverged so much from their own. The year I subsequently spent at the University of Ottawa (1995–6) was likewise stimulating: I profited from discussions with Richard Burgess in particular, while Thanos Fotiou, Roger Blockley and Eleanor Dickey all provided advice and support. Mention should also be made of the excellent library facilities available there, and in particular the map library of the University of Ottawa. The transformation was completed at the Department of Religious Studies and Theology at the University of Wales, Cardiff, during tenure of a Cardiff fellowship. There I learnt much from discussions with Frank Trombley and John Watt, whose knowledge of epigraphy and Syriac respectively have proved most useful; their research for a forthcoming translation and commentary on the Chronicle ascribed to Joshua the Stylite has given rise to many interesting discussions, of great benefit to the present work.

A particular debt of gratitude is owed to Maurice Clayton, who spent long hours drawing up the maps and plans for the book. His remarkable eye for detail revealed surprising inconsistencies in earlier maps, which, it is hoped, have been avoided in this work.[1] If mistakes remain, they are to be ascribed rather to the author than to the cartographer. The battle plans, it should be stressed, are schematic, since the precise site of the engagements is uncertain.

Thanks are due also to Theodora Antonopoulou, Jonathan Bardill, Elizabeth Beaumont Bissell, Freddie Beeston, Peter Heather, Robert Hoyland, Barbara Levick, Sam Lieu, Anne McCabe, Fiona Nicks, Zeev Rubin, Irfan Shahîd and Marina Wilks for advice, suggestions and references; and to Lorise Topliffe, the sub-librarian of Exeter College, Oxford, for her help and willingness to purchase relevant works. Michael Whitby kindly read through a draft of chapters five and six and made valuable comments. Much needed assistance in improving my prose style I owe to Francis Cairns, Sandra Cairns, Robin Seager and (at proof stage) Neil Adkin; for its remaining infelicities I remain culpable.

The text aims at clarity: I have tried to set out concisely my views on events, their sequence and their chronology, even where controversial and complex issues lie behind my decisions, in the hope of preventing disputes and minutiae from impeding the progress of the narrative. The reader will find the sources and detailed argumentation for a paragraph or half-paragraph of my text accumulated in a single

---

[1]   As an example: on map 3 (of the eastern frontier, p.20), the passes of Saphcae and Illyrisis have been placed in sequence, rather than in parallel, following Honigmann, *Ostgrenze*, Karte 1. Dillemann, *Mésopotamie*, 235–6 and fig.33, puts Illyrisis by the fort of Aphoumon, north of Pheison, Saphcae on the Batman Su (Qulp) by Attachas, and the Bitlis pass further east; however Proc.'s text (*Aed.* III.3.3) strongly implies that travellers had to pass through both Saphcae and Illyrisis, which would mean that Honigmann's map is correct. The uncertainty about the location of these passes may be seen by comparing the maps of Honigmann and Dillemann with that of Whitby, *Maurice*, 255 (cf. idem, *History*, map 4), who places Saphcae east of Illyrisis, but nowhere near Akbas or Attachas (or the Batman Su); in 'Arzanene' he gives some consideration to the topography of the region, but does not deal with the passes.

The map of the eastern frontier provinces in 529 (p.167) omits Theodorias, a province carved out from Syria I and II in that year: the change had no significant impact on the defences of the east.

footnote (which can as a result sometimes be rather lengthy); this method was adopted so as to keep the text free of references to primary and secondary material, while also avoiding excessive numbers of footnotes.

The glossary is based in part on the one I prepared for *Theophanes: Chronographia* tr. C. Mango and R. Scott (Oxford, 1997), and the material is re-used by permission of Oxford University Press.

Lastly it remains to thank the various institutions which have contributed financially to the publication of the book: the Department of Classical Studies at the Open University; the Faculty of Arts, University of Ottawa; and the Department of Religious Studies and Theology, University of Wales, Cardiff.

Cardiff, May 1997

Addendum

Since the completion of this book, several relevant important works have come to my attention. Nearly all of them are concerned with the Arabs and bear chiefly upon my appendix devoted to southern Arabian affairs. F. de Blois, 'The date of the "martyrs of Najran" ', *Arabian archaeology and epigraphy* 1 (1990), 110–28, argues strongly in favour of dating the death of the martyrs at Najran to 523 rather than 518. He would therefore place the start of the Himyarite era in 110 rather than 115 B.C., whereas I have preferred 110 (cf. p.226 n.4 below). De Blois' chronology is accepted by C. Robin, 'La Tihama yéménite avant l'Islam: notes d'histoire et de géographie historique', *Arabian archaeology and epigraphy* 6 (1995), 222–35, who also offers translations of several of the Himyarite inscriptions mentioned in the appendix. M. Whittow, 'Rome and the Jafnids: Writing the History of a Sixth-Century Tribal Dynasty', *JRA* 11 (1998), likewise accepts this chronology, which may be developing into a consensus. Those inclined to accept the later dating should note that the two main events affected are the martyrdoms themselves (in 523) and the subsequent conference at Ramla, to be placed in 524 rather than 519. In contrast, the date of the Ethiopian invasion of Himyar is securely fixed in 525 (see below, pp.230–31). One further important contribution on Arab matters generally, also by C. Robin, should be noted — 'Le royaume Hujride, dit "Royaume de Kinda", entre Himyar et Byzance', in *Comptes rendus de l'Académie des Inscriptions et Belles-Lettres* (1996), 665–714; I have not, however, seen this article myself. I regret also that A. Luther's doctoral thesis, *Die syrische Chronik des Josua Stylites* (Berlin, 1997), appeared too late for me to take into account.

One point of detail in de Blois' article should be addressed here, since it serves only to confuse unncessarily the already problematic chronology of events in southern Arabia. de Blois (p.120) argues from Procopius' words at I.20.1 — ὑπὸ τοὺς χρόνους τοῦ πολέμου τοῦδε ('at about the time of this war') — that the Ethiopian invasion of Ella Asbeha and the installation of Sumyaf'a Ashw'a as king of Himyar took place in 531, the precise moment at which Procopius' digression is inserted. He therefore argues for two Ethiopian invasions, one in 525 (or possibly 527) and another in 531, which installed Sumyaf'a Ashw'a (Esimiphaeus) as king. There is, however, no need to multiply the number of Ethiopian interventions. Procopius' vague phrase refers just to 'this *war*', not the battle of Callinicum in 531; and although it is not entirely clear when Procopius would have placed the start of 'this war', the events he narrates at I.12.1–4 concerning the renewal of hostilities between Rome and Persia in the Transcaucasus probably took place c.524 (see below, p.142). Procopius' words thus provide no grounds for inferring an additional Ethiopian invasion in 531.

Lastly, it has come to my attention that I omitted to mention one re-markable clause said to have been included in the treaty which brought the war to a conclusion (dealt with in ch.10.ii). According to Agathias, the Persian king Khusro required that Justinian allow back to their homes the Roman philosophers who had recently sought refuge at his court; and he further insisted that they enjoy intellectual freedom within the empire. Since no other source records the episode, however, it must be viewed with caution; even if true, it was clearly not an important element of the treaty.[1]

November 1997

---

[1]   Agathias II.30.3–4 with Evans, *Justinian*, 70 (inclined to accept the episode) and Cameron, *Mediterranean World*, 134 (more sceptical).

A note on conventions adopted

(1) Articles and books are cited by an abbreviated title; the full reference will be found in the bibliography, although short entries in encyclopaedic works are not included there. Likewise abbreviations of primary sources are to be found in the bibliography; generally an attempt has been made to follow those used in the *Prosopography of the Later Roman Empire (PLRE)*, although references simply to Proc. refer to the *Wars*.

(2) Diacritics have in general been avoided in non-classical names or titles, such as Kadishaye (for Kadišāyē) or *marzban* (for *marzbān*).

(3) References to sources in Arabic or Syriac include page references to the standard translation, as indicated in the bibliography; any exceptions to this rule are noted there. Where reference is made to the original text, this is clearly indicated in the footnote. Armenian sources are cited from the translations by R. W. Thomson, with the page number of the standard edition in square brackets.

(4) References to *PLRE* are by the name of the individual concerned, with the singular exception of Belisarius, whose entry is so lengthy that page numbers have been given for ease of reference.

(5) The term 'Mesopotamia' is used in several senses. On the one hand, it may refer to the whole area known as the Fertile Crescent; on the other, it may designate the Roman province of Mesopotamia, which was divided by the Emperor Diocletian into two smaller provinces, Mesopotamia and Osrhoene. The term 'Mesopotamia' consequently became somewhat ambiguous, referring sometimes to both Mesopotamia and Osrhoene (i.e. the old province of Mesopotamia), sometimes only to the former; this ambiguity remains in the text, but has been avoided wherever possible. See Dillemann, *Mésopotamie*, 105–7 with p.109 n.101 below.

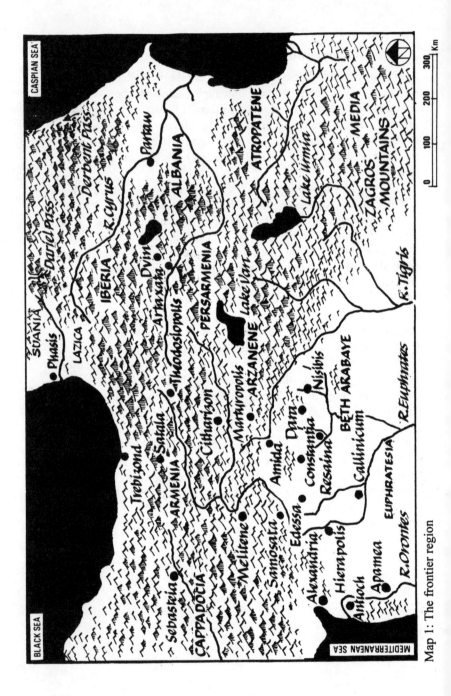

Map 1: The frontier region

xvi

I
Introduction

The war of 502–532 may be compared in certain respects to the Peloponnesian War. It lasted only three years longer than the conflict between Athens and Sparta, and like it caused great damage to both protagonists. Both wars were interrupted by a substantial break in hostilities; and lastly, the war of 502–532 attracted in Procopius a historian in the mould of Thucydides, the contemporary recorder of the Peloponnesian War.[1] Yet, although Thucydides' work was designed to be definitive, historians have been scrutinising the Peloponnesian War ever since: numerous modern histories are available. No such attention has been accorded to the war of 502–532, despite much recent interest in the east Roman frontier in late antiquity.[2]

The present work is divided into three sections. The first aims to sketch the background to the outbreak of hostilities from both the Roman and the Persian perspective; consideration is also given to the sources employed in drawing up an account of the war. In the second section, the opening phase of the conflict — usually referred to as 'the Anastasian War' — and its aftermath are recounted; thanks mainly to a detailed Syriac history of these years, the Chronicle once attributed to Joshua the Stylite, a full and nuanced picture emerges.[3] The third and final section covers the concluding years of the war, sometimes known as the first Persian war of Justinian, for which our chief source is Procopius. The last chapter considers the peace which brought the war to

---

[1] See below ch.4 on the sources for the war; ch.4 iii.a on Procopius in particular. That the war of 502–532 was regarded by contemporaries as a single conflict, despite the lengthy period of peace in the middle, is clear from both Mal. 478 and the inscription found at Hierapolis (on which see ch.10 iii). On the devastating nature of the war, cf. Theoph. A.M. 5998 (149.5–6).

[2] A century ago, several German scholars analysed episodes of the war in detail, cf. e.g. Hofmann, *Zur Kritik*, Haury, *Zur Beurteilung*, part III, *idem*, 'Procopiana (2)', Kirchner, *Zur Beurteilung*, and Merten, 'De bello'. Since then the war has only been dealt with briefly in larger scale works, such as Stein II, 92–101, 267–73, 283–96, Bury, *HLRE* II, 79–89 and Evans, *Justinian*, 114–18.

[3] I have been fortunate to have had access to a new translation of this work (Trombley–Watt, *Chronicle*) and to have been able to discuss points of detail with the translator and commentator.

an end and the brief period which elapsed before conflict broke out
anew in 540. An appendix concerning the Roman attempt to involve
the kingdoms of the southern Red Sea in the war is included. This was
a bold and not hopeless initiative by the Emperor Justinian, and hence
deserves consideration; but since it failed to yield any tangible results,
it was felt that it should not intrude on the main narrative of events.[4]

Since this work focuses on the war of 502–532, other contemporary
events inevitably receive little mention. Numerous general histories of
the sixth century, and of Justinian's reign in particular, are available,
and provide a more rounded treatment of the period.[5] One of the most
important issues to contemporaries of the war, though it played no
significant role in it, was that of doctrinal affiliation;[6] a brief overview
of the matter may be of service nonetheless. By the late fifth century
the eastern Roman empire, for the most part Christianised and subject
to a Christian emperor, was polarised over the outcome of the Fourth
Ecumenical Council. This had taken place at Chalcedon, near Constantinople, in 451 and had acknowledged Christ 'in two natures',
human and divine. To many Christians, particularly those in Egypt,
such a definition verged on the heresy of Nestorius, and they resolutely
refused to accept the decision of the Council. These opponents of
Chalcedon, commonly termed Monophysites by modern historians,
gained ground as the fifth century progressed: the Emperor Anastasius,
during whose reign the war broke out, was highly unpopular in the
imperial capital and elsewhere because of his rejection of the Council.[7]
But on his death in 518 the throne fell not to any of his nephews — the
most eligible, Hypatius, was absent from the capital at the time — but

4   Proc.'s excursus on the region, one of our main sources, interrupts his narrative of the
war, and has been regarded as an attempt to deflect attention from Belisarius' defeat
at Callinicum; so Smith, 'Events', 448 and Cameron, *Procopius*, 147. Cf. Whitby,
Maurice, 215–16 on the importance attached to the region by both powers: when
Khusro I finally annexed Himyar (Yemen) c.575, '[t]he Romans regarded this
peripheral Persian success as an attack on their vital interests; it therefore increased
Justin II's suspicions of Persian intentions and his own enthusiasm for war' (Whitby,
op. cit., 216; cf. also Proc. II.3.40–41).
5   E.g. Bury, *HLRE* II, Stein II; more recently, Moorhead, *Justinian*, Evans, *Justinian*.
6   Cf. Whitby, *Maurice*, 213–14: Christians usually presented a united front when faced
by non-Christian adversaries.
7   A good basic introduction to the disputes over Christ's nature in this period is
available in Evans, *Justinian*, 72–8. For more detail cf. Daniélou–Marrou, *The First
Six Hundred Years*, 348–68 and Gray, *The Defense of Chalcedon*, 17–61. On the term
Monophysite, cf. e.g. *ODB* II.1399. Stein II, 157–85, on Anastasius' anti-
Chalcedonian stance and the consequent unrest in parts of the empire (most notably in
the Balkans, caught up in the revolt of Vitalian from 513 or 514).

to the *comes excubitorum* Justin.[8] He lost no time in reviving the
fortunes of the Chalcedonian camp, assisted by his nephew Justinian.
Early in Justin's reign the anti-Chalcedonians were harshly persecuted,
but well before Justinian came to the throne in 527 a more conciliatory
line had evolved.[9] The opening years of Justinian's rule were not without hope of some sort of reconciliation between the two sides; the
opposition of the emperor's wife Theodora to the Council was significant in paving the way to a rapprochement. As the war drew to a close
and Constantinople recovered from the devastation of the Nika riot in
January 532, negotiations between the representatives of both sides got
underway in the capital. They came to nothing, however, and four years
later the eastern provinces witnessed a renewed persecution of prominent anti-Chalcedonians.[10]

It remains in this introduction briefly to set the war of 502–532 in
the broader context of the struggles between Rome and Persia in the
sixth century. Superficially, little changed between the opening of this
war in 502 and that of the next in 540. In both cases the Persians
invaded to find the Romans woefully unprepared, and succeeded in
capturing or holding to ransom several important cities. Although
Roman defences were greatly improved after the Anastasian War and
during the late 520s, it appears that the lessons of 502 were quickly
forgotten. Fortifications, particularly those west of the Euphrates, were
left unrepaired, and troops were sent away to serve in the west. Yet an
important change in the circumstances, and perhaps also the attitude, of
the Sasanian kingdom had taken place. Whereas in 532 the Romans
believed it possible to return to the peaceful days of the fifth century,
the Persians viewed the situation in a different light. No longer so
occupied in warding off the Hephthalite Huns, their enemy on the
central Asian steppes, they not unnaturally turned their attention to
other neighbours. Justinian's engagements in the west did not escape
King Khusro, nor the fact that the emperor had been prepared to pay
11,000 lbs. of gold to secure peace in 532. The opportunity to gain

---

[8] See Vasiliev, *Justin I*, 68–77 and Greatrex, 'Flavius Hypatius', 120–21 on Justin's
     accession. Greatrex, *art. cit.*, 135–6, for an attempt to explain his election.
[9] Cf. Vasiliev, *Justin I*, 221–50, Stein II, 223–35, Evans, *Justinian*, 108–10.
[10] Stein II, 235–6 (on Theodora), 376–85 (on the negotiations and their aftermath); also
     Evans, *Justinian*, 110–11, and Brock, 'The Conversations', 87–91. On the Nika riot,
     Evans, *op. cit.*, 119–25 and Greatrex, 'Nika riot'. John of Tella (on whom see ch.10
     iii) was one of those who suffered in the renewed persecutions of the late 530s.

further large quantities of gold from the Romans was too tempting for Khusro to pass over.[11]

By starting two wars in the sixth century gratuitously — at least in the opinion of the Romans — the Persians irremediably altered the atmosphere of great power relations. The twenty-one year war unleashed by Khusro in 540 inflicted much more serious damage on Roman territory than the previous conflict, and left many Romans eager for revenge, unhappy with the continuing payments to the Persian treasury.[12] Justin II's decision to take the offensive must be seen in this light, as a reaction against the more pacific policy of Justinian in the east. The next conflict, at the start of the seventh century, was to be no longer a struggle over boundaries, but a war of annihilation. The war of 502–532 was therefore not a turning point in Roman-Persian relations: Justinian, along with the inhabitants of the east, sincerely believed that the peace concluded in 532 would be enduring, if not eternal.[13] Khusro, as far as is known, had no pressing reason for renewing hostilities in 540; his raid was essentially opportunist. But it was that invasion of 540, and the sack of Antioch in the course of it, which shattered the notion of potential peaceful co-existence between the two powers. Thenceforth war, punctuated by temporary truces, became the normal situation in the east: only from 561 to 572 and from 591 to 602 were the two powers at peace before the overthrow of the Sasanian kingdom by Heraclius.[14]

---

[11] See Trombley, 'War and Society', *ad init.* on the predatory warfare of Khusro and his successors; also Whitby, *Maurice*, 208 on Roman views on Persian opportunism. Evans, *Justinian*, 118–19 notes Proc. I.26.1–4, testifying to Khusro's awareness of Justinian's western ventures and to his continuing appetite for payments. It is highly unlikely that Khusro was concerned about whether Justinian would eventually turn against the Persians; the speeches to Khusro, where this is suggested, are highly rhetorical (Proc. II.2.9–11, 3.38–53). The Goths and Armenians may indeed have sought to spur the king to action by emphasising Justinian's ambition, but the unprepared state of the eastern frontier belies their insinuations.

On the waning of the Hephthalite grip on Persia by the mid-540s see Marquart, *Erānšahr*, 62–3, followed by Christensen, *L'Iran*, 297 n.2; they were destroyed in the late 550s, cf. Whitby, *Maurice*, 218 and *CHEIA*, 301.

[12] Trombley, 'War and Society', II and V, draws attention to the damage inflicted on northern Syria by the Persian invasions of the 540s, and the accompanying deportations, evident from the epigraphy.

[13] See below ch.10 iii, esp. on the evidence of John of Tella in the mid-530s, who clearly felt that the peace was secure.

[14] Cf. Isaac, 'The army', 125–9, on hostility towards the Persians at the Roman court, though he seems to regard it as inherent, rather than developing over time. Whitby, *Maurice*, 206, sees the 502–532 war as marking the opening of a new phase in Roman-Persian relations.

II
Historical Background

i) Introduction

> And the Persians will arise in his [Anastasius'] times and will over-
> turn with the sword the cities of the East together with the multitudes
> of the soldiers of the Roman Empire.[1]

Such was the declaration of the prophet of Heliopolis (modern Baalbek), writing soon after the first assaults of Persian armies against
Roman cities in the East at the opening of the sixth century A.D. For
this Sibyl 'in Greek dress' the Persian successes were merely the prelude to the imminent end of the world. In their wake various kings
would emerge, the Assyrians would overrun and despoil the entire east,
and so events would proceed until Christ returned to earth. The opening
of the sixth century was an anxious time for many Christians, marking
the six thousandth year since Creation. God had created the earth in six
days, and, according to the Psalmist, a thousand years were like a day
in the sight of God (Ps. 90.4); since Christ's incarnation was reckoned
to have occurred halfway through the sixth day in the life of the world
— i.e. 5500 years after the Creation — the world might be expected to
end 6000 years after the Creation, i.e. some time around A.D. 500,
opinions differing as to the precise year of the Creation.[2]

---

[1] Καὶ ἀναστήσονται ἐν τοῖς καιροῖς αὐτοῦ Πέρσαι καὶ καταστρέψουσι τὰς πόλεις
τῆς Ἀνατολῆς μετὰ τοῦ πλήθους τῶν στρατιωτῶν τῆς Ῥωμανίας μαχαίρᾳ, tr. Alexander, *Oracle*, ll.170–72, p.28 (and for what follows).

[2] Cf. Mango, *Byzantium*, 192–3, 202–4 or Lane Fox, *Pagans and Christians*, 267 for
these figures. See also Alexander, *Oracle*, 118–20, Magdalino, 'The uses of the
future', 4, and now Brandes, 'Anastasios', 26–9, 39–40 and 53–6.

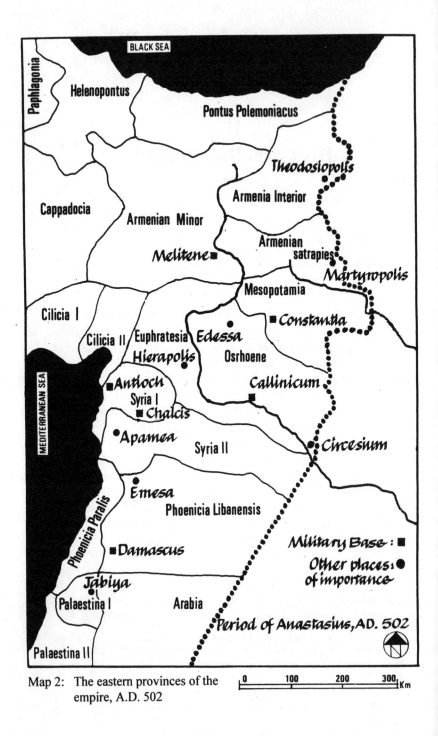

Map 2: The eastern provinces of the
        empire, A.D. 502

The prophet of Heliopolis was not alone in giving voice to such gloomy sentiments.[3] And for those living in Edessa, the chief city of one of Rome's eastern frontier provinces, the events leading up to the Persian invasion can only have seemed to confirm their concerns: the 490s witnessed plagues of boils, crop failures, a swarm of locusts, and an earthquake. Signs were seen in the heavens in November 499, and again in January 500. On the second occasion the sign resembled a spear: 'some said it was a broom of destruction, others a spear of war'. Neither group was wrong.[4]

The spear of war was raised by the Persian king Kavadh I, who entered Roman territory late in the summer of 502. No thoughts of the imminent end of the world will have clouded his mind, nor was it his objective to be the instrument of destruction of the Roman empire. Rather, Kavadh was motivated chiefly by a desire to replenish the exhausted Persian treasury; he had only just been restored to his throne with the help of powerful allies from the central Asian steppes, who expected some reward for their assistance. To prevent the possibility of these new allies, the Hephthalite Huns, turning against him, Kavadh approached the Emperor Anastasius with a request for money, but was refused; the emperor's advisers pointed out that it was hardly in Rome's interests to help the Persian king establish friendly relations with the Hephthalites.[5]

Kavadh was thus obliged to raise money by other means. Having only just recovered his throne, and with various subject peoples in revolt, he had little room for manoeuvre. He therefore united the Hephthalites and the rebellious peoples, as well as the Persians themselves, against a common enemy — the Romans. There, within the grasp of Persian forces, lay rich cities defended only by unmaintained

---

[3] Other contemporary prophecies of doom come from a 'Vision of Daniel', originally in Greek, but which survives only in Armenian, in Macler, 'Les apocalypses', 290–309 (esp. 305 on the period of Anastasius), on which see Alexander, *Oracle*, 118 and Mango, *Byzantium*, 203 (dated to c.500). Cf. the 'Tübingen Theosophy', written under the Emperor Zeno, p.167 §§2–3 with Nicholson, 'Golden Age', 11–13; see also Harvey, 'Remembering Pain', 298–301 (noting that contemporary Syriac sources were less preoccupied with the end of the world).

[4] Josh. Styl. §§28–37 (quotation from §37) for the catalogue of disasters, culminating in a further plague of locusts in 500 (§38) and a terrible famine (§§38–44). Note also the earthquakes which struck Ptolemais, Tyre and Sidon in August 501 (§47).

[5] Josh. Styl. §19 on the emptiness of the Persian treasury, §23 for Kavadh's final request for money; Proc. I.7.1 on Anastasius' advisers. *Ibid.* for Kavadh's debt to the Hephthalites, and see Blockley, 'Subsidies and Diplomacy', 68 on Persian financial problems at this point; also below, ch.3, on the situation in Persia.

fortifications and unpractised soldiers. A swift invasion, seizing the most readily available booty, and perhaps a few cities as bargaining chips, would yield rich pickings. News of the attack might in itself suffice to bring the emperor to terms and make him hand over the sums required by the Persian king: the last Persian invasion, in 440, had produced just such an outcome.[6]

To the surprise of many, however, the war thus begun would last for thirty years. The end of the world did not bring hostilities to an end, nor were sums quickly extracted from the Romans. Moreover, although peace terms were finally agreed, by which the Emperor Justinian handed over 11,000 lbs. of gold to Kavadh's successor, Khusro I, it is difficult to imagine that this compensated the Persians for the years of warfare and frontier raids which Kavadh had unleashed.[7] Worse, great damage had been done to the whole tone of Romano-Persian relations, which would henceforth be marked by ever increasing suspicion. When one side believed it had the advantage, it would now exploit it un-hesitatingly even if that meant breaking an agreement. Thus Khusro profited from Justinian's engagement in the west to attack the eastern provinces in 540 and the following years, while Justin II sought to take advantage of an Armenian uprising by attacking Persia in 572. Only with the final victory of Heraclius over Khusro II in the late 620s was the cycle broken; but the impact of the Roman success was quickly overtaken by the emergence of the forces of Islam.[8]

ii) The historical setting

The Romans arrived in the Near East in the first century B.C., when the principal power in the Lower Euphrates was the kingdom of Parthia.[9] Although the Parthians inflicted a memorable defeat on the Romans at Carrhae (53 B.C.), the Romans tended to gain the upper hand in the intermittent conflicts which arose thereafter. These wars, which took

---

[6] See below. On the incident in 440, cf. Greatrex, 'Fifth-century wars', 2.

[7] Proc. I.22.3 for the sum handed over; under Anastasius some money had also been paid to the Persians (e.g. for the return of the city of Amida, on which see below, ch.5 viii).

[8] On Khusro's attack in 540, Proc. II.5.1–13.29 with Stein II, 485–502. On Justin's in 573, Theoph. Sim. III.9.3–11 with Whitby, *Maurice*, 250–54. *Ibid.*, 206 and Howard-Johnston, 'Great Powers', 163–4, on the deteriorating relations between Rome and Persia over the sixth–seventh centuries.

[9] Debevoise, *Parthia*, 78–81 and Bivar, 'The political history', 45–68. See also Gray, 'Eastern *limes*' for a good survey of Roman relations with Parthia and Persia from this period onwards.

place under Nero (52–63), Trajan (114–17), Marcus Aurelius and Lucius Verus (161–5), Septimius Severus (194–8) and Caracalla (215–17), will not be dealt with in depth here. But it may be noted that in the first three the *casus belli* lay in Armenia.[10] Each side sought to nominate the king of this region, and reacted aggressively to any attempt by the other to foist a ruler on the country unilaterally.[11] A dispute over Armenia could thus lead to a war which might at first be played out in Armenia, but often only as a prelude to a wider conflict in Mesopotamia. From an early stage, therefore, Mesopotamia — i.e. the area of the Fertile Crescent — became the chief battleground of the two powers, although the seeds of the dispute lay elsewhere. This was also to be a feature of wars in the early sixth century. In the earlier period it had the further effect of bringing much of Upper Mesopotamia — the Roman province of Mesopotamia — under Roman control.[12]

As was realised at the time, the annexation of Upper Mesopotamia was an important development in Roman policy in the east, marking a significant extension of the empire. It did not meet with universal approval. The historian Dio Cassius disagreed with the arguments of Septimius Severus, who claimed that his newly acquired lands would protect Syria. Rather, according to Dio, they involved the Romans in wars which otherwise would not have concerned them. Dio's verdict still tends to be preferred to that of Severus, albeit on different grounds. Broader geopolitical arguments are now advanced against Severus: the Fertile Crescent, it is argued, inevitably invites conflict if two powers each control part of the region. This supposition is unconvincing. As noted above, wars fought in Mesopotamia were frequently the result of disputes which arose elsewhere, in particular in Armenia and the Transcaucasus. Moreover, following the treaty of 363 Mesopotamia enjoyed a long period of peace, as will be seen below. Dio's verdict may be applied with more justice to the further extension of Roman

---

[10]   Isaac, *Limits*, 28–30, offers a useful summary of these conflicts; see also Millar, *Near East*, 66, 99–104, 111–14, 121, 143–4, for further details and bibliography.

[11]   On this role of Armenia, see Isaac, *Limits*, 11, aptly citing Tacitus, *Annals* II.22, on the position of the Armenians.

[12]   For a description of the area in question cf. Fowden, *Empire*, 15–19. Dillemann, *Mésopotamie*, 223, argues that Mesopotamia took on the role of battleground from 363, but this development can be placed earlier. I am sceptical of Isaac's view (*Limits*, 31) that Rome displayed 'consistent expansionism' in Mesopotamia: were it not for the persisting dispute over Armenia, it seems highly questionable whether Trajan or Lucius Verus would have embarked on campaigns against Parthia. On the extension of Roman rule into Mesopotamia, Isaac, *op. cit.*, 31–2, Millar, *Near East*, 124–6.

territory in 299, but the view that two powers sharing the Fertile
Crescent must inevitably come into conflict should be rejected.[13]

At the start of the third century the Sasanian Persians emerged from
southeastern Iran to seize control of the disintegrating Parthian kingdom. By 226 Ctesiphon was in their hands, and it was not long before
their more belligerent attitude to Rome became apparent.[14] Lengthy
wars between Rome and Persia followed, for the most part ill docu-
mented by contemporary sources.[15] Decades of campaigning in Mesopotamia were brought to an end by the treaty of 363, which has often
been regarded, quite justifiably, as a turning-point in Roman-Persian
relations.[16] For almost a century and a half after this treaty only one
brief war disturbed the peace on the eastern frontier; and when, in the
sixth century, Mesopotamia once again became a battlefield, the conflicts had a rather different background from those of the fourth
century.

For this reason the circumstances of the treaty of 363 are of some
importance. The immediate background was the disastrous invasion of
Lower Mesopotamia by the Emperor Julian (361–3), who died during
the Roman retreat from Ctesiphon, and was succeeded by Jovian (363–
4). In order to extricate his army from Persian territory without overwhelming losses, Jovian was forced to agree to the terms dictated by
the Persian King Shapur II (309–79).[17] The chief Persian demand was

---

[13]   Dio Cassius LXXV.3.2–3, cited, e.g., by Millar, *Near East*, 124, who adds 'But in
       essence Dio was correct', cf. Fowden, *Empire*, 18, Lauffray, *Halabiyya*, 27–8 and
       Isaac, *Limits*, 251 (cf. 266), 'the conquest and annexation of part of this area brought
       about a state of permanent conflict between Rome and Persia.' While Isaac is right to
       emphasise the homogeneity of the inhabitants of the same area under Romans and
       Persians, this need not have heightened tension; cf. Lee, *Information*, 51–62, stressing
       the permeability of the frontier. See Gray, 'Eastern *limes*', 35, and Parker, 'Two
       books', 468, for a more positive assessment of the Roman occupation of the area. On
       Armenia as a source of dispute in late antiquity, cf. e.g. Blockley, *ERFP*, 115–17.
           The term Transcaucasus is used in the present work to refer to the region south of
       the Caucasus mountains, cf. e.g. *Merriam-Webster*, 1456 with the interesting dis-
       cussion of the ambiguity of the term in *Caucaso*, 81.
[14]   Howard-Johnston, 'Great Powers', 159–61, on the emergence of the Sasanians, cf.
       Schippmann, *Grundzüge*, 10–17 and the sources assembled in Dodgeon–Lieu, *East-
       ern Frontier*, 9–15.
[15]   See e.g. Dodgeon–Lieu, *Eastern Frontier, passim*; also 1–4 for a historical summary
       of the events, cf. Millar, *Near East*, 141–79; see too the useful brief analysis of
       Whitby, *Maurice*, 202–4. From 354, however, Ammianus Marcellinus provides a de-
       tailed account of the wars between the two sides.
[16]   Cf. e.g. Dillemann, *Mésopotamie*, 228, Isaac, *Limits*, 250–51 and Whitby, *Maurice*,
       204.
[17]   Cf. e.g. Matthews, *Ammianus*, 184–7, Blockley, *ERFP*, 26–9.

for the restoration of territory, in particular of the lands to the east and west of the Tigris in the vicinity of Nisibis. Shapur had written to Constantius II in 358 that it was his duty to recover Armenia and Meso-potamia;[18] and for much of the reign of Constantius (337–361) he had made strenuous, though largely unsuccessful, efforts to capture the various Roman fortified cities which defended the area. With the defeat of Julian he at last had the opportunity of removing the Romans from their salient in the upper Tigris region, an area which had largely passed from Persian hands by the treaty of 299 following a similarly decisive victory of the Romans.[19] After 363 no subsequent treaty between the two sides made any alteration to their borders in Meso-potamia.[20] The Sasanians, for all their earlier apparent claims to the heritage of their Achaemenid forebears, made no further attempts (until the seventh century) to annex Roman territories in the Near East.[21]

Three further points may be made with regard to the treaty of 363. First, it did not provide a solution for all the potential areas of dispute between the two sides, in particular leaving some ambiguity in the case of Armenia and Iberia, regions which therefore later brought the two powers back into contention.[22] Second, it took away an important commercial advantage hitherto enjoyed by the Romans: the most unpopular demand forced by the Romans upon the Persians in 299 was that Nisibis should be the only permitted point of entry into the Roman empire for goods emanating from Persia. From various sources it is evident that the frontier provinces of the east had prospered considerably from this situation. The cession of Nisibis to Shapur

---

[18] Ammianus XVII.5.6. Ammianus also alludes to wider Persian claims, on which see below, n.21.

[19] On the treaties of 299 and 363 see Blockley, 'Romano-Persian Peace treaties', 28–49, who stresses that there were differences in the territories involved in the two treaties, cf. *idem*, *ERFP*, 25–9; cf. also Dillemann, *Mésopotamie*, 210–20, Millar, *Near East*, 178–9, Winter, 'On the regulation', 555–71, and Warmington, 'Objectives and Strategy', 510–14. Eadie, 'The transformation', 75, notes that the Romans had made little effort to occupy the territories gained in 299 in any case.

[20] The next frontier adjustment (excluding the partition of Armenia), in 591, extended Roman control to the east, but only to the north of Mesopotamia: cf. Whitby, *Maurice*, 304.

[21] The nature of Persian aims is still disputed, as is their knowledge of their Achaemenid heritage: Fowden, *Empire*, 27–31 and Whitby, 'Persian king', 234–5 emphasise knowledge of Achaemenid affairs, while Potter, *Prophecy and history*, 370–80 and Blockley, *ERFP*, 103–4 play down Persian claims.

[22] Ammianus, XXVII.12 (warfare in Armenia between Rome and Persia, 368–70), on which see Blockley, 'The Romano-Persian Peace treaties', 36–8; also Ammianus, XXX.2.4–8, for continuing hostilities in the region in the 370s.

naturally removed this advantage.[23] Third, no payments were conceded by the Romans in 363, and there is no evidence that any were demanded by Shapur. His primary aim was clearly the recovery of territory, which in itself would bring some revenue. In the past, Shapur I had extracted a large indemnity from Philip the Arab (244–9), but at no point in the fourth century did financial matters play a part in occasioning hostilities.[24] This is in stark contrast with the fifth and sixth centuries, when, as will be seen, the question of Roman payments to the Persians takes centre stage.

The transfer to the Persians of the 'trans-Tigritane' lands, and especially of the Roman bulwark in the area, Nisibis, proved deeply unpopular with the local inhabitants.[25] But little was done to infringe the peace, and some degree of cooperation between the two powers is indicated by a law of 408, probably still in force in the sixth century, which limited to three border cities the places where goods could be imported into the Roman empire.[26] To the north, however, old scores remained unsettled. Shapur considered himself at liberty under the treaty of 363 to intervene in Armenia, an interpretation not shared by Jovian's successor in the east, Valens (364–78); the Sasanian ruler also tried to wrest control of the central Transcaucasus from the Roman-backed Iberian king Sauromaces. As a result Iberia was partitioned between the two powers,[27] although hostilities continued for most of the 370s until Valens determined to take the initiative and invade Persia. But that invasion never took place: events in the Balkans intervened, which led to the fateful Roman defeat by the Goths at Adrianople in 378.[28] Less than a decade later, in 387, an arrangement was negotiated which split Armenia between the two sides in the same

---

[23] Cf. Blockley, *ERFP*, 6–7, and Synelli, *Diplomatikes skheseis*, 86–7, with Petr. Patr. frg.14, tr. in Dodgeon–Lieu, *Eastern frontier*, 133. On the prosperity of the region, *Expositio* §22, p.156 with Blockley, *ERFP*, 29, Lee, *Information*, 62–4, and Winter 'Handel und Wirtschaft', 50–8.

[24] On Philip's payments, see Dodgeon–Lieu, *Eastern Frontier*, 45–6 with the comments of Winter, *Friedensverträge*, 97–106; see below, ch.10 n.10 on the sum handed over by Philip.

[25] Blockley, *ERFP*, 29–30, for the unpopularity of the surrender, cf. Whitby, *Maurice*, 205 and n.14 and the vivid description in Matthews, *Ammianus*, 3–4.

[26] *C.J.* IV.63.4, discussed in Isaac, *Limits*, 407. Cf. Lee, *Information*, 62 on this law and trading relations between the two sides; Synelli, *Diplomatikes Skheseis*, 94, for its continued application in the sixth century.

[27] Ammianus XXVII.12 on the events of 368–70; 12.16–17 on Iberia and its partition. Cf. Blockley, *ERFP*, 34 and 189 n.27, and Braund, *Georgia*, 260–1.

[28] Cf. Blockley, *ERFP*, 34–7, with Ammianus XXX.2.1–8.

way as Iberia had been divided. The Romans received rather less territory than the Persians, but it proved an enduring solution nonetheless.[29]

The apogee of Roman-Persian relations came at the opening of the
fifth century, when the Roman Emperor Arcadius (395–408) entrusted
the safety of his infant son Theodosius II (408–450) to the Persian king
Yazdgerd I (399–420). Even if the historicity of this episode is im-
pugned, there are many other indications of close contact between the
two powers in this period.[30] The tranquillity of the eastern provinces
was only briefly interrupted by the war of 421–422. The Persians attacked first, with some initial success; but once Roman reinforcements
were despatched the balance was restored and terms were soon
agreed.[31] While there is no evidence that the Persian monarch who led
the invasion, Bahram V (420–38), had any financial motives, it is
highly likely that his precarious position as king influenced his conduct. For, like Kavadh in 502, he had only just taken control of the
kingdom, following a period of internal strife.[32] A war against an
external foe, whose Christian proselytising was causing significant
desertions among Arabs previously loyal to Persia, would undoubtedly
prove popular. But Bahram had no need to maintain hostilities after a
few initial victories, and the sharp Roman response ensured a rapid
conclusion to the war.[33] By the time of the next Persian invasion (in
440), the needs of the Persian treasury were becoming more evident.
Yazdgerd II made an irruption into Roman territory, but was soon
dissuaded from continuing hostilities: the Roman envoy Anatolius, one
of Theodosius II's most high-ranking officials, accomplished this by
the judicious use of financial blandishments.[34]

---

[29] On this division, see esp. Blockley, 'The division', 222–34 with *idem*, *ERFP*, 42–5
(rightly stressing that the boundary was probably not precise, and only solidified
gradually).

[30] See Bardill–Greatrex, 'Antiochus', part I, for a full discussion of the episode and its
context.

[31] On this war, Greatrex, 'Fifth-century wars', 1–8, with Whitby, *Maurice*, 204 and
Holum, 'Pulcheria's Crusade', 170–71, on the terms agreed.

[32] On the disputes over the succession following Yazdgerd's death, see Christensen,
L'Iran, 279–81 and Nöldeke, *Tabari*, 91–8.

[33] Both sides claimed victory: cf. Socr. *HE* VII.20, with Nöldeke, *Tabari*, 108, according to which Bahram's emissary Narses accomplished all the king wanted in his
dealings with the Romans.

[34] Greatrex, 'Fifth-century wars', 2 and 9 n.4 for the ancient sources on this 'war', to
which add *NTh* V.3 (441), a piece of legislation on the erection of defences in
Armenia following a Persian attack. *Contra* Rubin, 'Diplomacy', 683, I cannot view
this as an aggressive measure. An invasion of some sort is described in two sermons

Sixty years of peace followed Yazdgerd's departure from Roman soil; not since the first century A.D. had the eastern frontier enjoyed such an extended period of tranquillity. Two reasons for this novel situation may be advanced. First, the sheer difficulty for both sides of making inroads into enemy territory, especially in Mesopotamia. On the Roman side of the frontier there was a mass of strongly fortified cities, which had been developed, particularly over the fourth century, as a counter to Persian invasions;[35] on the Persian side, from 363 on, lay the formidable fortifications of Nisibis, which never fell to Roman arms, despite several attempts. Second, and more important, were events extraneous to the eastern frontier: in the course of the fifth century the Roman and Sasanian governments had to face numerous opponents who endangered the very survival of each state. The eastern Roman empire, although it had freed itself from the Hunnic threat in the middle of the century, was soon confronted by other difficulties: armies of Goths in the Balkans,[36] dynastic rivalries linked to doctrinal affiliation,[37] conflicts with Vandals and Isaurians.[38] The principal menace for the Persians lay in their neighbours to the north-east, first the Kidarite, then the more powerful Hephthalite, Huns, whose power increased throughout the fifth century and encouraged instability among peoples subject to the Sasanians, such as the Armenians.[39]

Romans and Persians also shared a common foe — Huns from the area to the north of the Caucasus, including the Sabir Huns, who would sally forth periodically and cause devastation in the Transcaucasus region, an area of interest to both powers.[40] Confronting the same adversary might have been expected to bring peoples together, as it did

---

of Isaac of Antioch (XI and XII): Persians and Arabs laid waste the area around Beth Hur, identified by Dillemann, *Mésopotamie*, 232 with Kafer Hawar, close to the frontier to the north of Nisibis. Whether this raid took place during the war of 440 or later is unclear, cf. Nöldeke, *Tabari*, 116 n.1, Shahîd, *BAFIC*, 38 and Segal, *Edessa*, 168 (who dates it, without explanation, to 457); its significance should not be overrated.

[35] Cf. Lee, *Information*, 112–28 and 139–42, esp. 118, stressing advance knowledge of attacks and 141 on the role of fortifications. See also Isaac, *Limits*, 268, 425 and below, iv.c, on Roman defences (which did, however, deteriorate over the fifth century).

[36] On which see Heather, *Goths and Romans*, chs.4 and 7, Demandt, *Spätantike*, 167–9, and Blockley, *ERFP*, 35–42, 50–60, 62–7.

[37] Heather, *Goths and Romans*, ch.8, Demandt, *Spätantike*, 183–95, Stein II, 20–39.

[38] Demandt, *Spätantike*, 189, 191, Stein II, 181–5.

[39] Blockley, *ERFP*, 103–5 (on Persian constraints) and *CHEIA*, 171–2, 299–301 (on the Kidarites and Hephthalites); see below, ch.3.i and ch.6.ii.

[40] On the Sabir Huns, see *CHEIA*, 200, with Whitby, *Maurice*, 205.

with the Avars and the Persians during the siege of Constantinople in 626.[41] But in the case of the Sabir Huns it drove the two sides further apart. The issue of defence against these northern foes, in particular at the so-called 'Caspian Gates' through the Caucasus range,[42] is of fundamental importance to the outbreak of war in 502 and to the whole nature of Roman-Persian relations throughout the fifth century; it also remains a subject of dispute among scholars today. The point of contention, in the fifth century as now, is whether the Romans ever undertook to provide the Persians with some sort of financial subsidy to shore up the defences of the Caspian Gates. Whatever view is adopted on this matter will colour the whole interpretation of the exchanges between the two sides in the second half of the fifth century, when the Persians made frequent requests for money. Were the Romans opportunistic treaty-breakers in refusing many of these demands, or were they merely unwilling to submit to Persian blackmail? Was Kavadh's invasion of 502 provoked by Anastasius' unjustified intransigence, or was it undertaken 'for no reason', as Procopius (I.7.3) claims? An examination of the evidence is required.

According to the chronicle of Joshua the Stylite

> Furthermore, Romans and Persians had entered into an agreement that if they had need of each other while at war with another nation, they would assist by giving either three hundred fighting men along with their weapons and horses, or three hundred staters for each man, with the choice being made by the partner in need.[43]

He goes on to explain that only the Persians had needed to take advantage of this agreement, and that they had indeed received money from the Romans. The existence of such a treaty is apparently confirmed in a letter of Kavadh quoted by the chronicler John Malalas: the king claims to have found it mentioned in the Persian records.[44] A date for this treaty is lacking, although Joshua (§8) implies that it was in place at the latest by Peroz's day (459–84). Some scholars have sought to adduce an obscure passage of the sixth-century writer John the Lydian, but it does no more than show that the issue of the Caspian Gates was being discussed in the late fourth century. It is therefore preferable to suppose

---

[41]   On this collaboration, Howard-Johnston, 'The siege of Constantinople', 131.
[42]   On the Caspian Gates, Anderson, 'Alexander' and Braund, *Georgia*, 269, rightly equating them (in this period) with the Dariel Pass.
[43]   Josh. Styl. §8, tr. Watt.
[44]   Mal. 450. Cf. Peroz's request for either money or men, reported at Priscus frg.47.8.

that the arrangement, if there was one, was made towards the middle of the fifth century, perhaps during the reign of Peroz.[45] We know also of various embassies sent by Peroz to Leo and Zeno, as reported by the fifth-century historian Priscus of Panium. The relevant surviving fragments of his work tell of several attempts by Peroz's ambassadors to secure financial aid from the Romans; careful examination, however, shows that on each occasion the Persians had to make a case for their demands. So, if any arrangement existed, it was clearly loose in form: there was no obligation on the Romans to make contributions whenever called upon, still less had any regular payment been agreed, a claim not made by any source.[46]

It is highly unlikely then that the Romans were bound by any treaty to contribute on a regular basis to the maintenance of defences in the Caucasus. Although most of the points made above have been put forward before, they are nonetheless worth restating, since many scholars still believe in a permanent Roman obligation to pay annual subsidies to the Persians throughout the fifth century. If this were the case, then the negative responses of Leo, Zeno and Anastasius would represent clear breaches of the treaty, and Kavadh's invasion would be a long overdue act of revenge. Further, the Roman refusals to pay the sums due would imply a contempt for the Persian king and his efforts to preserve his kingdom: such a policy might then be thought to be 'indicative of a mood that prevailed in the imperial court, which was one of aversion to the very notion that the Roman Empire, which regarded itself as a universal political power, should depend for its security on the goodwill of another power with identical pretensions.'[47]

---

[45] So Blockley, 'Subsidies and Diplomacy', 63–6 on John Lydus (de Mag. III.53 [142]). Mari, 36, refers to Leo and Peroz making peace (cf. Blockley, ERFP, 75 n.32), apparently relatively early in Peroz's reign, though this is a late source (cf. Sako, L'hiérarchie, 51 and below, ch.4 n.26). Synelli, Diplomatikes Skheseis, unlike Blockley, firmly believes in the existence of this treaty, 109–111, dating it to 408/13; cf. Wirth, 'Anastasius, Christen und Perser', 128 and n.246, placing it in 442.

[46] The figure of 300 staters in Joshua is remarkably low, being the equivalent of 400 Sasanian dirhams, in turn roughly equal to only eight solidi (cf. Morony, Iraq, 39 for these ratios) and clearly is intended as an occasional sum, contra Isaac, Limits, 261. According to Josh. Styl. (§9) Peroz 'very often received money from the Greeks, not however demanding it as tribute'. Cf. Priscus frg. 41.1.9–18 and 47.9–12 for the arguments of Persian ambassadors at Leo's court in 464/5 and 467 respectively with Blockley, 'Subsidies and Diplomacy', 66. See also now Braund, Georgia, 268–71, for a good overview of the issue.

[47] Rubin, 'Dilemma', 36 (referring in this case to the Roman acceptance of Arab allies of Persia in 420). In general cf. idem, 'Diplomacy', 677–95.

It would thus become possible to suppose that the Romans had ideological objections to making payments to the Persians, even if the sums were small and the advantages great; and that throughout the fifth and sixth centuries an atmosphere of hatred pervaded Rome's dealings with the Sasanians.[48]

Yet what actually stands out from the fifth century is the favourable attitude of Roman emperors to repeated Persian requests for financial help. Theodosius II, admittedly hard pressed by circumstances, quickly offered money to Yazdgerd II in 440, as has been seen.[49] Marcian not only failed to give any support to an Armenian revolt against the Persians in 451, but is also said to have ransomed Peroz from captivity among the Hephthalites.[50] Leo and Zeno, according to the evidence of Priscus, seem to have been less accommodating; but Joshua the Stylite clearly states that Peroz had succeeded in obtaining funds from Zeno at least.[51] This evidence of more amicable Roman-Persian relations can be placed in a wider context of great power diplomacy. The sixth-century diplomat and writer Peter the Patrician likened the two powers to the two eyes or lights of the world, who should not aim at the destruction of the other.[52] From the fourth century the monarchs of either empire were in the habit of addressing one another as 'brother', and after the

---

[48] Isaac, *Limits*, 262, 265–6, 420–25, now expanded in 'Army', 127–9, 136–7.

[49] See above, n.34. Theodosius had to cope with attacks from many quarters in this year, cf. Marc. *com.* a.441.1 with Blockley, *ERFP*, 61–2 and Cröke, *Chronicle*, 85.

[50] Mari, 35, on Marcian ransoming Peroz, adding that Marcian cited the precedent of Yazdgerd I's help to Arcadius, and sent off a *dux* to ransom the king; the chronology is impossible, so if the report is credited, it must be placed under Leo or Zeno, since Peroz's reign did not overlap with Marcian's; cf. Blockley, *ERFP*, 68, on Jordanes, *Rom.* 333, concerning a peace made with the Persians under Marcian. An inscription at the Derbent pass (next to the Caspian Sea) attests Marcian's assistance in the construction of fortifications there, although doubts have been expressed regarding the trustworthiness of this evidence: Marquart, *Erānšahr*, 105, doubted by Braund, *Georgia*, 271 n.14. See also Howard-Johnston, 'Great Powers', 191–3 on the fortifications at Derbent.

[51] Blockley, *ERFP*, 74–5, believes that Priscus' account implies that no money was paid, though at 211 n.32 he notes that others consider that Leo did pay up (e.g. Synelli, *Diplomatikes Skheseis*, 111–12, Rubin, 'Dilemma', 40). See n.46 above on Priscus' evidence, Josh. Styl. §8 on Roman payments in general, §10 on Zeno ransoming Peroz. The Persians also received significant contributions from the rebels Illus and Leontius, who hoped to enlist their support against Zeno; thereafter the emperor was unwilling to offer any more money (Josh. Styl. §§15, 18).

[52] Petr. Patr. frg.13 (tr. in Dodgeon–Lieu, *Eastern frontier*, 131–2), on which much has been written. Note e.g. the references collected by Fowden, *Empire to Commonwealth*, 18 n.21; also Whitby, *Maurice*, 205 and n.15. *Contra* Isaac, *Limits*, 265, it is surely not significant that Peter attributes the simile to a Persian.

peace of 363 relations between the two sides improved still further.[53] Contacts grew more frequent, especially once the Christians of Persia were accorded freedom of worship by Yazdgerd I at the start of the fifth century.[54] An elaborate diplomatic protocol emerged for the despatch and receipt of embassies from either side; and each ruler expected formal notification if his opposite number were replaced.[55] These close relations are reflected in the Roman sources of the fifth and sixth centuries, who display a marked interest in Persian affairs, even if they are not always accurate. They attest that the Romans felt a certain respect for the Persians and were aware that harmonious co-existence was possible, although Persian demands for payments were disapproved of.[56] So while Anastasius refused to give money to Kavadh outright, this need not have been on account of any ingrained contempt for an inferior neighbour; and throughout the sixth century hostilities often ceased as quickly as they had started.[57]

---

[53] Cf. Chrysos, 'Some Aspects', 4–20 on the mutual recognition of the two sides. Blockley, *ERFP*, 115, 125 and Helm, 'Untersuchungen', 378–80, 385, rightly also stress the flexibility of titulature according to circumstance.

[54] On the role of the Christians of Persia, and of the Roman bishop Marutha, see Sako, *L'hiérarchie*, 32–45, 59–70, Christensen, *L'Iran*, 270–73 and Blockley, *ERFP*, 117–19.

[55] Whitby, *Maurice*, 204, makes this point and notes that Menander provides the best evidence for the conduct of embassies, e.g. frgs. 6.1, 9.1–3, 18.6.1–8. Note also the chapter, probably from Peter the Patrician, preserved in the *De Cerimoniis* (I.89, 398–400), which details how a Persian embassy should be received at the frontier and accompanied to the capital. On the notification of a change of ruler, also practised with other powers, see e.g. Mal. 447–8: in July 529 the *magister officiorum* Hermogenes brought Kavadh gifts to commemorate Justinian's accession (in 527). On the practice, see Chrysos, 'Byzantine Diplomacy', 32, Kazhdan, 'The notion', 13–14 and Lee, *Information*, 169.

[56] Note (for instance) Proc. I.6.19, 7.34: praise for Kavadh (and I.3–6 on Persian history), Blockley, *Menander*, 23, pointing to frg.16.1.26–8, 56, on Menander's condemnation of Justin II's unprovoked declaration of war in 572, with Whitby, *Maurice*, 253. Note too the speech Theophylact assigns to Khusro II at IV.13.6–7 (cf. IV.11.7), in which the dangers of leaving the Persian kingdom to be destroyed are set out; cf. also Frézouls, 'Les fluctuations', 224–5, on Roman realism in the east. On the Roman distaste for payments, cf. Menander frg.20.2.16–23 with Blockley, *Menander*, 25 n.106.

[57] Thus the phase of the 502–532 war which started under Anastasius was effectively over by 505 (see below); and Justin II's war begun in 572 was soon suspended by a truce in 574, extended in 575, cf. Whitby, *Maurice*, 254, 258–9. Cf. Chrysos, 'Some Aspects', 4, 11, for a similar view; for a different interpretation, see Isaac, 'Army', 129–32 and Rubin, 'Diplomacy', 678–9, 686.

iii) Geographical setting

The preceding section dealt with the broad sweep of Roman-Persian relations over the centuries. This section will discuss the impact that the military campaigns and diplomatic manoeuvrings of the two powers had on the frontier zone. A brief overview of the geography of the area will be followed by a consideration of the state of defences at the close of the fifth century, including physical structures in the form of city fortifications, and manpower, i.e. the army on the ground.[58]

From the Transcaucasian kingdom of Lazica, the ancient Colchis, to the frontier post of Circesium at the confluence of the rivers Khabur and Euphrates, the territories of the two powers adjoined one another. To the south of Circesium lay the Syrian desert, an area which both powers were content to leave in the hands of Arab tribesmen.[59] The nature of the frontier north of Circesium varied considerably, depending largely on geographical and demographic conditions. Thus, to proceed northward from Circesium, the area of southern Osrhoene as far as Thannuris was sparsely inhabited. Here Arabs were accustomed to launch raids across the Khabur, taking advantage of the dense woodland, and the Persians also tried to use this as a screen for an invasion in 354.[60] Between Thannuris and the area around Nisibis lies the central plain of Mesopotamia. Situated inside the *isohyet* — the area within which more than 200 mm of rain falls each year — the clay soil is amenable to cultivation. Significant tracts of the area were desert, however, and the danger of invasion was always present.[61] The whole plain is punctuated by impressive *tells*, mounds where once fortresses had been placed. In late antiquity too cities and forts of

---

[58] Cf. the useful survey of Lee, *Information*, 49–66, esp. on movement across the frontier. A broader geographical outline of the region may be found in Isaac, *Limits*, 9–12, Fowden, *Empire*, 15–19 and Kennedy–Riley, *Desert Frontier*, 24–7.

[59] Cf. Proc. *Aed.* II.8.3–4, cited by Isaac, *Limits*, 251, and below on the Arabs. On the term Transcaucasia, see n.13 above.

[60] Dillemann, *Mésopotamie*, 35 on this area, with Millar, *Near East*, 484; cf. Dillemann, *op. cit.*, pl.V and 66 on the meagre remains of the woodland today. *Ibid.* 108–10 on the forts of the region, cf. Proc. *Aed.* II.6.14–16 (on Saracen raids) and Ammianus XIV.3 (esp. 3.4 on the *solitudines Aboraeque amnis herbidas ripas*). Note, however, Lauffray, *Halabiyya*, 51–63, on irrigation systems further up the Euphrates (towards Callinicum), allowing considerable prosperity there.

[61] Dillemann, *Mésopotamie*, 35 and 68–9 on cultivation, chiefly in the foothills of the Tur Abdin; also *ibid.* 71, playing down the extent of cultivation in this area. For a good illustration of the *isohyet* and the climatic zones in the area, see Whittaker, *Frontiers*, 96 fig.26 or Kennedy–Riley, *Desert Frontier*, 26 fig.2. See also Lauffray, *Halabiyya*, 26–32, for a description of Mesopotamia and Osrhoene.

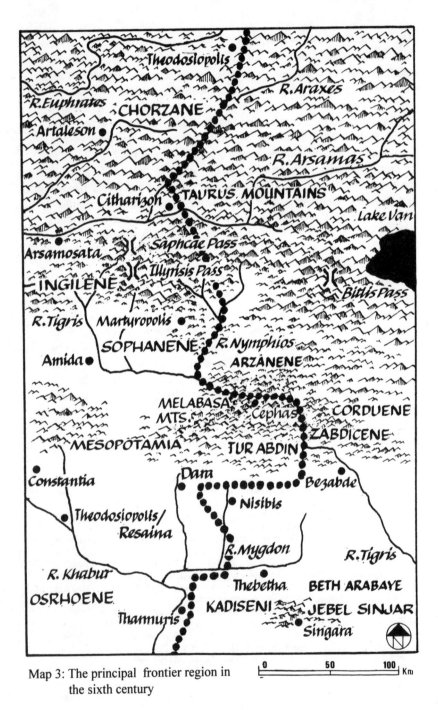

Map 3: The principal frontier region in
      the sixth century

importance were to be found here, such as Nisibis, Constantia, and (from 505) Dara.[62]

Further north, a greater density of population could be found in the Tur Abdin, the plateau separating the Mesopotamian plain from Sophanene and Arzanene. This is a limestone area, bounded to the east and west by extinct volcanoes. It provided ideal shelter for Christian communities from both persecuting emperors and invading Persians, as well as furnishing excellent building material. Since it stretches as far east as Bezabde (on the Tigris), ceded to the Persians in 363, the boundary between the territory of the two powers was not everywhere straightforward: probably for this reason Procopius believed that one Roman fort, that of Rhabdion, actually constituted an enclave within Persian territory (*Aed.* II.4.4–13). More likely it lay right on the border, which followed the Tigris past the Tur Abdin, but continued southwards where the Tigris veers east; at this point lies a basalt plain several miles wide, from which it is necessary to proceed uphill to reach the rest of the Tur Abdin plateau, an approach well guarded by Roman forts. The border then followed the foothills of the Tur Abdin to the west, past Rhabdion as far as Dara, where it turned south once again. This elevated region thus constituted an important Roman salient, flanking Persian held Arzanene to the north and the Mesopotamian plain to the south.[63]

To the north of the Tur Abdin the frontier followed the river Nymphius (modern Batman Su), a tributary of the Tigris flowing in from the north. Some 80 km to the west of the confluence of the Nymphios and Tigris lay the vital Roman border city of Amida, the cornerstone of Roman defences in northern Mesopotamia. Roman-controlled Sophanene to the west of the Nymphios was protected above all by Martyropolis; Persian-held Arzanene across the river, a personal fiefdom of the king, fell a frequent victim to Roman raids. These southern regions of Armenia were bounded to the north by the Taurus

---

[62] Dillemann, *Mésopotamie*, 35–7, 50–62 and 72–3.

[63] Dillemann, *Mésopotamie*, 29–35 for a physical description of the area with fig.2. On the inhabitants of the region, cf. *ibid.* 69, and Proc. *Aed.* II.4.14–18, noting the fertility of the foothills; also Theoph. Sim. II.1.1–3 with Whitby, *Maurice*, 200. For a convincing explanation of Proc.'s error about Rhabdion and a perceptive picture of the Tur Abdin's numerous monastic communities, see Palmer, *Monk and Mason*, 1–6. Whitby, *op. cit.*, 199–200, gives useful information on the practicalities of campaigning in this area. On the frontier line, Mango–Bell, *Churches*, iii–iv (and the map on p.185).

mountains, through which a limited number of passes permitted access; most lay in Roman hands, notably those at Saphcae and Illyrisis, facilitating north-south communications. The Persians, however, controlled the Bitlis pass, just to the west of Lake Van.[64]

As we move further north, into the Armenian satrapies, the notion of a frontier becomes more improbable. Movement grows difficult, confined to less than half the year, and even then to certain routes (usually along river valleys). Roman forts become more scattered, and are generally to be found guarding important river routes; Citharizon is an example, built during the war of 502–532 and dominating the Arsanias or (perhaps) Artaleson on the Murat Su. Before Justinian's day, moreover, no Roman forces at all were stationed in the Armenian satrapies.[65] Four days' march north from Citharizon lay Theodosiopolis, founded early in the fifth century (modern Erzurum), the first target of Kavadh in 502. In the highland region between here and the Black Sea Roman control was further attenuated: annual subsidies were paid to the wild Tzani, who nonetheless ventured forth to attack Roman cities from time to time.[66]

It was here, at the north-east frontier of the empire, that the most important developments of the Justinianic phase of the 502–532 war took place. This was due at least in part to the fluidity of the borders in this area: the boundary between the two powers in Armenia differed

---

[64]   Dillemann, 38–9 (with fig.3) and 115–24 on this region with Proc. *Aed.* III.3.1–6 (on the passes); see above Preface, n.1, on the location of the passes. Cf. Matthews, *Ammianus*, 53–5 and Adontz, *Armenia*, 9–14; Zach. IX.6 (227–8) on Arzanene being a crown possession (with considerable revenues). See also Whitby, *Maurice*, 200–1, who notes the problems caused on occasion to campaigning here by swollen rivers.

[65]   On the two forts (the location of the second is uncertain), see Proc. *Aed.* III.3.7–8, 14 and Howard-Johnston and Ryan, *Scholar*, 44 and 53–4 (Citharizon dominating the Bingöl plain); also Howard-Johnston, 'Citharizon', 203, Adontz, *Armenia*, 14–21. See too Howard-Johnston and Ryan, *Scholar*, 78–81, for a vivid description of the physical geography of this area. On the difficulties of campaigning in Armenia, Whitby, *Maurice*, 201–2 and Isaac, *Limits*, 231. Proc. *Aed.* III.1.17–29 for the lack of Roman troops stationed here until Justinian's day: the Armenian satraps provided their own forces. Cf. Winter, 'On the regulation', 559–60, on these forces in Diocletian's time and Adontz, *Armenia*, 26–37, 88–95.

[66]   Proc. *Aed.* III.5.1–12 on Theodosiopolis and the upgrading of its defences by Anastasius and Justinian, with Adontz, *Armenia*, 22–4; Proc. II.24.13 on the distance from Citharizon to Theodosiopolis. *NTh* V.3 (441) explicitly mentions Theodosiopolis in conjunction with the area recently attacked by the Persians. Proc. *Aed.* III.6.1–5 on the Tzani before their subjugation under Justinian, cf. *Wars* I.15.21–3 and Braund, *Georgia*, 289. See also Bryer–Winfield, *Pontus*, ch.1, for a description of this region.

markedly in nature from that in Mesopotamia, as Procopius observed. In Chorzane, between Citharizon and Theodosiopolis, there was no clear dividing line between the populous communities subject to each power, a situation remedied by the Emperor Justinian, who solidified the frontier by the erection of the fortress of Artaleson (Proc. *Aed.* III.3.9–14); Justinian also marked out Roman territory in Tzanica and sent troops to Lazica. This Roman tendency towards direct government had begun already in the fourth century, with the suppression of the royal house of Armenia, the Arsacids. In 488 the Emperor Zeno greatly reduced the independence of all the satrapies (bar one) in Armenia by depriving them of their hereditary rulers.[67] The Romans thus still had gains to make in the north, both by internal integration and by external conquests.

South of Martyropolis the situation was different. The location of the frontier was much better defined, particularly in the vicinity of Nisibis: Procopius refers to Dara being built at a location 28 stades from the border (I.10.14). No swift campaigns were possible here. Concentrations of forces were viewed with suspicion, and the construction of forts near the border was forbidden.[68] Perhaps on account of this delicate balance, both sides proved unwilling to disturb the *status quo* unless provoked; and when Kavadh did break the peace in 502, it is significant that he did not choose to make his initial attack here. In the area south of the Tur Abdin the fifth century witnessed quite cordial relations between inhabitants on either side of the border, which was in any case an artificial division of a region united by a common culture and language.[69] A good illustration of this comes in the 530s, when the Roman authorities were seeking to track down the anti-Chalcedonian bishop John of Tella (Constantia). He had fled to the Jebel Sinjar, a mountainous area to the south of Nisibis, in the region known as Beth Arabaye, which, like the Tur Abdin, was a haven for religious communities. The Romans informed the Persian commander

---

[67] On the fluidity of the frontier here, see Wheeler, 'Rethinking the Upper Euphrates frontier', 505–9. On the developments in Armenia, Blockley, *ERFP*, 85, *idem*, 'The divison', 231–4 and Adontz, *Armenia*, 88–95.

[68] See Lee, *Information*, 112–18, on the difficulty of concealing campaign preparations here. The ban on fortifications was probably introduced after the war of 421–422, see Greatrex, 'Fifth-century wars', 8. On the linear frontier which evidently existed here, Kaegi, 'Reconceptualizing', esp. 84–5; also Arrignon–Duneau, 'La frontière', 20–21.

[69] See Lee, *Information*, 56–64, making good use of Syriac material, cf. Millar, *Near East*, 481–8, Segal, 'Mesopotamian communities', 109–10 and Fowden, *Empire*, 18 (a grander-scale view).

at Nisibis of this, and he sent a task force of Roman, Persian and local troops to capture John. When the holy man was interrogated by the commander as to why he had crossed into Persian territory, he replied that in the peaceful times that prevailed between the two powers the frontier was scarcely evident.[70]

In fact, the chief dangers for those living on either side of the border were drought and raids by Arab tribesmen; the former could indeed cause the latter, since drought would force the tribesmen towards inhabited areas with better access to water. Such a sequence of events, described in a letter of Bar Sauma, a controversial metropolitan of Nisibis, occurred around 484, less than twenty years before the war of 502–532. Following two years of drought, Arab tribes, nominally allied to the Persians, moved up from the south with their animals and ravaged the villages in the area, intruding on Roman territory. In response, the Romans assembled a large army, summoned their own Arab allies, and demanded compensation for the actions of the Persian Arabs. The Persian commander at Nisibis, the *marzban* Kardag Nakoragan, defused the situation by persuading the Persian Arabs to restore the booty they had taken from the Romans; at the same time, the Arabs allied to the Romans were to hand back what they had seized on their expeditions. Despite further complications, a confrontation was avoided, and the two sides agreed to clarify the border so as to avoid future disputes; it may safely be presumed that the Arab allies of each side claimed they were unaware that they were encroaching on the other power's territory.[71]

---

[70] On the Jebel Sinjar, see Dillemann, *Mésopotamie*, 35 and 68. On John of Tella, cf. the *V. Ioh. ep. Tell.*, 42–6, with Lee, *Information*, 59; see below ch.10.iii for a more detailed consideration of this episode. On the porousness of the frontier, cf. Lieu, review of Lee, *Information*, *BSOAS* 59 (1996), 134–5 (with particular reference to the School of Nisibis); also Matthews, *Ammianus*, 67–8 and Elton, 'Defining Romans', 130–31 (drawing attention to the defection to the Persians of the merchant Antoninus in 357/8).

[71] *Ep.*2 of Bar Sauma in *Syn. Or.*, part 3, 532–4, a fascinating text, with Blockley, *ERFP*, 85, Isaac, *Limits*, 242–3, Fiey, *Nisibe*, 44 and Gero, *Barsauma*, 34–7 on the incident. Nisibis always retained some Roman sympathisers, cf. Segal, 'Mesopotamian communities', 133–5 and Lee, 'Evagrius', 575, 583; Bar Sauma, however, maintained close contact with the Persian king, cf. Gero, *Barsauma*, 34–7 and Lieu, review of Lee, *Information*, *BSOAS* 59 (1996), 135. Around this time, moreover, Zeno laid claim to the city: Josh. Styl. §18 with Whitby, *Maurice*, 206–7. A comparable modern fear from the 1920s of nomads being forced by drought to encroach on settled areas is noted by Lighfoot, *Eastern Frontier*, 268. Marc. *com.* reports a similar movement of tribes in 536. On Bar Sauma, see Fiey, *Nisibe*, 40–46 and

iv) Roman defences

In the period when the Roman empire was expanding, until the third century at least, to speak of Roman defence might give a misleading impression. Offence was the prime concern of emperors and generals, and early legionary camps were established at points from which strikes into enemy territory might most opportunely be made.[72] But by the sixth century the situation had changed. The strength of the Romans no longer lay chiefly in their troops, but in the walls of their cities. After Julian's invasion of 363, the Romans preferred to concentrate their resources on defence, mainly through the erection of new forts and cities, a process already under way in the reign of Constantius II.[73] The solidification of the frontier was thus begun, although, as noted above, its rate of progress varied from one area to another. The primary objective was to defend Roman lands and possessions — the Ῥωμαίων γῆ — against raiding Arab tribes (particularly in Osrhoene and Syria) or Persian armies (in Mesopotamia and further north).[74]

a) Roman allies

A vital component in the defence of the eastern frontier, alongside the regular military forces, the inhabitants of the cities, and the fortifications of the cities, was furnished by the allies of the Romans. At an

---

Labourt, *Christianisme*, 145–6. The *strata* dispute also had its origins in territorial claims by Arabs: see Isaac, *Limits*, 244–5 and Whitby, *op. cit.*, 211.

[72] Though note Severus' defensive considerations in annexing Mesopotamia, as reported by Dio, on which see n.13 above. The classic exposition of this defensive strategy is the now much criticised work of Luttwak, *Grand Strategy*, cf. also (e.g.) Lepper, *Trajan's Parthian War*, 172–3, with the criticisms of Isaac, *Limits*, 50–53.

[73] Dillemann, *Mésopotamie*, 219–22, Matthews, *Ammianus*, 54 on Constantius II's work, e.g. at Constantia and Amida.

[74] For the term γῆ Ῥωμαίων (from Proc.), see Arrignon–Duneau, 'La frontière', 19. Isaac, *Limits*, 255–60, 265–8, and Whittaker, *Frontiers*, 139–41, agreeing with Isaac, are particularly opposed to the notion that there was even any concept of a frontier. Isaac in particular seems not to be able to countenance the idea that the Romans may have wanted to defend their territory, e.g. 266: 'it is in fact obscure what the strategic aim of the Byzantine rulers was in fighting Persia'. As has been seen, his assertions are determined by his view of Roman-Persian relations on the larger scale. The arguments of the previous section have, it is hoped, demonstrated that there was a notion of a frontier, and that it was taken seriously, cf. the criticisms of Isaac by Wheeler, 'Methodological Limits', esp. 215–23 (with the articles of Kaegi and Arrignon–Duneau referred to above, n.68). Around Thannuris and to the south, however, the borders were much less clear-cut.

earlier point these had been known as *foederati*, bound to the empire by a *foedus* or treaty. In the fourth century, for instance, the Goths were recruited as *foederati*, and fought *en bloc* for various emperors; in return they received gifts from the Romans, although this did not necessarily imply any weakness on the Romans' part. In the late fifth century, however, Roman payments had become more regularised: for example, some of the Goths remaining in the Balkans in the 470s under Theodoric Strabo received pay and victuals from the Emperor Zeno. So by the sixth century *foederati* were scarcely distinguishable from *stratiotai*, ordinary soldiers.[75] But the Arab tribal groupings with which we shall be concerned, the Ghassanids and Kindites, who entered Roman service later, at the turn of the sixth century, should not be termed *foederati*; rather, they were allies, *symmachoi*, who fought under their own commanders — their phylarchs — and were not enrolled among the *stratiotai* or *foederati*.[76]

Of the allies of the Romans in the east the most important, to become yet more so over the sixth century, were the Arabs, or, as they were usually known, Saracens. These were nomadic tribesmen, who migrated with their livestock according to the seasons; they were regarded by contemporary sources — city-dwelling officials, for the most part — with distrust at best.[77] Modern writers too have been inclined to stress the threat posed by such nomads; and it is clear from ancient writers and from inscriptions that nomadic raids on Roman territory

---

[75] On the evolution of the term *foederatus* over the fourth and fifth centuries, see Heather, *Goths and Romans*, 109–15 (4th century, stressing that Roman payments need not be seen as a sign of weakness), 253–5 (5th century), with *ODB* II.794, Grosse, *Militärgeschichte*, 280–82 and Stein II, 87–8. Proc. III.11.3–4 and VIII.5.13 on the term in the sixth century; cf. also Blockley, *ERFP*, 149–50, on Roman payments.

[76] Cf. Grosse, *Militärgeschichte*, 291–4. As he points out, these *symmachoi* were the old *foederati* in all but name. See also Shahîd, *BAFIC*, 51–2, on Arab *foederati* in the fifth century; and Isaac, *Limits*, 444 on the correctness of the term 'ally'. Shahîd, *BASIC* I, xx, prefers the term *foederati* (though aware of its shift in meaning). They come under Blockley's category 2, *ERFP*, 149.

[77] On the seasonal migrations of these transhumant pastoralists, see MacDonald, 'Nomads and the Hawran', 320–22, cf. *idem*, 'The seasons and transhumance', 1–11; also Millar, *Near East*, 484–5 and Donner, 'The Role of Nomads', 73–85, esp.74–5 on the differing types of nomadism. As Shahîd, 'Ghassanid and Umayyad structures', 299–300 and 303, notes, the Ghassanids did erect buildings in the sixth century and hence cannot be viewed as purely nomadic; cf. Donner, *art. cit.*, 83, on the inevitable sedentarisation of nomads and vice versa. See also Peters, 'Byzantium and the Arabs', 102–7 on the migration routes of the Ghassanids.

were greatly feared along a line from Egypt to Osrhoene.[78] But co-operation with the Arabs was possible and was practised, for instance, in the Sinai peninsula, where one group of Arabs was paid to defend the community of Pharan from other potential raiders. For the dreaded Saracens were to be found not just outside the empire, far off in Arabia Felix, but within the provinces, such as Palaestina III, which incorporated the Sinai peninsula. The Roman authorities set up forts in various places to check depredations, which happened even well within the provinces, away from the frontiers — a testament to the ubiquity of the raiders. Yet the forts never succeeded in controlling the movement of the Arabs. A new solution had to be devised.[79]

Over the fifth and sixth centuries a more successful strategy was indeed developed. The empire decided to enlist the tribesmen as allies to supplement imperial forces, a technique long employed by the Romans with other peoples in the east and elsewhere.[80] In fact, both Rome and Persia turned to tribal groupings to strengthen their grip on territories liable to Arab raids, as well as to support their own armies in battle. While the Persians recruited the assistance of the Lakhmids, who proved valuable allies for some three centuries, the Romans used various groups at different times.[81] At the close of the fifth century came a period of change for Constantinople in her relations with Arab tribal groupings, marked by several attacks by tribesmen on various provinces, which had to be fended off by imperial commanders. The tribe which had hitherto been allied to Rome, the Salîhids, seems to have been unequal to the task of warding off these raids, and a new configuration of alliances arose. The emergent Byzantine diplomatic

---

[78] Note, e.g., Proc. I.17.48 and van den Ven, *V. Syméon Stylite*, §187, for the fear inspired by the Lakhmid king al-Mundhir, with Shahîd, *BASIC* I, 244–5. Whittaker, *Frontiers*, 137–8, for some of the earlier evidence on these incursions; also Kennedy–Riley, *Desert Frontier*, 36–9. On the wide scope of their raids, see Proc., *loc. cit.*, and Mayerson, 'Saracens and Romans', 73.

[79] Cf. Mayerson, *art. cit.*, 71–81 with *idem*, 'The Saracens and the *limes*', 35–47 on the Arabs generally, 44 on Pharan. MacDonald, 'Nomads and the Hawran', 323–7, also opposes the view that posits an inevitable hostility between nomads and cultivators. Isaac, *Limits*, 68–77, plays down the threat posed by the nomads, but cf. Parker, 'Two books', 468–70, who rightly argues that they were a cause for concern. Whittaker, *Frontiers*, 135–8, is more cautious.

[80] Cf. e.g. Braund, *Friendly King*, 91–3, on the use of allied kingdoms in the east in the first century B.C.; also Isaac, *Limits*, 235–51, on the use of nomad allies in general.

[81] On the Persians and the Lakhmids, cf. Rothstein, *Lahmiden*, 38–44 and Bosworth, 'Iran and the Arabs', 596–602. Note the presence of a large Arab contingent in the Persian army in 421–422, discussed by Shahîd, *BAFIC*, 28–31.

corps achieved a considerable success in bringing this about: the envoy Euphrasius was able to secure peace with both the Ghassanids, henceforth the principal allies of Constantinople, and the Kindites.[82]

The importance of such allies was recognised by both sides. The defection of the Arab chieftain Aspebetus in 420 had led, it appears, to a clause in the peace terms of 422, by which each side undertook not to accept any allies who defected from the other.[83] The Emperor Leo infringed this clause in 473, when he entertained in Constantinople a certain Amorcesus (Imru' al-Qays) who had moved out of the Persian orbit, and gave him the title of 'phylarch', i.e. leader of a tribe. He thus consolidated Imru' al-Qays' power on the borders of Palaestina III, where the chief had already gained control of the island of Iotabe, previously under direct Roman administration. The impression given by the whole episode — admittedly from a source thoroughly hostile to Leo — is of imperial weakness in the face of Imru' al-Qays' demands.[84]

The case of Imru' al-Qays illustrates two points about Roman dealings with Arabs: first, the weak position of the imperial authorities, and second, stemming from this, the need to reward these allies with subsidies. As long as the tribesmen were satisfied with their treatment by the Romans, they proved, on the whole, useful allies. The Ghassanids, based well within Roman territory, could be used for internal security (against Samaritan rebels, for instance), as well as for reprisal raids against Persian allied tribes.[85] They also served alongside

---

[82] On the raids on Roman territory c.500 and Euphrasius' mission, cf. Shahîd, *BAFIC*, 120–30, and *BASIC* I, 3–12; also Kawar, 'Ghassan and Byzantium' 232–55 and 'The Last Days of Salîh', 145–58, Sartre, *Trois études*, 156–62. But see now Whittow, 'Rome and the Jafnids', text to nn.2–7 for doubts on the treaty of 502. One of the attacks c.500 was conducted by the Lakhmids, which may have been an attempt to put pressure on the Romans, cf. the raids into Mesopotamia at the start of Zeno's reign (Theoph. A.M. 5966 [120.9–11]).

[83] On Aspebetus, cf. Shahîd, *BAFIC*, 40–49, for an exhaustive discussion; Blockley, *ERFP*, 57 and 200 n.38, with Rubin, 'Dilemma', 34, on the clause in 422. Note also the anger of Khusro at what he perceived to be Justinian's attempts to suborn al-Mundhir, Proc. II.1.12–13.

[84] Malchus frg. 1, on Imru' al-Qays' capture of Iotabe in 473. On his seizure of the island and its significance, cf. Letsios, 'The case of Amorkesos', 530, Shahîd, *BAFIC*, 61–90, and below, appendix. On the title 'phylarch', cf. Shahîd, *BAFIC*, 517–18 and below.

[85] Liebeschuetz, 'Defences', 495–6, on the base of the Ghassanids at Jabiya in the Golan, cf. Sartre, *Trois études*, 178–88. Cf. Paret, 'Note sur un passage de Malalas', 251–62, Sartre, *op. cit.*, 168–70, Lee, *Information*, 52–3, Isaac, *Limits*, 243 on the functions of Arab allies.

Roman forces, though here their efficacy is more open to doubt.[86] Whatever the terms of the treaty by which the Ghassanids entered Roman service — if there was a formal arrangement — it marked the beginning of an advantageous relationship for both sides. The Ghassanids, although unable to fend off every incursion by their Lakhmid adversaries, became an increasingly important element in the defence of the south-eastern frontier. When the Emperor Maurice severed relations with them in the 580s, many eastern provinces suffered considerably.[87]

The Romans placed great reliance on the Ghassanids to secure the nebulous frontier south of the Euphrates. Under Diocletian a network of forts had been erected along a road, the *strata Diocletiana*, running up from Damascus, via Palmyra, to Sura on the Euphrates — perhaps to defend the populous region west of the Euphrates (Syria and Phoenicia) which had been exposed to Persian attacks in the third century.[88] Over the fifth and sixth centuries the Roman presence here diminished, so that in 540 it was a matter of dispute between Lakhmids and Ghassanids as to who owned grazing rights in the area. The absence of Roman troops can be overstated, however, since there were units based at Damascus and Palmyra under Justinian; at Sergiopolis, on the other hand, the inhabitants had to defend themselves with the aid of fewer than 200 imperial troops in 542.[89]

---

[86] Shahîd, *RA*, 22–3 for a determined defence of Rome's Arab allies, cf. *idem*, 'Procopius and Arethas again', 335–7. Devreesse, 'Arabes-Perses', 299, for instance, is more sceptical of their worth, cf. Goubert, *Byzance*, 260 (citing Devreesse with approval).

[87] On the treaty, Shahîd, *BAFIC*, 480–81, 284, *BASIC* I, 3–12 and Whittow, 'Rome and the Jafnids', text to nn.2–7. On Maurice, Sartre, *Trois études*, 189–91, Goubert, *Byzance*, 256–7 and Shahîd, *BASIC* I, 548–9. Cf. Theoph. A.M. 6123 (335–6) on the disastrous consequences of Roman unwillingness to pay tribesmen in Palestine in 633/4 (with Kaegi, *Conquests*, 90). An enactment of 443 attests *annona* (evidently the *annona foederaticia*) being paid to Saracens, although this was being abused by local commanders, *NTh* XXIII.2 (443), on which cf. Shahîd, *BAFIC*, 49–50 and Isaac, 'Army', 131.

[88] Cf. Liebeschuetz, 'Defences', 488–9, with Isaac, *Limits*, 163–71 on the *strata*, though the latter views the forts as staging posts on a military road rather than a system of defence; but see also Gawlikowski's review of Millar, *Near East*, *JRS* 84 (1994), 246.

[89] On the *strata* dispute, reported by Proc. II.1 (note the lack of Roman interest in the area, 1.11), cf. Liebeschuetz, 'Defences', 489 and Isaac, *Limits*, 211–17, who is cautious as to the extent of the Roman withdrawal, as is (e.g.) Parker, 'Retrospective on the Arabian frontier', 648–52 and Whittaker, *Frontiers*, 137; cf. Isaac, 'Army', 149, playing down troop reductions in Palestine before the seventh century. But see now Casey, 'Justinian and the *limitanei*', 221–2, who argues for the progressive devolution of Roman defences in Syria and Palestine to the Arabs in the sixth century,

Thus from Egypt to Mesopotamia Arab tribesmen were of considerable importance to the defence of the empire. For most of the war of 502–532 they were under the command of various phylarchs, each in charge of a particular contingent of Arabs based in one province; towards the end of the war Justinian elevated one of their number, al-Harith the Ghassanid, to a supreme command.[90] The increasing role of Arabs on the frontier brought certain dangers; raids across the borders in the 480s, and the resultant tension, have already been noted. In the Anastasian war, Arabs allied to both sides launched raids while negotiations were in progress, and were punished for their actions. They derived much profit from hostilities between the two sides, which provided them with a license to raid at will. The fact that the dispute between Lakhmids and Ghassanids over ownership of the *strata* area soon embroiled both great powers will therefore not have been unwelcome to either tribe; not surprisingly therefore, the treaty of 561 which brought to an end the war begun in 540 incorporated a clause barring the Saracen allies of each side from attacking one another, a clear acknowledgement of their importance in relations between the two sides.[91]

The Arabs, while certainly the most numerous allies of the Romans in the war of 502–532, and probably the most important, were not the only people to serve in this capacity. The others may be dealt with more briefly. The Tzani, subdued during the reign of Justin and Justinian, may have furnished contingents during this war, although there is firm evidence of their participation only in the war of 540–61.[92]

---

based on numismatic and archaeological evidence. Mal. 441 and 426 on Damascus and Palmyra respectively; Isaac, *Limits*, 253 on Sergiopolis (Proc. II.20.11–15).

[90] Sartre, *Trois études*, 164 and 170–73 and Shahîd, *BASIC* I, 95–8, on the separate commands and the elevation of al-Harith; even after this, there remained separate phylarchs in each province. Kaegi, *Conquests*, 40–41, offering numerical estimates for the 630s, shows how numerous these Arab forces could be. Treadgold, *Army*, 47 (and elsewhere) fails even to consider this element of the army, though a quarter of the total he gives for the Army of the East was comprised of Ghassanid allies (see below).

[91] See n.71 above on the raids in the 480s. Josh. Styl. §88 for the raids in winter 504/5; §79 on the Arabs profiting from the war, with Matthews' comment, *Ammianus*, 352. Proc. II.1 on the *strata* dispute, cf. Menander, frg. 6.1.320–22 on the clause on Saracen allies, with Blockley, 256 n.50, Kawar, 'The Arabs in the Peace Treaty', 197–208, Shahîd, *BASIC* I, 267–8, and Isaac, *Limits*, 263.

[92] Mal. 461 gives a figure of 5000 men serving under the phylarch al-Harith in 531. On the Tzani, Proc. II.29.10, 41; cf. Grosse, *Militärgeschichte*, 294. Proc. I.15.25 states that the Tzani were enrolled in the main body of the Roman army, though at what point it is unclear; cf. Rance, *Tactics*, 123.

More significant were the Heruls, frequently mentioned by Procopius in the latter phase of the 502–532 war. This Hunnic tribe inhabited Pannonia, where they had been settled in the area around Bassiana by the Emperor Anastasius; under Justinian they were granted better lands around Singidunum, while their king was baptised into the Chalcedonian church in 528. In return they furnished the emperor with troops which proved remarkably effective against the Persians, despite their light armour and poor equipment.[93] Various other Huns of uncertain provenance also served in the Roman army in this war; probably, like the Heruls, they came from the Balkans, since the term is a loose one by this period. They too proved of great worth, as will be seen from the battles fought under Justinian.[94]

b) Roman forces

All the troops east of Constantinople were under the overall command of the *magister militum per Orientem*; and at the time of the *Notitia Dignitatum* he is reported to have had a significant army of his own. Beneath him were *duces* (dukes) in every province, who had charge of military affairs, and were not always on good terms with the civilian governor.[95] In 502 the three *duces* most important for defence against the Persians were those of Osrhoene (based at Callinicum), Mesopotamia (based at Constantia until the construction of Dara) and Armenia Minor (based at Melitene).[96] During the 502–532 war Justinian

---

[93]   Stein II, 305–6 and 306 n.1, assembles the evidence; see Proc. VI.14.28–36 on their position under Anastasius and Justinian (note the use of the term *symmachos* at 31). Also Grosse, *Römische Militärgeschichte*, 293, and Bury, *HLRE* II, 71 on their status as allies; but see below ch.8 n.16 for evidence that some also served as *foederati*. On their equipment, Proc. II.25.27–8, doubted by Delbrück, *Barbarian Invasions*, 348.

[94]   Proc. I.13.20–22 for Huns (referred to as Massagetae) at the battle of Dara. Note *Aed*. IV.1.5 for Huns in the vicinity of the Danube, cf. *Wars* II.4.4–12 for a 'Hunnic' invasion of the Balkans in 540 (which Stein however interprets as a reference to Bulgars, II, 309). It is unlikely that there were any Caucasian Huns, such as the Sabirs, in the Roman army during this war; it was not until later in Justinian's reign (Proc. VIII.11.22–5) that they came to the assistance of the Romans.

[95]   On the *magister militum per Orientem* and the *duces* beneath him, Jones, *LRE*, 655–6, Lee, *Information*, 53, Grosse, 'Die Rangordnung', 152–7 and Ravegnani, *Soldati*, 73–5, 79–81; see n.101 below on the *Notitia Dignitatum*. Note too that there were forces belonging to the praesental armies of Constantinople (i.e. those under the *magistri militum praesentales* based in the capital) stationed in the east, *C.J.* XII.35.18 (under Anastasius); these came under the authority of the *duces*, cf. Ravegnani, *op. cit.*, 95 and Haldon, 'Administrative Continuities', 49.

[96]   See e.g. Lauffray, *Halabiyya*, 31; on Melitene, Proc. *Aed*. III.4.15–20 and note Josh. Styl. §57 on the *dux* of Osrhoene being based at Callinicum (rather than Edessa,

decided that the eastern frontier was too extended to remain under one
magister militum, so a new commander was set up in Armenia, the
magister militum per Armeniam (et Pontum Polemoniacum et gentes),
with new subordinate *duces*.[97]

That all was not well with this system of defence is made clear by
the following passage, concerning the Persian invasion of 542:

> And all the Romans, both officers and soldiers, were far from enter-
> taining any thought of confronting the enemy or standing in the way
> of their passage, but manning their strongholds as each one could,
> they thought it sufficient to preserve them and save themselves.[98]

By this point, it is clear, a markedly defensive mentality had set in, not
without reason.[99] First, there was a shortage of manpower: although in
the fourth century Julian could assemble a force of some 65,000 men
for his invasion of Persia, this was the last time that the eastern frontier
would see such a massive force.[100] Somewhat later than Julian one
source, the *Notitia Dignitatum*, offers some indication of (theoretical)
troop numbers throughout the empire. For the eastern half of the empire
the figures are thought to date from c.408, still a century before the war
of 502–532. A recent calculation using this document puts around
65,000 men still available on the eastern frontier at this time.[101] This

---

    contra e.g. Ravegnani, *Soldati*, 74). Under Justinian places closer to the frontier, such
as Martyropolis and Citharizon, became more important. According to Proc. II.13.14
there were no soldiers in Constantia in 503; but Josh. Styl §51 refers to troops of the
dux operating nearby.

[97] Jones, *LRE*, 656, Stein II, 290, Adontz, *Armenia*, 106–13 and Treadgold, *Army*, 15.
See n.65 above on the absence of Roman troops in the area under satraps in Armenia
Minor.

[98] Proc. II.20.19, tr. Dewing, cited by Kaegi in *Conquests*, 47. For another survey of
Roman forces at this time, see Bury, *HLRE* II, 75–8.

[99] Though it should also be borne in mind that the passage immediately precedes
Belisarius' entry into this war and thus serves to highlight his success still further.

[100] Note also that Julian spurned the use of Arab allies, whereas in calculations of Roman
troop numbers in the sixth century Ghassanid allies are usually included. See
Howard-Johnston, 'Great Powers', 166 and Matthews, *Ammianus*, 167 for figures for
Julian's army.

[101]See Treadgold, *Army*, table 1, p.51 (with map 6, p.48), for the most recent consideration of the *ND*; he estimates 36,000 *limitanei* (a term to be explained below)
stationed in Mesopotamia, Osrhoene and Armenia (to which 9000 in Syria could be
added). He estimates that the Army of the East under the *magister militum per Orientem* comprised a further 20,000 men (p.50), but see n.90 above for problems with
his calculations. Contrast Jones, *LRE*, map IV, a calculation of troop dispositions according to the *ND*, and Appendix II on the date of the *ND*. *Ibid.*, 1450, for inflated
figures for Roman forces along the frontiers, criticised by MacMullen, 'How big was

figure is, however, an upper estimate — from an official document — and of limited help when considering frontier defences at the opening of the sixth century. If sixth-century sources are consulted, a few more plausible estimates are possible. The army assembled by the Emperor Anastasius against the Persians probably amounted to (at least) 30–40,000 men; Belisarius' army at Dara in 530 numbered 25,000 (with no Arab allies present), and at the same time another Roman force, perhaps 10–15,000 strong, was defending Armenia. An army defeated in Armenia in 543 by a much smaller Persian force contained 30,000 men; Agathias offers a figure of 50,000 troops operating in Lazica in the 550s, but he is generally thought to have exaggerated here.[102] Military manuals, in particular that of Maurice, corroborate these numbers for the later sixth century, viewing an army of 15–20,000 as on the large side.[103]

Regardless of the precise numbers involved, one point stands out — the discrepancy between the number of troops to be found guarding the east in time of peace and the number of men who could be summoned to serve there should the need arise. From the second century onwards Rome's eastern wars had tended to begin badly: an attack from Parthia or Persia would overwhelm local forces, and it might take over a year before Roman reinforcements arrived to restore the situation. Even in the mid-fourth century, when the Mesopotamian provinces were geared for war, Shapur's unexpected attack on Amida found only a few thousand soldiers there.[104] The church historian Theodoret of Cyrrhus recounts how in 440 a Persian invasion was thwarted only by inclement weather, which gave Roman troops time to react: again, the implication is that there were few men *in situ* ready to ward off invaders. So it comes as no surprise that Kavadh was able to traverse the frontier with

the Roman army?', 451–60, esp. 457; cf. also Whitby, 'Recruitment', 75 n.50. Treadgold's estimates should be preferred.

[102] Howard-Johnston, 'Great Powers', 166–7, believes the Roman army mustered by Anastasius to have been larger; see ch.5 below on this. Dara army: Proc. I.13.23; I.15.11, 14 on the attack in Armenia. Cf. now Treadgold, *Army*, 47, 60–63 with map 7, p.62. Whitby, 'Recruitment', 101 on Agathias' exaggeration (II.8.2–3).

[103] Whitby, 'Recruitment', 73–4, 100–1, on Maurice, cf. Stein II, 89 and n.1 and Treadgold, *Army*, 61. See also Turtledove, 'True size', 216–22, Kaegi, *Conquests*, 40, and Bury, *HLRE* II, 78 for more estimates.

[104] Ammianus XIX.2.14 gives a figure of 20,000 for the total population of the city (which some have emended to 120,000), but I follow Matthews, *Ammianus*, 66, in accepting the lower number; at least half the 20,000, and probably more, will have been civilians.

ease in 502 and besiege Amida; nor that the Roman commanders in 542, when many forces were engaged in a war in Italy, were loath to meet Khusro in pitched battle.[105] Nonetheless it should not be supposed that there were no Roman troops on the eastern frontier in the fifth century: while Kavadh laid siege to Amida, local commanders were able to launch counter-attacks against the Persians.[106]

The second problem facing the Romans was one of troop quality. The first line of Roman defences in late antiquity, on the eastern frontier as elsewhere, was held by the *limitanei*, i.e. 'soldiers serving in a *limes*, a frontier district'; they were, however, 'simply soldiers serving anywhere in the area assigned to the relevant *dux* and their duties were not necessarily connected with frontier defence.'[107] Once despised as a rather ineffectual force of 'peasant-farmers', the *limitanei* are now held in higher esteem. While it is clear that they did cultivate lands on the borders for their own use, they were still viewed by the Emperor Justinian as sufficiently useful to be installed in the newly reconquered provinces of Africa in 533. But the effectiveness of the *limitanei* can be overestimated: evidence from Egypt suggests that a soldier there might have an alternative career while still serving as a *limitaneus*. Although the *magister officiorum* was supposed to inspect the condition of frontier defences annually and to ensure that the *limitanei* were properly drilled, it seems as if discipline suffered in peace time; for the duties of the *limitanei* were then confined generally to police and guard duties, as an inscription from Cyrenaica dated to Anastasius' reign bears out. No doubt the effectiveness of units of *limitanei* varied, since some were apparently able to accompany field armies on campaign.[108]

---

[105] On Theodoret *HE* V.37.5–6, see Greatrex, 'Fifth-century wars', 3–4. See n.98 above for the commanders in 542; Belisarius too refused to engage the Persians on this occasion, so great was the shortage of men, though this was after the eastern empire had been hit by the plague in 541 — cf. Teall, 'The barbarians in Justinian's armies', 303–7 (with Treadgold, *Army*, 167 and table 11, p.165) on the various problems confronting the empire at this point.

[106] Josh. Styl. §§51–2.

[107] For the definition of the *limitanei*, see Isaac, *Limits*, 208, with *idem*, 'The meaning', 143. The quotation regarding their functions, *ibid.* 146.

[108] On the continuing use of *limitanei* by Justinian, see Ravegnani, *Soldati*, 95–7 and Isaac, 'The meaning', 145–6. Patlagean, 'L'impôt', 307, claims that *limitanei* could own land, but were not entitled to work it; but Isaac, *art. cit.*, 145, rightly argues that they were entitled to cultivate land, as is clear from *NTh* XXIV.1.4 (443). Isaac, *art. cit.*, 144, and Jones, *LRE*, 662, on the policing duties of *limitanei* in Cyrenaica, from *SEG* IX.356 = Oliverio, *Il decreto*, 142 §11. On the doubtful quality of *limitanei* (and field army soldiers) in Egypt and the role of the *magister officiorum*, see Jones, *op.*

The *limitanei*, like the soldiers of the field army, were divided into units (*numeri*, ἀριθμοί or κατάλογοι) comprising some 200–500 men.[109] These units were stationed throughout the provinces — not just along the frontier — under the control of *duces*. Some were probably stationed in forts, such as those along the Euphrates like Circesium and Zenobia,[110] while others provided garrisons for larger cities, such as Amida, Edessa and Constantia. The *limitanei* will for the most part have been recruited locally, though service may no longer have been hereditary.[111] In addition to their land-holdings, which were exempt from imperial taxes, they received pay through the provincial governor. Deductions were made from their pay for the *dux* and his *officium* (staff), but emperors sought to limit such siphonings. Payment was generally made in kind: the goods would come from the local *possessores* (landlords) and be handed over to the governor. He would then give them to the *optiones* or *actuarii* of the *limitanei*, upon being presented with the appropriate requisition order.[112]

---

cit., 661–3 and Liebeschuetz, 'Defences', 489–90; the *duces* were also supposed to drill the *limitanei*, cf. Ravegnani, *op. cit.*, 80 and n.32 (citing *C.J.* I.46.4 [443]). On *limitanei* campaigning alongside field army forces, Isaac, *art. cit.*, 145 and n.89 and *Limits*, 210–11. Whitby, 'Recruitment', 113–14, offers a more positive view of the *limitanei* in the sixth century.

[109] Maspero, *Organisation*, 69–70, on the division of the forces in this period. On the numbers involved, cf. *ibid.* 69–70, 115–17, Müller, 'Heer', 104–6, Treadgold, *Army*, 87–97, and Haldon, 'Administrative Continuities', 51 n.13. The commanding officer of such a unit was a *comes* or tribune, cf. Ravegnani, *Soldati*, 36; in the *Strategikon* a group of several *numeri* is known as a *moira* and is commanded by a *dux*, *ibid.* 62. On the command structure in general, *ibid.* 29–39 with Treadgold, *loc. cit.*

[110] Evidence for the garrisoning of these forts is, however, lacking: see Liebeschuetz, 'Defences', 494 and Lauffray, *Halabbiya*, 37. For *limitanei* not just on the frontier, Isaac, 'The meaning', 143. But note that Proc., when describing Justinian's repairs to Circesium (*Aed.* II.6.1–11), does not state that it had hitherto been ungarrisoned.

[111] Liebeschuetz, 'Defences', 494, on Egyptian evidence, where much of the population was on the roll of the *limitanei*, cf. Jones, *LRE*, 662 and Ravegnani, *Soldati*, 19. Isaac, *art. cit.*, 145, argues that service was not hereditary, but cf. Whitby, 'Recruitment', 69 and 79–81 (who argues that conscription, and probably hereditary service, were maintained in the sixth century). Garrison at Edessa: Josh. Styl. §43 (in 500/1), cf. Segal, *Edessa*, 117–19, on *limitanei* there.

[112] Ravegnani, *Soldati*, 105, Jones, *LRE*, 626–7, Whitby, 'Recruitment', 111–12 on the procedure; Patlagean, 'L'impôt', 303–9, Ravegnani, *op. cit.*, 108, 114, and Jones, *op. cit.*, 662–3, on the payments to *duces* and the attempts of Anastasius and Justinian to limit them. Carrié, 'L'Etat', 36–7, on payments in kind to the *limitanei* (*contra* Jones, *op. cit.*, 671); the soldiers preferred to be paid in cash, however, and apparently frequently got their way, cf. Isaac, *Limits*, 287–9. It is worth noting that in Mesopotamia at least, the *dux* received his pay — the *annona* and *capitus* — from the *commerciarius* there, implying that sufficient revenue was raised through trade (presumably across the border): see Sartre, *IGLS XIII*, 114–15. Justinian later attempted

Superior to the *limitanei* were the soldiers of the field army, the *comitatenses* or στρατιωταί (*stratiotai*), as they were known in the sixth century. The field army was the descendant of the old Roman legion, and it consisted for the most part of men from within the confines of the Roman empire. Better remunerated than the *limitanei*, they were excluded from cultivating fields or keeping livestock. They were expected to remain in their barracks and to keep in training so as to be able to ward off enemies attacking the empire.[113] They could be stationed in the same place as *limitanei* in order to bolster defences, such as at Palmyra in 527; as a result of this, in order to maintain a unified command of local defences, the *duces* came to hold authority not just over *limitanei* but also over field army units of the *magistri militum praesentales* or *magister militum per Orientem*. As such units became more static, it is not unlikely that their efficiency deteriorated, although, as with the *limitanei*, this should not be exaggerated.[114] Payment and supplies for the *stratiotai*, when on the frontier, were also channelled through the local governor.[115]

Two further categories of troops remain. The *foederati*, alluded to earlier, had, by the sixth century, become almost synonymous with the

---

to abolish payments to *limitanei* altogether, cf. Durliat, 'Armée', 31–2, Maspero, *Organisation*, 107–13 and Treadgold, *Army*, 150–51 (who also discusses the amounts involved).

[113] Maspero, *Organisation*, 43–4. *C.J.* XII.35.15 (458) on the proscriptions from farming etc.; it also informs us that the soldiers were armed and fed by the state, cf. Durliat, 'Armée', 32. Cf. *Nov.* 116 (542), *proem.* on the duties of soldiers, with *C.J.* IV.65.35.1 (?530), the definition of a soldier. That Roman soldiers — of the field army and *limitanei* — had a tendency not to turn up for drill emerges from Justinian's insistence on this in North Africa, *C.J.* I.27.2.9. On the recruitment of *comitatenses*, see Whitby, 'Recruitment', 75–87, esp. 81, arguing that they (and the *limitanei*) were raised by conscription and (probably) hereditary obligation, *contra* Haldon, *Recruitment*, 21, 24–5; cf. also Ravegnani, *Soldati*, 18–19.

[114] Jones, *LRE*, 686, Ravegnani, *Soldati*, 95 and Whitby, 'Recruitment', 71 with *C.J.* XII.35.18 (on which see above n.95).

[115] Durliat, 'Armée', 31–3, Jones, *LRE*, 626–7 (who notes that special arrangements might be made for supplying a particularly large force, as happened during the Anastasian war). Treadgold, *Army*, 147–8, 153–5, calculates pay at 20 *nomismata* (*solidi*) a year under Anastasius, paid in cash rather than kind; before his reign, however, with deductions for arms and equipment, pay had been rather less generous. On *adaeratio* (the commutation of payment in kind for cash), cf. Jones, *op. cit.*, 671–2, Ravegnani, *Soldati*, 106–7 and Kaegi, *Conquests*, 36–7, who believe that a significant proportion of soldiers' wages was paid in cash; Carrié, 'L'Etat', 36–7, is more cautious. Supplies from the province were deductible from imperial taxes, cf. Ravegnani, *Soldati*, 105–6; but note also Isaac, *Limits*, 287 (on the non-reimbursable *annona*).

stratiotai, the only difference being that there were more soldiers of barbarian origin in the *foederati*. Like the *stratiotai* the *foederati* were barred from cultivating land, received their pay from the state and served under Roman generals. They were more highly regarded than *stratiotai*, and figured more in offensive wars than defensive; they are seldom attested in the east.[116] Finally, there were the *bucellarii*, troops who were attached primarily to a particular general, but swore an oath of allegiance to the emperor and in the final resort were at his disposal. Some, it appears, were supported on the domains of large landowners, who as a result developed a tendency to use them for their own purposes, a practice condemned by both Leo and Justinian.[117] Certain generals, notably Belisarius, assembled thousands of such soldiers; they were, in effect, attached to the commander's *oikos* or household, from which they received their pay. They were subdivided into two categories, *doryphoroi* and *hypaspistai*. Despite the literal meanings of these terms, the former were used extensively as leaders of *numeri*, while the latter were generally employed in a more limited capacity, for instance as bodyguards for the commander.[118] They were élite troops of high standing, who stood to be well rewarded by their commander and could themselves attain high office through their prominent role in campaigns: Belisarius and Sittas, it may be remembered, had both once been *doryphoroi* of the Emperor Justinian. The *bucellarii*, recruited both inside and outside the empire, were thus an important component

---

[116] Cf. Maspero, '*Foederati*', 97–109, esp. 99, 104–8; note, however, that there were probably more 'barbarians' in the army than he supposes — see Carrié, 'L'Etat', 53–6 with the remarks of Whitby on the category 'barbarian' in 'Recruitment', 104–6. Cf. also Jones, *LRE*, 663–5, on *foederati* under Justinian; as he notes, some were allowed to remain Arians, unlike other soldiers (*C.J.* XII.5.12.17). On the rarity of *foederati* in the Persian wars, Müller, 'Heer', 114. I follow Maspero, *art. cit.*, and Bury, *HLRE* II, 77 n.1, in viewing the *foederati* as soldiers of the state, not private *condottieri*, as, e.g., Müller argues, *art. cit.*, 115–16.

[117] The evidence for the position of *bucellarii* supported by the landowners is assembled by Carrié, 'L'Etat', 57, who sees them as occupying an intermediary position between the élite field army and the *limitanei*, to be called upon and formed into units when needed. Cf. Gascou, 'L'institution des bucellaires', 143–56, also on the evidence from Egypt. Whitby, 'Recruitment', 116–19 on the laws of Leo (*C.J.* IX.12.10 [468]) and Justinian (*Nov.* 116 [542]) and the oaths.

[118] Gascou, 'L'institution des bucellaires', 149–50, on their status, cf. Whitby, 'Recruitment', 116–19. Müller, 'Heer', 117 on their pay. Maspero, *Organisation*, 66–8, on the two categories, cf. Bury, *HLRE* II, 77–8 and Jones, *LRE*, 667, who refers to them as 'officers' and 'privates'.

in Roman armies, although their numbers in the war of 502–532 are
entirely unknown.[119]

A brief analysis of the nature of these forces can now be made. The
majority of Roman troops were infantry, whose quality is usually
poorly rated. The *Strategikon* of Maurice, however, is aware of the
usefulness of infantry later in the sixth century; and there are instances
in the war of 502–532 of infantry formations being adopted for
defence, such as at the battle of Callinicum in 531. It appears, however,
that the infantry was often inexperienced in battle, which would explain
why it tended to play a lesser role.[120] Infantry equipment is described
by Maurice and Magister Syrianus (writing under Justinian); the
leading ranks at least were well armoured and supplied with large
shields to protect against enemy missiles. All the soldiers were to be
instructed in the use of the bow, which was the prime instrument of
attack; Roman archery, while less swift than that of the Persians, was
believed to be more powerful.[121]

The Roman cavalry was the prime force in offence. Already in the
fourth century the cavalry was held in high esteem,[122] and Procopius in
the sixth century presents a glowing picture of its capabilities:

[119] Whitby, 'Recruitment', section 9, cf. Müller, 'Heer', 118–19 and Jones, *LRE*, 665–7;
also Whittaker, *Frontiers*, 271–4. Proc. I.12.21 on Belisarius and Sittas.

[120] On Roman infantry in the sixth century and its uses, see Rance, *Tactics*, 211–38, who
assembles the evidence, cf. Coulston, 'Later Roman armour', 150 and Ravegnani,
Soldati, 58–62; note, e.g., Proc. VIII.29.16–21 for a dense infantry formation beating
off cavalry (at Busta Gallorum). Callinicum: Proc. I.18.41–8. Inexperience: the *Epitedeuma* of Urbicius, written under Anastasius, explicitly refers to this, cf. Rance,
Tactics, 7–8 on this treatise and his tr. of it, 266–8. Proc. I.18.39 for raw recruits at
Callinicum. Ravegnani, *op. cit.*, 58–60, rightly points out that certain generals, such
as Belisarius, distrusted the infantry more than others, like Narses, who were prepared
to make more use of it (with considerable success). The proportion of infantry to
cavalry (two to one) may be gauged from the expedition sent to North Africa, Proc.
III.11.2. Among the *limitanei* a considerable increase in the proportion of cavalry to
infantry seems to have occurred over the fourth century, cf. Treadgold, *Army*, 57–9.

[121] Maurice, *Strategikon* XII B 1–5, 16 (418–22, 442) on infantry, with *Peri Strategias*
16 and Ravegnani, *Soldati*, 45–8. On the attribution of this work to Magister
Syrianus, see Zuckerman, 'The military compendium', 209–24 and Rance, *Tactics*,
10–27; it in any case probably belongs to the sixth century, cf. Zuckerman, *art. cit.*,
216, Elton, *Warfare*, 270, *contra* (e.g.) Shahîd, *BASIC* I, 582–3. On the importance of
archery, note *Strategikon* I.1 (74–6), Περὶ Τοξείας in *Peri Strategias*, 128–35,
Rance, *op. cit.*, 153–6, Ravegnani, *op. cit.*, 45, 86–7 and Dagron, 'Modèles', 279–82;
Bivar, 'Cavalry Equipment', 286 on Procopius' claim (I.18.32) for more penetrating
Roman archery (rejected completely by Delbrück, *Barbarian Invasions*, 346–7). See
also Boss, *Justinian's Wars*, 50–60, for some illustrations.

[122] Cf. Vegetius, *Epitoma* III.26 (p.124); tr. Milner, xxv–xxix on the date of the work
(probably late fourth century).

But the bowmen of the present time go into battle wearing corselets and fitted out with greaves which extend up to the knee. From the right side hang their arrows, from the other the sword. And there are some who have a spear also attached to them and, at the shoulders, a sort of small shield without a grip, such as to cover the region of the face and neck. They are expert horsemen, and are able without difficulty to direct their bows to either side while riding at full speed, and to shoot an opponent whether in pursuit or in flight. They draw the bowstring along by the forehead about opposite the right ear, thereby charging the arrow with such an impetus as to kill whoever stands in the way, shield and corselet alike having no power to check its force. (I.1.12–15, tr. Dewing)

These horse-archers possessed the long-range effectiveness of Hunnic warriors, but could also fight efficiently at close quarters; they were rather lighter than the *clibanarii* or *cataphracti* of previous centuries, but with the corresponding advantage of greater manoeuvrability.[123] Such cavalry were hardly to be found among the *limitanei*. Probably most were enrolled among the *bucellarii* of the generals, while others served as *foederati* or *symmachoi* — such as the Huns who played so important a role at the battle of Dara (530).[124]

Finally, the morale and discipline of the troops stationed requires examination. From the quotation at the start of this section it seems that in 542 at least the soldiers and generals were in no mood to confront the Persian invaders; the fact that some units were owed several years' back pay may have contributed to their unwillingness to fight.[125] Anastasius' concern for the army is clear from some of his laws, but the short treatise of Urbicius implies that neither the generals nor the

---

[123] On the cavalryman described, cf. *Strategikon*, tr. Dennis, ix–x, Haldon, 'Some Aspects', 12–25, Grosse, *Militärgeschichte*, 314–15, and Rance, *Tactics*, 161–5 (who points out that not all Roman cavalry matched the ideal here portrayed by Proc.); also Ravegnani, *Soldati*, 54–8 and Boss, *Justinian's Wars*, 46–9. Dagron, 'Modèles', 282–3, notes the development of the cavalry since the fourth century. Ravegnani, *op. cit.*, 49–51, details the rest of the cavalryman's equipment, including a lance, a quiver, a sword, and armour. The prominence of the bow is generally attributed to Hunnic influence, cf. Bivar, 'Cavalry Equipment', 282. For a representation of Khusro II firing a bow, see plates 17 and 23 in Bivar's article; Haldon, *art. cit.*, 19, notes the absence of any armour for the horse, which the heavier cataphracts had possessed. Agathias offers a much briefer description of Roman cavalry equipment at II.8.1. The stirrup, it should be noted, had yet to be developed in Europe — Bivar, *art. cit.*, 286 and A. Cutler and E. McGeer in *ODB* III.1958.

[124] Grosse, *Militärgeschichte*, 291; Proc. I.13.19–21 on Huns at Dara. The mounted *limitanei* (see n.120 above) will have been more geared to policing duties.

[125] Above, p.32 for the quotation. On the lack of pay, see Proc. II.7.37 (at Beroea), Fotiou, 'Recruitment shortages', 66 and Ravegnani, *Soldati*, 108–9.

infantry soldiers were of the highest calibre. Furthermore, relations between soldiers and civilians were poor, as emerges, for instance, from Joshua the Stylite (§§93–4), who recounts tension between the inhabitants of Edessa and Roman soldiers stationed there during the war.[126] The east had been thought to have an enervating effect on the discipline of soldiers from as far back as the first century B.C. But although this became a cliché in the literary sources, there can be no doubt that there was considerable disorder and insubordination among imperial forces in the early sixth century. Hence great stress is placed on training in military manuals, as also by the Emperor Justinian himself; and so in 530 the Persians were surprised to find the Roman army encamped at Dara in such a well-ordered condition (*Wars* I.14.14).[127]

c) Roman fortifications

In 542 the fortifications into which the Romans fled so precipitately were in a far better state than at the start of the century, when Kavadh was able to take Theodosiopolis and Martyropolis without difficulty; and although Amida held out for three months, other cities in Mesopotamia and Osrhoene preferred to enter negotiations with the invaders. That city walls should have fallen into disrepair over the fifth century should occasion no surprise: not only had it been a period of peace, as has been seen, but extensive repair work would have been against the spirit of the agreement between the two sides not to build new fortifications along the frontier. So, as soon as there was a lull in the fighting, Anastasius made haste to repair the walls of some cities, and to begin the construction of a major new border fortress at Dara. Likewise Justinian embarked on an ambitious programme of upgrading

---

[126] For Anastasius' concern, Kaegi, *Unrest*, 43, citing the inscription from Cyrenaica (see n.108 above), cf. *C.J.* XII.35.18; on Justinian's measures, Kaegi, *op. cit.*, 45, Fotiou, 'Recruitment shortages', 69–70. On the relations with the civilian population, Kaegi, *op. cit.*, 60, Fotiou, *art. cit.*, 68–9 and Segal, 'Mesopotamian communities', 113–14.

[127] On the supposed degenerative effects of the east, see Coulston, 'Later Roman armour', 149 with instances at 155 n.144, and Isaac, *Limits*, 23–5. On training, see Rance, *Tactics*, ch.4 (on the military manuals), Ravegnani, *Soldati*, ch.4, Kaegi, *Unrest*, 37, 95 and Justinian, *Nov.* 26.3 (535). Kaegi, *op. cit.*, 64–7, on discipline problems in the east in the sixth century generally. Note also Heraclius' training of his army before his campaigns, Theoph. A.M. 6113 (303–4) and Maurice's in 577/8 (Whitby, *Maurice*, 268). Belisarius may have spent the year 529 (otherwise empty) in similarly preparing his army, as Chassin, *Bélisaire*, 31, suggests.

fortifications in the late 520s when fighting had resumed between the two sides.[128]

A few examples will demonstrate the poor state of fortifications at the turn of the century. Callinicum, endowed in Ammianus' day with a *munimentum robustum* (XXIII.3.7), and rebuilt by the Emperor Leo in 466, was nevertheless browbeaten by Kavadh into handing over a captured Persian general in late 503.[129] Joshua the Stylite actually records some of the decay which had affected the defences of Edessa before the outbreak of war. In October 499 a breach appeared in the south wall during a solar eclipse, so that when the Persians approached the city three years later urgent repairs were undertaken; the gates had decayed to such an extent that they had to be blocked up with stone. In 505 further work was undertaken on the fortifications.[130] Batnae, also in Osrhoene, a prosperous city in the fourth century, fell to a squadron of Persian cavalry because its walls had crumbled; these too were restored by Anastasius.[131]

In a speech to Athenian troops stranded in Sicily in 413 B.C., the general Nicias pointed out that 'it is men that make a State, not walls nor ships devoid of men'.[132] But by the sixth century A.D. walled cities and forts had taken on an ever greater importance in the defence of the Roman state. This should not necessarily be perceived as indicative of the unreliable quality (and limited quantity) of imperial forces. True, there was a tendency on the part of some troops to confine themselves to forts and thus to permit invaders to bypass them on their way into Roman territory; but others forced Belisarius to give battle against his will in 531. Furthermore, as the agreement made after the 421–422 war implies, forts had an offensive as well as a defensive capability: they could provide the springboard for raids into enemy territory, and it was

---

[128] Whitby, 'Development', 717–35, is a useful survey of work in the early sixth century; cf. esp. 717, 726 on the situation in 502 and cf. *idem, Maurice*, 209–10. Capizzi, *Anastasio*, 206–24, reviews all the building work of Anastasius along the eastern frontier; see also Crow, 'Frontiers of Cappadocia', 82–7, on the northern sector. Rubin, 'Diplomacy', 683, on the other hand, believes that improvements were made to fortifications over the fifth century.

[129] Josh. Styl. §57 with Musil, *Middle Euphrates*, 328 and Whitby, 'Notes', 93–4.

[130] Josh. Styl. §§36, 52, 77 for these measures with Segal, *Edessa*, 157–8.

[131] Ammianus XIV.3.3 reports an annual fair at Batnae, attracting travellers from India and China; cf. also Petersen, 'A Roman prefect', 278–9. Josh. Styl. §§63, 89 on the fate of the city in the Anastasian war.

[132] Thucydides VII.77.7, tr. C.F. Smith (London, 1923), 159 (and note the parallels offered at 158 n.1).

for this reason that the Persians made such strenuous efforts to deflect Belisarius from constructing the fort at Minduos in 528.[133]

Gibbon's view of the condition of the empire under Justinian, 'never so weak as when every village was fortified', has perhaps been over-influential and requires tempering. Certainly there were numerous forts, many of which were without a permanent garrison; yet they served a useful function in providing refuge for country-dwellers in time of need. And the larger garrisoned cities presented a problem to any aggressor: they had to be either besieged, which would usually require a huge investment of time and resources, or bypassed, which left the supply lines of the invader in danger. Nevertheless Nicias' dictum remained true: men were required for defence. Cities could hold out for months, even years, but eventually they would fall. Only if in the inter-vening time reinforcements were mustered — as happened in the Anastasian war — could the tide be turned and the offensive capability of border forts be put to good use. If, on the other hand, no further troops were forthcoming, then resistance crumbled — as happened to a certain extent in 540 and 542, and on a massive scale under the Emperor Phocas (602–10).[134]

---

[133] On the purpose of forts, see the list of Isaac, *Limits*, 255–6 and Josh. Styl. §90. Proc. I.13.1–8 and below on Minduos, with Whitby, *Maurice*, 212–13 on the offensive potential of such forts. Note also the problems faced by Shapur I's retreating army when they had to pass by Edessa, Petr. Patr. frg.11, tr. in Dodgeon–Lieu, *Eastern Frontier*, 67. Isaac, *Limits*, 263 and Rubin, 'Diplomacy', 683 and n.12, put the agreement in 441 rather than 422.

[134] For the downbeat assessment of fortifications, see Crow, 'The Long Walls', 120–21, who cites Gibbon (*Decline*, IV, 250–53), cf. Lauffray, *Halabbiya*, 35–7. On the lack of a garrison in many forts, Liebeschuetz, 'Defences', 491–4. See Napoli, 'Ultimes fortifications', 69–72, on the importance of fortifications in this period. More positive are Lee, *Information*, 141, following Liebeschuetz, 'Defences', 499, and Treadgold, *Army*, 205–6. Note also Menander frg.26.1.40–43, a speech by the Persian am-bassador Andigan, in which he points out how the Persians are aware of the state of Roman defences.

III
The Persian Perspective

It was not only on the Roman side of the border that some expected the imminent end of the world. In the mid to late fifth century certain followers of Zoroaster, the founder of the Persian state religion, believed that the end of the millenium of Zoroaster was approaching.[1] Such a view, as will be seen, was not without foundation, given the enormous problems facing the Sasanian state at the time.

From the Roman standpoint, the invasion of Armenia by Kavadh in 502 was inexplicable and unjustifiable.[2] Relations between the two powers had indeed deteriorated as a result of the incessant wrangling over Roman payments for the Caspian Gates, but this was not what prompted the attack of 502; hence the Romans were caught off-guard. More immediate internal factors pushed Kavadh to launch his invasion then, and these may be clarified by a brief analysis of the condition of the Persian kingdom.

i) The Sasanian empire in the late fifth century

The Sasanian empire was scarcely smaller in area than the eastern Roman empire. It extended from the Transcaucasus and the plains of Gurgan in the north to Khuzistan and the Persian Gulf in the south, and from Armenia and Lower Mesopotamia in the west to the mountains of Khorasan in the east.[3] This immense empire was governed by the Sasanian rulers — all of them descendants of the first king, Ardashir I, if not of the shadowy Sasan — from their capital at Ctesiphon on the

---

[1] Morony, *Iraq*, 302–3 and Zaehner, 'A Zurvanite Apocalypse II', 611–12 (§49) on this apocalyptic tradition.

[2] Proc. I.7.3 and see ch.2.ii.

[3] Howard-Johnston, 'Great Powers', 180; cf. the description of Christensen, *Iranshahr*, 19–21. As Howard-Johnston notes, however, the resources provided by this empire were by no means the equal of those that could be drawn upon by the Romans, *art. cit.*, 168–9.

Mesopotamian plains.[4] The king was the representative of Ohrmazd, the Zoroastrian god of light, and enjoyed absolute authority.[5] Beneath him functioned an efficient bureaucratic hierarchy, incorporating military, financial and religious officials. There also existed a small group of noble families, traditionally seven in number, whose power could rival that of the king.[6] During the reign of a strong king, such as Shapur I or Shapur II, this system operated smoothly, giving rise to unprecedented levels of cultivation and habitation in Lower Mesopotamia and Susiana by the sixth century. The government appears to have played a key role in extending areas of cultivation through the construction and upkeep of canals, while kings also took the initiative in founding cities, sometimes as commercial centres, sometimes for defence.[7] But the remarkable prosperity of the agricultural heartland of the empire, the plains of Lower Mesopotamia, was fragile. Strong central control was necessary to maintain the canal system, and Roman armies, following well-trodden invasion routes along the Euphrates or Tigris, posed a serious threat to this region.[8]

---

[4]   Nöldeke, *Tabari*, 436a for a family tree of the Sasanian kings. On Sasan and the establishment of the Persian capital, Frye, 'The political history', 116–20. In the chaos of the early seventh century there were a few kings not descended from Ardashir, *ibid.* 170–71.

[5]   Morony, *Iraq*, 29–30, Christensen, *L'Iran*, 300–2.

[6]   On the officials, Morony, *Iraq*, 28 and Howard-Johnston, 'Great Powers', 218–19; on the seven families, Morony, *op. cit.*, 186, Christensen, *L'Iran*, 103–10. They held a monopoly of certain posts.

[7]   On the population levels and the role of the monarchy and central government see Wenke, 'Western Iran', 255–60, emphasising the government's strength, cf. Christensen, *Iranshahr*, 67–74. Cf. also Adams, *Land behind Baghdad*, 69–73 and *idem*, *Heartland of Cities*, 181, with the remarks of Howard-Johnston, 'Great Powers', 221–5 (cautioning against seeing too great a conflict between the monarchy and the seven families). Useful summary in Lee, *Information*, 19–20.
      On the founding of cities for commerce, see Wenke, *art. cit.*, 255, Adams, *Heartland of Cities*, 200–1. Lukonin 'Taxes and trade', 723, on the founding of cities for defence, cf. Christensen, *L'Iran*, 287 (Yazdgerd II founding Shahristan i Yazdgard, to the east of the Caspian Sea, for defence against steppe peoples); also Frye, 'Sasanian system', 13.

[8]   Adams, *Heartland*, 213, on the need for central control and the fragility of the system; also Wenke, 'Western Iran', 260. The canals could be put to defensive use: cf. Matthews, *Roman Empire*, 149–54, on the difficulties this caused Julian in 363. But the Sasanian kingdom never recovered from the devastation resulting from Heraclius' invasion in 628, cf. Adams, *Land behind Baghdad*, 82. Howard-Johnston, 'Great Powers', 214 and n.122, perhaps overestimates the strength of Persian finances, especially in light of what is known about their treasury at the end of the fifth century (on which see below).

Other neighbours, however, proved more dangerous to the Sasanian state in the fifth century. Chief among them were the Kidarites, also known as Kushans or Chols, who, following their demise in the 460s, were succeeded by the still more redoubtable Hephthalite Huns.[9] The peoples of the Transcaucasus, as well as the Armenians, also proved to be stubborn foes. Until 428 the portion of Armenia under Persian control continued to be ruled, however ineffectually, by Arsacid kings. At the request of the Armenians, the last Arsacid, Ardashir IV, was then removed and a Persian *marzban*, or military governor, installed at Dvin.[10] But it was not until Yazdgerd II made strenuous efforts to convert the Christian Armenians, Iberians and Albanians to Zoroastrianism that trouble broke out.[11] Even after the Armenians were decisively defeated in 451 hostilities continued; the Albanians were able to inflict serious damage on the Persians by opening up the Derbent pass next to the Caspian Sea, thus permitting the Huns from north of the Caucasus to irrupt into Persian territory.[12] By the time of Yazdgerd's death in 457 the Kidarites were still undefeated, and concessions had to be made to the Transcaucasian peoples.[13] This war on two fronts must have imposed a severe strain on Sasanian resources; and the civil war which erupted in the wake of the Yazdgerd's death points to the divisions resulting from his harsh policies.[14]

The younger son of Yazdgerd, Peroz, emerged victorious from the civil war and ascended the throne in 459.[15] His reign, and that of his

---

[9]   On the campaign against the Kidarites/Chols, Christensen, *L'Iran*, 287; Schippmann, *Grundzüge*, 44 and n.131, prefers to identify them with the Hephthalites. They were situated to the east of the Caspian Sea, cf. Marquart, *Eranšahr*, 51. On the Hephthalites, see below.

[10]   Grousset, *Histoire*, 182–8, Chaumont in *EIr* II, 428–9, Hewsen, 'An introduction', 87.

[11]   On the conversion of the Armenians see Chaumont, *Recherches*, 131–64; on the Iberians, *eadem*, 'Conquêtes Sassanides', 705–6. See also Braund, *Georgia*, 238–9, 246–53. The extent of Christianisation of the Albanians is uncertain, but of their resistance to the Persians there is no doubt: Chaumont, 'Conquêtes Sassanides', 707–8 and Movses Dasxuranci I.10, II.2. On Yazdgerd's attempts at conversion, see Lang, 'Iran, Armenia and Georgia', 521, Christensen, *L'Iran*, 283–8; also see ch.6.ii below.

[12]   Grousset, *Histoire*, 189–207, Dédéyan, *Histoire*, 162–5; also Marquart, *Eranšahr*, 97, Movses Dasxuranci, I.10, II.2, Elishe 242 [198].

[13]   Marquart, *Eranšahr*, 97–8, Grousset, *Histoire*, 212–13, Christensen, *L'Iran*, 287–9; also Chaumont, *EIr* II, 429–30.

[14]   Christensen, *L'Iran*, 289–90, Schippmann, *Grundzüge*, 43–4 on the war. Note Proc. I.16.6 for a Persian complaint on the difficulties of maintaining two armies.

[15]   Christensen, *L'Iran*, 290, noting the support he appears to have received from the Zoroastrian clergy and from one of the seven noble families. It is possible that, like

successor Balash, marked the nadir of the Persian monarchy before the turmoil of the seventh century. Initially Peroz enjoyed some success: he re-established peace in Armenia, releasing the Armenian nobles whom Yazdgerd had led off in captivity, although the Albanians remained refractory.[16] At some point the Lazi, the people situated on the Black Sea coast to the west of the Iberians, actually came into the Sasanian orbit. Attempts to convert the region to Zoroastrianism continued, and one Iberian ruler at least succumbed. This merely had the effect, however, of triggering a general uprising in Armenia and Iberia. The revolt began c.481 and was only brought to an end by substantial Persian concessions during the reign of Balash.[17]

The campaigns of Peroz against the Kidarites were crowned by success, but only after a sustained effort: as has been seen, the king had made frequent appeals to the Romans for funds throughout the 460s. Apart from the war against the Kidarites, and the need to guard the Transcaucasus (as well as the passes over the Caucasus mountains), the Persians had a further reason for seeking funds in the 460s. A lengthy drought afflicted the empire from 464, which according to the Arab tradition lasted seven years, and obliged Peroz to reduce taxes and organise emergency distributions of grain.[18] Once the Kidarites had been crushed, Peroz did not hesitate to inform the Romans. His embassy brought the news to Leo in Constantinople in 466: 'they reported their victory', according to Priscus, 'and in barbaric fashion boasted about it, since they wished to advertise the very large force which they had at present.' While the announcement may have been intended in part to dissuade the Romans from continuing to intervene in Lazica, the emphasis on the large number of forces assembled may also have been aimed at underlining their need for financial support.[19]

---

his son Kavadh, he received the backing of the Hephthalites in gaining the throne; this is doubted by Christensen, *L'Iran*, 289 n.5, accepted by Schippmann, *Grundzüge*, 44 and n.134. Cf. also Nöldeke, *Tabari*, 115 and 117.

[16] Grousset, *Histoire*, 212–13, Marquart, *Eranšahr*, 98, Frye, *Ancient Iran*, 321–2.

[17] Braund, *Georgia*, 283–4, on continuing Persian problems in controlling Iberia and the apostasy of Varsken; also Toumanoff in *CMH* IV, 600. Braund, *op. cit,*, 272–5, on the defection of the Lazi from Rome, probably in the 470s. On the revolt, Grousset, *Histoire*, 216–26, Thomson, *Lazar*, 15–16. See p.48 below on Balash's settlement.

[18] Ch.2 p.16. Christensen, *L'Iran*, 290–91, on the drought; Rawlinson, *Seventh Monarchy*, 441, following the Arab tradition, dates its outbreak to 464. See also Nöldeke, *Tabari*, 118–19, and Bal'ami II.24 (128–30); the latter reports that supplies were forthcoming from the Romans, among others.

[19] Priscus, frg.53 on the current war in Lazica (and Suania) and the embassy to Leo (cited in Blockley's translation); dated to 466 by Blockley, *FCH* I, 122. Blockley also

There can therefore be little doubt that the Sasanian empire was in serious difficulties at this time, even before the arrival of the Hephthalites. And no sooner had Peroz annihilated the Kidarites than he was forced to turn his attention to this new enemy threatening the north-east sector of his empire. At some point in the 470s he undertook a large expedition against the Hephthalites, but met with utter defeat. He was captured in battle and held to ransom.

> Boastfully promising to pay for his life a ransom of thirty mule-loads of drachmas, he sent the order for it back to his own realm but could hardly muster twenty loads, for by the previous wars he had completely emptied the royal treasury (inherited from) his predecessor. (Josh. Styl. §10, tr. Watt)

Peroz was therefore obliged to give the Hephthalites his son Kavadh as a hostage, while he gathered the ten outstanding loads; he also promised not to attack them again.[20] In light of this reverse, it is not surprising that the Armenians and Iberians determined to lift the banner of revolt once again in the early 480s. Worse was to follow.

In 484 Peroz, despite his promise, mounted another assault on the Hephthalite kingdom. He raised another army, which marched with reluctance into Hephthalite territory. There it was led astray by enemy spies and destroyed; much of the army perished upon falling into trenches constructed for that purpose by the Hephthalites. Peroz became the first and only Sasanian king to die in battle, and many of his children died with him; according to some sources, such was the slaughter that his body was never recovered. The fortunes of the Persian kingdom — and of the Persian monarchy — were at a low ebb.[21] The role of the seven noble families increased accordingly, and

---

draws attention to the strain on Persian resources in maintaining a large army, *FCH* II, 398 n.180.

[20] Many dates have been put forward for this initial campaign against the Hephthalites: Schippmann, *Grundzüge*, 44, prefers 469, but cf. Lippold, 'Hephthalitai', 134–5 and Blockley, *ERFP*, 253 n.39. Proc. I.3.8–22 clearly places this defeat during the reign of Zeno (i.e. after 474), as does Josh. Styl. (§10), who, however, reports that Peroz was captured twice; on the first occasion Zeno provided the funds to release him. Christensen, *L'Iran*, 293 n.4, is rightly sceptical of this version. For a recent brief treatment of the Hephthalites see Sinor in *CHEIA*, 298–301.

[21] Christensen, *L'Iran*, 294, Frye, *Ancient Iran*, 322, on the defeat, for which many sources are available, e.g. Proc. I.4, Lazar 214–16 [154–6], Nöldeke, *Tabari*, 119–32 (three different versions). See also Cameron, 'Sassanians', 153, on the various sources. Proc. *Wars* I.4.14 erroneously claims that all Peroz's sons were killed.

two of their number who were campaigning in Armenia rushed back to Ctesiphon to ensure the succession of a suitable ruler.[22]

Their choice fell upon a brother of Peroz, Balash, described by the Armenian historian Lazar P'arpec'i as a 'benevolent and gentle man': the time had come for conciliation with the Christians of the Transcaucasus. A considerable degree of autonomy was granted to the Armenians, as well as freedom of worship. Thus the region was pacified at last, and the Armenians gave Balash their support in crushing a revolt by a son of Peroz named Zarer.[23] But the financial pressure facing the king was overwhelming: 'he found nothing in the Persian treasury, and his land was laid waste and depopulated by the Huns ... and from the Greeks (i.e. the Romans) he had no help of any kind such as his brother had.'[24] Confirmation of the continuing hardship faced by those within the Persian empire may be found in an anecdote recounted by Tabari: whenever the king heard that a farm had been abandoned, he punished the *dekhan* (mayor) of the village concerned, on the grounds that he had failed to support the peasant, who had therefore been forced to leave. Evidently farmers were being forced by economic circumstances to quit their lands.[25]

Balash had been able to resolve the conflict in the Transcaucasus, but the replenishment of the state coffers remained beyond his grasp. The Hephthalites continued to drain Sasanian resources until the 540s,

---

[22] Christensen, *L'Iran*, 294–5, cf. Schippmann, *Grundzüge*, 45, and Frye, 'The political history', 149, on the rise of the noble families. Christensen, *L'Iran*, 263–6, notes the increased role of the nobility in selecting kings in this period. Noteworthy too is the attempt by the Karen house (one of the seven noble families) to claim that a certain Sokhra, a member of their family, avenged Peroz's defeat shortly afterwards; no contemporary sources justify this story, to be found in Tabari. Cf. Christensen, *L'Iran*, 294 n.5, 296 and Nöldeke, *Tabari*, 130 n.3.

[23] Lazar, [157], tr. Thomson 217, for the quotation, cf. the views of Josh. Styl. §18 and Agathias IV.27.6 (with Cameron, 'Sassanians', 155). Christensen, *L'Iran*, 295, Lazar 220–33 [160–72] on the settlement in Armenia; also Grousset, *Histoire*, 227–9, Blockley, *ERFP*, 84. Numismatic evidence suggests that Kavadh, Balash's successor in 488, may have made a bid for the throne already in 484: cf. Schipmann, *Grundzüge*, 46 n.140 and Göbl, 'Sasanian coins'.

[24] Josh. Styl. §18. According to two of the versions reported by Tabari (Nöldeke, 126, 132), the Persian treasury had fallen into Hephthalite hands in 484. The later Arab tradition appears to date the start of the accumulation of capital in the Sasanian treasury to the reigns of Kavadh and Peroz, cf. Morony, *Iraq*, 31 n.19, Christensen, *L'Iran*, 453 n.4. But the fact that 48 million *mithqals* are said to have been minted under the two rulers need not imply that the state was any more prosperous at the time, cf. Rubin, 'The Reforms', 263.

[25] Nöldeke, *Tabari*, 134. On the term *dekhan* see now Tafazzoli in *EIr* VII, 223.

forcing the Persian kings to make tribute payments to them.[26] Moreover, the Romans were not only failing to provide any financial aid, but
were also exerting pressure to recover Nisibis.[27] With the Armenians
conciliated and the Hephthalites triumphant, the Sasanian army,
inevitably demoralised, was in no mood to tolerate an absence of pay;
as Joshua the Stylite says, 'because he [Balash] had no money to
maintain his troops, [he] was despised in their eyes'.[28] Furthermore, he
had alienated the Zoroastrian priests (the Magi), and the high nobility
too were unhappy with the extent of his concessions to the Christians in
his kingdom. After only four years therefore Balash was removed from
the throne and blinded; his successor was Kavadh, son of Peroz.[29]

Kavadh's position upon mounting the throne in 488 could not have
been weaker. He owed his position to the noble families, in particular
Zarmihr/Sokhra of the Karen family and Shapur of Ray, of the Mihran
house, as well as to his good relations with the Hephthalites, with
whom he had spent some time as a hostage.[30] The lack of funds remained pressing, and in 491 Kavadh sent an embassy to the Roman
court to demand money; he menaced war if the demand was not met,
but did not carry out the threat immediately upon hearing of the emperor's refusal.[31] For he was still engaged in securing his own position
at the expense of the nobles who had promoted him to the throne. At
some point in the 490s he engineered the execution of Sokhra at the
hands of Shapur, then the commander-in-chief of his forces (the *Eran-
spahbadh*).[32] Kavadh's grip on his kingdom remained limited,

---

[26] Proc. I.4.35 seriously underestimates the duration of Persia's status as tributary to the
Hephthalites: see Christensen, *L'Iran*, 297 and n.2, Marquart, *Eranšahr*, 62–3 and
Schippmann, *Grundzüge*, 44. An example of a Sasanian coin with a Hephthalite
countermark, presumably part of a tribute payment, may be found in Allchin–
Hammond, *Archaeology of Afghanistan*, 250 fig.5.19.

[27] Josh. Styl. §18, and see above ch.2 n.71.

[28] Josh. Styl. §19.

[29] Josh. Styl. §19, Christensen, *L'Iran*, 296–7, *Le règne*, 92–3, Schippmann, *Grundzüge*,
45.

[30] Christensen, *L'Iran*, 297, Schippmann, *Grundzüge*, 46. On the identity of Zarmihr
and Sokhra cf. Christensen, *Le règne*, 92 n.1 and Nöldeke, *Tabari*, 120 n.3 and 140
n.2. He will henceforth be referred to as Sokhra. On Kavadh's tenuous position in
488, note Sebeos, p.4 (tr. R. W. Thomson): 'Because the power of his numerous army
had been broken, he did not wish to engage in war with anyone, but made peace on
all sides.'

[31] Josh. Styl. §19 for the embassy, sent out while Zeno was still alive, perhaps therefore
in 490.

[32] Christensen, *L'Iran*, 336, Frye, 'The political history', 150, Nöldeke, *Tabari*, 140.
Schippmann, *Grundzüge*, 46, places Sokhra's fall in 494/5.

however: the Armenians resisted his efforts to convert them to Zoroastrianism, while other tribes to the south also rose up against him. The Tamuraye, a highland tribe of Iran, engaged in some sort of revolt, while the Kadishaye, a people inhabiting the Jebel Sinjar and the lands to the north, actually attacked the city of Nisibis. Arab tribesmen, perhaps of the Kindite confederation, were also launching raids on Persian territory.[33] The one consolation for the Persian king was that his Roman counterpart was also involved in internal struggles: Anastasius waged a bitter war for much of the 490s against the rebellious Isaurians, who were only finally crushed in 498. Kavadh believed that he had now found the ideal opportunity to press the emperor for money, but the embassy he sent was only partly successful: Anastasius was willing to offer the king a loan, but not to give him money outright.[34]

Not long after this, probably in 496, Kavadh himself was ousted and imprisoned, and his brother Zamasp elevated to the throne in his stead.[35] Evidently the removal of Sokhra had failed to restore the authority of the monarchy, and the king had further undermined his own position by supporting a radical sect, the Mazdakites. The followers of Mazdak, who were eventually massacred in the early 530s, espoused a type of communism, holding goods and wives in common. Whether this movement was supported by Kavadh before his overthrow, or only afterwards, is unclear. It may reasonably be supposed, however, that the harsh circumstances within the kingdom helped give rise to the revolutionary sect, and that it suited the king to give it some support as a means of reducing the power of the nobility and the Zoroastrian clergy.[36]

---

[33] On the peoples in revolt, see Josh. Styl. §§21–2 with Nöldeke, 'Zwei Völker', 157–66 (158 n.4 on the Tamuraye); see below ch.8 n.32 on the Kadishaye. On the rising power of the Kindites, see Rothstein, Die Lahmiden, 87–9, Olinder, Kings of Kinda, 57–8.

[34] Josh. Styl. §23 on this request for money and the Isaurian war, cf. Stein II, 81–4. Blockley, ERFP, 89, dates this second request to 491 or 492, though it could have occurred at any time before Kavadh's expulsion.

[35] On the date of the coup, Christensen, L'Iran 348 n.5, Nöldeke, Tabari, 427–8, and Schippmann, Grundzüge, 49.

[36] The bibliography on this much debated question is extensive. See Christensen, Le règne, for an analysis of all the traditions, esp. 96–106 on the beliefs of the Mazdakites. Yarshater, 'Mazdakism', 991–3, reviews earlier treatments of the sect and goes on to consider Mazdakism in general. See also Schippmann, Grundzüge, 46–9, Wirth, 'Anastasius, Christen und Perser', 127–36, and Crone, 'Kavad's heresy', who doubts

It was these elements — the clergy and the nobility — that joined forces to overthrow Kavadh. One of the principal conspirators was Gushnaspdadh, a high-ranking general (*kanarang*) who controlled the region which adjoined Hephthalite territory. He had been entrusted by Sokhra with the task of negotiating with the Armenians after the defeat of Peroz, and was heavily critical of the king in his discussions. He now advocated the elimination of Kavadh, who, he feared, would otherwise return to power with Hephthalite help.[37] But the other assembled nobles were unwilling to shed royal blood and instead imprisoned Kavadh in the so-called 'Castle of Oblivion'. Some remained loyal to the deposed king, however, and he was able to escape. He fled to the Hephthalite kingdom, where he was supplied in due course with the forces necessary to wrest the throne from his brother. Zamasp, who had clearly done little to secure his own position, was pardoned by Kavadh, but some of the nobility were executed.[38]

Thus in 498/9 Kavadh found himself once more the master of the Sasanian state. The situation of the kingdom was no happier than it had been ten years earlier; indeed, it was probably worse. The Persians remained tributary to the Hephthalites, and now their king owed them his throne. The need to maintain the tribute payments to them was consequently paramount; and just at this moment we hear of another famine striking Persia. Under such circumstances the treasury was unlikely to recover. Moreover, the Tamuraye and the Kadishaye remained in a state of unrest: the latter were again besieging the city of

---

that any radical measures were proposed, save the sharing of wives, before Kavadh's expulsion.

   Christensen attributed Kavadh's support for the movement to his concern for the people (e.g. *L'Iran*, 345–6), while Nöldeke (*Tabari*, 461) regarded it as a means to counter the influence of the nobility; Yarshater combines these two views convincingly ('Mazdakism', 1020–21).

[37] Christensen, *L'Iran*, 295 on the negotiations in Armenia, cf. Lazar, 219, 226–7 [159, 165–6]. On Gushnaspdadh's role in Kavadh's overthrow, Christensen, *L'Iran*, 348–9, Schippmann, *Grundzüge*, 49, with Proc. I.5.4–7. On the position of *kanarang*, see Christensen, *L'Iran*, 107–8 n.3.

[38] On the reluctance to shed royal blood, see Whitby, 'Persian king', 251–2. The escape and return of Kavadh inspired many tales, e.g. in Proc. I.5–6, Tabari (Nöldeke), 135–8, 143–5, Josh. Styl. §24; see Christensen, *L'Iran*, 349–51, esp. 350 n.1. Agathias, IV.28.7–8, with Cameron, 'Sassanians', 157–9, on the sparing of Zamasp. Yarshater, 'Mazdakism', 1021 and n.3, on support for Kavadh among the aristocracy; Josh. Styl. §24 for the execution of some nobles.

Nisibis.[39] The time had evidently come for another appeal to Constantinople for money. Again the Persians were offered a loan rather than an outright payment: the emperor was, it appears, aware of Kavadh's plight, but reluctant to free him entirely from dependence on the Hephthalites.[40]

At this point the king's options were very limited. He had payments to make to the Hephthalites, some of whose troops remained with him, as well as to the Persian army. Only one easy source of revenue was available — the cities of the Roman East. A campaign directed against them would be sure to bring in large sums of money, whether as booty from captured cities or as payments extorted from frightened citizens.[41] So the king decided to strike at the Roman cities, and he compelled the local peoples to participate in the operation; some at least were not unwilling to serve, attracted by the riches to be gained from the surprise attack.[42]

ii) The Sasanian army

Little certain can be said of the Sasanian army. Its size, its structure and even its status (whether it was a standing army or not) are still debated. Some information can be gathered from later Arabic sources, but we are dependent for the most part on Roman writers, in particular Ammianus Marcellinus and Procopius.[43]

---

[39]   For the date of Kavadh's return to power cf. Nöldeke, *Tabari*, 427–8, Christensen, *L'Iran*, 350, Schippmann, *Grundzüge*, 50. On the famine in Persia, Frye, *Ancient Iran*, 323 and note Josh. Styl. §§33–44 on the famine which struck Roman Mesopotamia from 498–500. Josh Styl. §24 on the siege of Nisibis by the Kadishaye.

[40]   Theoph. A.M. 5996 (144), cf. Theod. Lect. *HE* 552, on the offer of a loan, and see Mango–Scott's notes, 224 n.1. Proc. I.7.1–2 on Roman awareness of Kavadh's situation, though he believes that the Persians only sought a loan in the first place. Blockley, *ERFP*, 89 and 218 n.25, suggests that the sources have conflated Kavadh's various demands for money, and that no request was made at this point. This is possible, though two independent sources (Theod. Lect. and Proc.) vouch for the fact that a demand was made at this point; and the Persians had sent numerous such embassies previously.

[41]   See above ch.2, pp.7–8 on this.

[42]   Josh. Styl. §24 on the role of the Kadishaye, the Tamuraye and the Arabs; the Armenians were more reluctant, but took part nonetheless. On the riches to be had from the cities see the evidence assembled by Iluk, 'The export of gold', 92 and Whittow, 'Ruling the late Roman city', 17.

[43]   On the sources available, Howard-Johnston, 'Great Powers', 169–80, pessimistic about both Arabic and Roman sources, but noting that information may be gained from Armenian and Jewish sources as well. Cf. also Adontz, *Armenia*, 339–43, for some comparative evidence from Armenia.

The commander in chief of the Persian army was the *Eran-spahbadh*, under whom various officers served, such as *kanarangs*, *spahbadhs* and *marzbans*. But the king himself frequently took charge of campaigns, in contrast to most East Roman emperors in late antiquity.[44] For a Persian king it was an important demonstration of his fitness to govern as well as an opportunity to unite his kingdom behind him, especially the potentially fractious nobility; undoubtedly these considerations will not have escaped Kavadh in 502.[45] The king's role in battle would usually be to observe and direct his forces from a distance, but on occasion he might enter the fray in person.[46]

The most important element of the Sasanian army was its cavalry. At the time of Khusro I each cavalryman is said to have been equipped with horse-armour, a hauberk, a breastplate, greaves, a sword, a spear, a circular shield, a mace strapped to his belt, an axe, and a quiver holding two bows with strings and 30 arrows; a lasso was also sometimes carried.[47] A massed array of such heavily armed cavalry, each unit distinguished by its own battle-standard, presented a formidable sight to any opponent. The élite corps of the Persian army, the ten thousand 'Immortals' — the name recalling that of the unit which fought against the Greeks at Thermopylae in 480 B.C. — will have offered just such a spectacle.[48]

---

[44] Christensen, *L'Iran*, 130–31, Nöldeke, *Tabari*, 444, on the commanders. *Marzbans* generally governed a frontier province, Christensen, *L'Iran*, 102, but the fourfold division of the Sasanian empire frequently posited in connection with the commands of the *marzbans* may be doubted, cf. Gignoux, 'L'organisation administrative', 4, 26. Gignoux sees the *marzban* as a military officer first and foremost, with some role in civilian matters; he was important at the local level, but not part of the central government, *ibid.* 26. On the role of the Persian king in war, see Whitby, 'Persian king', esp. 256–8 on the differences between Roman emperors and Persian kings in this period.

[45] Whitby, 'Persian king', 238–9, Frye, *Ancient Iran*, 323.

[46] Whitby, 'Persian king', 239–40, cf. Christensen, *L'Iran*, 212.

[47] Nöldeke, *Tabari*, 248–9, Christensen, *L'Iran*, 368, Shahbazi, 'Army', 497; see also the appendix in Bivar, 'Cavalry Equipment', 291. For illustrations of these warriors, *ibid.*, plates 5, 23 (Khusro I himself) and 30 (Khusro II). Lightfoot, *Eastern Frontier*, 134–7, notes the existence of light as well as heavy Persian cavalry.

[48] Christensen, *L'Iran*, 208, Shahbazi, 'Army', 497 on the Immortals; add Socr. *HE* VII.20 and the Armenian sources noted by Chaumont, *EIr* II, 430, to the list of sources in Christensen, *L'Iran*, 208 n.3, attesting the Immortals. Christensen, *L'Iran*, 210–11, for the banners. Ammianus XXV.1.12–13 and XXIV.6.8 for a description of the Persian forces, cf. the novelist Heliodorus' picture, *Aethiopica* IX.14.3–15, tr. in Dodgeon–Lieu, *Eastern Frontier*, 209–10 (on which see Eadie, 'Roman mailed cavalry', 170). Cf. also Chapot, *Frontière*, 48–50.

This heavy cavalry, while proficient with the bow, relied above all on its fearsome charges to overcome the enemy; and, as has been seen, the Romans too had incorporated such *clibanarii* into their forces.[49] If success was not achieved in the mêlée, the cavalry were prone to lose heart and disengage; they then covered their withdrawal by firing off arrows behind them.[50] The men who made up the Sasanian cavalry were for the most part members of the lesser nobility, for whom the burden of supplying and maintaining their equipment and mount was considerable. Following the reforms introduced by Khusro I, they could look to the state for a regular salary; but before these changes, and especially during the troubled years of the late fifth century, it is doubtful whether they received any regular remuneration. They did, however, stand to gain considerably more booty than infantrymen.[51]

The large discrepancy in the spoils offered to cavalry and to infantry was not without reason. Seldom did the Sasanian infantry (the *paygan*) play a significant part in a battle, and when it was involved it rarely acquitted itself gloriously. Perhaps the most useful type of infantryman was the archer, equipped with a bow and a large curved shield. Units of archers would advance in the wake of the cavalry, discharging volleys of arrows.[52] Alongside the archers there were other soldiers, often the servants of noblemen on campaign, wielding spear and shield, who might be used for scaling walls or tending to the baggage.[53] Ammianus'

---

[49] Schippmann, *Grundzüge*, 104, Shahbazi, 'Army', 497, Morony, *Iraq*, 210, cf. Bivar, 'Cavalry Equipment', 277–9. Garsoïan, 'Byzantium and the Sasanians', 580–81 on Sasanian influences on Roman military practice; Eadie, 'Roman mailed cavalry', 170–73, draws attention to the limited success of this Roman heavy cavalry. By the sixth century Roman cavalry was somewhat lighter, see above ch.2, 39 and n.123. Horse-archery among the Sasanians enjoyed a revival from the fourth century, cf. Bivar, *art. cit.*, 284–6.

[50] Ammianus XXV.1.18, accepted by Christensen, *L'Iran*, 207–8, Shahbazi, 'Army', 498. Bivar, 'Cavalry Equipment', 285 and n.52 for a representation of a cavalryman firing while seated backwards.

[51] Ammianus XXIII.6.83 is a key passage on the role of the nobility, cf. Shahbazi, 'Army', 497, Christensen, *L'Iran*, 367. Tabari (Nöldeke), 164 (noted by Christensen, *loc. cit.*), on the provisions made by Khusro, implying that hitherto the state had not made such payments. Morony, *Iraq*, 58 on the cavalry getting up to forty times more booty than infantry. On the situation after Khusro's changes, see Whitby, 'Persian king', 254–5 and Rubin, 'The Reforms', 290–91; it is not possible to retroject the institution of paying soldiers before Khusro's reign.

[52] Ammianus XXIV.6.8 with Shahbazi, 'Army', 497 and Lightfoot, *Eastern Frontier*, 137, 140.

[53] Christensen, *L'Iran*, 209 and Shahbazi, 'Army', 497. On their equipment, see Ammianus XXIV.6.83 and Proc. I.14.52.

picture of these ineffectual troops receives confirmation from Procopius: he reports that before the battle of Dara in 530 Belisarius and Hermogenes pointed out to the Roman soldiers how 'their [the Persian] infantry is nothing more than a crowd of pitiable peasants.' Their description was vindicated by the behaviour of the infantry in the battle: once the cavalry had been routed they threw away their shields and were cut down by the Roman cavalry.[54] The elephant, an instrument of war so feared by Ammianus, had become rarer in Sasanian armies by the sixth century. There is evidence that some were still in use, but the failure of Roman sources to make more than passing mention of them implies that they no longer enjoyed the prominence they had once held.[55]

To supplement these forces, the Sasanian kings made frequent use of neighbouring or subject peoples in their armies. Ammianus personally observed the units of Chionites under their king Grumbates, who were among the besiegers of Amida in 359; also taking part in the siege were Gelani, Albanians and Segestani (from Sistan in the east of Iran).[56] A century and a half later the auxiliaries had changed, but their importance remained. As has been seen, Kavadh's army contained Hephthalites, Arabs, Tamuraye, Kadishaye (Kadiseni) and Armenians. Sabir Huns from north of the Caucasus were also employed, as were the Sunitae (the Siwnik).[57] The forces supplied by these various peoples were mainly cavalry, often rather lighter than the Sasanian horsemen. Whether they came from within or from outside the empire they needed to be supplied and paid; the neighbouring peoples were, in effect,

---

[54] Proc. I.14.25, 52, noted by Nöldeke, *Tabari*, 442.

[55] Ammianus XXV.1.14–15, cf. XIX.2.3 with Matthews, *Roman Empire*, 63–4, Chapot, *Frontière*, 51–2 and Lightfoot, *Eastern Frontier*, 138–9. Kavadh rode into Amida in 503 on an elephant, see below ch.5 n.60, and (according to Josh. Styl. §62) employed them against the city of Edessa. But although Justinian, in strengthening the fortifications of Dara, foresaw that the Persians would attack the city using platforms positioned on elephants (Proc. *Aed.* II.1.11), Procopius records the Persians as using elephants only in campaigns in the Transcaucasus.

[56] Ammianus XIX.1.7 with Matthews, *Roman Empire*, 61–3 and Christensen, *L'Iran*, 209.

[57] Proc. I.15.1 for these last contingents. Little is known of the equipment of these allies, though Proc. describes the Hephthalites as having used bows (I.7.8); Tabari, on the other hand, implies that they did not use missile weapons, cf. Nöldeke, *Tabari*, 127 (with Bal'ami, II.26 [143]). Proc. should be preferred here, since the episode in Tabari (a victory by Sokhra over the Hephthalites) is an obvious fabrication, cf. Christensen, *L'Iran*, 296. Josh. Styl. §62 refers to the Huns (i.e. the Hephthalites) using thongs, but the reading of the word is uncertain.

employed as mercenaries, summoned when necessary and returning to their own territories upon the completion of the war.[58]

Among these auxiliaries the case of the Arabs is somewhat exceptional. Just as the Romans came to rely largely on the Ghassanid tribe, so the Persians had, since the fourth century, entrusted the Lakhmid dynasty with defending their interests in the desert regions to the west of Ctesiphon. The capital of the Lakhmids lay at Hira, on the edge of the desert near where the city of Kufa would later emerge; their domains came to spread over much of the Arabian peninsula.[59] Various Arab tribes served in the Lakhmid forces; and the dynasty was further assisted by the presence of one thousand Persian heavy cavalry at Hira. They proved valuable allies of the Sasanians, particularly under their ruler al-Mundhir who from 503/4 to his death in 554 struck fear into the hearts of all those living in the diocese of Oriens. Lakhmid rulers could also operate independently against the Romans so that the Sasanians were able to deny any involvement in their actions; Justinian therefore sought to negotiate with them directly, though with little success.[60]

The question of numbers, hitherto deferred, must now be addressed. Bound up with it is the issue of whether or not the Sasanians maintained a standing army. A sixth-century source, John the Lydian, explicitly denies the existence of such a force, drawing upon the tactician Celsus: 'for it is evident that the Persians do not maintain specific bodies of troops in a state of mobilization so as to be ready to do battle, as the Romans do.'[61] That no permanent bodies of forces existed, however, is highly unlikely. Mention has already been made of a thousand cavalry posted at Hira, and other cities in frontier regions were guarded by garrisons of various sizes: following the hand-over of Nisibis to Shapur II in 363, some 12,000 Persians were transplanted

---

[58]   Shahbazi, 'Army', 497, Christensen, *L'Iran*, 210, Schippmann, *Grundzüge*, 105–6.
[59]   Bosworth, 'Iran and the Arabs', 597–600, Morony, *Iraq*, 151 and Rothstein, *Lahmiden*, 14, 18–40, Howard-Johnston, 'Great Powers', 188–9.
[60]   Bosworth, 'Iran and the Arabs', 599–600 on the cavalry; note also the role played by the Lakhmids in assisting Bahram V in mounting the throne, Christensen, *L'Iran*, 274–5. Above ch.2 n.78 on the fear inspired by al-Mundhir; Shahîd, *BASIC* I.1, 17–18, on the date of his accession. Rothstein, *Die Dynastie der Lahmiden*, 127 on their importance and Justinian's dealings, cf. Shahîd, *BASIC* I, 273–4 (citing Menander frg.6.1.288–303). On occasion they played an important role in great-power diplomacy: Scott, 'Diplomacy', 163–4 with Mal. 466–7 and Shahîd, *BASIC* I, 142–3.
[61]   John Lydus, *de Mag.* III.34.3, tr. Carney. On this passage see Kaegi, 'Two notes on Heraclius', 225–6 and n.14.

there, many of whom will have formed the permanent garrison of the city. Our sources are too scanty to allow for certainty about the status of the Immortals, but it is unlikely that such an élite unit would have been disbanded at the end of every conflict.[62] The bulk of the Sasanian army, the infantry, was raised when the need arose, which would account for its inadequacy in battle. Whether it was assembled by the nobles according to a 'feudal' system or whether muster-rolls were kept by the state is unknown; it is equally unclear whether or not the infantrymen received any pay. From the time of Khusro I a greater degree of centralisation is evident, but uncertainty arises as to how different the army structure was before his reforms and how far the Arab sources retroject conditions which applied under Khusro to an earlier period.[63]

The Persians probably disposed of some 15,000 seasoned troops for war in the west before calling upon any levies; at least 5000 Arab horsemen could be added to that total.[64] This number could be greatly increased by the use of mercenaries and subject peoples, as well as by levies of infantry. Procopius refers to an army of 50,000 facing the Romans at the battle of Dara in 530, at the same time as an invasion of Roman Armenia was being undertaken by some 30,000 men.[65] An upper limit to the size of a Sasanian field army of around fifty or sixty thousand tallies with the Persian tradition; beyond this, problems of

[62] Morony, *Iraq*, 181 on the Persian forces at Nisibis (and Anbar); Howard-Johnston, 'Great Powers', 190 n.69 on the size of the garrison at Nisibis, which deterred Belisarius from attacking the city in 541. Note also the garrison at Pirisabora (Anbar), numbering at least 2500, Ammianus XXIV.2.22. Chapot, *La frontière*, 46–7, on the garrisons, following Nöldeke, *Tabari*, 442, against John Lydus. The garrison of Nisibis was under the command of a *marzban*, cf. Morony, *Iraq*, 131. Lee, *Information*, 19, argues that the 10,000 Immortals were a permanent force.

[63] Nöldeke, *Tabari*, 442, Chapot, *La frontière*, 47, and Lee, *Information*, 19 (with *idem*, 'Campaign preparations', 260–61), for the summoning of troops (likened by Chapot to a feudal system); Ammianus XXIII.6.83 asserts that the infantry received no pay, accepted by Shahbazi, 'Army', 497. Howard-Johnston, 'Great Powers', 219 and n.143 attaches greater value to the Arab sources, arguing that the troops were paid and that muster-rolls existed before Khusro. But the letter of Tansar, on which he relies, dates from the reign of Khusro I (cf. Christensen, *L'Iran*, 63–6 and Morony, *Iraq*, 184) and the description in it of conditions under Ardashir I actually reflects those of Khusro's reign.

[64] Mal. 461 reports al-Harith as being accompanied by 5000 men in 531 (cf. Shahîd, *BASIC* I, 136); the Lakhmids will certainly have been able to muster an equal number of troops. Socr. *HE* VII.18 offers the improbable figure of 100,000 Saracens killed during the war of 421–22. The figure of 15,000 is reached by combining the 10,000 Immortals and an estimate for the garrison of Nisibis.

[65] Proc. I.13.23, 14.1, 15.11, noted by Howard-Johnston, 'Great Powers', 165–6.

supply would have been almost insurmountable.[66] The bulk of these
many thousands would be provided by the infantry levies, and hence
was of limited use. But mercenaries and subject peoples will also have
furnished highly useful auxiliary cavalry in some numbers. Three
thousand Sabir Huns are said to have been recruited for the attack on
Satala in 530, while the Kadishaye (Kadiseni) were the mainstay of the
Persian right wing at the battle of Dara in the same year. Later in the
century Persian forces operating in the Transcaucasus received the
services of 12,000 Sabir Huns. Hephthalite numbers during the opening
phase of the war of 502–532 are less easily assessed; Procopius reports
that nearly eight hundred were killed by the Romans in 503, but this
was clearly only a part of their vanguard.[67]

It remains to stress the sophistication of the Sasanian military
machine. Unlike the Parthians, they were adept at siege warfare, a type
of operation requiring not only technical expertise but also an efficient
system of logistics to keep the besieging army supplied. Provisions for
the army were raised from the populace by means of taxes and rents;
payment was made in kind and deposited in storehouses until it was
required. In the west, depots are attested at Nisibis and Anbar.[68] And
just as the Romans had their military manuals, such as the *Peri Strategias* and Maurice's *Strategikon*, so the Persians had theirs: the *Ain-
nameh* (Book of Regulations) on the art of governing included much
information on military matters. The parts that have survived in a late
anthology offer advice on the deployment of an army, recommending

---

[66] Widengren, 'Sources', 1282 on the agreement between eastern and western sources,
cf. Schippmann, *Grundzüge*, 103 (with some higher figures) and Howard-Johnston,
167, 165 (for a later figure of an army just under 100,000 which had to be split into
three for the campaign). See also Shahbazi, 'Army', 497–8.

[67] Proc. I.8.13 on the 800 Hephthalites. According to Wirth, 'Anastasius, Christen und
Perser', 128 n.247, later sources refer to as many as 30,000, which may be closer to
the mark; yet although he describes this as a 'frequently cited figure', he fails to name
any sources. Proc. I.15.1 for 3000 Sabirs in 530; 14.38 on the Kadiseni. VIII.13.8 for
the 12,000 in 550 (most of which were dismissed by the Persian commander), cf. the
3000 Dilimnites under Nakhoragan's command somewhat later, Agathias III.17.6.
See also Christensen, *L'Iran*, 209–10, on the peoples employed by the Persians, and
the importance of the Armenian element. Note that both Proc. I.15.1 and Zach. IX.6
(228) explicitly attest the hiring of Hunnic forces by the Persians.

[68] Morony, *Iraq*, 61–2 and Lee, *Information*, 19–20 with *idem*, 'Campaign preparations', 259–60. Note the large quantity of provisions seized by Julian in 363 after
he had captured Pirisabora (Anbar), Ammianus XXIV.2.22. On the sophistication of
Persian siege techniques, see Christensen, *L'Iran*, 212–13, Chapot, *Frontière*, 52; a
vivid demonstration of their capabilities at an early stage is furnished by the evidence
from Dura Europus, on which see Leriche, 'Techniques de guerre', 83–100, esp. 86.

that combat be offered on the right rather than the left, as well as on archery techniques.[69]

It can be concluded that the Persians, for all their internal difficulties, remained a formidable power. Once mustered, their army might indeed be spoken of in boastful terms by ambassadors to the Constantinopolitan court. It remained an expensive instrument, however, which could not be employed over long periods. This in turn had an effect on the type of campaigns which could be waged. Long-term wars of attrition were impossible; swift invasions, the capture of poorly defended cities and the extortion of funds from others constituted the preferred alternative. Such, as will be seen, was the pattern of Persian campaigning in this war, as it would remain for the rest of the century.[70]

---

[69] Christensen, *L'Iran*, 62 with *EIr* I, 692, s.v. Ain-nameh, and Bogdanov, 'The Sasanian Military Theory', 7–10, 13, 35, 39–40. The *Peri Strategias* may not date from the sixth century, however: see above ch.2 n.121. The *Ain-nameh*, it has been suggested, may have been translated into Greek and influenced the *Strategikon*: *EIr* I, 692 and Miyakawa–Kollautz, 'Abdelai', 119.

[70] See above p.46 on the ambassadors' boast. The diminishing returns from the campaigns in the face of accumulating Roman forces also help to account for the swift termination of the first phase of the war in 505.

IV
The Sources

i) Introduction

In the ancient world wars seldom lacked a historian. Wars fought against 'the barbarian' were particularly popular, and most attractive of all were those waged against the Persians. For historians writing in Greek, the opportunity to follow in the footsteps of Herodotus was hard to resist. In the wake of the successful campaigns of Lucius Verus in 162–5 against the Parthians (often termed Persians by historians) many histories were produced; so inaccurate were they, and so excessive in their descriptions of Roman feats and eastern wonders, that they inspired the satirist Lucian to write his parodic *On how to write history*.[1] In the later Roman empire eastern campaigns had lost none of their allure: Julian's invasion of Persia, despite its failure, generated numerous accounts, while the more successful war of 421–22 was celebrated by the empress Eudocia herself in a poem.[2]

But by the opening of the sixth century, in the absence of successful wars against external foes, Roman historians (writing in Greek, it should be noted) were beginning to concentrate more on diplomatic affairs; this tendency is detectable, for instance, in Malchus of

---

[1] Millar, *Near East*, 112. Lucian, *Quomodo Historia conscribenda sit, passim*, with Jones, *Culture and Society*, 59–67. On the popularity of war, see Grant, *Greek and Roman Historians*, 76–80 with Woodman, 'From Hannibal to Hitler', 121. Fornara, *Nature of History*, 63–4, on the popularity of notable deeds (with Proc. I.1.1–2), cf. 102–3 (on histories of eastern campaigns).

[2] Ammianus is the most obvious source on Julian's expedition, but note also Magnus 3 (of Carrhae), Oribasius, Seleucus 1, Eutychianus 3 (authors of prose histories) and Callistus 1, author of an epic poem, all in *PLRE* I, and cf. Fornara, 'Julian's Persian expedition', 1–2; Zosimus, a surviving later source, probably followed Oribasius' account, Fornara, *art. cit.*, 13. On Eudocia's poem see Socr. *HE* VII.21.8 with Eudocia 2, *PLRE* II; note also Holum, 'Pulcheria's Crusade', 171–2, on the propaganda generated by this war.

Philadelphia, at work probably in the 490s.[3] Chroniclers, interested in the more distant past, were flourishing, and one military theorist at least was offering advice to the emperor, perhaps based partly on Roman experiences during the war.[4] Panegyrists under Anastasius, before the outbreak of war in 502, had little in the way of martial exploits to recount; the emperor had, it is true, finally subdued the troublesome Isaurians of south-east Asia Minor, but these were an inconsiderable people from within the empire. His war against the Blemmyes in southern Egypt may have attracted a panegyric, but only fragments survive.[5] The first phase of the war of 502–532 therefore provided panegyrists, poets and aspiring historians with a welcome opportunity to display their skill in lauding the emperor and his generals; Justinian for his part was sufficiently pleased by the conduct of the last phase of the war of 502–532 for him to ensure that it was recorded.[6]

ii) Lost sources

As with the earlier eastern wars mentioned above, some of the contemporary sources for the war of 502–532 no longer survive. We know of a lost epic poem by Colluthus of Lycopolis, which probably dealt with the war under Anastasius, and a lost history (perhaps just on the final phase of the war) composed by John the Lydian at Justinian's behest. The works of Eustathius of Epiphaneia, on the other hand, have not vanished entirely: he wrote a chronicle which covered all of world history up to 503, including a description of the siege of Amida in 502–3. Although none of his original works survive, he was cited by other writers, such as John Malalas and Evagrius, and hence is of some importance.[7]

---

[3]   Blockley, *FCH* I, 84, 93 (on diplomatic affairs), 71–2 (on the date of composition).
[4]   Chroniclers — e.g. Eustathius of Epiphaneia (see ii below) and Hesychius of Miletus, on whom cf. *PLRE* II, Hesychius 14 with Greatrex, 'Lawyers and Historians'. The military theorist was Urbicius, whose *Epitedeuma* seeks to compensate for the weakness of the Roman infantry; the author alludes also to the old age of the Roman commanders and the inexperience of their forces. See Rance, *Tactics*, 7–9 and Dain, 'Les stratégistes', 341 on Urbicius.
[5]   Vasiliev, *Justin I*, 285–6 and 286 n.49.
[6]   The Roman successes in the east are alluded to in the panegyric of Priscian, 254–60 (with Chauvot, 136–7, rightly connecting this passage with the Anastasian war), cf. 300 (on Hypatius' deeds against the Persians). On Justinian's efforts to commemorate the war, see below n.7 and iii.f; he also had an inscription set up to commemorate the peace treaty which ended the war, see v below.
[7]   Cameron, 'The date', 108, on Colluthus, cf. *ODB* II.1137 (more sceptical as to whether the lost work was concerned with the war). Joh. Lyd. *de Mag.* III.28

iii) Contemporary sources

a) Procopius

Our principal source for the whole war is Procopius. He was an eye-witness to certain events, a fact which prompted him to write his work; for the events of his own day at which he was not present he could consult his contemporaries, while for earlier times (such as the opening phase of the war) he was reliant, at least partly, on written sources. Some consideration of the author, his methods and his sources is therefore required.[8]

Procopius, 'a writer who must be accounted the most excellent Greek historian since Polybius', was born at Caesarea in Palestine early in the sixth century. Before his appointment as the *assessor* of the *dux Mesopotamiae* Belisarius in 527 it is uncertain what sort of training he received —legal or literary, or quite probably both.[9] It is clear at any rate that he accompanied Belisarius on his campaigns until 540 and possibly up to 542. Thereafter he is believed to have set to work composing his *Wars* and *Anecdota*, which were both completed by 550–51. The latter work was never published in his lifetime, and it contains much which contrasts with what is said in the *Wars*; no corrections, however, are made to *Wars* I, although there is further clarification of some points. The former work, the *Wars* or *Bella*, provides an account of the campaigns fought under Justinian up to 550–51: against Persians (books I–II), Vandals (III–IV) and Goths (V–VII). Procopius followed the success of *Wars* I–VII with an eighth book of *Wars* and the *De Aedificiis* or *On Buildings*, both published around the year 554. The final book of the *Wars* took the history of Justinian's wars up to that

---

(116.10–15) on the request that he write a history of the Persian war; McCormick, *Eternal Victory*, 64 n.100 suggests that the work may have been a panegyric rather than a history. On Eustathius, see Eustathius 10 in *PLRE* II with Jeffreys, *Studies in Malalas*, 180 and Allen, 'An early epitomator', 1–3. Cameron, 'The date', 107, argues that Eustathius need not have died in 503, and may have lived until the 520s; but, as *PLRE*, *loc. cit.*, notes, Mal.'s mistake (presumably following Eustathius) concerning Constantinus 14, implies that Eustathius died before the general returned to the Roman side (see ch.5 iii below).

[8] I.1.3, with Greatrex, 'Lawyers and Historians'; as will be seen (below ch.5.i), Proc. was less interested in earlier military history (e.g. the Anastasian war).

[9] On the post of *assessor* and the possibility of a legal background, see Greatrex, 'Lawyers and Historians'. On his possible connection with the Gaza school and Procopius 1 in *PLRE* III, see Greatrex, 'Stephanus', 128–33. The quotation comes from Bury, *HLRE* II, 419.

year, while the *De Aedificiis*, which may have been commissioned by the emperor, detailed the lavish building programme initiated by him. Most probably Procopius died not long afterwards, and he should not be identified with the prefect of Constantinople in 562–3.[10]

Procopius probably started making notes for his history at an early stage in his service with Belisarius; hence, it may be supposed, the wealth of detail in the central sections of *Persian Wars* I (12–22), particularly in his description of the battle of Dara (13–14), at which he was present in person. As was the custom of 'classicising' historians, he failed to specify from whom he derived his information for events not known to him by autopsy; one possibility is that the chronicler Eustathius furnished at least some of the material, in particular concerning the siege of Amida in 502–3. Although Procopius' coverage of the Anastasian War is cursory, it should be stressed that this most probably stemmed from conscious choice rather than ignorance: he was more interested in reporting matters from his own day.[11]

Oral informants no doubt played an important role; two probable contributors were the younger Kavadh, grandson of king Kavadh, who fled to the Byzantine court around the year 541 (I.23.23), and Peranius, son of the Iberian king Gourgenes, who fled to Constantinople during Justin's reign (I.12.11–14). Both these men went on to command units of the Roman army in Italy, where Procopius also served as an aide to Belisarius. Given that Procopius, Kavadh and Peranius were all serving at a high level in the Italian campaigns, there is every reason to suppose that they knew one another, and that Procopius acquired material for his work from the two exiles.[12] It is uncertain whether Procopius made use of 'official' or 'court' documents — reports from generals or diplomats to the emperor in Constantinople; but there is no doubt that archives were stored not only in the imperial capital but also at the

---

[10] For the most recent account of Proc.'s career, cf. *PLRE* III, Procopius 2, which rejects the identification with the city prefect, Procopius 3; also Cameron, *Procopius*, ch.1. On the (much disputed) question of the dating of Proc.'s works, see now Greatrex, 'The Dates' (with *idem*, 'Procopius and Agathias', 125–9), supporting the traditional view *contra* Scott, 'Justinian's Coinage', 215–21, and Whitby, 'Sangarius Bridge', 129–48.

[11] See n.7 above on Eustathius. Ch.5 p.74, on Proc.'s treatment of the Anastasian war; cf. Soyter, 'Glaubwürdigkeit', 541–5, who aptly describes Proc. as a 'Gegenwartmensch' (545). Bury, *HLRE* II, 420 n.2, suggested that Proc. I.12–22 (the Justinianic phase of the war) represents an earlier stage of composition than the rest of the *Wars*, because the account is so patchy.

[12] *PLRE* III, Cavades, on Kavadh; also *PLRE* III, Peranius.

headquarters of the *comes Orientis* at Antioch. Procopius' contemporary Malalas appears to have made extensive use of the latter
archive, while Menander Protector, writing later in the sixth century,
probably used the one at Constantinople to record the terms of the
Romano-Persian treaty of 561/2. Whether such archives were
employed by Procopius must remain in doubt, since he nowhere quotes
any official documents *verbatim*. But given that it was at
Constantinople that he worked on his *Wars*, it is *prima facie* likely that
he took advantage of the records stored there: a good example of
material which he may have acquired from such archives (if not from
the persons involved) is his excursus on southern Arabia (I.19–20).[13]

Notwithstanding the high opinion of Bury, Procopius' reliability as a
historian is not universally acknowledged. He is accused of showing
undue partiality to his commander, Belisarius, as well as equally undue
hostility to Justinian and (for instance) the Ghassanid allies of Rome.
That he held strong views on the empire and its rulers has never been
doubted and is amply attested by the *Anecdota*.[14] But that he either
included false information in his histories or consciously omitted
important events is less certain. Nevertheless, his alleged prejudices
will be borne in mind in making use of the evidence he offers.[15]

b) 'Joshua the Stylite'

The Syriac chronicle conventionally attributed to Joshua the Stylite
provides a remarkably detailed account of the Persian war fought under
Anastasius, written from an Edessene perspective. Although the work
was in fact not composed by Joshua, but rather just copied by a monk
of this name, there is no doubt that it was written very soon after the
truce brought hostilities to a halt in 506. The author gives a year by

---

[13] Cameron, *Procopius*, 156, suggests Proc. used 'official' sources for the list of army
commanders at I.8.1–3. On the archives in Constantinople, see now Lee, *Information*,
35–40, noting that it was the practice of ambassadors to deposit their accounts there;
also Kelly, 'Later Roman bureaucracy', 161–3 on the location of the archives. On those
of the *comes Orientis*, see Croke and E. Jeffreys in *Studies in Malalas*, 9–11, 208.

[14] Note *Wars* I.24.11–16 for a forthright expression of Proc.'s opinions. His partiality
towards Belisarius waned over time: Belisarius emerges with little credit from the
later books of the *Wars* and the *Anecdota*. On Proc.'s biases (esp. in favour of Belisarius): Cameron, *Procopius*, 230 (noting the change in attitude), with Shahîd,
'Procopius and Kinda', 74–8, 'Procopius and Arethas', *passim*, esp. 380–82, and
'Procopius and Arethas again', 313–19, and now *BASIC* I, 49–53.

[15] E.g. Shahîd, 'Procopius and Arethas', 366 (accusing Proc. of an 'utterly and deliberately false statement') and 380–82.

year description of events in Mesopotamia from the 490s to the end of
the war, and regards the Persians as the instruments of God's
punishment of the region. He is clearly well informed about military
and political affairs, deriving his information 'from meeting with men
who served as envoys to the two rulers [Anastasius and Kavadh]', as
well as from eye-witnesses and written texts (§25); the very making of
such a claim, alongside the speeches attributed to generals and other
touches, points to a familiarity with the genre of classicising history. It
has been suggested that the author made use of the work of the
historian Candidus the Isaurian; and Joshua may in turn have been used
by the chronicler Theophanes. The work is preserved in the chronicle
of Pseudo-Dionysius of Tel Mahre, and it appears to be independent of
all the other Syriac sources on the war.[16]

c) 'Pseudo-Zachariah' of Mytilene

The work which has come down to us as the *Ecclesiastical History* of
Zachariah is an important, but complex, source. The historical
Zachariah, bishop of Mytilene, was probably the author only of books
III–VI, composed during the reign of Anastasius. These books, written
originally in Greek but surviving only in Syriac, cover the period 451–
91 and were extensively used by the later church historian Evagrius.
The books of relevance to the present work are VII–XII, covering the
period 491–569. This portion of the *History* seems to have been put
together in 569: at XII.4 (321) there is a reference to the year 561,
while at XII.7 (327) there is one to 555, and I.1 (16) alludes to the year
569. But there are a number of indications in the text that point to use
of earlier sources: at VII.5 (161) a reference is made to a certain
Gadono in the Anastasian War who was known to the author. Perhaps
it was this same author who was acquainted with Dominic, a refugee in
Constantinople from the war being waged in Italy against the Goths

---

[16] On 'Joshua' (henceforth referred to as Joshua or Josh. Styl.), see Watt's preface in
Trombley–Watt, *Chronicle* (arguing for familiarity with classicising historiography).
Wright, *Short History*, 78, regards him as the best source on the Anastasian war, cf.
Witakowksi, *The Syriac Chronicle*, 34–6. Palmer, 'Who wrote the chronicle of
Joshua?', argues, 279, that the author of the work was the steward of a hospice
mentioned at §42 (named Stratonicus), but this is rejected by Watt, *loc. cit.* See also
Witakowski, *Chronicle*, xx–xxiii. Pigulewskaja, 'Theophanes' Chronographia', 57,
on Joshua's use of Candidus (and Eustathius). See ch.5.i below on Theophanes and
Joshua.

(IX.18 [264]).[17] It follows that the compiler of the work in 569 had
access not only to Zachariah himself, but also to other contemporary
sources. Among these may have been the chronicle of Eustathius of
Epiphaneia, for instance for the very detailed account of the siege of
Amida; and if Procopius too had used Eustathius, then the similarity
between his account and that of 'Zachariah' is explicable. Since the
work ascribed to Zachariah incorporates earlier sources, its account
merits careful consideration.[18]

d) John Malalas

Recent research has done much to boost the reputation of the *Chronographia* of John Malalas, at any rate for events close to his own day.
John was probably born in the reign of Zeno, and since he is termed
rhetor by Evagrius (a term similar to the Syriac root *mll* — Malalas) it
is supposed that he had some legal or rhetorical training. From the
wealth of information which he provides on the city of Antioch in
particular, as well as from the detail in his accounts of military and
foreign affairs relating to the east, access to the records of the *comes
Orientis* has been inferred. The first edition of the chronicle was
probably published in 532, and soon afterwards Malalas moved to
Constantinople.[19]

While Malalas has little to say about the Anastasian War, he offers a
very circumstantial report of the campaign of 531, culminating in the

---

[17] On Pseudo-Zachariah (henceforth Zach.), see Honigmann, 'Patristic Studies' XXI,
194–204, Kugener, 'La compilation', and Brock, 'Syriac historical writing', 4–5. A
brief biography of Zach. may be found in *PLRE* II, Zacharias (the Rhetor) 4 and *ODB*
III.2218. On Evagrius' use of him, see the introduction to the translation by Hamilton
and Brooks, 4–5 and Allen, *Evagrius*, 8–9. There is also a Latin translation by Brooks
and an inferior German one by Ahrens and Krüger.

[18] Kugener, 'La compilation', considered that the chapters on the Anastasian war were
written by a monk of Amida, and that Michael the Syrian later attributed the whole
work to Zach., not knowing who was its author, 202–3. See also Allen, 'Zachariah
Scholasticus', 471–3 and the introduction to the translation of Hamilton and Brooks,
4–7 for a discussion of the compiler's sources. Haury, *Bella* I, xix–xx, suggests that
Eustathius was the common source of Zach. and Proc. for the siege of Amida, cf.
Allen, 'An early epitomator', 3. Note also Allen, 'Zachariah Scholasticus', 472 on the
library of Mare, bishop of Amida, which was probably available to the compiler.

[19] On Malalas generally, see *Studies in Malalas*; on his life, the debate over the first
edition and the use of the archives of the *comes Orientis*, Croke, 'Malalas', 3–4, 17–
22 and 9–11 (with Witakowski, 'Malalas in Syriac', 305–6 on his name). On the
version of the text of Malalas which has survived, see Jeffreys, 'Malalas in Greek',
245–8.

battle at Callinicum, which has frequently been contrasted favourably
with Procopius' version of events. Although his information on the
events leading up to the battle is invaluable, it should be stressed that
his account may be just as partisan as that of Procopius: among his
informants was the *magister officiorum* Hermogenes, who will have
had his own perspective on the causes of the Roman defeat. Hence
even if Malalas was making use of official reports which passed
through the office of the *comes Orientis*, these documents themselves
will scarcely have been objective; and this in turn must be borne in
mind in assessing his account.[20]

e) Marcellinus Comes (and his continuator)

Marcellinus' Chronicle was initially published in 518, but was later
extended by the author up to 534; a continuation to 548 by another
writer also survives. Marcellinus served as the *cancellarius* of the
future Emperor Justinian during the reign of Justin, and it has long been
observed that his account reflects an official perspective. Although his
chronology is not always accurate — for example he places the fall of
Amida in 502 rather than January 503 — he can on occasion help to
compensate for the failure of other sources to date events explicitly.[21]

f) John the Lydian

The *de Magistratibus* of John the Lydian, a 'disgruntled civil servant
and antiquarian', contains a few relevant pieces of information, such as
his comments on the generals who served during the Anastasian War.[22]

iv) Later sources

The importance of sources later than the sixth century naturally lies in
their access to contemporary sources no longer extant. Sometimes these

---

[20] On Mal.'s sources, see Jeffreys 'Malalas' sources', esp. 209–10 on his use of Hermogenes and on the 531 campaign (and see ch.9.i below). Also of importance is his
information on diplomatic affairs — both between Rome and Persia, E. Jeffreys, *art.
cit.*, 210 and cf. Scott, 'Diplomacy', 159–65 — and on southern Arabia, cf. E.
Jeffreys, *art. cit.*, 200.

[21] See Croke, *Chronicle*, xix–xx with *PLRE* II, Marcellinus 9, and Croke, *op. cit.*, 111
for his error on the fall of Amida. On his official stance, see Scott, 'Malalas and his
contemporaries', 76.

[22] Maas, *John Lydus*, 1 for the quotation; see also *PLRE* II, Ioannes Lydus 75 on his
career. Scott, 'Malalas and his contemporaries', 72–5, notes similarities between his
outlook and that of Malalas.

lost sources can be pinpointed accurately, but usually they remain elusive.

The *Chronographia* of Malalas proved to be a popular work, and later chroniclers in the Byzantine period made extensive use of it. John of Nikiu, writing in the late seventh century, appears to have depended considerably on Malalas, incorporating many sections of the work into his own text. The *Chronicon Paschale*, dating from earlier in the seventh century, also relied heavily on Malalas for the period with which we are concerned. But sometimes, as for instance in the case of the Nika riot, the *Chronicon Paschale* preserves material lost from our text of Malalas.[23]

The chronicler Theophanes (early ninth century) made use of a range of sources, including Procopius and Malalas, but he also provides a few unique items of information concerning the Anastasian War. He probably had access to an earlier version of Malalas, as he often gives more precise dates for events reported by Malalas than the text of Malalas now available. Subsequent chroniclers seldom have anything to add to Theophanes and Malalas; among them may be noted the fourteenth-century writer Nicephorus Callistus Xanthopulus, who composed an ecclesiastical history from the time of Christ to 911, of which the portion up to 610 survives; he evidently relied much on Evagrius and earlier church historians, but also had access to all of Procopius' works.[24]

A chronographical tradition also emerged in Syriac, where later sources such as Michael the Syrian, Gregory Bar Hebraeus, Pseudo-Dionysius of Tel Mahre and the *Chronicon ad annum Christi 1234 pertinens* can preserve details from sixth-century sources now lost or fragmentary. Hence the loss of the second book of John of Ephesus' *Ecclesiastical History* is compensated for to some extent by these later works, which also make much use of Zachariah. The siege of Amida proved to be a particularly popular story, and accounts of it — generally differing little from that in Zachariah — can be found in

---

[23]   On John of Nikiu, see iii–iv of Charles' translation. On the *Chronicon Paschale* (henceforth *CP*), see the helpful translation and commentary of M. and M. Whitby (henceforth *CPW*), ix–xiv on the work and xv–xxii on its sources (esp. xviii–xix on the fifth–sixth centuries).

[24]   On Theophanes, see Mango–Scott, *Theophanes*, lxxxi. On Nicephorus (henceforth Nic. Call.), see Gentz, *Die Kirchengeschichte* and *ODB* III.2207 (A.-M. Talbot).

many Syriac chronicles.[25] Later still, Arab chronicles too occasionally furnish information not found elsewhere, although they must be approached with circumspection.[26]

Armenian sources do not contribute much to sixth-century history: Łazar P'arpec'i's work terminates in 485, while Sebeos' *History of Heraclius* gives only very cursory treatment to events before the reign of Maurice.[27] The section of the Georgian chronicles concerning *The History of King Vakhtang Gorgasali* deals with events in the Caucasus in the late fifth century, but needs careful handling: it was composed several centuries later by Juansher Juansheriani and naturally places great emphasis on the role played by the Iberians and their king.[28]

The Iranian tradition has little to say directly about the war of 502–532. The principal Sasanian traditions were recorded in the Royal Annals, set down in the Pahlavi *Khvadaynamagh* during the reign of Yazdgerd III (632–51). Both the original version of this work and the translation of it into Arabic by Ibn Moqaffa in the eighth century are lost. But an early version of the annals survives in Agathias' excursus on Sasanian history, which can be compared with later Arabic and

---

[25] On the Syriac chronicles and their sources, see e.g. Witakowski, *The Syriac Chronicle*, chs. 3 and 4 (on Pseudo-Dionysius) and *idem*, 'Chronicles of Edessa', 495–6. Pigulewskaja, 'Theophanes' Chronographia', 58–60 and Witakowski, *Chronicle*, xv–xvi, xxvi–xxix, on the use of John of Ephesus; also Brock, 'Syriac historical writing', 5–6 on John and 7–21 on later chronicles. See now Palmer, *Seventh Century*, xxviii–xxxii and 95–104 (on Pseudo-Dionysius and *Chron. 1234*, though for a slightly later period). Note also the Chronicle of Edessa (composed in the mid-sixth century, Witakowski, 'Chronicles of Edessa', 487), the Chronicle of 724 (on which see Palmer, *Seventh Century*, 5–12, who dates it to 639–40) and that of Elias of Nisibis (an eleventh-century work, Palmer, *op. cit.*, 41, Morony, *Iraq*, 567). The *Lives of the Eastern Saints* of John of Ephesus also give useful details of life on the eastern frontier, for instance concerning the monk of the monastery of Mar John, who survived the siege of Amida in 503 (see ch.5 n.33 below). His fiercely anti-Chalcedonian account must be handled with care, as Whitby, *Maurice*, 213 n.29, notes; see also Harvey, *Asceticism*, 28–42.

[26] E.g. the Chronicle of Seert, a tenth- or eleventh-century Arabic translation of a lost Syriac chronicle (Morony, *Iraq*, 568 and Sako, *L'hiérarchie*, 51). Note too Eutychius (tenth century, see Breydy, *Annalenwerk*, v–ix) and Agapius (tenth century, *ODB* I.35). Even later chronicles in Arabic, such as that of Mari ibn Sulayman (twelfth century), and to a lesser extent, those of 'Amr ibn Matta and Salîba ibn Yuhannan (fourteenth century), can add some useful pieces of information: see Sako, *op. cit.*, 51–2.

[27] On Łazar, see Thomson's translation, 6–8, 18–31; on Sebeos, see Thomson in *ODB* III.1863.

[28] See now Thomson, *Rewriting Caucasian History*, xxxviii–xxxix, to be used with Toumanoff, *Studies*; also Martin-Hisard, 'Le roi géorgien', 212 and van Esbroeck, 'Lazique', 196–209 on the life of Vakhtang.

Persian texts.[29] Chief among these are the Annals of Tabari (d. 923), which often preserves several versions of events, probably following the *Khvadaynamagh* in this; other even later sources, such as Bal'ami (in Persian) and Eutychius (in Arabic), occasionally offer further information deriving ultimately from the Royal Annals. The eleventh century Iranian epic of Firdausi, the *Shahnameh*, and the Arabic work of al-Tha'alibi (d. 1038) differ considerably from the royal tradition, however, and hence attest the continued existence of other sources for Persian history.[30]

v) Other sources: epigraphic, numismatic, archaeological

Epigraphy furnishes at least one piece of evidence directly relevant to the war of 502–532: to celebrate the Eternal Peace agreed in 532 a series of four inscriptions was engraved in Hierapolis. They not only thank the emperor for having put an end to the 'measureless wretchedness of life' occasioned by the war, but also mention the length of the war (thirty years) as well as the money handed over to bring it to an end.[31] Inscriptions from Syria date building work, in some cases defensive, to the period of the war, confirming the continuing threat of Lakhmid raids.[32] But closer to the front much less remains. Some inscriptions may come from the period 502–32, but, because they

---

[29] Cameron, 'Sassanians', 111–13 on this and Nöldeke–Bogdanov, *Iranian National Epic*, §13 p.24.

[30] On the Sasanian tradition, see Nöldeke–Bogdanov, *Iranian National Epic*, esp. §14, p.25 and §27, p.63, on the divergence of the *Shahnameh* and al-Tha'alibi; also now Davis, 'The problem', 53. In general see the introduction to Nöldeke, *Tabari*, Christensen, *L'Iran*, 59–74 (where he also discusses the various works apart from the *Khvadaynamagh*); also *idem*, *Le règne*, 22–5 and Yarshater, 'Iranian National History', 359–64. For a useful assessment of the importance of Tabari and Nöldeke's translation and commentary of the part of his work concerning the Sasanians, cf. Shahîd, 'An evaluation', 117–20. On Bal'ami see D. M. Dunlop in *El²* I, 984: he does not derive his material exclusively from Tabari.

[31] Roussel, 'Un monument', 367–8 and see ch.10.iii below. A translation will be provided in Greatrex–Lieu. Note also the statue put up in the hippodrome in 530, and the inscriptions carved upon it, on which see ch.8.ii below.

[32] *IGLS* IV, 1630–31 (defences from 509/10 at Taroutia emporon), cf. 1702 (from Androna, 528/9), 1725 (Oumm et-Tin, 516). The inscriptions from Cyrrhus mentioning Belisarius and others probably date from 542 (*IGLS* I, 145–7 with notes on p.91). Vasiliev, *Justin I*, 273 connects an inscription at Ghour (*IGLS* V, 2155, cf. *IGLS* IV, 1610), on the road between Emesa and Apamea (from 524/5) with defensive preparations by the Romans. For a useful assessment of defence inscriptions from this region, see Trombley, 'War and Society'.

are generally undated, their dating often depends on the identification of individuals.[33] Archaeology is no more specific, and discussion of the dating of fortifications tends to start from Procopius' *De Aedificiis* and then to seek to prove or disprove his claims. Given the similarity of building techniques under Anastasius and Justinian, it is not surprising that greater attention has been paid to the literary than to the archaeological record.[34]

Numismatics likewise contributes little directly to an account of the war: there are no emissions from local mints which may be connected with imperial campaigns, nor were any Roman mints affected by the Persian invasions, as happened a century later.[35] The study of Sasanian coinage has revealed that neither Balash nor Zamasp issued any gold coins; but silver drachms of Peroz, countermarked by the Hephthalites, have been found. The emptiness of the Persian treasury, so emphasised by Joshua the Stylite, thus receives some confirmation.[36]

[33] Mango, 'Inscriptions', collects the relevant material and remarks (465) on the scarcity of inscriptions in the area. Among them note no.4, 469, from Hisarkaya, referring to a general, possibly Belisarius, and nos.5–7, 470, from Amida, ascribing fortifications to a general Theodore. C. and M. Mango favour identifying Theodore with Heraclius' brother; but the Greek term στρατηλάτης can refer to a duke, a tribune or others (Durliat, 'Magister Militum', 316, *contra* Mango, *loc. cit.*), and so it could refer to a Theodore who served at Amida in 503 (*PLRE* II, Theodorus 53, a tribune or *comes rei militaris*).

[34] Cf. Whitby, 'Defences', 719–20.

[35] See Ziegler, 'Civic Coins', 121–4, for linkage between local emissions and Roman campaigns in the first–second centuries A.D. Foss, 'The Persians in Asia Minor', 729–30, is able to suggest dates for Persian campaigns in Asia Minor in the reign of Heraclius based on the closing and re-opening of mints. The mint at Antioch issued bronze coinage, but functioned only from late in Anastasius' reign, cf. Grierson, *Byzantine Coins*, 66.

[36] Göbl, *Sasanian Numismatics*, 49–51 and see above, ch.3 n.26, on Persian payments to the Hephthalites.

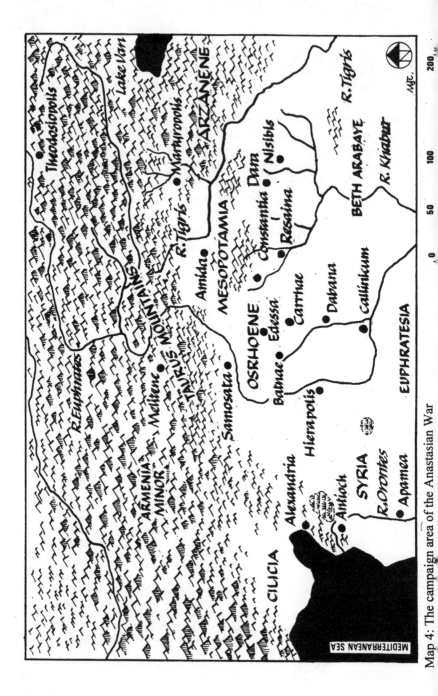

Map 4: The campaign area of the Anastasian War

V

The Anastasian War

i) The sources

By far the most important source for the initial phase of the war of 502–532 is the chronicle attributed to Joshua the Stylite, clearly the work of an eye-witness based at Edessa, with access to detailed information on events elsewhere.[1] His account appears to have been unknown to other sources, except probably the ninth-century chronicler Theophanes. For it is remarkable that Theophanes, often so inaccurate and brief on this period, gives precise information on the war, some of which is corroborated only by Joshua, and some of which is not found in any other extant source. If this link is accepted, it must be supposed either that Theophanes was using Joshua (and other sources), or that both had access to some sort of official report on the whole campaign.[2]

Two other important sources, Pseudo-Zachariah of Mytilene and Procopius, also appear to be connected. Both concentrate on the conflict at Amida, offering limited coverage of events further south. The author of the relevant chapters of the work ascribed to Zachariah was a contemporary, and perhaps an eye-witness, of this part of the war. Since Zachariah himself wrote originally in Greek, it is possible that the author of this section of the work also did so; in such a case, Procopius might have been able to draw upon it when composing his

---

[1]   Trombley–Watt, *Chronicle*, intro. (on §25) with Howard-Johnston, 'Great Powers', 166 and n.13; see also above ch.4 pp.64–5.

[2]   The link is well demonstrated by Chekalova, 'Jesu Stilit', 73, rejecting earlier theories of Rubin and Pigulewksaja. Cf. also Mango–Scott, *Theophanes*, lxxxiv–lxxxvii on Theoph.'s use of Syriac material in this period. Howard-Johnston, 'Great Powers', 166 n.13, argues for the existence of an official source, designed to highlight Roman achievements; cf. *idem*, 'The official history', 70, on the form that such a work might take. Since Theoph. preserves material not in Joshua (or any other surviving source) the case for the existence of some sort of detailed official source is strong, cf. also Cameron, *Procopius*, 156 and n.35. Proc. too might have used it for his list of generals at I.8.1–3, cf. Cameron, *ibid.*

history.[3] The narrative of Procopius, it should be noted, is extremely selective and, on occasion, even inaccurate. Of the three chapters on the Anastasian War, two concern the sieges of Amida (in 502–3 and 504). The other gives a catalogue of the commanders who took part in the war, perhaps drawn from an official list, and an account of the battle at Apadna.[4] Procopius' competence as a historian has been attacked because of his patchy treatment of the war, but such criticism is misleading. There is no doubt that he chose to relate far less about the events than he actually knew. In other works, for instance in *Wars* II or in the *De Aedificiis*, he introduces details completely omitted from *Wars* I. And at I.8.20, for instance, he asserts that '[the other Roman army] did nothing worth recounting...' as a result of the lack of a unified command, strongly implying that he could have written more, but thought it of little interest.[5] Procopius' *Wars* were explicitly designed to describe the wars waged by the Emperor Justinian — not by Anastasius. The purpose of the introductory chapters was to entertain the reader, rather than to examine earlier events; such information was in any case readily available in other historians. Hence only remarkable and little-known episodes were related by Procopius.[6]

Among the sources on the war which might be consulted by the sixth-century reader were the epic poem of Colluthus, already mentioned, as well as chronicles by Hesychius of Miletus and Eustathius of Epiphaneia.[7] The last of these is of some importance, since it has been postulated as a source for nearly all the surviving accounts of the war, including Joshua, Procopius and Theophanes.

---

[3]   On the link between the two, Chekalova, 'Jesu Stilit', 74. See above ch.4 n.17 on Zach.'s work with VII.5 (161) for contemporary information. Haury, *Zur Beurteilung*, 21 n.1, on Proc.'s use of Zach., cf. 22–23 for a detailed comparison of the two writers on the siege of Amida. Eustathius of Epiphaneia has been posited as their common source, but see above ch.4 n.7 and below n.8.

[4]   Merten, *De Bello*, 153, on Proc.'s sources for the leaders; also Kirchner, *Bemerkungen*, 6, noting that only Proc. mentions Bessas and Godidisclus, cf. Cameron, *Procopius*, 156 (also suggesting use of oral sources by Proc.).

[5]   Howard-Johnston, 'Great Powers', 175–6, for criticism. *Wars* II.13.8–15 and *Aed.* III.2.4–9 for episodes not reported in I.7–9.

[6]   Proc. I.1.1 sets out his objective: to write the history of the wars of Justinian. I.2.1–10 offers an example of an episode nowhere else reported (the guardianship of Yazdgerd), cf. Agath. IV.26.3–4. See on this Cameron, *Procopius*, 156 and Greatrex, *Procopius*, 272–4. A further reason for the lack of detail on the war will be suggested below.

[7]   See above ch.4 n.6 on Colluthus and Eustathius; ch.4 n.4 on Hesychius. There may also have been some sort of official source, as noted above.

There is one awkward problem for those who wish to assign such a prominent role to Eustathius — the fact that the chronicler died in the middle of the war, soon after the battle at Apadna (503). Moreover, only Malalas, whose account is in any case very brief, is apparently affected by Eustathius' demise.[8] The narratives of Procopius, Joshua, Zachariah and Theophanes are as detailed for the year 504 as for 502–3. Hence, while it can be conceded that Eustathius may have been a common source for the Persian siege of Amida, where all our sources show considerable congruence, his influence should not be overrated.[9]

A few later authors may be mentioned more briefly. John the Lydian and Marcellinus *comes*, both writing under Justinian, offer a few useful items, while the later Syriac sources (such as the *Chron. 1234*) tend, in the main, to follow Zachariah. It should be noted that all three sources dating from Justinian's reign — Procopius, John and Marcellinus — have a tendency to downplay Roman successes in the war under Anastasius. John offers little detail, but is heavily critical of the leadership particularly of Areobindus, and scarcely less so of Hypatius and Patricius. Marcellinus contains a few more items of interest, and no specific criticism of generals; nevertheless he reports that the Romans fought *sine audacia* at the battle near Syficum castellum (Apadna). While this need not be taken as criticism, and is probably true, the way in which he describes the recovery of Amida is certainly unfavourable: he says that the Roman generals bought back a deserted city for a large price.[10] Procopius likewise stresses the disgraceful purchase of the Persian withdrawal from Amida as well as the poor performance of the Roman commanders, and mentions no Roman victory.[11] In fact, of the three Justinianic sources so far discussed, only Marcellinus mentions something approaching a Roman success — Celer's raid into Persian

---

[8] Mal. 398.11–399.12 (also on the death of Eustathius). Pigulewskaja, 'Theophanes' Chronographia', 57–8, for an overestimation of Eustathius, cf. Chekalova, 'Jesu Stilit', 72. Cameron, 'The date', 107, argued that Eustathius may have lived long after 503, since Evagrius (III.41) merely states that he died when his history reached the year 503. But Mal.'s text (399.4–5) strongly implies that he died soon after the events related; and his mistake concerning the death of the Roman leader Constantine (noted by *PLRE* II, Eustathius 10) appears to confirm this.

[9] Cf. e.g. Haury, *Prolegomena* to his edition of the *Wars*, xix–xx on Proc.'s use of Eustathius, esp. for the siege of Amida.

[10] Joh. Lyd., *de Mag.* III.53 (142.4–6), Marc. *com.* a.503. Note Croke, *Chronicle*, 112, for the suggestion that Marcellinus relied on Celer, a fellow-Illyrian, for information about the war. On the Syriac sources, see below n.34.

[11] I.8.19 (cowardice of Hypatius and Patricius), I.9.19–23 (the Romans fooled into allowing the Persians to leave Amida).

territory — and even this is ambiguously portrayed.[12] Yet, as will be seen, there is no doubt that the Romans did gain the upper hand in the final campaigns.

It is not hard to explain this tendency to pass over Roman victories. The Justinianic writers were naturally seeking to make their emperor's achievements the more remarkable through an unfavourable comparison with those of his uncle's predecessor. In Procopius' *Wars*, for instance, Belisarius' victory at Dara seems all the more unexpected and notable since no previous Roman success is mentioned. Both Marcellinus and John were faithful servants of the régime, and it may confidently be supposed that, if John's lost account of Justinian's Persian war dealt with these events, it would have been no more flattering to the Roman generals.[13]

ii) The immediate background

The courses of action open to Kavadh, newly restored to the throne of Persia, were limited, and governed almost exclusively by the needs of his treasury. Anastasius' refusal to accede to another of his requests for money provided the final trigger for war.[14] It is possible, as one source claims, that on this occasion Kavadh sought only a loan from the emperor; but more probably this was the counter-proposal tabled by the shrewd Anastasius, as others report.[15] That Anastasius was consciously

---

[12] Marc. *com.* a.504: *plurimos agrestes rusticis intentos laboribus more pecudum trucidat* 'He killed like cattle very many farmers engaged in their rural labours ...' (tr. Croke).

[13] Note Proc. I.14.54, where he draws attention to the considerable lapse of time since there had been a Roman victory (before Dara). See above ch.4 p.67 on Marcellinus, nn.7, 22 on John. While the incompetence of Hypatius, and, to a slightly lesser degree, Patricius, are apparent in all sources, some have perceived a special targeting of Areobindus by Justinianic writers: Joh. Lyd. *de Mag.* III.53 (142.4–5), Proc. I.9.1 (mistakenly claiming that it was he who was recalled in 503), cf. Lamma, 'La politica', 179 n.80, Kirchner, *Bemerkungen*, 6. Despite attempts to establish a link between generals brought back from exile by Justin and enemies of Areobindus, it is likely that Areobindus seems to incur more criticism because, unlike his two colleagues, he actually had victories which could be passed over.

[14] On his previous demands, see Josh. Styl. §§19 and 23, Lamma, 'La politica', 176–7, and above ch.3 n.40. As noted there, not all accept that a demand was made in 502. The Persians may have put forward other justifications for their invasion, reflected in Zach. VII.3 (153), where the Romans are blamed by Kavadh for the Hephthalite invasion which defeated Peroz.

[15] Proc. I.7.1–3 for Kavadh seeking a loan; Theod. Lect. 552, followed by Theoph. A.M. 5996 (144), on the offer of a loan, cf. Josh. Styl. §23 (an earlier case of a loan being offered). Nic. Call. XVI.36, *PG* 147, 197, prefaces an account similar to that of

aiming to provoke the Persians by such an offer, as some scholars believe, is highly unlikely given the unprepared state of Roman frontier defences. Furthermore, when an opportunity to take advantage of Persian weakness had arisen — in the form of an Armenian uprising in the 490s — Anastasius had refused to exploit it. His offer should there-fore be seen as an attempt to give some assistance to the Persians, without conceding the principle of not yielding to demands for money.[16]

As has been seen, Kavadh's decision to attack Roman territory neatly resolved several problems for him.[17] The Tamuraye were invited to take part in the invasion, and broke off their rebellion; and the Kadishaye, who had been besieging Nisibis, followed suit. The Armenians, however, proved less pliant. They had revolted against the imposition of Zoroastrianism in the 490s and had defeated an army sent to crush them. If Kavadh was to be able to launch a successful campaign against the Romans, he could not risk leaving his northern flank exposed to rebellious Armenians. He assembled his men and marched northwards; a brief demonstration of force proved sufficient to cow the Armenians and to extort from them some contingents for his army.[18] It was, then, at the head of a heterogeneous army that he launched his invasion from Persarmenia. His first target was the capital of Armenia Interior, Theodosiopolis, which was captured in August 502. The king must have spent the earlier months of the year mustering his forces for the attack, an undertaking of such a scale that it cannot have escaped Roman intelligence. According to Joshua the Stylite the news was reported to Anastasius, who responded by despatching his envoy Rufinus to the frontier, probably in late summer, with orders to give Kavadh some money if he forbore from invading. But no military

---

Theodore Lector with mention of a peace being agreed between the two sides in the eleventh year of Kavadh's reign.

[16] Blockley, 'Subsidies and Diplomacy', 68 n.19, Stein II, 93, Bury, *HLRE* II, 11 and n.1, for the offer as a snub. Josh. Styl. §21 for Anastasius' refusal to aid the Armenians. A persecution of Christians in Persia in 498 (reported by *Chron. Arbela* XIX, p.101, perhaps alluded to by Joh. Eph. *Lives, PO* 17 [1923] 143) also failed to elicit an armed response from the emperor; cf. Wirth, 'Anastasius, Christen und Perser', 128 n.246.

[17] See above ch.2 pp.7–8, ch.3 p.52. Cf. also Pigulewskaja, *Villes*, 216–17.

[18] Josh. Styl. §24; on the Cadusii/Kadishaye/Kadisenoi see Nöldeke, 'Zwei Völker', 157–66. He places the Kadishaye by Šiggar (Singara) and Tebeth (Thebetha), in the area around Dara; see below ch.8 n.32. The Tamuraye he views as a mountain tribe of Iran, 158 n.4.

preparations were made by the Romans: they were well aware of the troubles in Persarmenia, and will no doubt have inferred (quite reasonably) that this was the destination of Kavadh's army. Khusro employed a similar ruse in 541, spreading the word that his forces were being assembled to deal with a Hunnic tribe, while in fact he was preparing an invasion of Lazica.[19]

For their part, the Persians were not without intelligence about Roman affairs. In 498 several Arab tribes, amongst whom were the Persian-aligned Lakhmids, had undertaken raids against Roman territory. The Lakhmid king al-Nu'man had been able to penetrate into Syria before being brought to battle and defeated by the *dux* Eugenius at Bithrapsa.[20] It is highly likely that al-Nu'man was acting on instructions from Kavadh and seeking to put pressure on the Romans to accede to Persian requests for money; he could also gauge the strength of Roman defences.[21] The raids by the other two tribes, the Ghassanids and the Kindites, should not be linked to that of al-Nu'man; although the Kindites attacked again in 501/2, both tribes were brought into the Roman orbit in the following year. They were to prove their usefulness to the Roman cause in the ensuing war.[22]

---

[19] Josh. Styl. §21 on Roman awareness of the Armenian revolt; §50 on Rufinus (who arrived at Cappadocian Caesarea in October 502, after the Armenian satrapies had been laid waste). Lee, *Information*, 115 on this episode, 116–17 for Khusro's trick (Proc. II.15.35–16.4). In 531 Rufinus was allowed 70 days to get to Constantinople from the frontier and back (Proc. I.22.7); hence Anastasius knew of the invasion by early September at the latest.

[20] Theoph. A.M. 5990 (141) on these raids, also in Evagrius III.36, with Shahîd, *BAFIC*, 121–130. He identifies the place where al-Nu'man was defeated, Bithrapsa, with Sergiopolis, 123–4 (although Theoph.'s text seems to place Bithrapsa in Syria). Stein II, 91 n.5, however (cf. Nöldeke, *Tabari*, 169 n.1), wished to place al-Nu'man's raid in 499 or later, since Arab sources attribute to him only a very brief reign (followed by *PLRE* II, Eugenius 5). On the other two incursions, by Kindites and Ghassanids, see above ch.2 n.82.

[21] Shahîd, *BAFIC*, 124–5; cf. the raids into Mesopotamia at the start of Zeno's reign (Theoph. A.M. 5966 [120]), and Zach. VIII.5 (206) for Kavadh's later use of the Lakhmid king al-Mundhir against Justin. Cf. also Proc. I.17.30–9 for a Lakhmid king apprising the Persian ruler of the weakness of Roman defences in this area in 531 (albeit in a rhetorical account).

[22] Shahîd, *BAFIC*, 125–30, *BASIC* I, 3–9, Sartre, *Trois études*, 160–1 with the reservations of Whittow, 'Rome and the Jafnids', text to nn.2–7; see also above ch.2 n.82. Theoph. A.M. 5994–5 (143–4) for the raid (cf. the more general entry of Evagrius at III.36 and Nonnosus, *FHG* IV, 179) and the peace treaty (with Shahîd's comments on Theoph.'s text at *BASIC* I, 6–7).

iii) Kavadh's invasion (502)

On 22 August 502 Kavadh crossed into Roman territory. He will very soon have reached Theodosiopolis, the chief city of Armenia Interior. Founded by the Emperor Theodosius II around the year 420, it was an important border fortress and a considerable source of irritation to the Persians: later in the century Menander describes Khusro's attempt to capture it 'since he realised that he could not regain Persian Armenia and Iberia unless he took possession of the strongest of the Roman cities and, establishing himself there, protected Persarmenia and Iberia in its rear.' Having just had to suppress a revolt in Persarmenia, and with Iberia still in turmoil, Kavadh's choice of target was quite logical.[23]

Furthermore, unlike his son Khusro in 576, Kavadh had chosen a moment to attack when the city was ill prepared to resist him: not only were the fortifications installed by Theodosius inadequate, but they had also been allowed to fall into disrepair.[24] Although a Roman governor, Constantine, was stationed at the city, he probably had few, if any, Roman troops at his disposal; he was the *comes Armeniae*, who had charge of civilian matters.[25] It was not long therefore before he

---

[23] Josh. Styl. §§47–8. On the conflicting accounts of the foundation of Theodosiopolis (Erzerum), see Greatrex, 'Fifth-century wars', 5–6. Menander, frg.18.6.80–85 for the quotation (tr. from Blockley, 169) with Whitby, *Maurice*, 201, on the importance of the city. On Iberia, see below ch.6 p.128–9. August, it may be noted, was the traditional time for the Sasanians to campaign in Armenia, cf. Whitby, *Maurice*, 202 and see below ch.8 n.39.

[24] Cf. Whitby, 'Development', 717–35, *Maurice*, 209–13, and Gray, 'The Roman Eastern *Limes*', 30, on the generally poor state of fortifications. As soon as the war was interrupted by a truce Anastasius set about improving the defences of Theodosiopolis; see Proc. I.10.18–19 on Theodosius' and Anastasius' work, with *Aed.* III.5.1–8 and Whitby, 'Development', 726. The doubts of Croke and Crow regarding the weakness of the walls in 502 ('Procopius and Dara', 159) are effectively rebutted by Whitby, 'Notes', 106–7.

[25] Adontz, *Armenia*, 93–6 on the *comes Armeniae*, an entirely civilian officer, like the *comes Orientis*. The *comes Armeniae* was the successor of the Arsacid kings, nominated by the emperor himself; Adontz, *Armenia*, 94 (following Proc. *Aed.* III.1.15–16) on the absence of troops (with Adontz, *op. cit.*, 412 n.43 and Toumanoff, *Studies*, 195). Note too that the term used by Josh. Styl. for governor, *hegemon*, is the same as that for the governor of Mesopotamia (at Amida) and of Osrhoene (at Edessa). However *PLRE* II, Constantinus 14 (followed by Mango–Scott, *Theophanes*, 224 n.3) believes that Constantine was a *comes rei militaris* or even a *magister militum vacans*; but the fact that he held the rank of *illustris* (as Theoph. A.M. 5996 [144.27] seems to indicate) need not imply that he was too high-ranking for the post of *comes Armeniae* (cf. Ephraemius, *PLRE* II, who was *comes Orientis* and acquired the *illustris* grade shortly afterwards).

surrendered the city to the Persians. The swift hand-over of the city
soon gave rise to rumours of treachery, and Constantine was accused of
having delivered it into Kavadh's hands because of a grudge against the
emperor.[26] These allegations will have received confirmation from the
fact that he was granted a military command by Kavadh; and so well
did he adapt to the Persian way of life that by the time of his return to
the Roman camp in June 504 he had acquired two wives. Whatever the
condition of Theodosiopolis' defences, there is nothing implausible in
the accounts of Constantine's treachery. A similar betrayal was effected
in 589 by Sittas, an officer in the Roman garrison of Martyropolis, who
is said to have harboured a grudge against one of his superiors. He too
was then granted a command by the Persians. Sittas, it is known, was
an Armenian, as Constantine may also have been, and one who felt that
his interests were best served by collaborating with his compatriots in
Kavadh's army.[27]

The fate of the surrendered city is uncertain. That it was utterly laid
waste, as Joshua reports, may be doubted, since Kavadh judged it
feasible and worthwhile to leave a garrison to defend it.[28] From
Theodosiopolis Kavadh headed southwards. To the north lay only more
mountainous territory and unsubjugated highlanders; to the west a
lengthy march would be necessary to get as far even as the Roman
military base of Satala. But by moving south he could gain much booty
from the rich and poorly defended Armenian satrapies. On his way he
would pass through the region of Chorzane. The populousness and
vulnerability of this territory, which extended for three days' journey
south from Theodosiopolis, is noted by Procopius; here communities

---

[26] Josh. Styl. §48 and Theoph. A.M. 5997 (144) for the allegation; Josh. was writing
very soon after the truce of 506, see above ch.4.iii.b. See above n.2 on the possible
link between the two sources.

[27] Josh. Styl. §74 on Constantine's return. On Sittas' betrayal see Theoph. Sim. III.5.12–
13, IV.15.13–16 with *PLRE* III, Sittas 2. Cf. also the defection of the Persarmenians
Narses and Aratius to the Romans in the 520s, Proc. I.12.22. An alternative tradition
on Constantine may stem from Eustathius of Epiphaneia, who appears to have
believed that he perished in Persian territory, cf. Mal. 398 and Eustath. frg.7 (142).
The brief accounts of Zach. VII.3 (153) and Proc. *Aed.* III.4.3 make no mention of
treachery.

[28] Josh. Styl. §48 (accepted by Stein II, 94), who adds that the inhabitants were led into
captivity. But Zach. VII.3 (153) insists that Kavadh was generous in his treatment
because he had not been insulted by the inhabitants, although Zach.'s reliability is
open to doubt here, since he may be seeking to contrast the city's fate with that of
Amida (narrated immediately afterwards): see Merten, *De Bello*, 162, who is
suspicious of Zach.'s pro-Persian bias.

from both sides of the border lived in harmony, with no expectation of war. It was the ideal invasion route for an indigent king and a rapacious army.[29] From Chorzane Kavadh will have entered Asthianene, traversing the passes of Saphcae and Illyrisis on his way south. Beyond lay the fertile satrapies of Ingilene and Sophanene, both of which were ravaged by his forces.[30] The king first directed his army to Martyropolis, the chief city of Sophanene, whereupon the satrap Theodore and the inhabitants of the city presented themselves to Kavadh and offered him the public taxes of the last two years; their fortifications were too weak to be defended, as was subsequently acknowledged by the emperor himself. Kavadh, impressed by the gesture, spared the city and surrounding area, and confirmed Theodore in his position as satrap; Sophanene he now regarded as Persian territory.[31]

---

[29] See above ch.2 p.23 on Chorzane; Proc. *Aed.* III.3.9–13.

[30] Josh. Styl. §50. On the prosperity of Ingilene, cf. Dillemann, *Mésopotamie*, 238, citing *Aed.* II.4.14–18; see also his map, 235. Josh. Styl.'s Aggel is clearly a reference to Ingilene, cf. Markwart, *Südarmenien*, 107–8. On the passes through which Kavadh advanced, see above Preface, n.1.

[31] Proc. *Aed.* III.2.4–9; see also Whitby, 'Martyropolis', 178, Theodorus 52 in *PLRE* II. The 'public taxes' (δημοσίοι φόροι) mentioned by Proc. imply that the satrapies were no longer immune from Roman taxation, cf. Adontz, *Armenia*, 91–3 with 411 n.33b (Garsoïan) and Toumanoff, *Studies*, 194–5. Cf. also Nöldeke, *Tabari*, 146 n.1, on two oriental sources which note the capture of the city. Another source, the Armenian 'Life of bishop Marutha of Maipherkat' (Martyropolis), a work perhaps of the late sixth century, tells how the inhabitants of the city presented Kavadh with a gold cup given to them by Yazdgerd I, cf. Marcus, 'The Armenian life', 54, 69. The author of the 'Epic Histories', probably writing in the 470s, regarded Sophanene as traditionally Persian, cf. Garsoïan, *Epic Histories*, 11, 457: Kavadh's decision to regard the satrapy as his own is quite comprehensible, since he had been acknowledged as its overlord by the hand-over of its taxes.

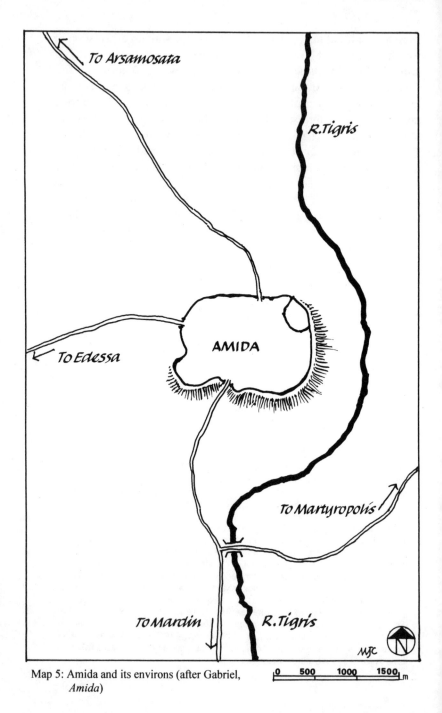

Map 5: Amida and its environs (after Gabriel,
        Amida)

iv) The siege of Amida (502–3)

Little more than one day's march away from Martyropolis lay Amida, the prosperous capital of Roman Mesopotamia. It was surrounded by wealthy farms and thriving monasteries; the city itself, 'Amida the Black' as it was known from the colour of its dark stone, still dominates the west bank of the Tigris. Protected to the east and the south by steep banks, the city is situated on a wide plateau at a bend of the river; Roman engineers had compensated for the lack of natural defences on its north and west sides. The arrival of refugees from Nisibis in 363 had swollen the city's population to a figure in the tens of thousands. An illustration of Amida's prosperity is furnished by the bishop of Mesopotamia, John Sa'oro, who built a Church of the Forty Martyrs (of Sebaste) in the city, as well as a bridge over the Tigris, less than twenty years before Kavadh's attack.[32]

It was perhaps by way of this very bridge that Kavadh arrived outside Amida and began to invest it on 5 October. News of his invasion had already reached the Amidenes, and so there will have been little for the king to plunder in the city's territory; John of Ephesus, for instance, tells how most of the four hundred monks of the monastery of Mar John Urtaye sought shelter inside the walls. Despite the riches to be had from the city, Kavadh's decision to undertake a siege is surprising, and probably reflects his continuing need of booty. For the inauspicious constellation of the Kids, then visible, presaged the onset of winter and the end of the campaigning season; according to a proverb, 'At that time (i.e. winter) the Mede does not even put his hand outside his cloak'.[33]

---

[32] Ammianus XVIII.9.1–2 on Amida and the rich lands around it, cf. Matthews, *Ammianus*, 55. On the fortifications of the city see Strzygowski-van Berchem, *Amida*, 6–7, 277–85, van Berchem, 'Recherches', 266–7, Lightfoot, *Eastern Frontier*, 80–2 and Sinclair, *Eastern Turkey*, III, 166–9; whether the walls now remaining are mainly of fourth or sixth century date is disputed, although Gabriel, *Voyages*, 176–82, argues convincingly that most are Justinianic. On the monasteries, see Harvey, *Asceticism and Society*, 57–9 with Palmer, *Monk and Mason*, 83; also Mango-Bell, *Churches*, 105–6. Proc. *Aed.* III.1.4 on the distance between Martyropolis and Amida. On bishop John Sa'oro, Palmer, *Monk and Mason*, 116, from *Chron. 819*, a.795 (p.4).

[33] Joh. Eph., *Lives*, *PO* 19 (1925), 218–19 with Harvey, *Asceticism and Society*, 60. John himself was later a monk of this monastery, cf. Ginkel, *John of Ephesus*, 27. Ammianus XIX.9.1 on the coming of winter in 359 (and the constellation), cf. Matthews, *Ammianus*, 58; Proc. I.7.3 on Kavadh's arrival at Amida in winter (but with too much emphasis on the unexpectedness of his appearance). Segal, *Edessa*, 115 for the proverb (from Socr. *HE* III.21.1); cf. Lee, *Information*, on the problems caused to Romans and Persians by the cold weather.

The siege of Amida, which was to last three months, had a great impact on contemporaries and posterity alike. One old monk of the monastery of Mar John, having witnessed the capture of the city, passed the rest of his life in Palestine, vowing never to revisit the place. Contemporary sources describe the siege in detail, and the later Syriac chronographers, usually so terse, become quite prolix in their narration of this episode. It was not only the enormity of the disaster which stimulated such interest, but also the moral lesson that could be drawn from it. John Sa'oro died a few days before Kavadh's arrival, as had been prophesied to him; his people were accordingly deprived of the prudent counsel of a bishop in their resistance to the enemy. During the siege, as will be seen, they unwisely taunted the Persians, and, according to some accounts, Christ even appeared to Kavadh to assure him that he would capture the city. It should therefore be remembered that, while we are fortunate to have numerous accounts of the siege, many of them are clearly more interested in the edification of the reader than in historical accuracy.[34] Our two principal sources for the siege are Joshua the Stylite and Zachariah; Procopius, although for the most part in agreement with Zachariah, adds some detail.[35]

Not long after the Persians had encamped outside Amida the Roman envoy Rufinus arrived. He offered the king the gold he had deposited at Caesarea, but Kavadh preferred to pursue the siege and detain the ambassador. Although winter had come, he believed that the capture of the city was within his grasp. His reckoning was hardly unjustified. Procopius notes that there were no forces stationed in the city, and although he may be thought to have exaggerated, it is significant that no source refers to Roman soldiers among the defenders. And, as elsewhere on the eastern frontier, the city's defences had suffered neglect during the years of peace. For these reasons, as well as his need for the riches contained in it, Kavadh was determined to gain possession of Amida.[36]

---

[34] Josh. Styl. §§50–53 on the siege, cf. Zach. VII.3–4 (153–60). Zach. is the first source to place great emphasis on the death of John Sa'oro, on which cf. Palmer, *Monk and Mason*, 117. Later sources: Mari, 41, Chron. Seert, *PO* 7 (1911), 40, one of the *Narrationes Variae*, XVIII, 261–2, *Chron. 1234*, ch.51, 147–150. Proc. I.7.17–18 also stresses the vaunting behaviour of the Amidenes. Joh. Eph., *Lives*, *PO* 19 (1925), 219 on the monk's vow.

[35] The similarity of the accounts of Proc. and Zach. concerning the siege of Amida may stem from their use of Eustathius of Epiphaneia, see above p.75. The later Syriac accounts are based on Zachariah, *ibid*.

[36] Josh. Styl. §50 on Rufinus; Proc. I.7.4 on the lack of soldiers, with Theoph. A.M. 5996 (144.29). In 359, by contrast, a considerable body of forces had defended the

To the king's surprise, however, the Amidenes 'were quite unwilling to yield to the enemy, and showed an unexpected fortitude in holding out against dangers and hardships'. Right from the start the citizens of Amida matched siege engines and mounds with devices of their own, thwarting every attempt to take the city by storm. Kavadh's first enterprise was to bring his battering-rams to bear on the city walls, probably on its northern side; the monastery of Mar John provided some of his building materials.[37] The Amidenes countered by strengthening and increasing the height of the walls at the point of attack. The Persian battering rams, once deployed, had limited success. The defenders, like those at Plataea in 431 B.C.,[38] broke off the heads of the rams by means of timbers manipulated from the walls. Although the newly added section on top of the wall did collapse, the defences were not breached.[39]

The most straightforward method having failed, Kavadh next determined to construct a mound close to the city walls from which beams could be laid across to the ramparts, so providing a gangway for his forces; dampened hides were employed to shelter those involved in building the mound. By just such a means had Amida fallen to the Persians in 359: the defenders had attempted to erect a type of glacis within the walls as a counter-measure, but the Roman mound collapsed, bridging the gap to the attackers' mound and exposing the city to all their forces. Perhaps recalling this unsuccessful tactic, the defenders of 502 devised a more subtle expedient: they secretly set about under-

---

city, as Ammianus (XVIII.9.3) notes; cf. also *ND*, *Oriens* XXXVI, 78, for *equites* stationed at Amida. Proc. *Aed.* II.3.27 on the ageing walls of the city.

[37] Quotation from Proc. I.7.4 (tr. Dewing). On the monastery of Mar John, Joh. Eph., *Lives*, *PO* 19 (1925), 216–18. The monastery lay north of the city; given that the city was most accessible from the north and west, it may be conjectured that Kavadh built the mound on the north side (probably on the western side of the north wall, since a well fortified citadel lies in the north-east corner, cf. the map on p.82). The author of the *Peri Strategias* offers detailed advice to citizens on the defence of their cities, and makes no reference to soldiers, 13.22, 30.

[38] Thuc. II.75–8. Haury, *Zur Beurteilung*, 5–6, long ago refuted the view that Proc. was merely imitating Thucydides' description of the siege of Plataea and was therefore not credible; Zach.'s terminology is very similar to Proc.'s here, cf. *ibid.*, 22–3 and Merten, *De Bello*, 164–74. Cf. the debate about Priscus' description of the siege of Naissus (frg.6) with Blockley's notes, *FCH* II, 380–1.

[39] Proc. I.7.12–13, Zach. VII.3 (153), cf. *Peri Strategias* 13.121–35. Josh. Styl. §50 reports the (limited) damage inflicted by the battering-rams. Zach., *loc. cit.*, also tells how the defenders muffled the force of the rams by hanging bundles of rushes from the ramparts (cf. Ammianus XX.11.15 and *Peri Strategias* 13.115–20 with Elton, *Warfare*, 261 and Runciman, *Fall of Constantinople*, 97).

mining the Persian mound.[40] Their ingenuity was amply rewarded. While the Persians laboured to build up their mound, the Roman miners extracted the earth beneath it, supporting their tunnels by means of wooden beams. It must have taken some weeks for the besiegers to match the height of the walls with their mound. As they laboured through October and perhaps much of November, the lightly-clothed Persians suffered in the cold; the condition of their bows deteriorated and morale sagged.[41] Much was staked on the impending assault.

Eventually the mound surpassed the height of the walls. On the day of the attack five hundred select Persian troops assembled on top of the mound. Wooden beams were at hand, ready to serve as bridges from the mound across to the ramparts. Archers were positioned to give covering fire to the assault troops. Kavadh and his army were deployed around the city, ready to take advantage of any gap the attack might open up elsewhere on the walls. At a given signal, the beams were thrown down and the soldiers rushed across. Few will have made it as far as the ramparts, for the defenders were ready. No sooner had the beams come down than lengths of ox-skin and pieces of vetch, doused in myrrh-oil, were thrown upon them, rendering them extremely slippery; at the same time the props supporting the mound were set on fire. Fighting continued all day, but eventually the fire beneath the mound ate away its foundations and consumed much of the material used in its construction. Its sudden collapse cost the lives of large numbers of Persians still deployed on it and brought joy to the

[40]   Josh. Styl. connects the erection of a mound with the use of the battering-rams (§50); it is possible that the mound was used in conjunction with rams, in order to hit the higher (weaker) portion of the walls. Proc. I.7.14 places the assault of the battering-rams first, while Zach. VII.3 (153) simply catalogues the whole range of Persian initiatives. *Ibid.* on the protection required for the mound-builders, cf. Ammianus XIX.7.3. *Ibid.* XIX.8.1–2 on the collapse of the Roman mound in 359. Cf. Leriche, 'Techniques', 85–6, on the extensive Roman mines dug under the Persian ramp during the siege of Dura Europus in 256.

       Unlike Shapur in 359, Kavadh does not seem to have made any use of siege engines. He was presumably unwilling to spend the time needed for their construction, hoping to take the city more swiftly; and since the city's population had expanded since 359, there may have been fewer suitable sources of building materials (such as forests) in the vicinity.

[41]   Zach. VII.3 (153) on the effects of the weather; the effect on morale may safely be inferred. According to Proc. (I.7.20) Amida fell 'not many days after' this failure; the city fell on 10 January (see below). This would imply that the attack from the mound took place in late December; but Proc.'s phrase cannot be pressed and other sources (e.g. Josh. Styl. §53) report a further failure of Kavadh before the city finally fell.

defenders. Such was their elation that they mocked the Persian king
from the ramparts in an ill-omened display of hubris.[42]

While the mound was being constructed, Kavadh had not remained
idle: various contingents of his army, less suited to siege warfare, were
despatched to ravage the surrounding countryside and to forage for
those undertaking the siege. Some of his Hephthalite forces, who
headed northwards into Ingilene, came upon the shelter of a local holy
man, Jacob. Finding their attempts to kill him ineffectual, they
summoned the king. Impressed at the power of Jacob, he acceded to the
holy man's request that his shelter might act as a refuge for those
fleeing the war.[43] Another force, under the command of the Lakhmid
chief al-Nu'man, was sent southwestwards to overrun the territory of
Carrhae and Edessa. Yet another, comprising Persians, Hephthalites
and Arabs, headed directly southwards and, skirting the Tur Abdin,
made first for Constantia. On 19 October, with their forces dispersed
outside the city, the Persians found themselves at a disadvantage when
they came under attack from the *duces* of Armenia and Mesopotamia,
Eugenius and Olympius respectively.[44] Not for the last time in the sixth

[42] Zach. VII.3 (154) for the most detailed account, followed by *Chron. 1234*, 148.
Proc.'s account (I.7.14–15) is briefer but very similar; cf. Josh. Styl. §50 (very
cursory). Proc. I.7.17–19 is the most detailed on the mocking of Kavadh, cf. Zach.
and *Chron. 1234, loc. cit.*

[43] Proc. I.7.5–11 is the only source for this; his specific allusion to Hephthalites
confirms that these must be the Huns referred to in the Syriac sources. He places
Jacob at Endielon, which is taken by Dillemann, *Mésopotamie*, 87 n.1 to refer to
Ingilene (cf. Markwart, *Südarmenien*, 107 and n.2). Thierry, 'Monuments chrétiens',
195–6, connects Jacob's shelter with a convent of St Jacob the Recluse near Seert;
since he oddly seems to believe that Jacob was no longer at Endielon at the time of
Kavadh's invasion. According to Proc., Jacob froze the Hephthalite who was about to
shoot him; for this 'well-known miracle motive' (Maenchen-Helfen, *Huns*, 240
n.250), cf. Joh. Eph., *Lives, PO* 17 (1923), 20–1 and Soz. *HE* VII.26.8 with Harvey,
Asceticism and Society, 66 and 173 n.59 (citing other examples). Cf. Kavadh's
respect for Bar-Hadad in the same war, Proc. II.13.15. Haury, *Zur Beurteilung*, 23,
suggests Proc.'s use of Christian Syrian sources here, cf. Cameron, *Procopius*, 156.
John of Ephesus, born in Ingilene c.507, was entrusted to a holy man who, like Jacob,
lived in an enclosure north of Amida, cf. Palmer, *Monk and Mason*, 81.

[44] Josh. Styl. §51 (also for the date). On Eugenius, cf. *PLRE* II, Eugenius 6. On
Olympius (Theoph.'s Alypius, A.M. 5996 [144.30]), *ibid.*, Olympius 14: he was,
contra PLRE, *dux* of Mesopotamia, since (cf. *ND, Oriens* XXXVI, 77–9) Constantia is in Mesopotamia, not Osrhoene, cf. Mango–Scott, *Theophanes*, 224 n.5.

That it was not al-Nu'man's force which was engaged near Constantia is implied by
his being sent to Carrhae, a long way southwest of Constantia; and when he
approached Carrhae, he did so from the south (Josh. Styl. §52), not from the north-
east. Further, the commanders of the Persian forces engaged at Tell Beshme are
referred to as *marzbans* (with no reference to al-Nu'man).

century, however, the initiative of a Roman commander was thwarted by the indiscipline of his men. As the Romans were returning to Constantia, they were informed of a further detachment of Persians nearby. Although evening had fallen, Olympius gave a signal to muster the Roman forces, but they had scattered to despoil the Persian dead. The delay in mobilising proved fatal. Observing the *dux*'s beacon signal from Tell Beshme, the Persian commanders were well prepared for the Roman attack. The Roman cavalry fled when they realised they were outnumbered; the infantry, hemmed in by the mountainous terrain, resisted the enemy cavalry in *testudo* formation, but were finally broken. 'Thus many of the Romans were killed and the rest were taken captive'.[45]

Faithful to his orders, on 26 October al-Nu'man, arriving from the south, started to ravage the territory of Carrhae. Kavadh had chosen his target well: it was the vintage season, and many of the inhabitants of both Carrhae and Edessa were out in the villages, where they were easy prey to the raiding Arabs. Carrhae itself was spared by the Arabs, who were unaccustomed to siege warfare; in fact, the city's defences were in poor condition, much as they had been in 359, when, in the face of Shapur's impending attack on Roman territory, the inhabitants had been forced to flee the place, described by Ammianus as an *oppidum invalidis circumdatum muris*. In Edessa, threatened by the Lakhmid attack, emergency measures were implemented to put the city defences in working order; basic maintenance work on the walls and gates, long put off, was rapidly completed.[46]

---

[45]   Josh. Styl. §51 (and for the quotation, tr. Watt); the engagement took place to the east of Constantia, near Tell Beshme. See Dillemann, *Mésopotamie*, 189 and n.5 (with fig.10, p.76) for the location on the route between Amida and Constantia; Ps. Dion. II, 5 mentions an engagement at Tell Beshme in 502/3 (though he may be referring to the defeat of Patricius and Hypatius later in the year, which also took place near Tell Beshme, see below n.81).

The *testudo* formation, consisting of densely packed infantry behind a shield wall, though no longer referred to as such, was commonly used against cavalry, often with success; cf. Ravegnani, *Soldati*, 63–4 and Rance, *Tactics*, 219–24, citing (e.g.) *Peri Strategias* 32, 36 and *Strategikon* XII A 7 (410–12). Ideally archers would rain arrows on the enemy from behind the infantry wall; but since this was a night battle, the Roman infantry will not have been able to do so.

[46]   Josh. Styl. §52. Proc. II.19.12, cf. *Aed.* II.9.3–4 (with Isaac, *Limits*, 236–7) on the Arab inability to capture fortifications, doubted, however, by Kaegi, *Conquests*, 56–7. Ammianus XVIII.7.3 on the abandonment of Carrhae in 359. Josh. Styl. also notes the seizure of 18,500 captives by the Arabs, which will have had a significant impact on local population levels; cf. Trombley–Watt, *Chronicle*, note *ad loc.*

Eugenius, the *dux* of Armenia, was however able to launch a successful counter-strike. From Constantia he marched northwestwards, probably passing through Samosata and Melitene (his headquarters); there he will have turned northeast and headed for Theodosiopolis. The garrison left by Kavadh was unable to resist his attack, and the city passed into Roman hands once more.[47]

At Amida meanwhile, despite the failure of the attack from the mound, Kavadh refused to abandon the siege. He persisted in his determination to make use of the mound, ordering the Persians to build it up again. Stones, wood and earth were employed in raising the structure once more. This time the king's intention, it appears, was to set it up right against the city walls, in order to allow his battering-rams to strike their upper sections, which were usually thinner and weaker. But again he found his efforts foiled by the resourcefulness of the defenders: they employed a 'scorpion', a machine which projected rocks using torsion springs of sinew, against the building work. The machine, known to the Persians as 'the crusher', rendered their work nearly impossible and devastated much of what had already been accomplished. And whereas other devices, such as fire-arrows, had failed to damage the battering-ram, which was protected by a wet cotton covering, the massive stones hurled by the scorpion wrecked that too. In very much the same way the skilful deployment of four such scorpions during the siege of 359 had destroyed the siege-towers being deployed by Shapur. For Kavadh, this development was the last straw. Demoralised and having sustained heavy losses, his army prepared to withdraw.[48] But he did not forget the original aim of his

---

[47] Josh. Styl. §52. It is possible, if unlikely, that the Theodosiopolis retaken was that in Osrhoene (Resaina), cf. *Chron. Arbela* XIX, p.101; Resaina, not far from Constantia down the Khabur, could already have been captured by the Persians. But Josh. Styl. calls this place Resaina, rather than Theodosiopolis, and Eugenius, as *dux* of Armenia, is more likely to have operated close to his territory.

[48] Josh. Styl. §53 alone on this (putting Persian losses at 50,000, clearly an exaggeration). Ammianus XXIII.4.4–6 for a description of the 'scorpion' (wild ass, *onager*, was another term), XIX.7.6–7 on its use in the siege of 359 with Matthews, *Ammianus*, 291–2 and Marsden, *Artillery*, I, 197–8 and II, 249–65. Constantius, when Caesar, had deposited some of these machines in Amida, cf. Ammianus XVIII.9.1 and Elton, *Warfare*, 171. Josh. Styl., *loc. cit.*, states that the rocks weighed 300 (presumably Roman) lbs. (= 98.25 kg), an amazing figure, if accurate; the heaviest balls noted by Marsden, *op. cit.*, I, 81 weighed between 35 and 40 kg (and cf. his table of weights and measures, xix). With 'the crusher' may be compared a catapult employed by the defenders of Theodosiopolis against Bahram V in 421/2 which was named 'the apostle Thomas' by the city's bishop (Theod. *HE* V.37.8).

invasion: he sent a message to the Amidenes, requesting from them a payment in return for his departure. The governor (*praeses*) of Mesopotamia, Cyrus, in consultation with the city council, refused the king's request. In their reply the Roman leaders even demanded money from him, to compensate for the damage he had caused to the region. Whether because of this final insult from the Amidenes, or a vision of Christ (as he himself subsequently claimed, according to Zachariah), or fresh intelligence from one of his men, Kavadh did not depart. Within a few days Amida had fallen.[49]

Probably even before Kavadh had made his request to the governor, the fate of the city had been sealed. One of the Persian commanders,[50] stationed on the western side of the city, had observed the repeated raids undertaken by a certain Amidene known as Kutrigo. He then traced the route of the raider, and discovered a hidden way into the city; according to Zachariah, it was one of the streams next to the Tripyrgion, a tower in the west wall. A similar passage had been used by the Persians during the siege of 359 in an ultimately unsuccessful attempt to storm the city.[51] The commander duly reported his discovery to the king, and plans were laid for a final assault the following day, 10

---

[49]   Zach. VII.4 (155–6), cf. *Narratio* XVIII (p.261), offering more details on the vision of Christ and placing the capture three days afterwards; also Chron. Seert, *PO* 7 (1911), 40 and Mari, 41. Mich. Syr. IX.7 (158) attributes the fall of the city to the sins of the defenders. *Chron. 1234*, 148, omits the vision of Christ and ascribes Kavadh's decision to stay to the defenders' insults, cf. Proc. I.7.19 (the lewd behaviour of the prostitutes of Amida is interpreted by the Magi as a sign of the imminent fall of the city). *PLRE* II, Cyrus 5, on the governor.

[50]   The Persian commander, a *marzban*, is named as Kanarak by Zach. and the sources dependent on him. This is, as so often in non-Persian sources, almost certainly a misunderstanding of the title *kanarang*, on which cf. Christensen, *L'Iran*, 107 n.3. The *kanarang* was the *marzban* in charge of the troublesome north-east frontier of the Persian kingdom; but now that the Persians' neighbours here, the Hephthalites, were the backers of Kavadh, the *kanarang* was free to take part in the expedition. According to Proc. (I.6.14–16) the newly appointed *kanarang* at the time was Adergoudounbades (Adhurgundadh); hence it is just possible that it was he who made the discovery.

[51]   Zach. VII.4 (156), followed by *Chron. 1234*, 148–9, Barhebraeus, 72; cf. Proc. I.7.20. Hamilton–Brooks refer to 'aqueducts' in their translation, but the Syriac *bybwtha* is best translated as 'streams': the only aqueduct on Gabriel's plan, *Voyages*, 93, enters the city on the northern side, by tower X, while there is a ravine on the western side, with several postern gates leading down to it, cf. *ibid.*, 98–9, between towers XXIV and XXVI. One of these might be Zach.'s Tripyrgion. Ammianus XIX.5.4 describes a stairway leading down to a channel of the Tigris on the south side of the city. Even if he has confused the southern and eastern sides of Amida (cf. XVIII.9.2 with Matthews, *Ammianus*, 55), he is probably referring to one of the towers in the southeast corner of the city, cf. the plans of Gabriel, *Voyages*, 93, 100.

January 503. The defence of the tower had been entrusted to monks of the monastery of Mar John Urtaye.[52] That Friday evening they had enjoyed a good meal and some wine, in celebration of a feast or to resist the cold, and were soon overtaken by sleep. Even if they had been keeping a look-out, it would have been difficult for them to descry any moves being made by the Persians, for it was a cloudy wet night. But they would have been able to defend themselves against the small company of Persians who ascended the passage to the bottom of the tower. The Persian commander, realising that they had not been observed from the tower, had scaling-ladders brought. His men then scaled the Tripyrgion from within the walls and swiftly overpowered the monks.[53]

So far all had gone smoothly for the attackers. But the cries of the monks as they were slaughtered alerted the guards in neighbouring towers. Cyrus, the governor, was summoned; foolishly, his aides lit his way with torches, which made him an easy target for the Persian archers. He was wounded and quickly withdrew. Day dawned, and the Persians hastened to press their advantage. Kavadh launched his infantrymen up scaling ladders propped against the exterior of the Tripyrgion and the neighbouring battlements. As they ascended they came under fire from the defenders of the adjacent towers, and many perished. Those who climbed back down the ladders to escape the missiles were cut down as cowards by their fellow soldiers, just like

---

[52] Dillemann, *Mésopotamie*, 313 on the monastery, which he oddly chooses to render as John of Abarnia (Zach. VII.4; Hamilton-Brooks render it as John of Anzetene, 156), but the Syriac text has Urtaye (ed. Brooks, 25.18, cf. Palmer, *Monk and Mason*, 83 and Witakowski, *Chronicle*, 5 n.38). The archimandrite of the monastery was a Persian, which seems to have given rise to allegations of treachery by the monks, cf. Marc. *com.* a.502 and Theoph. A.M. 5996 (145.7–8). Joshua (§53) notes general rumours of a betrayal, cf. Merten, *De Bello*, 168.

[53] Proc. I.7.21–5 and Zach. VII.4 (156–7). There are minor discrepancies between the two sources. Proc. is in general less detailed, but mentions the feast; Josh. Styl. §53 gives the date, and ascribes the consumption of wine to the cold. Zach. represents the commander, whom he calls Kanarak, as launching his attack without consulting Kavadh; the king was informed only when the Persians had reached the base of the Tripyrgion. Proc., *loc. cit.*, more plausibly has Kavadh informed well before the attack. Zach. also states that Kanarak followed Kutrigo up the passage on the night of the attack. Given the similarity between this episode and that of 359 (Ammianus XIX.5.4–6), where a deserter led the Persians up a passageway under cover of darkness, it is possible that Kutrigo likewise had turned traitor; see above n.52 on rumours of treachery.

In 503 Easter fell on 30 March (cf. Grumel, *Chronologie*, 269); hence 10 January was a Friday, Epiphany having been celebrated the previous Monday (*ibid.*, 312).

Bashi-bouzouks during the siege of Constantinople in 1453.[54] The king himself took up position near the foot of the ladders. Such stern measures, combined with the presence of Kavadh so close to the fray, stiffened the attackers' resolve and they pursued their onslaught with renewed vigour. The battle on the ramparts, hitherto proceeding to the advantage of the Romans, turned in the Persians' favour.[55] While the defenders sought to bring about the collapse of the tower, the Persians, passing along the battlements in one direction, gained control of one tower after another. In the other direction a burly Roman soldier impeded their progress for a long time, but gave way once he saw so many towers on the other side falling to the Persians. Night fell, leaving the besiegers in command of one wall. It took them that night and the following day (12 January) to clear a path to one of the gates, which they then opened for the rest of the army.[56]

Amida had fallen. The siege had lasted 97 days and cost the Persians dearly.[57] A massacre ensued, which Kavadh permitted to go on for three days. The one place where he allowed the citizens to find refuge was the Church of the Forty Martyrs, and this was only after being approached by a suppliant.[58] Once the soldiers had finished plundering the city, the bodies of the slain were deposited outside the north gate; the Syriac sources are unanimous for a total of 80,000 corpses taken

---

[54] Runciman, *Fall of Constantinople*, 134 on the Bashi-bouzouks (the irregular Turkish infantry).

[55] The repulse of the attack in 359, when the Persians gained control of the tower and scaled the battlements in force, shows that the capture of one of the towers need not prove fatal to the city. But the defenders in 359 had been able to bring several *onagri* (scorpions, cf. n.48 above) to bear against the attackers (Ammianus XIX.5.6); those in 503 clearly could not move any into place in time.

[56] Zach. VII.4 (157–8) for a most vivid description; Proc. (I.7.25–9) was clearly using the same source, but more sparingly, cf. Merten, *De Bello*, 147–8.

[57] Elias Nis. a.814, *Chr. Edess.* 80 (a.814), put the length at 97 days, which accords with Joshua's dates, cf. Merten, *De Bello*, 174. *Chron. 724*, a.814 (115, 21), on the other hand, places the fall of Amida on 24 December (502), cf. Marc. *com.* (a.502). Joshua's date should be preferred.

[58] For a vivid account of the massacres cf. Joh. Eph., *Lives, PO* 19 (1925), 219–20; see above p.83 on the Church of the Forty Martyrs. According to Zach. VII.4 (158) the suppliant was a prince of Arran (Albania), cf. Mich. Syr. IX.7 (159). Ps. Dion. II, 5 (clearly from Joh. Eph.) notes that ninety monks of the monastery of John Urtaye were slaughtered by Persian scouts in the school called 'of the Urtaye'. Proc. I.7.30–2 records that a priest (ἱερεύς, his usual term for a bishop, as F. Trombley has pointed out to me, cf. II.13.13) prevailed upon Kavadh to call a halt to the slaughter; Merten, *De Bello*, 173, rightly doubts his account (the bishop having died before the siege, see above p.84), but it is accepted by Christensen, *Le règne*, 108–9.

from the ruins.[59] Once this was accomplished, Kavadh rode into Amida through the south gate on an elephant. He despoiled the city of all its treasures, including those housed in its churches; larger items were placed on rafts and sent down the Tigris. The chief councillor Leontius and the governor Cyrus, the leaders who had survived and had earlier rejected the king's request for a payment, were clothed in rags, forced to carry pigs about and publicly exposed to ridicule. Most of the survivors were gathered together to be deported to Persia; some, however, were sacrificed to the troops' continuing thirst for revenge.[60] Some of those led away into captivity founded a new city, Veh-az-Amid-Kavadh (the 'better Amida of Kavadh'), south-east of Khuzistan; others, it seems, were sent to the Caucasus, no doubt to help garrison that region against raiders from the north.[61] The Roman envoy Rufinus was then at last released to inform the emperor; on his way to the capital he brought the news to all the cities through which he passed, causing a panic in the area east of the Euphrates.[62]

Since Amida had been captured without demolishing the walls or gates, Kavadh decided to garrison it against the Romans. A certain Glon was placed in command of a force of no more than 3000 men, and governors were appointed to take charge of the few remaining

---

[59] Zach. VII.4 (158), Josh. Styl. §53, Elias of Nisibis, a.814 (80,000) and Joh. Eph. in Ps. Dion. II, 5 (85,000). The figure appears rather high, although the population of Amida is unknown. Ammianus XIX.2.14 is of no help, since the figure he offers for those in Amida in 359 has been emended by some from 20,000 to 120,000.

[60] Zach. VII.4 (158-9), cf. Josh. Styl. §53 on the 80,000, not including others stoned outside the city or killed by other means (but apparently placing the removal of the corpses after the departure of Kavadh). Theoph. A.M. 5996 (145.10-12) alone reports Kavadh's entry on an elephant, clearly relying on a detailed (but unknown) earlier source. Proc. I.7.34 reports that Kavadh soon released the captives, but evidently many remained in Persia; his gesture may have been part of an attempt to win the favour of the people of the frontier area (cf. Anastasius' concessions to the Amidenes later on, Proc. I.7.35), on which see Lamma, 'La politica', 178.

[61] On the deportations, Josh. Styl. §53, Zach. VII.4 (159), Joh. Eph., Lives, PO 19 (1925), 219, Nöldeke, Tabari, 138 and n.3, 146 and n.2, and Christensen, L'Iran, 353. A Sasanian administrative seal referring to Kavadh's new city by name is shown in Maricq, 'Classica et Medievalia', pl. IV (b), cf. 104-5; see also Lieu, 'Captives', 499 and Luther, 'Die syrische Chronik', 184 n.322. The city's location may be seen on TAVO B VI 3. On the survivors at the Caspian Gates, Zach. XII.7 (329), cf. Merten, De Bello, 173.

[62] Josh. Styl. §54. The periodeutes (visitor) Jacob of Sarug helped to rally the people; one of the letters he despatched at this point, to the people of Edessa, survives, reminding them of the impregnability of their city (on which see below n.93), ep.20, 129-35, cf. Segal, Edessa, 170.

inhabitants.[63] Kavadh and the bulk of his army then retired southwards. He probably divided his forces for the rest of the winter and the spring; a vanguard occupied a position between Amida and Constantia, poised to move to the southwest against Edessa and Samosata or to the northwest against Melitene, while others were quartered in the Jebel Sinjar. The king himself withdrew to Nisibis.[64]

v) The first Roman counter-offensive

Anastasius, learning of the siege of Amida, immediately despatched an army to garrison the cities east of the Euphrates over the winter.[65] The arrival of a messenger from Kavadh in April demanding money decided him in favour of a counter-offensive; now that Amida had fallen it would be an admission of defeat, and a dangerous precedent, to pay any money to the Persians. In order to forestall the further attacks which would attend non-payment, counter-measures were required. The emperor's solution was to follow up the forces already sent out with a battery of important generals. Not only would this show his determination to exact vengeance on the aggressors, but the various commanders would bring with them their own *bucellarii* to supplement the imperial forces. In May the two *magistri militum praesentales*, Hypatius and Patricius, and the *magister militum per Orientem* Areobindus were sent forth. They were accompanied by many other officers, listed by Procopius and Theophanes, among them the future Emperor Justin and the redoubtable Lazic general Pharesmanes.[66] The

---

[63]   Zach. VII.4 (160) puts the garrison at 3000; Proc. I.7.33 gives a figure of 1000. Theoph. A.M. 5996 (145.12) mentions Glon.

[64]   Theoph. A.M. 5996 (145.13–15) on Kavadh's return to Nisibis and the position of the army (between Amida and Constantia), if, unusually, δυναστεία here refers to something as concrete as an army; Dillemann, *Mésopotamie*, fig. XVII (p.148) offers an excellent map of the area. Josh. Styl. §53 (cf. §55) places Kavadh's forces in the Jebel Sinjar. The divergence between Josh. Styl. and Theoph. can only be resolved by supposing a division of forces; Josh. Styl. §55 appears to confirm this, referring to a part of Kavadh's forces stationed in the Jebel Sinjar.

[65]   Anastasius must have known of the siege of Amida before Rufinus reached him, despite Josh. Styl. §54; and troops could hardly winter in the east if they only set off in late January. Proc. I.8.1 is therefore probably right in describing Anastasius as reacting during the siege, though he may be wrong about the measures taken at that time; *contra* Merten, *De Bello*, 176 n.1.

[66]   Josh. Styl. §54 for the chronology. Proc. I.8.1–3 for his list of commanders, cf. Theoph. A.M. 5997 (145.17–146.5), probably from the same source as Proc., as noted by Mango–Scott, *Theophanes*, 227 n.3, see above n.4; Proc. alone refers to Godidisclus and Bessas, while Theoph. is the only source to mention Zemarchus. Cf. also Zach. VII.4 (160), Joh. Lyd. *de Mag.* III.53 (142.4–10).

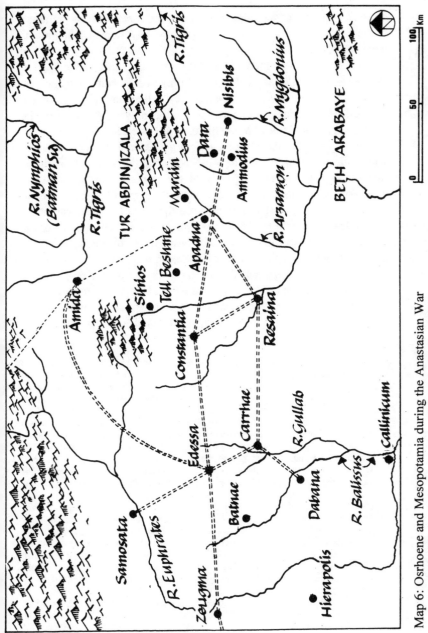

Map 6: Osrhoene and Mesopotamia during the Anastasian War
(note that construction at Dara did not begin until 505)

mustering points for the commanders and the forces already stationed at the front were Edessa and Samosata; by July Roman preparations were complete.[67]

The host thus gathered was an imposing one; according to Procopius, it was said to be the largest army ever assembled against the Persians. There is, however, a discrepancy in the numbers given by the sources: Marcellinus *comes* puts the total at only 15,000 men, while Joshua suggests 52,000.[68] Marcellinus' figure is clearly too small, even though he adds that the *magister officiorum* Celer was later dispatched with a further 2000 troops; the most likely solution to this disparity is that Marcellinus is referring only to the soldiers sent out with the *magistri militum* in May, and excluding those who had been sent to winter in the east. Joshua's figures, on the other hand, appear rather high; even if 630,000 *modii* of *bucellatum* (biscuit) were baked for the forces,[69] this amount may have been based on an overestimate by the praetorian prefect in charge of provisions, Apion.[70]

The Roman strategy for 503, insofar as there was any co-ordinated plan of action, seems to have been two-fold. One force, under the two *magistri militum praesentales*, was to move northeast and wrest Amida from Persian hands. The other, under Areobindus, Romanus and the

---

[67] Theoph. A.M. 5997 (146.6–7) for the places; Josh. Styl. §55 for an engagement in July. Julian, with at least some of his army, had marched from Litarba (Syria) to Hierapolis in five days (5 to 9 March 363), a distance of some 120 km (75 miles), cf. *TAVO* B VI 4 with Dodgeon–Lieu, *Eastern Frontier*, 231–2. The distance from Constantinople to Antioch, comparable to that to the frontier, was 750 miles, which could plausibly be traversed by the generals and their (mounted) *bucellarii* within two months; cf. Ramsay, 'Roman Imperial Post', 62–3 and cf. map 2.2 in Luttwak, *Grand Strategy*, 82–3 (estimating the time for forces to move from Rome to Antioch at 124 days overland and a further two at sea) and Whitby, *Maurice*, 261. Proc. I.8.6, referring to the slowness of the mustering, is comparing it to the siege of Amida: he is emphasising that the army was too late to deal with Kavadh's first invasion.

[68] Marc. *com.* a.503, Josh. Styl. §54, cf. Proc. I.8.4.

[69] Josh. Styl. §54 for the quantity of *bucellatum*. Jones, *LRE*, 231–2, calculates that the quantities of wheat specified by Joshua for the Roman army would provide an army of 32,500 to 40,000; see also Howard-Johnston, 'Great Powers', 166, the most recent discussion of these figures, who favours acceptance of Joshua, arguing (n.13) for his use of an official source. See the note in Trombley–Watt, *Chronicle*, for a detailed discussion. At II.24.16 Proc. refers to a Roman army in the 540s as being 30,000 strong: for the claim to be made that the force in 503 was the largest ever assembled, it can hardly have fallen short of this number.

[70] On the position of Apion (and his successor Calliopius) cf. Stein II, 95 n.2, Josh. Styl. (tr. Wright), p.44 n.3 and *PLRE* II, Apion 2. He was clearly invested with considerable authority, cf. Joh. Lyd. *de Mag.* III.17 (104.16–17) and Proc. I.8.5 (using very similar phraseology).

phylarch al-Aswad, was to take the offensive and strike into Persian
territory. Neither of the operations enjoyed great success. Areobindus
crossed into Persian territory near Nisibis with around 12,000 men. He
was met by the Persian force, 20,000 strong, which had been quartered
for the winter in the Jebel Sinjar. He nevertheless emerged victorious in
several minor engagements, and even laid siege to Nisibis; but although
at least some of the Nisibenes favoured the Roman cause, he was
unable to capture the city. In July Kavadh, perceiving the small size of
Areobindus' army, committed further troops under the command of the
renegade Constantine. It was enough to push the *magister militum per
Orientem* back in retreat; as he withdrew, he despatched a certain
Calliopius of Beroea to summon help from his colleagues at Amida.[71]

Meanwhile Hypatius and Patricius, having failed to force an entry
into Amida by setting fire to the south gate, had resorted to the lengthy
and expensive measure of constructing siege-engines. Their task was a
formidable one, since the Persians, well aware that the Romans would
try to recapture the town, had stockpiled large quantities of provisions
for themselves; the remaining inhabitants will also have been able to
store up supplies from the market held just outside the city. The task of
investing the city had not been welcomed by the two *magistri militum
praesentales*, and Patricius may have led off some detachments to
ravage Arzanene, leaving his colleague to prosecute the siege.[72] Just
when the three siege-towers, clad with iron to protect them from fire,

---

[71] Josh. Styl. §55, Zach. VII.5 (161), Theoph. A.M. 5997 (146.9–19). Zach. states that
all the leaders initially participated in the siege of Amida, which is possible, if unlikely; Theoph. implies that Kavadh was actually driven out of Nisibis, but the sense
is not altogether clear, cf. Mango–Scott, *Theophanes*, 227 n.4. He is also the only
source to mention Romanus and al-Aswad. Shahîd, *BASIC* I, 20–1, argues that al-
Aswad was a Kindite chieftain; he also suggests that Theoph. was using Eustathius
here, though an official source (see above n.2) is also possible. On the pro-Roman
attitude of at least a section of the population of Nisibis, see Lee, 'Evagrius', 575, 583.

[72] Zach. VII.4–5 (160–61) on the siege and the raid on Arzanene (always an easy target
for the Romans), with Josh. Styl. §§55–6 and Theoph. A.M. 5997 (146.7–8). It was
probably in the course of this raid that the future Emperor Justin captured the young
Peter, who later became the emperor's secretary and who served Justinian in the war
in Lazica; see Proc. II.15.7–8 and *PLRE* II, Petrus 27. Cf. Proc. I.8.22, where he reports an attack on Arzanene late in 503 by Celer; since Celer does not seem to have
taken the field until 504 (see below pp.108, 110), this could be a garbled reference to
Patricius' raid. Zach., *loc. cit.*, seems to believe that Hypatius accompanied Areobindus against Nisibis, while Proc. (I.8.7), noting the unwillingness of the generals to
besiege Amida, says that all the generals advanced into Persian territory. But the
more detailed (if not independent) accounts of Theoph. and Joshua should be
preferred. On the market outside Amida, Zach. VII.5 (162).

were almost ready, Calliopius came with Areobindus' message asking for help. Unsurprisingly, the generals were reluctant to abandon their siege; but when they heard of Areobindus' sudden retreat, they burnt their engines and hastened southwards. They were too late. Areobindus' men, outnumbered by the Persians, had abandoned their camp near Apadna and fled to Constantia and Edessa. Defeat failed to turn into rout only because the Persian soldiers, no less rapacious than their Roman counterparts, prefered to pillage the Roman camp and return eastwards. By the time Hypatius and Patricius arrived, the Persians had gone.[73] Quite apart from their capture of the Roman camp, the Persians had inflicted a serious blow to the Roman high command. Areobindus, feeling himself betrayed by his colleagues, threatened to leave for Constantinople at once; only the praetorian prefect of the force, Apion, was able to restrain him. Hypatius and Patricius, no doubt vexed at having had to break off their siege for no gain, soon returned to Amida.[74]

The absence of the *magistri militum* from Amida had tempted the Persian garrison into negligence. They made excursions from the city into the countryside for the purpose of plunder; and so the Lazic leader Pharesmanes, one of the subordinate Roman generals, overtook and killed many of them when he suddenly returned to the city. Pharesmanes, a figure dreaded by the Persians, was then approached by a certain Amidene. The Amidene, a 'crafty fellow, Gadono by name', was a trusted henchman of the Persian commander Glon. He offered to lure out a detachment of Persians, including Glon, to be ambushed by the Romans. His plan worked admirably. The Persian commander, persuaded that some poorly guarded Roman animals lay near at hand, set off with four hundred cavalry. Pharesmanes' forces were lying in wait at Thilasamon, southwest of Amida, and the surprised Persians were utterly defeated. Glon or one of the other Persian commanders (he is referred to only as a *marzban*) was captured alive, and offered to surrender the city to the Romans; Hypatius and Patricius apparently

---

[73] Josh. Styl. §§55–6. Areobindus, having retreated from Nisibis, must have been somewhere on the road between Ammodius (adjacent to the frontier) and Constantia. Dillemann, *Mésopotamie*, 314–16, the most detailed discussion of these manoeuvres, wrongly connects Theoph. A.M. 5997 (146.25–147.3) with this episode. There is no evidence that Kavadh led this incursion (in July); rather, the Persians were led by Constantine (Josh. Styl. §55).

[74] Theoph. A.M. 5997 (146.21–4) and Josh. Styl. §56. Theoph. alleges that Hypatius and Patricius spurned Areobindus' request out of jealousy.

returned at this point, when the city's surrender looked likely. After the garrison nevertheless refused to come to terms, the *marzban* was executed.[75]

Around this time Roman arms enjoyed further successes. Lakhmid tribesmen allied to Persia made an incursion towards Osrhoene, advancing as far as the Khabur. But Timostratus, the *dux* of the province, defeated them and forced them to withdraw.[76] It was now the turn of the Roman-allied Arabs to pass to the offensive. An expedition was undertaken, which took them as far as Hira, the principal base of the Lakhmids. Although the inhabitants evacuated the encampment in advance, the invaders were able to plunder what remained and to intercept a caravan on its way to al-Nu'man. Given that Anastasius had concluded an agreement with both Kindite and Ghassanid Arabs shortly before the outbreak of war, the identity of these raiders, termed Tha'labites by Joshua, has been the subject of much discussion. It seems most likely that they were in fact Ghassanids: the father of the Ghassanid chief Jabala was called Tha'laba.[77]

With Areobindus' force dispersed in flight and the other commanders occupied in the siege of Amida, it was Kavadh's turn to seize the initiative. The quarrels of the Roman generals had come to his attention, further prompting him to exploit his opportunity. In August

---

[75] Zach. VII.5 (161–2), cf. Proc. I.9.5–19 (a detailed anecdotal account, giving Patricius the role of Pharesmanes); also Josh. Styl. §56. Pharesmanes may have left the siege with the *magistri militum* in order to lure the defenders out. Zach. is much better informed concerning the ruse, his source having been acquainted with Gadono personally. Although Joshua states that the bait was a flock of sheep and Zach. refers to 500 horses, they are clearly recounting the same incident: both put the Persian expeditionary force at 400 men, while Proc. (9.11) puts it at 200. Zach. and Proc. have Glon killed in battle with the Romans, while Zach. adds that his head was sent to Constantia; Joshua reports that a *marzban* was captured, but could not arrange the hand-over of the city. Proc. I.8.14 places the ambush at Thilasamon, for the location of which cf. Honigmann, *Ostgrenze*, map 1; Zach. VII.5 (162) puts it at a place called 'Afotho Ro''en, which Hamilton-Brooks suggest (n.1) may mean 'the fold of the shepherds'.

[76] Josh. Styl. §57 (presumably also in July, so Shahîd, *BASIC* I, 13); *PLRE* II, Timostratus, rather unambitiously places the engagement 'in late 503'.

[77] So Shahîd, *BASIC* I, 13 with *idem*, 'Ghassan and Byzantium', 251–5; see above n.22 on the treaty. See also Sartre, *Trois études*, 161, arguing that Tha'laba was in charge of the tribe in 503, hence Joshua's use of this term to refer to the Ghassanids; cf. Nöldeke, *Ghassanischen Fürsten*, 6 and Aigrain, 'Arabie', 1197. The connection of the Kindites to the Tha'laba tribe, part of the Bakr tribal group, has inclined other scholars to infer that Joshua's Tha'labites are Kindites, cf. e.g. Olinder, *Kings of Kinda*, 52–3, Rothstein, *Lahmiden*, 91–2, Rubin, *ZI*, 272, and (most recently) Potts, *Arabian Gulf*, 226; Shahîd, *BASIC* I, 5, effectively rebuts this line of argument.

he regrouped his force of Hephthalites, Armenians, Arabs and Persians, and followed the main road west from Nisibis. The *magistri militum* moved to block his advance. With Hypatius and Patricius moving south from Amida, and Areobindus coming from the west (presumably from Constantia), the logical place to effect a junction was just to the south of Apadna, where the two roads met. Such may have been the plan of the Roman commanders, but it was thrown into disarray by the sudden arrival of Kavadh. Areobindus was the first to reach Apadna, also known as Arzamon, and established his camp there. The forces of the two *magistri militum praesentales*, however, set up camp at Sifrios, a considerable distance west of Apadna.[78] Areobindus, hearing of the imminent approach of Kavadh's army, could not resist the invader unsupported. He had no option but to beat a hasty retreat westwards once again, leaving his camp to be pillaged by the enemy.[79] So swift was his withdrawal, or so poor the communication between the Roman armies, that Hypatius and Patricius knew nothing of this development; they therefore proceeded eastwards. A chance encounter with a detachment of 800 Hephthalites brought them an easy victory, and they inferred that Kavadh had retreated. Confident of their position, the Romans settled down to their midday meal by a stream, probably the Arzamon. But their ablutions, swept downstream, alerted the Persian king to their location; he had already been informed of the defeat of the Hephthalites.[80] The Persian troops followed the stream northwards, and charged the Romans as soon as they came upon them. The result was an utter rout. The Romans, caught unprepared in a valley, fled

---

[78] Proc. I.8.10, cf. Zach. VII.5 (161) and Josh. Styl. §57 for these positions, with Dillemann, *Mésopotamie*, 315 and fig.38, p.293; the roads intersected at Tell Armen, a few miles south of Apadna, cf. *ibid.*, 82 with fig.30, p.215 and Dussaud, *Topographie*, 493. Dillemann, *op. cit.*, 314, oddly applies Proc.'s passage to the Roman dispositions before Areobindus' invasion of Persian territory; given that this passage corresponds with other sources concerning the site of the battle in August, such an interpretation seems unnecessary.

[79] Proc. I.8.11–12, Zach. VII.5 (161). This therefore was Areobindus' second such retreat; Josh. Styl. §57 does not mention his role in the battle, while Zach.'s version of events precedes his account of Pharesmanes' ruse against the Persians at Amida. That there were two Persian invasions in 503, the second of which was led by Kavadh, is clear, cf. also Theoph. A.M. 5997 (146–7); and that the two Roman armies on each occasion sought to block the enemy advance may reasonably be inferred from the sources. On the identification of Arzamon and Apadna see Dillemann, *Mésopotamie*, 159.

[80] Proc. I.8.14–17; the Romans ate around noon, cf. Proc. I.14.34. Dillemann suggests that the stream was the Arzamon; Kavadh, downstream from the Romans, was therefore further south, perhaps still at Apadna, *Mésopotamie*, 315.

precipitately; it was alleged that their commanders were the first to flee. In an attempt to escape the slaughter some soldiers climbed up the sides of the valley, but many fell to their deaths. Others, led by the *comes* Peter, returned to Sifrios for refuge, but were handed over to the Persians by the inhabitants and executed; only Peter was spared. On the Persian side, the Lakhmid chief al-Nu'man was wounded in the head; he died a few days later, after urging Kavadh to pursue his invasion westwards, towards Edessa.[81]

vi) Kavadh's renewed invasion

While the praesental army sought shelter behind the Euphrates and Areobindus' men fled westwards, Kavadh pressed home his attack. He proceeded towards Edessa in the trail of the retiring columns of the *magister militum per Orientem*. Two days' march from Apadna, a little less from Sifrios, lay the city of Constantia, fortified by Constantius II and the seat of the *dux* of Mesopotamia, Olympius.[82] But the *dux* seems not to have been present there at the time: he is not referred to by any sources. In his place Leontius, a *comes (rei militaris)*, was stationed in the city with a garrison; he and the citizens, inspired by their bishop Bar-Hadad (Baradotus), were resolved to defend the place. Unlike the Amidenes, however, not all were united in opposing the Persians: the Jews of Constantia attempted to tunnel under the walls from their

---

[81]   Proc. I.8.17–19, Zach. VII.5 (161), Josh. Styl. §57 (the sole source concerning Peter); Joshua does not mention Hypatius, stating only that Patricius retreated hastily to Samosata. Both Proc. and Zach. refer to soldiers falling off cliffs (presumably in the mountains of the western Tur Abdin). Marc. *com.* places the battle *iuxta Syficum castellum*, a.503 (one manuscript has 'Syfream', cf. Honigmann, *Ostgrenze*, 9 n.7). Sifrios is also mentioned in George of Cyprus, 64 no.918. The precise location of Sifrios is uncertain, but remains of a fort have been found at Rabbat Kalesi, at the entrance of a pass west of Derik (northwest of Tell Beshme), on which see Wiessner, *Ruinenstätten*, 34–6 and Honigmann, *Ostgrenze*, 13 n.2.

      Al-Nu'man was replaced as leader of the Lakhmids by a certain Abu Ya'fur (not named by Josh. Styl. §47), but he ruled only briefly. The legitimate son of al-Nu'man, al-Mundhir, did not accompany the expedition; cf. Rothstein, *Lahmiden*, 74–5 and Shahîd, *BASIC* I, 26–7.

      Proc. (I.8.19–21), drastically abridging his source here (as he admits, 8.20), believes that Kavadh withdrew after the battle on account of a Hun invasion (on which see below n.104).

[82]   Mango-Bell, *Churches*, 154–5 on Constantia; Theoph. A.M. 5996 (144.30–145.1) on Olympius. That the city was founded by Constantius, not Constantine (to whom Mal. attributes it, 323.14–19) is clear: see Burgess, *Cont. Ant.* a.350 and Mango–Scott, *Theophanes*, 59 n.1 (Theoph. A.M. 5832 [36.10–12]). Ammianus XVIII.9.1 may refer to Constantia, but is unclear: see Matthews, *Ammianus*, 54.

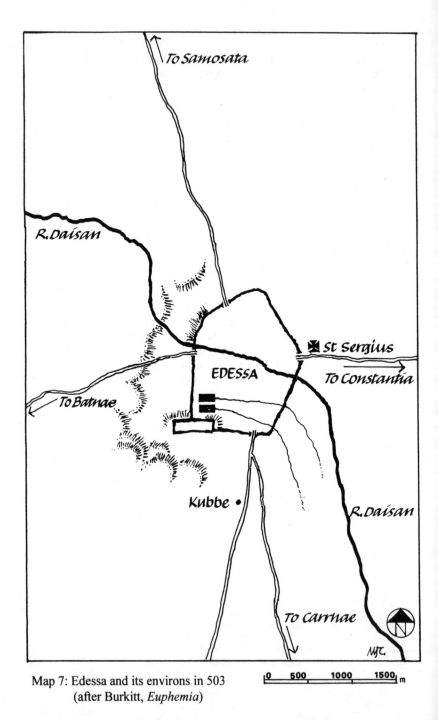

Map 7: Edessa and its environs in 503
(after Burkitt, *Euphemia*)

synagogue and thus hand the city over to Kavadh. Their plot was foiled only when Peter, the *comes* captured by the Persians at Sifrios, learned of it, and succeeded in informing the defenders about it. Once the tunnel beneath the synagogue was discovered, a massacre of the Jewish population immediately ensued; it was only with difficulty that the *comes* Leontius and Bar-Hadad brought an end to the bloodshed.[83]

Once the opportunity to capture the city had been lost, Kavadh was persuaded to depart. It was perhaps not so much a visit from Bar-Hadad that induced him to leave as a scarcity of provisions: the region around Constantia, never fertile, had already suffered from earlier depredations. Maintaining his army outside the city for any length of time was therefore difficult; furthermore, he had no wish to allow the Roman armies an opportunity to regroup. And so, assuaged by the gift of some supplies from the citizens, he pursued his way westwards. Here lay more fertile lands and a wealthy city, Edessa, famous for its sacred pools and for its supposed invulnerability to enemy attack; the ailing al-Nu'man vigorously urged Kavadh to besiege Edessa, so as to destroy the legend for good.[84] The king set up camp some 25 km east of the city, on the river Gullab, doubtless a mere stream in late August. Here he remained, threatening both Edessa to the west and Carrhae to the south.[85]

On 6 September the Edessenes, under the leadership of Areobindus, destroyed all the buildings surrounding the city and brought within the walls the relics of the martyrs which had lain in the churches there. Three days later Kavadh sent an emissary to Areobindus to discuss a venue for a meeting of the two leaders. Whether or not the king was planning treachery, as Joshua alleges, Areobindus was reluctant either

---

[83] Josh. Styl. §58 recounts the episode in detail, as well as Peter's ruse in communicating with the garrison. On Leontius, cf. *PLRE* II, Leontius 21; see also Segal, 'Mesopotamian communities', 122–4, on the status of Jews in this period.

[84] Josh. Styl. §58 for the visit of Bar-Hadad and Kavadh's lack of provisions, also for al-Nu'man's insistence on attacking Edessa. On the barrenness of the area around Constantia see Ammianus XVIII.7.9 and Theoph. Sim. II.1.5 (referring to lands further east, but still relevant) with Whitby, *Maurice*, 200 and Dillemann, *Mésopotamie*, 72–3. Proc. II.13.8–15 highlights the role of Bar-Hadad and plausibly asserts that supplies were handed over to the Persians. His emphasis on the weakness of the defences should not be preferred to Joshua's account; Proc. was more interested in anecdotal material at this point, as is demonstrated by his belief that Kavadh came to Constantia from Edessa. Matthews, *Ammianus*, 51, on the sacred pools of Edessa; on the legend of the city's impregnability, see below n.93.

[85] Josh. Styl. §58 with Dillemann, *Mésopotamie*, 94 for the location of the river (with fig.17, p.148).

to leave the city or to allow a Persian delegation inside it. In the end he agreed to meet the Persian envoy, Bawi, in the Church of St Sergius, just outside the Great Gate on the east side.[86] Bawi demanded 10,000 lbs. of gold from Areobindus and the ratification of a treaty by which the Romans would give an annual sum of gold to the Persians; remarkably similar terms would be accepted by Justinian just under thirty years later.[87] But it was too much for Areobindus. He put forward a counter-proposal of 7000 lbs. of gold; the resulting discussions took up much of the day. Since any treacherous plans the Persian delegation may have harboured had proved impossible to execute, the king turned his attention to the surrounding area. The Persians and Hephthalites made for Carrhae, while the more swiftly moving Lakhmids were sent forward to Batnae (Sarug). The garrison of Carrhae proved no less valiant than the defenders of Amida, Constantia or Edessa: a sudden sally was made, which resulted in the capture of the leader of the Hephthalites. He was soon returned to the Persians, however, for the inhabitants judged the town unable to withstand a siege.[88] The Arabs, on the other hand, met no check to their incursion, and continued their plundering westwards as far as the Euphrates; but they got no further, since by now further Roman reinforcements were reaching the opposite bank. The newly arrived troops, under Patriciolus and his son Vitalian, crossed the river and at once engaged the Arabs. The Romans came off the victors, and wished to press eastwards to relieve Edessa; but when they heard that Kavadh had now surrounded the city, they headed instead for Samosata.[89]

---

[86]   Josh. Styl. §59 with the map of Edessa in Burkitt, *Euphemia*. Bawi is described by Joshua as an *astabid* (which he equates with the Roman *magister*); on this post (*astabadh*) see Christensen, *L'Iran*, 136 and Appendix 2, 521. Chaumont, however, doubts the existence of such an office, 'Un Astabad', 234 and *EIr* II, 825–6; she regards it as an error for the post of *spahbadh* (on which office see above p.53).

[87]   Bawi, according to Josh. Styl. §59, referred to a 'customary' payment of gold — presumably a reference to the treaty mentioned earlier, which, however, had not stipulated an annual payment; but this need hardly have barred Bawi from making the claim. See above ch.2.ii for a discussion of the treaty.

[88]   Josh. Styl. §59; see above n.46 on the weak fortifications in 359. As Whitby, *Maurice*, 200, notes, the lands west of Edessa were particularly fertile, and hence a tempting target for Kavadh; cf. also Segal, *Edessa*, 141, on the prosperous plains near Edessa. The leader of the sally from Carrhae was a certain Rifaya, presumably an Arab. Shahîd, *BASIC* I, 14, places the Lakhmid raid in August, but Josh. Styl. clearly dates it to September.

[89]   Josh. Styl. §60, cf. *PLRE* II, Patriciolus, Vitalianus 2. Since Josh. Styl. (§60) represents Kavadh as moving against Edessa from the Euphrates, it is possible that he

The realisation that further Roman forces were mustering at Samosata, less than 50 km to the northwest, stirred the Persian king to action, and at last he moved to surround Edessa. His forces were deployed on 17 September, encamping on all sides of the city. But according to Joshua they did not attempt an assault, although the city gates remained open. Kavadh, probably hoping to overawe the defenders, never gave the signal to attack; the campaigning season was nearing its end, and his troops were some distance from Persian territory. A defeat at this point could leave him dangerously cut off. Eventually, late in the day, a few Edessenes made a sortie and inflicted some casualties on the Persians. It was enough to persuade Kavadh to withdraw to the south.[90]

From his camp at the village of Kubbe, just south of Edessa, Kavadh made his final demand. He asked for hostages to guarantee an unmolested retreat, the return of the soldiers captured the previous day, and the 7000 lbs. of gold offered earlier by Areobindus. But his bargaining power had been seriously diminished by the failure of his attempt on the city: in the end he was induced to depart by the hand-over as a hostage of the *comes* Basil (and perhaps also the *dux* Olympius), the return of fourteen Persian prisoners and the promise of only 2000 lbs. of gold, to be paid after the elapse of twelve days.[91]

Next Kavadh, no doubt seeking fresh provisions for his army, moved to Dabana. On the following day, 19 September, perhaps realising the scarcity of supplies available, he sent an envoy to demand the gold immediately. While Areobindus was prepared to consider the demand, the 'noblemen of the city' — the city councillors — refused outright. The *magister militum* therefore demanded back the hostage

---

himself led these forces, now that al-Nu'man was dead; yet if he did, it is surprising that he is not named here.

[90] Josh. Styl. §60, an eye-witness account for these events, attributing the king's failure to take the city to the blessing of Christ. It is unclear why the city gates were left open. It may be that some of those in need of repair had not been filled in and that the defenders therefore had little choice; see above p.41 and Josh. Styl. §52. For the dispositions of the Persian troops, see the helpful map of Burkitt, *Euphemia* and the topographical notes of Wright, p.51 (not always in agreement with one another).

[91] Josh. Styl. §61 with *PLRE* II, Basilius 7; he was a native of Edessa. Theoph. A.M. 5997 (147.11–12), reports that Kavadh kept his hostages Basil and Olympius. The latter may also have been handed over at this point; Josh. Styl. (§80) states simply that he had been seized while taking part in an embassy to Kavadh.

and accused Kavadh of conduct unbecoming of a monarch.[92] The
Persian king, determined not to leave Edessa empty-handed, resolved
to make one final attempt on the city. He marched back northwards and
surrounded it on 24 September. As before, the gates remained open, but
the Roman soldiers did not make a sortie. This time the Persian
infantry, supported by elephants, made an assault on the walls, while
local villagers came forth from the city and engaged the enemy cavalry.
But again the legend of Edessa was vindicated, according to which
Christ himself had promised king Abgar in writing that the city would
never fall into an enemy's hands. By the sixth century, despite a recent
decree of Pope Gelasius to the contrary, the story was widely believed;
the text of the letter was even inscribed on the city gates and the lintels
of houses. Both Kavadh's infantry and his cavalry were defeated in
their attacks, although it may reasonably be doubted whether none of
the defenders were killed, as Joshua insists. All that the Persians could
do was destroy the remaining buildings around the city and withdraw.[93]

Kavadh's position was difficult. A retreat directly eastwards from
Edessa would take him past the hostile city of Constantia, as well as
leading him through lands already ravaged several times by his own
forces. Not far away to the north the Romans were assembling in
Samosata, as well as to the west, in Hierapolis. This left him only one
direction — south. He therefore headed southwestwards, towards
Batnae, which fell to some Persian cavalry; the inhabitants surrendered
because of the dilapidated condition of their walls.[94] Lakhmid tribesmen crossed the Euphrates and ravaged the province of Euphratesia;

---

[92] Josh. Styl. §61 (the Syriac word is *rawrbane*); cf. Segal, 'Mesopotamian
communities', 112–13, and *idem*, *Edessa*, 125–7, on the role of the Senate (council)
in Mesopotamian cities.

[93] Josh. Styl. §62 with Theoph. A.M. 5997 (147.5–8), who reports an unexpected
victory of Areobindus. Segal, *Edessa*, 73–8, on the legend of Abgar's letter and the
decree of Gelasius (*Decret. Gelas.* V.8, p.13) in 494; the story is retold by Proc. at
II.12.7–30, on which cf. Cameron, *Procopius*, 116 and *eadem*, 'The Sceptic', 6 (with
20 n.22 on the inscription of the letter in the city). Note also the allusion to the story
in Jacob of Sarug, see above n.62, and cf. Josh. Styl. §58.

[94] Josh. Styl. §63. Although by referring to the place as Batnae (rather than Sarug, as
earlier) Joshua might be supposed to mean the Bathnae in Syria I, the mention at §89
of a Batnan-kastra in Sarug with a dilapidated wall would seem to favour the Batnae
in Osrhoene, already attacked by the Arabs. On the danger of Kavadh's position, cf.
the anxiety of Shapur I's army during its retreat eastwards when confronted by the
city of Edessa: Petr. Patr. frg.11, *FHG* IV, 188–9, tr. in Dodgeon–Lieu, *Eastern
Frontier*, 67. Josh. Styl. §65 for Roman forces at Hierapolis; §64 for Kavadh's
awareness of the arrival of reinforcements.

and Kavadh even sent messengers to Anastasius to tell of his advance. It was a clever feint, for he soon followed the Euphrates south and east.[95] The only Roman troops blocking his return to Persian territory were those at Callinicum, the base of the *dux Osrhoenae* Timostratus. Again the initial Persian assault failed; the *marzban* in charge was even captured by the defenders. But the garrison thought it best to return the prisoner, once Kavadh arrived with his army; and thence he proceeded downstream to Lower Mesopotamia.[96]

Neither side had achieved its objective in 503. Kavadh had defeated the Romans in the field on more than one occasion, but such victories were by no means as profitable as the capture of cities; and since the fall of Amida he had not been able to capture any city of consequence. The Romans, for their part, had opened the campaigning season with the intention of wresting the initiative from the Persians. But apart from Patricius' raid into Arzanene and Areobindus' brief foray as far as Nisibis, they had spent most of the time retreating and reacting to Kavadh's movements; they had failed to recover Amida, and the lack of co-ordination between their generals had led to needless defeats and confusion. All this would change in the following year. Before that, however, they had to endure one more invasion.

Probably late in 503, but possibly early the following year, al-Nu'man's son al-Mundhir, who had now succeeded him to the Lakhmid throne after the interregnum of Abu Ya'fur, undertook an expedition against Arabia and Palestine. The moment was well chosen, for the *dux* of Palestine, Romanus, was taking part in the campaign in Mesopotamia; and even this redoubtable leader had failed to check the Kindite raid here just three years earlier. According to the only source to report the attack, al-Mundhir inflicted great damage on the provinces, and carried off many captives.[97]

---

[95] Josh. Styl. §§63–4. Theoph. A.M. 5997 (147.3–4) refers to Kavadh raiding as far as the two Syrias (though before his failure against Edessa); if this is not exaggeration, then it is possible that the Arabs penetrated some distance beyond the Euphrates. Despite Jarry, 'Une prétendue invasion', 197–201, the report that Kavadh reached as far as Syrian Alexandria (Alexandretta) after capturing Amida, found only in Eutychius (*PG* 111, 1061 = Breydy, p.98), may safely be rejected.

[96] Josh. Styl. §64; Beth Aramaye is Lower Mesopotamia, cf. Wright's tr., p.55 n.*.

[97] Cyr. Scyth., *V. Ioh.* 211.15–17 for al-Mundhir's raid, cf. Shahîd, *BAFIC*, 204, and now *BASIC* I, 17–18, 27–8, dating the raid most probably to August-September 503 (Cyril's chronological indicators are confused). Proc. I.17.41 offers a general description of al-Mundhir's raids in very similar terms to Cyril. *PLRE* II, Romanus 7,

vii) The second Roman counter-offensive (503–4)

Reports of the indifferent performance of the Roman generals will have reached Anastasius by late summer 503. Further reinforcements were therefore sent out, along with a supreme commander, the *magister officiorum* Celer. Although the *magister officiorum* had charge of inspecting the *limitanei* annually, his main role by this period was the conduct of foreign policy. Celer's position as *magister officiorum* thus had little to do with his appointment as supreme commander; he owed it rather to the trust placed in him by the emperor, attested to by his lengthy period in office.[98] Evidently the reinforcements, probably transferred from Thrace, arrived piecemeal in the east; hence in September the Lakhmid tribesmen raiding as far as the Euphrates encountered newly arrived units under Patriciolus and Vitalian.[99]

By late September, when Kavadh was moving down the Euphrates, Celer had reached Hierapolis, a traditional marshalling point for eastern campaigns. Since it was too late to undertake any campaigning that year, he contented himself with rebuking the *magistri militum* for their lack of co-operation and dismissing them to various cities to spend the winter. Hypatius, though he was the oldest nephew of the emperor, was

---

oddly believes that Romanus, because of his role in the war to the north, was no longer *dux* of Palestine; but, as it notes, he is termed *dux* by Josh. Styl. §92.

[98] *PLRE* II, Celer 2 (cf. the Fasti, 1258 and Clauss, *Magister officiorum*, 150–1) believes that he was only now appointed *magister officiorum*; but since the previous incumbent is last attested at the end of 497, Celer's appointment may well have been earlier. On the post, see Lee, *Information*, 41–7 esp. 43 and Austin–Rankov, *Exploratio*, 224–5. On Celer's long career, see now Greatrex, 'Hypatius', 126–7.

While Celer did not outrank the *magistri militum* as *magister officiorum*, his close contact with the emperor as a member of the consistory will have strengthened his authority, cf. Stein II, 97 and n.1. Jones, *LRE*, 339, 342–3, Clauss, *op. cit.*, 63 on the consistory (the *magistri militum praesentales*, when in Constantinople, were also members). The palace troops (*scholae palatinae*) under Celer mentioned by Proc. (I.8.2) may, despite Clauss, *op. cit.*, 40–2, have been battle-worthy, cf. M. Whitby, 'On the Omission', 465–6.

Celer was designated commander-in-chief, to act in consultation with Areobindus (Theoph. A.M. 5998 [147.32–148.1]). Proc. I.8.2 gives the misleading impression that all the *magistri militum* and Celer held equal power, cf. Zach. VII.4 (160); but since both Proc. and Zach. also believe that Celer was sent out at the same time as the other commanders (though note Proc. I.8.10), their information is clearly unreliable.

[99] Josh. Styl. §60. That many of these troops were drawn from Thrace is an inference based partly on the associations of these two commanders with the region (cf. *PLRE* II, Patriciolus and Vitalianus 2) and partly on the invasions of the Balkans which took place around this time, probably exploiting the withdrawal of Roman troops, cf. Stein II, 146: the *magister militum per Thracias* Sabinianus could still raise 10,000 men in 505, but most of these were Bulgars.

recalled to the imperial capital, and Apion was replaced as the expedition's praetorian prefect by Calliopius; their hostility to Areobindus had proved too costly.[100] The strains imposed both by the war and by the billeting of so many soldiers in the region were alleviated at the end of the year, when it was announced that the emperor had resolved to cancel the taxes due from Mesopotamia and Osrhoene, the provinces most affected by the war.[101]

A greater spirit of enterprise now animated the Roman commanders. Patricius, wintering in Melitene, reacted vigorously to news reaching him of the confidence of the Persian garrison in Amida: they had opened up the city and set up a thriving market outside it, importing whatever victuals they could. He marched there at once, slew the merchants he came upon, and seized all their goods, as well as those of Persians bringing up supplies to the city. In response, Kavadh despatched a *marzban* against him, probably from Nisibis. Patricius' men, remembering their defeat the previous summer, appealed to him to withdraw as battle approached; perhaps wisely, and certainly typically, he agreed. That a Roman army should retreat eastwards is certainly remarkable, yet it was in this direction, towards the river Nymphius, that Patricius' men headed. They probably had little choice. The *marzban*, coming from Nisibis or the Jebel Sinjar, will have made for Amida by the most direct route — westwards through Roman territory, turning northwest at Apadna through the Tur Abdin. At the moment they arrived, probably in March, Patricius' troops may have been operating across the Tigris from Amida, intercepting the supply convoys coming to the city, presumably from Arzanene. With the Persians holding the bridge south of the city and the river unfordable,

---

[100] Josh. Styl. §65. Goossens, *Hiérapolis*, 149–53, 168–9 on Hierapolis as a frequent mustering point from the fourth century onwards. Theoph. A.M. 5998 (148.2–6) and Mal. 399.6–7 on the recall of Apion and Hypatius; Josh. Styl. §70, however, reports, probably correctly, that Apion went to Alexandria, from where he could despatch supplies to the army. *Expositio* 36 (172) notes Egypt's role in supplying grain for wars in the East in the fourth century. Proc., at his most careless in his account of this war (cf. Howard-Johnston, 'Great Powers', 176), gives Areobindus as the commander recalled (I.9.1). It seems likely that Pharesmanes later succeeded Hypatius as *magister militum prasentalis* (Josh. Styl. §88), cf. Merten, *De Bello*, 185, and *PLRE* II, Pharesmanes 3. On Calliopius, Croke, 'Marcellinus and Dara', 83–4 and 86–8.

[101] Josh. Styl. §66 (edict of 25 December 503) with Jones, *LRE*, 237 and Segal, *Edessa*, 119, 160–3. Josh. Styl. refers only to Mesopotamia, by which, however, he clearly means both Mesopotamia and Osrhoene (he never refers to the latter); cf. Dillemann, *Mésopotamie*, 105. On the tax reductions accorded to the region during this period, Leclainche, 'Crises économiques', 98–9.

the way west was barred. The Tigris also blocked their path south, while to the north lay the unwelcoming heights of the Anti-Taurus mountains. The way east was thus the most promising option. Once the Romans reached the Nymphius, however, they found it to be impassable on account of the season; there, no doubt to the surprise of the Persians, they rallied, turned on their pursuers and utterly routed them. The victorious Romans then returned to besiege Amida.[102]

In March the main Roman force, under Celer, took up position at Theodosiopolis (Resaina); morale had received a further welcome boost meanwhile from the discovery of a miraculous egg near Zeugma, which was inscribed with the cross and (so it was believed) foretold a Roman victory. Among Celer's subordinate commanders were the *magister militum* Areobindus and the *duces* Bonosus, Timostratus and Romanus.[103] The arrival of a supreme commander on the Roman side coincided with the disappearance of the Persian king from the front; an invasion by the Sabir Huns required Kavadh's presence in the Caucasus region.[104] Before he left, he despatched a further force of 10,000 men to dislodge Patricius from Amida, but it advanced no further than Nisibis. The presence of Celer's army at Resaina had effectively prevented the Persians from reaching Amida. If they followed the route used earlier by Persian forces, via Apadna, they would be vulnerable to attack from Celer's men to the south, as well as Patricius' to the north; other routes

---

[102] Josh. Styl. §66; he explains that the Roman forces took little thought as to where they were fleeing. He does not report whence the *marzban* came. The Kallath of Joshua is the Nymphius, cf. Wright's tr., p.56 n.*; but given the distance between Amida and the Nymphius (at least 60 km), it is possible that another tributary of the Tigris halted the Romans (e.g. the Ambar Tchai or the Hazru Su, cf. Dillemann, *Mésopotamie*, fig.3, p.39). Since both Proc. and Ammianus place the Nymphius north of Amida, Patricius' men may have thought they were heading in this direction (*ibid.*, 49). The flood season here lasts from March to June (Whitby, *Maurice*, 201), which suggests the battle took place in March, if not earlier.

[103] Josh. Styl. §§66–7, with Theoph. A.M. 5998 (148.6–8) and Mango–Scott, *Theophanes*, 229 n.4. As they suggest, Bonosus, not otherwise attested, was probably a local *dux*, perhaps of Euphratesia (cf. *PLRE* II, Bonosus 4). Olympius (*dux* of Mesopotamia) was still in Persian hands, while Eugenius (*dux* of Armenia) will have been operating further north.

[104] Proc. I.8.19 on the Hun invasion, also referred to at 9.24, 10.15, and *Aed.* II.1.5. Cf. Christensen, *L'Iran*, 352, Stein II, 97–8, and Marquart, *Eranšahr*, 63 n.4, on the war against the (Sabir) Huns, who irrupted again around 515–16, see below ch.6 n.29. *Contra* the views of (e.g.) Whitby, 'Defences', 717, Kavadh's war was not against the Hephthalites: Proc. would have named them, if he were referring to them (and they were serving in Kavadh's army in any case). Joshua does not mention Kavadh conducting any military operations after his despatch of an army against Patricius at Amida in early 504 (§69).

to Amida through Persian territory were lengthy and difficult.[105] They
may also have had to face local unrest: Theophanes mentions a revolt
of the 'Kadousioi', who before the war had even laid siege to Nisibis.
The Persian garrison at Amida could expect no relief.[106]

Already Celer's strategy had borne fruit. Next he sent 6000 cavalry
under the *dux* of Osrhoene Timostratus to seize the livestock belonging
to the garrison at Nisibis, which was being pastured in the Jebel Sinjar.
The operation was a complete success. Celer's forces now moved
north, to assist Patricius in the siege of Amida. With the entire Roman
army encamped outside the city, a swift resolution to the siege might
have been hoped for.[107] Patricius' men had been trying to undermine
the city walls by tunnelling, and they achieved a partial success when
the outer section collapsed. Since, however, the inner section remained
standing, Patricius continued the tunnelling to gain entry into the city.
The tunnel finally emerged within the walls, and Roman troops
prepared to pour forth. But when the first soldier came out, the cry of a
joyful Amidene alerted the Persians to his presence; and, before he
could gain a foothold, the Persians slew him and forced his companions
back. The tunnel was flooded, then sealed up, and the surrounding area
filled with water to prevent further tunnelling.[108] The joy of the
Amidene woman who witnessed the emergence of the Roman soldier
may easily be understood from the description of the tribulations of the
Amidenes furnished by Zachariah. The Amidenes had been deprived of
their sole means of acquiring victuals when the Persians had shut down
the market following the death of Glon; although it had re-opened
during the winter, Patricius' attack had forced it to close down again.
Later many, ten thousand according to Zachariah, were imprisoned in
the amphitheatre without food; those who survived the dreadful

[105] Whitby, *Maurice*, 201 on the inaccessibility of Arzanene (the nearest Persian territory
to Amida) from the south.
[106] Theoph. A.M. 5998 (148.14–15) on the revolt of the 'so-called' Kadousioi; cf. Josh.
Styl. §§22, 24 on the activities of the Kadishaye before the war, and see above n.18.
Josh. Styl. §69 states that the Persians sent their flocks to pasture in the Jebel Sinjar,
the Kadishaye heartland, which would seem odd if they were in revolt; it is more
plausible nonetheless to identify the 'Kadousioi' with the Kadishaye than to suppose
Theoph.'s tribe was situated near the Caspian Sea (as Whitby, *History*, 78 n.18, does).
See also ch.8 n.32 below.
[107] Josh. Styl. §69. At §70 Joshua informs us that the new praetorian prefect of the army,
Calliopius, had 850,000 *modii* of *bucellatum* baked at Edessa, while Apion was to
arrange for more to be sent from Alexandria. It may therefore be inferred that the
army of 504 was considerably larger than that of 503.
[108] Josh. Styl. §71. Similar counter-measures are noted in *Peri Strategias* 13.34–5.

conditions there were eventually released into the city; but still no sustenance was offered them.[109]

Despite the defenders' lack of provisions, the siege was costing the Romans more heavily than the Persians; a skirmish which broke out after the failure of the tunnel caused many more losses to the besiegers than the besieged. Celer therefore gave orders not to engage the enemy, who, if the rest of the Persian army were defeated, would have to yield the city or survive an indefinite blockade.[110] That such Roman optimism was not without foundation is shown by the return to their side in June of the former governor of Armenia Interior, Constantine, disillusioned with the Persian performance in the war. He was soon joined by an Arab chieftain, who defected to the Romans with all his forces.[111] Notwithstanding Celer's decision, further fighting took place outside Amida in July, in which the besiegers inflicted numerous casualties on the Persians; but the *dux* of Arabia, Gaïnas, having loosened his armour on account of the heat, fell victim to arrows shot from *ballistae* on the walls.[112] This appears to have incited Celer to take the initiative rather than wear down his army against a small number of defenders. While Patricius was left in charge of the siege, two Roman invasions into Persian territory were organised. Both inflicted heavy damage, no doubt in a spirit of revenge for the fall of Amida. Areobindus took charge of an expedition into Persarmenia, which yielded a copious quantity of prisoners and booty, as well as the

---

[109] Zach. VII.5 (162–3) and Josh. Styl. §§76–7, who give a detailed account of the plight of the Amidenes; Proc. alludes to this too, I.9.22. The incident described by Josh. Styl. at §72 illustrates the defenders' want of supplies, cf. Proc. I.9.21. Thanks to the efforts of Calliopius at Edessa and bakers elsewhere, the besiegers experienced no supply difficulties, cf. Josh. Styl. §77.

[110] Josh. Styl. §§72–3.

[111] Josh. Styl. §74 for the details; Constantine was summoned to Constantinople from Edessa, ordained a priest, and sent to Nicaea, cf. *PLRE* II, Constantinus 14. Josh. Styl. §75 on the Arab chief, Adid (though the name is uncertain) with Shahîd, *BASIC* I, 14 (who suggests that he may have been a Christian).

[112] Josh. Styl. §75, cf. the death of Julian, who had omitted to put on all his armour (Bowersock, *Julian*, 116). But even a suit of armour might not protect a man from the powerful shot of a *ballista*: the arrow which slew the son of Grumbates in 359 penetrated right through his breastplate (Ammianus XIX.1.7).

   Wright, in his tr. of Josh. Styl, p.61, states that Gaïnas had charge of the area around Damascus, cf. *PLRE* II, Gainas 2. But if Romanus, who may have still been *dux Palaestinae* (see above n.97), was among the Roman commanders in Mesopotamia, there is no reason why the *dux Arabiae* may not also have been summoned north (although Sartre, *Trois études*, 152, believes that the term Arabia is being used loosely here).

defection of one leading Armenian. The Roman army returned to Amida past Nisibis, where it succeeded in ambushing a large portion of the garrison by a ruse.[113]

The other Roman expedition, which probably took place in October,[114] was led by Celer in person. While Areobindus had headed northeastwards from Amida, Celer apparently moved to the southeast, albeit by an indirect route. It seems that initially he went to Callinicum, whence he moved into Persian territory, most probably along the Euphrates, following the path of Kavadh's retreat one year previously. How far he proceeded is unclear. A lengthy march down the Euphrates and then back up the Tigris might be inferred from Marcellinus *comes*' mention of a *Pons Ferreus*, identified with a bridge across the Tigris in the heights above Ctesiphon.[115] More likely, however, he soon cut northeastwards into Beth Arabaye, a fertile region hitherto largely untouched, where he caused widespread devastation. The *magister officiorum* gave the order to spare no man above the age of twelve and to do as much damage as possible. Buildings, vineyards and trees, including olive-trees, were destroyed. The Persian forces in the area retreated before the Romans, seeking refuge across the Tigris. There they met with some friendly cavalry and attempted to make a stand. But Celer's army crossed the river after them, overcame the enemy cavalry, and laid waste to the lands on both sides of the river; laden with spoils, it then returned to Roman territory.[116] While such damage

---

[113] Josh. Styl. §75, who claims that 7000 Persians from the garrison of Nisibis were killed. Theoph. A.M. 5998 (148.12–13) reports that Nisibis was nearly captured.

[114] A.G. 816 begins in Josh. Styl. at §76 (on 1 October 504); Celer's expedition takes place after this.

[115] Josh. Styl. §79 with Ps. Dion. II, 6, specifying the lands between Nisibis and Beth Arabaye. Marc. *com.* (a.504) on the invasion passing through Callinicum and the mention of *Pons Ferreus*. This is said by Honigmann, *Ostgrenze*, 10 n.1, to bridge the Euphrates above Ctesiphon in Beth Arabaye; yet the bridge in Joh. Eph. to which he refers crosses the Tigris, not the Euphrates, cf. Whitby, *Maurice*, 273. Marcellinus' account, perhaps relying on information from Celer, a fellow Illyrian (so Croke, *Chronicle*, 112), cannot be dismissed lightly. Although Celer may have been using the same invasion route as Maurice in 580 (on which see Whitby, *ibid.*), it seems more likely that his was a more limited operation (involving the Mesopotamian citizenry according to Marc. *com.*) between Nisibis and the Tigris. Croke, *ibid.*, refers to an invasion of Arzanene by Celer as well as the assault from Callinicum, presumably relying on Proc. (see above n.72); but Arzanene lies well to the north of the area attacked by Celer.

[116] Josh. Styl. §79 with Ps. Dion. II, 6, on the massacre of those over twelve. The destruction of olive-trees was a particularly heavy blow, because they take so long to recover, cf. (e.g.) Hornblower, *Greek World*, 107. On the fertility of Beth Arabaye,

was being inflicted on Persian territory, the inhabitants of Roman
Mesopotamia and Osrhoene were cheered by the cancellation of taxes
for a further year; and on this occasion the residents of Hierapolis were
also granted a reduction in their contributions.[117]

viii) The Persian surrender of Amida

For Kavadh the whole object of the war had been the replenishment of
his treasury. Now that his own territories were being methodically
pillaged by the Romans, and his forces were unable to prevent it, he
realised that it was time to open negotiations. He sent forth a *spahbadh*
to Celer for this purpose, accompanied by 20,000 men, doubtless to
prove that the Persians were still able to field a large force. All the
Roman hostages were returned, including Peter, the officer captured at
Sifrios, and Basil of Edessa; the body of Olympius, who had died in
captivity, was also handed back.[118] In exchange the *spahbadh* asked
that Celer release the men besieged in Amida, now desperately short of
food. When the *magister officiorum* refused, the Persian requested that
he be allowed to send supplies to those in the city. Celer and his
general staff duly swore that they would permit the supplies to reach
Amida unmolested; but one general, the *dux* Nonnosus, was not present
for this very reason. He it was therefore who intercepted the camels
laden with supplies and concealed weaponry making their way to
Amida. The *spahbadh* naturally complained of the infringement of the
oath, but was powerless to do anything more.[119]

Just as Kavadh's troops had been discomfited by the cold during
their investment of Amida, so now the Roman soldiers suffered, and
the army started to disperse. Some, presumably the *limitanei*, withdrew
to their own homes, while others returned to winter quarters in
Constantia, Resaina or Edessa, all carrying off whatever booty they

---

see Whitby, *Maurice*, 200: being a well watered area, it was suitable for campaigning
later in the year than elsewhere.

[117] Josh. Styl. §78. Note at §82 the sufferings of the Edessenes in winter 504–5 as they
attempted to convey supplies to Amida, cf. Segal, *Edessa*, 160–1.

[118] Josh. Styl. §80 with Theoph. A.M. 5998 (148.26–7), who, telescoping these events,
places the return of the hostages during the negotiations at Dara (on which see
below). He therefore describes the war as having lasted only three years (149.5). Note
too Proc. I.9.24 on continuing Persian difficulties against the (Sabir) Huns.

[119] Josh. Styl. §80. Nonnosus was probably Olympius' replacement as *dux Mesopotamiae*; cf. also *PLRE* II, Nonius (the precise form of the name is uncertain). It may
be supposed that the negotiations took place outside Amida; note that the hostages
were 'sent on' to Edessa (Josh. Styl.), which implies a location further east.

could. The *spahbadh* saw his chance. He offered an ultimatum: either Celer should now choose peace or he must accept a renewed offensive by the Persians. Celer attempted to reassemble the Roman army, but was obliged to agree to the Persian terms when this proved impossible. A truce was therefore agreed. The return of Amida accomplished in this way (probably in January 505) was scarcely a triumph for the Romans: not only was the garrison allowed to depart freely from the city, but a substantial sum of money was also paid for the evacuation.[120]

ix) Peace negotiations (505–6)

Peace did not immediately follow the hand-over of Amida: the agreement concluded between the *spahbadh* and Celer had to be ratified by the two monarchs, and in the meantime Anastasius set about securing the frontier. Rebuilding work was carried out at Edessa, Batnae, and Amida, and a wall was constructed at Europus.[121] Perhaps because of all this Roman activity, Kavadh refused to ratify the agreement at once, but kept the gold he had received. It soon became apparent, however, that he was unable to prosecute a war against the Romans at the same time as quelling internal unrest; as well as the troubles already mentioned, the Tamuraye had again risen in revolt.[122] Meanwhile Anastasius strove to maintain the morale of the region hit by the war; not only were the taxes for Mesopotamia remitted once again, but in addition the venerable former *praepositus sacri cubiculi* Urbicius visited Amida and Edessa, distributing largesse to the inhabitants. Discontent nonetheless remained rife among the residents

---

[120] The sum is put at 1100 lbs. of gold by Zach. VII.5 (163) (who highlights the role of Pharesmanes), at 1000 lbs. by Proc. I.9.4, and at 3 talents (with a manuscript variant of 30) by Theoph. A.M. 5998 (149.25). Marc. *com.* a.503 merely states that a large sum was handed over. Although Joshua refers to no such agreement, he does mention presents given to Kavadh, including a golden service for his table (§81). Merten, *De Bello*, 192–3 and Stein II, 98 and n.3 dismiss Theoph.'s figure, accepting those of Zach. and Proc., cf. Mango–Scott, *Theophanes*, 229 n.6. It is odd, given the detailed nature of his narrative, that Joshua is not more specific: he may have wished to suppress a fact so unfavourable to the Roman side (cf. his insistence at §§8–9 that the Romans had not given money to the Persians as tribute). See above n.33 for the difficulties caused by the winter weather; Proc. I.9.20 on the recovery of the city two years after its capture, an implied date of January 505.

[121] Josh. Styl. §§89, 91 and Zach. VII.5 (163) on the building work, cf. Capizzi, *Anastasio*, 214, 224. Note also the construction of a wall at Birtha on the Euphrates (just to the west of Batnae) by its bishop Sergius, Josh. Styl. §91 with Dillemann, *Mésopotamie*, fig.11, p.106.

[122] Zach. VII.5–6 (163, 165), accepted (e.g.) by Blockley, *ERFP*, 91.

of Mesopotamia because of the behaviour of the soldiers billeted in the cities; for Celer's army remained in the frontier region, although it was stationed west of the Euphrates for at least part of 505. Joshua describes in some detail how soldiers took over houses, ejected citizens from their beds, and refused to obey those who tried to impose discipline on them.[123] While the Romans kept a defensive posture, and the Persians did likewise, the Arabs allied to each side preferred not to acknowledge the cessation of hostilities, but continued to raid the territory of the opposing side. No doubt to their surprise and consternation, their leaders were apprehended and executed by their erstwhile allies in war.[124]

Later that year, since an agreement had still not been signed, a more ambitious building project was undertaken at the instigation of the Roman generals. Celer, who had returned to Constantinople during the year, may have been the one who persuaded Anastasius. A major new fortress was to be built right next to the frontier; after some discussion, a site was chosen at Dara, to the north of Ammodius. Since the Persians at Nisibis would sally forth to interrupt the building process, the Roman army took up position near the frontier; Pharesmanes, now *magister militum*, was stationed at Amida, while Romanus took his place at Edessa.[125] In April 506 Celer mustered his forces once more, probably at Hierapolis, and proceeded to Edessa on his way to the frontier to conclude the peace negotiations. There he was informed that the *spahbadh* with whom he had been negotiating, presumably Bawi, had died, and he was asked to stay until a successor was appointed by Kavadh. For the Edessenes the five-month wait of the Roman army entailed enormous expense and suffering; so large was the army that soldiers had to be stationed in the villages and monasteries outside the

---

[123] Josh. Styl. §92 for the remission of tribute; Zach. VII.5 (163) reports that for the Amidenes it was remitted for seven years. Josh. Styl. §§86, 93–4 on the behaviour of the Goths (but as Jones points out, *LRE*, 1263 n.53, the term 'Goth' in the Syriac sources refers quite generally to a soldier), and cf. Segal, *Edessa*, 162–3. The remarkable story of Euphemia illustrates the same problem, a century earlier, cf. Burkitt, *Euphemia*, 131. As Jones, *op. cit.*, 631–2 and 1262–3 n.51, and Isaac, *Limits*, 297–300, make clear, there were restrictions on what could be required of citizens, even if they were frequently ignored (note *CTh* VII.11.1–2 for a case of exactions by a *dux* of Euphratesia for his bath in 414 and 417; *C.J.* XII.31.1 is the only law on this in the Justinianic codex).

[124] Josh. Styl. §87 on the location of the Roman commanders; §88 on the Arab raids, with Shahîd, *BASIC* I, 14–16.

[125] Josh. Styl. §92. On the construction of Dara see below ch.6.i.

city. After the citizens posted anonymous complaints throughout the city about the soldiers' intolerable behaviour, Celer wisely decided to leave; by September he was at Dara.[126]

The two sides then exchanged hostages and negotiations began. The numerous ruses and betrayals of the war had, however, created an atmosphere of mistrust, and this was to prove an increasingly serious stumbling block to negotiations for the rest of the century. On this occasion, because the Romans feared to come unarmed to the negotiations, Celer stationed the whole army close by in case of Persian treachery; and, when one of the negotiating team noticed that the Persian envoys were wearing armour, it was enough to cause Celer to signal to the troops to attack. The *spahbadh* and his men were seized, and the Persian troops who were still in their camp fled to Nisibis. Only the insistence of Celer restrained the troops from slaying the *spahbadh* and his colleagues, who were released unharmed and returned to Nisibis. Such was the size of the Roman army, however, that the *spahbadh* was no longer willing to negotiate alone, nor could he induce his troops to accompany him. As a ruse, according to Joshua, the *spahbadh* summoned his daughter to Nisibis to take her in marriage, thereby providing himself with an excuse for failing to attend the negotiations.[127]

Eventually, in November 506, the *spahbadh* came forth to negotiate, while Celer removed the preconditions upon which he had hitherto insisted. An agreement was accordingly drawn up, establishing a cessation of hostilities between the two sides for seven years. News of the truce was greeted with rejoicing by the troops, and no doubt with still greater happiness by the citizenry of Mesopotamia. But exactly what had been agreed? Joshua the Stylite unhelpfully alludes only to 'written terms', while Procopius provides the figure of seven years. It has reasonably been assumed that the ban on fortifications near the frontier was reiterated; this would be acceptable to the Romans, since most of their refortification work had been carried out already. It is

---

[126] Josh. Styl. §§95–7. Theoph. A.M. 5998 (149.2–3) places the discussions on the border, between Ammodius and Mardin, corresponding to the site of Dara; he does not name Dara because he puts its foundation in A.M. 6000 (150.24–5). Cf. also Proc. I.9.24 on the negotiations; he names the Persian negotiator as Aspebedus, clearly (*pace PLRE* II, Aspebedus) the post of *spahbadh* (see above n.86), not a personal name.

[127] Josh. Styl. §97. Marriage with daughters was practised by the Persian nobility, cf. Christensen, *L'Iran*, 323 (*contra* Mango–Scott, *Theophanes*, 261 n.7).

probable that Anastasius offered a considerable sum to appease Persian pride, but there is no evidence whatsoever that he agreed to regular payments for the duration of the seven years of the truce.[128] No source makes this claim, and it is difficult to see why Anastasius would have agreed to such a term, considering the strong position of the Romans during the negotiations, as well as Kavadh's preoccupation with another war.[129]

Celer and Calliopius, empowered by Anastasius to decide whether to remit taxes for that year, did so for Amida and reduced the contribution of the Edessenes by a half.[130] On his return westwards Celer was reconciled with the citizens of Edessa; for, although he had planned to bypass the city on account of their earlier complaints, bishop Bar-Hadad of Constantia persuaded him nonetheless to pass through it. He therefore sent his army on westwards and was received in the city amidst general rejoicing.[131]

---

[128] Josh. Styl. §§98–9; Proc. I.9.24 on the seven years of the truce. Unusually, Proc. gives a precise figure, whereas Joshua just refers to a 'definite time' (tr. Watt). Joh. Lyd. mentions modest concessions by Anastasius, *de Mag.* III.53 (142.13–14). Blockley, *ERFP*, 91, places the agreement in October or November 506, and asserts (without argument) that it was a full peace treaty, rather than a truce, 220 n.42.

[129] *Contra* (e.g.) Blockley, *ERFP*, 91 or Stein II, 99, who claims that 550 lbs. of gold a year would fit well with the 11,000 lbs. handed over in 532. Blockley adduces Joh. Lyd. *de Mag.* III.53 and Zach VIII.5 (206) for the figure of 500 lbs. But the former in fact offers no figure at all, while Zach. refers to a later demand of Kavadh to the Emperor Justin (not necessarily in connection with this agreement, which will in any case have expired in 513); the same applies to the passage of Mich. Syr. (IX.16 [178]) noted by Blockley. It was not until 561 that the Romans finally consented to pay a yearly sum to the Persians, see above p.18.

Blockley, 'Subsidies and Diplomacy', 68, wonders whether the sums mentioned by Procopius at I.10.17 are to be equated with truce payments, but they are better viewed as an *ex gratia* payment to ensure that hostilities were brought to a definitive close in 506; Dara was not completed until 508/9 (Whitby, 'Dara', 751), and Persian interference was not desirable (cf. Merten, *De Bello*, 201).

[130] Josh. Styl. §99.

[131] Josh. Styl. §100.

The Anastasian War: a chronology

502	August	Kavadh takes Theodosiopolis and Martyropolis
		Start of the siege of Amida
	November	Battle near Constantia and Tell Beshme, Romans defeated
		Persian forces move on to Carrhae and Edessa
		Eugenius recaptures Theodosiopolis (Erzurum)
503	January	Fall of Amida: Kavadh returns to Nisibis, while his army stays between Amida and Constantia
	? May	Anastasius' army arrives in the East
	June	Persian army besieged at Nisibis by Areobindus
	July	Areobindus forced to retreat by Persian reinforcements
	(August)	Hypatius and Patricius beaten at Apadna
		Kavadh advances, fails to take Constantia, then encamps at the river Gullab
	September	Kavadh lays siege to Edessa; Persian contingents lay waste as far as Batnae. Kavadh moves to Dabana, near Carrhae. Kavadh besieges Edessa again. He withdraws southwards to the Euphrates, but fails to take Callinicum on his way back
	(winter)	Celer arrives at Hierapolis
		Patricius moves from Melitene to attack Amida
504	(spring)	Roman forces assemble at Resaina
		Timostratus' raid into the Jebel Sinjar
	(summer)	Celer and his army join in the siege of Amida
		Areobindus raids Persarmenia
	(winter)	Celer leads a raid on Beth Arabaye
		Negotiations start for the hand-over of Amida
		Amida returned to the Romans
505		Work started on Dara; Anastasius strengthens other forts and cities
		Kavadh initially rejects truce terms (?)
506	November	Terms for the truce finally agreed at the frontier

VI
The aftermath of the Anastasian War

i) The eastern frontier, 506–518

For twenty years following the truce in 506 the inhabitants of Mesopotamia enjoyed a period of peace. Although technically the agreement expired in 513, there was no attempt to renew hostilities. Even if both sides had not then been occupied with other matters, it is doubtful whether the Persian king would have been inclined to repeat his invasion of 502. The Romans, having learnt their lesson from the ease with which Kavadh had overrun Roman territory and captured certain cities, had quickly taken steps to remedy the situation. Some cities were strengthened before the truce was signed, while other projects, such as the building of Dara, took longer to realise. Nor did the process cease with the death of Anastasius; it was carried on energetically under Justin and Justinian. Consequently it is difficult in many cases to determine who initiated construction work at a site, and Anastasius may deserve more credit than is accorded him in Procopius' *De Aedificiis*.[1]

The significance of this fortification work should not be underestimated. The building of Dara in particular was a constant source of complaint from the Persians, and, as they pointed out, a flagrant contravention of the treaty of 422. Kavadh later asserted that its existence required him to maintain two standing armies, one at the Caspian Gates and one to counter the Roman forces at Dara.[2] The city lay menacingly close to Persian territory: it is described by Procopius in the *Wars* as an ἐπιτείχισμα (an offensive stronghold), while in the *De Aedificiis* he portrays it as openly threatening enemy lands. The need for such a Roman base had been emphasised by Anastasius' generals in their report to him on the war; they had complained that it was difficult to

---

[1] Cf. Whitby, 'Dara', 'Development', esp. 719–20, and 'Notes', esp. 110–12 *contra* Croke and Crow, 'Procopius and Dara'.

[2] Proc. I.16.6 with Blockley, 'Subsidies and Diplomacy', 69. Proc. I.10.16, and see above p.23, on the terms of the peace of 422; given that the Persians had openly violated the peace by their invasion, their complaints, as reported by Proc., are somewhat ingenuous.

lay siege to Nisibis from their far-off base at Constantia, and had
pointed out that what forts there were in the vicinity were too small to
house the army.[3] But the motivation for the construction of Dara was
by no means purely offensive. According to Zachariah, the generals
who had served during the Anastasian war urged the emperor to build a
new base 'as a refuge for the army in which they might rest, and for the
preparation of weapons, and to guard the country of the Arabs
(*'Arbaye*) from the inroads of the Persians and Saracens (*Tayyaye*)'.
Dara thus served both as a powerful deterrent to Persian aggression and
as a useful springboard for Roman forces in any attack on Persian
territory.[4]

By 507/8 the circuit walls of the city were complete, the emperor
having spared no expense to ensure the speediest possible implemen-
tation of the project. Kavadh, perhaps hoping that he would be able to
destroy the fortress before it was ready, had agreed to the truce in spite
of the construction work already in progress. But he remained engaged
elsewhere for too long, and by the time he made an attempt to halt the
builders they were able to shelter behind the walls. Kavadh's bid to
interrupt the construction may in any case have been merely a show of
force, for he was soon dissuaded from his attacks by a combination of
payments and threats; doubtless the former were more efficacious than
the latter. Work then continued on the fortress, which became the seat
of both the *dux* of Mesopotamia and a bishop.[5]

---

[3]   Proc. I.10.19 and 16.6, cf. *Aed.* II.1.13. Cf. John the Lydian's description of the city
      as ἦν ὁ πολὺς Ἀναστάσιος [ταῖς φά]ρυγξι τῶν πολεμίων ἐπιτέθεικεν ('which the
      great Anastasius placed at the throat of the enemy', tr. Carney), *de Mag.* III.28
      (116.12–13), cf. III.47 (137.15–18). Zach VII.6 (164) on the generals' complaint, cf.
      Whitby, *Maurice*, 212 and n.28 on the offensive role of some Roman forts. Dara lay
      10.4 km from the frontier and 26 km from Nisibis. For a discussion of the distances
      (and Proc.'s errors in this regard, I.10.14) see Dillemann, *Mésopotamie*, 226–8,
      Whitby, 'Dara', 758 (putting the distance to the frontier at just 5 km) and George of
      Cyprus, no.912 (six miles).

[4]   Zach. VII.6 (164) for the quotation. On the Syriac terms *'Arbaye* and *Tayyaye*, see
      Segal, 'Mesopotamian Communities', 119; also Shahîd, *BASIC*, 17 n.74 and Dille-
      mann, *Mésopotamie*, 76–7, who equates the country of the *'Arbaye* with the northern
      part of Mesopotamia (in the vicinity of Constantia), cf. Segal, *Edessa*, 142–3. Isaac,
      Limits, 254–5, lists the various functions of fortifications, cf. Whitby, *Maurice*, 212–
      13, Elton, *Warfare*, 157, and *Peri Strategias* 9. Even if Anastasius intended the city as
      a means of defence, the Persians will hardly have been likely to interpret his actions
      thus, cf. Lee, *Information*, 24–5 on Persian suspicions of Roman aims.

[5]   The construction of Dara and its remains are dealt with in detail by Whitby, 'Dara',
      Mango–Bell, *Churches*, 102–5, Capizzi, *Anastasio*, 216–21, Stein II, 101 n.1.
      Whitby, *art. cit.*, 751 on Anastasius' (substantial) bribes (Proc. I.10.17) and the

Further from the main eastern front defences were strengthened, in some cases even before the truce came into effect.[6] For the most part such activity will have caused no unease among the Persians: fortifications were also erected or strengthened in Phoenicia (at Emesa) and Syria, no doubt chiefly to guard against Arab raids.[7] More work was carried out in the northern sector of the frontier, though not all was completed by the end of Anastasius' reign; Theodosiopolis was certainly extensively refortified, and work was begun at Melitene, but new bases close to Persian territory, such as Citharizon, were probably not constructed until Justinian was on the throne.[8]

ii) The north-eastern frontier and the Transcaucasus (to c.518)

The second decade of the sixth century saw both powers turn their attention to the Transcaucasus, a region which had never been fully integrated into the Roman or Sasanian orbit; north of it lived tribes who would issue forth periodically to inflict great damage upon the territories of both empires. Towards the end of the fifth century and the beginning of the sixth the region had become particularly troublesome: the Romans had been struck by raids of Tzani and Sabir Huns as well as by an Armenian uprising, while the Persians had had to contend with rebellions in Iberia, Armenia and Albania, and with the Sabir incursion.[9] Many of these problems originated considerably earlier.

---

suggestion (with 774 n.18) that the walls were completed before the buildings. Zach. VII.6 (166) for Kavadh's attack.

[6] See above ch.5 p.115.

[7] Capizzi, *Anastasio*, 225–6 on work on the citadel at Emesa (*IGLS* V, 2204, from 509); *ibid.* 226–8 for forts elsewhere attested epigraphically, with Trombley, 'War and Society'. As Capizzi notes, the foundation of the border fortress of Thannuris is assigned to Anastasius by Michael the Syrian; but since it already existed, and received further attention under Justin I, then if Michael's report is accurate Anastasius can merely have strengthened it, *ibid.*, 223–4.

[8] Howard-Johnston, 'Citharizon', 218–20, prefers an early start to construction at Citharizon and elsewhere; but Whitby, 'Development' 727 argues persuasively that Citharizon and Martyropolis were built/restored during the 527–532 war, cf. *idem*, 'Martyropolis', 178–9 and 'Dara', 758. Reconstruction was started at Melitene probably not long after 505 (Howard-Johnston, 'Citharizon', 219 and n.14, Proc. *Aed.*, III.4.19–20). On the work at Theodosiopolis (in Armenia) see Proc. I.10.18 with Capizzi, *Anastasio*, 206–7 and Whitby, 'Notes', 106–7.

[9] These events will be discussed in detail below. On the term Transcaucasus (the region south of the Caucasus mountains), see above ch.2 n.13.

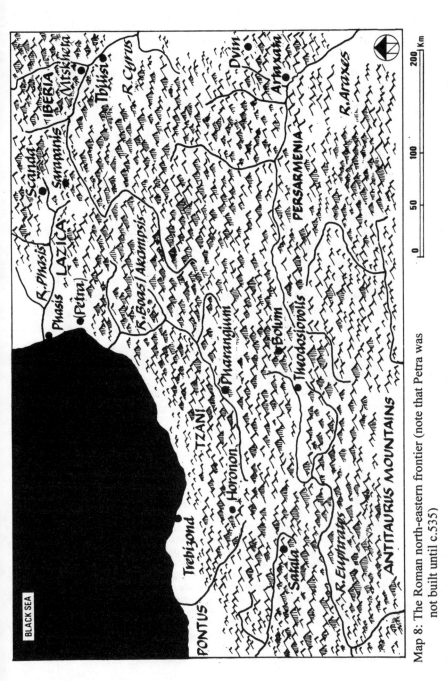

Map 8: The Roman north-eastern frontier (note that Petra was not built until c.535)

By the end of the fourth century the Persians were the dominant power in the region, controlling most of Armenia and all of Iberia; the Romans were confined to Lazica (ancient Colchis) and western Armenia.[10] But the extent of great-power control was limited. The Armenians and their neighbours, inhabiting a harsh mountainous region, were far from obedient subjects. Iberia and Armenia had a system of government similar to that of the Persians, a monarchy with a limited number of very influential noble families; the Arsacid dynasty of Armenia, which ended only in 428, was related to the kings of Parthia.[11] But this potential bond with the Persians was counterbalanced by the adherence of both kingdoms to Christianity from the fourth century onwards. As a result there were often internal differences within the kingdoms, a circumstance which tended to play into the hands of the great powers and helped bring about their partition.[12]

As Sasanian rulers in the fifth century discovered, control of the Transcaucasus was not an unalloyed advantage. The more a Persian king sought to integrate the kingdoms there into his empire, the less tractable they proved. The first to experience this was Yazdgerd II. An intolerant Zoroastrian, he was determined to convert the Christian Iberians and Armenians to his religion. In the 440s he had some success in Iberia, but his harsh measures to enforce Zoroastrianism in Armenia sparked a major rebellion in 451, which was suppressed only with much bloodshed.[13] Roman control of Lazica was no more secure. It took at least two campaigns to persuade the Lazic king Gubazes to

---

[10]   Braund, *Georgia*, 268–9.

[11]   Russell, *Zoroastrianism*, 119–20, M.-L. Chaumont in *EIr* II, 433 (on Armenia); *eadem, EIr*, I, 809, for a similar system of government in Albania. Also Toumanoff, *Studies*, 108–32 on Armenia, 141–4 on Iberia. According to *HVG* 181, 184, the Iberian king Vakhtang claimed to be a relative of the Sasanian dynasty, cf. Martin-Hisard, 'Le roi géorgien', 215. Howard-Johnston and Ryan, *Scholar*, 78–80, on the effects of the geography of Armenia on its government.

[12]   Russell, *Zoroastrianism*, 125–9, 139–40, Martin-Hisard, 'Le roi géorgien', 210–11, Chaumont, *EIr* II, 428, Braund, *Georgia*, 259–61. According to the Roman chroniclers, the Lazic king Tzath also reverted to allegiance to Constantinople because of his distaste for Zoroastrian rituals (see below n.29). See above ch.2 pp.12–13 on the division of Iberia and Armenia in the late fourth century.

[13]   Grousset, *Histoire*, 189–211, Russell, *Zoroastrianism*, 136–8 and Lordkipanidse–Brakmann, 'Iberia II', 36; cf. also Fowden, *Empire*, 104–9. *HVG* 145–6, for the spread of Zoroastrianism in Iberia (while King Vakhtang was a child); it survived until the seventh century, cf. Braund, *Georgia*, 261 and Lordkipanidse–Brakmann, *art. cit.*, 58–60. See also Yuzbashian, 'Le Caucase', 156–8, on the common features of the various Transcaucasian revolts against the Sasanians.

abdicate in favour of his son around 456.[14] The effects of Yazdgerd's proselytism continued to trouble the Persians even after his death in 457: taking advantage of the civil war which ensued between Peroz and Hormizd III, the king of Albania, Vach'e II, revolted, having been forced to convert to Zoroastrianism by Yazdgerd. Vach'e turned to allies north of the Caucasus for help, opening the Derbent pass to them; the Persians, after unsuccessfully trying to start negotiations, retaliated by admitting some Huns through the Dariel pass. A peaceful settlement followed, and Vach'e resigned his throne; for the next quarter of a century Albania was ruled by Persian *marzbans*.[15]

The use by both Albanians and Persians of allies from beyond the Caucasus illustrates a further difficulty for whoever controlled the region: the constant threat of an irruption by these peoples. They could, on the other hand, be employed as a powerful instrument of war, albeit a risky one since they might be suborned by the opposing power.[16] Control of the key passes across the Caucasus was therefore of great importance to Transcaucasians and Persians alike. It was rather less relevant to the Romans, whose empire lay at some distance from the zone most vulnerable to Hunnic incursions. The devastation caused by the Hunnic raid of 395/6 was nevertheless long remembered throughout Rome's eastern provinces; and the Sabir raid of 515 extended as far as Armenia and Cappadocia. The Persians thus had some justification in

---

[14]   Priscus, frgs.36.1–2 (c.456, cf. *FCH* I, 120 and 170 n.59 with *PLRE* II, Gobazes); as Burgess, 'A new reading', 357–8, has shown, Hydatius' chronicle is not relevant to this episode. Toumanoff, *Studies*, 363, connects *HVG* 157 (a three year campaign by Vakhtang against Roman forts in Abkhazia) with this campaign. Certainly the fort of C'ixe-Goji mentioned as the furthest point of Vakhtang's attacks by the *HVG* is in Lazica, cf. Hewsen's map in Thomson, *Rewriting Caucasian History*, liv (A3). I follow Toumanoff (*Studies*, 362), Martin-Hisard ('Le roi géorgien', 213–14) and van Esbroeck ('Lazique', 210–11) in dating the birth of Vakhtang to 439/40. Braund, apparently misunderstanding Martin-Hisard, *loc. cit.*, and calculating from an erroneous date for Vakhtang's death (491, see below n.25), prefers c.431 (*Georgia*, 283). While Toumanoff, *Studies*, 363 believes that Gubazes was seeking to leave Persian control at this point, it seems more probable that he had always been aligned with Rome, but had recently been trying to negotiate with both powers (so Braund, *Georgia*, 272–3 and Zuckerman, 'Byzantine strongholds', 543).

[15]   Elishe provides the details concerning this war, 241–3 [197–199] with Thomson's notes *ad loc.* on the Massagetae allies of the Albanians (Armenian Mask'ut'k) and Garsoïan, *Epic Histories*, 389–390; cf. also Movses, I.10, Toumanoff, *CMH*, 600 and Grousset, *Histoire*, 213–14. On Vach'e's resignation and the rule of the *marzbans*, Toumanoff, *Studies*, 262–3.

[16]   Braund, *Georgia*, 64; the case of Zilgibis (discussed below) shows the danger of such allies changing sides.

seeking subsidies from the Romans for the maintenance of defences against such raids, while the Romans for their part felt that the matter was more the concern of the Persians.[17]

In the reign of Leo Roman interest in the Caucasian passes must have waned still further. Around 467 the Lazi under Gubazes lost control of Suania, a region whose kings had traditionally been appointed by the ruler of Lazica; the Romans, in conjunction with Gubazes, wrested some forts from the Suani, but apparently failed to retake Suania. With Suania independent, Lazica was vulnerable from the north; and when Leo, preoccupied with his attempt to recapture North Africa, failed to intervene, it soon lapsed from Roman control. Although the Suani rapidly reverted to their allegiance to Rome, the Transcaucasus now lay almost entirely in Persian hands.[18] But their grasp was hardly secure. Almost at once the region fell prey to a wide-ranging invasion of the Saraguri. The invaders were halted briefly by Persian defences at the Caspian Gates, but soon found an alternative route into Iberia.[19] Meanwhile, even at this nadir of Roman fortunes in the Transcaucasus, the groundwork was being laid for an eventual

[17] Josh. Styl. §9, with Burkitt, *Euphemia*, 130–31 and Greatrex, 'Ziatha', on the destruction caused in 395/6. See below n.29 on the Sabir raid of 515. Note Anastasius' decision not to try to take control of the Dariel pass, when given the chance, Proc. I.10.9–11 (on which see below). The Caucasus mountains can however be penetrated elsewhere than Derbent and Dariel, cf. Braund, *Georgia*, 45–6; as a result of either the permeability of the Caucasus range or the inadequate defences of the Derbent and Dariel passes, numerous raids by the northern peoples are attested, e.g. by the Ossetians (Alans) in the late 440s (cf. *HVG* 145–6 with Toumanoff, *Studies*, 362) or the Saraguri c.467 (Priscus frg.47, dated by Blockley, *FCH* I, 121). On Roman indifference to the Caucasus defences (the ambiguously termed 'Caspian Gates'), see Braund, *Georgia*, 270–71.

[18] Priscus frg.51.1 (dated to 467, *FCH* I, 122). From Menander frg.6.1.565–84 it is clear that at some point in Leo's reign the Romans lost control of Lazica; but the kings of the Suani stayed loyal to Rome (*ibid.* 553–4). See on this Zuckerman, 'Byzantine strongholds', 542–4, who rightly emends Blockley's text of Priscus to read that the Romans and the Lazi were seizing forts of the Suani (51.1.4); also Toumanoff, *Studies*, 364 and Braund, *Georgia*, 273. The Suani may have temporarily favoured the Persians so as to free themselves from the Lazi, but evidently preferred allegiance to Rome once the Lazic king was appointed by the Persians.

  Although Leo may have promised to give help to the Armenians under Sasanian control in the 460s (Lazar, 165 [113]), it is significant that none ever materialised; Grousset, however, suggests that some unofficial assistance was forthcoming during Zeno's reign, *Histoire*, 226.

[19] Priscus, frg.47, dated by Blockley, *FCH* I, 121 to c.467. It is unclear whether the Caspian Gates referred to by Priscus were at the Dariel or the Derbent pass, cf. Anderson, 'Alexander', 136–7, Isaac, *Limits*, 230 and n.62, Marquart, *Eranšahr*, 102; also Synelli, *Diplomatikes Skheseis*, 160 n.14.

recovery, for just then a campaign was launched against the Tzani, an unruly tribe based in the mountains to the south of Trebizond.[20]

Peroz combined Yazdgerd's religious intolerance with disastrous incompetence in his wars against the Hephthalites. Apparent initial success in the Transcaucasus soon came to nothing. Varsken, the *vitaxa* (governor) of Gogarene, to the south of Iberia, apostasised from Christianity to Zoroastrianism in 475, but was executed seven years later by Vakhtang, the Iberian king. This triggered a renewed revolt in Iberia and Armenia, which was countered only by a sustained effort on the part of the Persians. Large Persian armies inflicted defeats on both Armenians and Iberians in 483 and 484, but failed to quell the uprising.[21] And so, once news of Peroz's defeat and death reached the region, the Persians swiftly withdrew. The commanders who had led the forces attempting to crush the rebels now ensured the election of Peroz's brother Balash, and persuaded him to seek Armenian support. The 'peace of Balash' of 485 brought immediate benefits to all parties. The Armenians regained their autonomy, and their leader Vahan was greatly honoured by Balash; the Iberians, it appears, were also left unmolested, and the Arsacid dynasty was restored in Albania. Balash, for his part, received armed assistance from the Armenians in defeating a rival for the throne, his nephew Zarer.[22]

The peace of Balash provides the immediate background to the renewed interest of both powers in the Transcaucasus in the early sixth century. For it meant that Balash's successor Kavadh was obliged, in effect, to reconquer the region to restore it to full Persian control. Naturally the kingdoms which had won their autonomy in 485 were most unwilling to relinquish it, and so several preferred to turn to the Romans rather than reenter the Sasanian orbit. Furthermore, since

---

[20] Joh. Ant. frg.206.2 (= *Exc. de insidiis* 90, p.130), probably from Priscus (Blockley's frg.51.2, dated by him, *FCH* I, 169–70, to 467). Stein I, 360, overinterpreting Joh. Ant., asserts that Zeno led the campaign, but cf. *PLRE* II, Zenon 7. On the Tzani in general see Bryer, 'Some notes' I, 187–8 and Braund, *Georgia*, 289.

[21] Toumanoff, *Studies*, 364–5 with Thomson, *Lazar*, 15–16, Grousset, *Histoire*, 216–26 and Lordkipanidse–Brakmann, 'Iberia II', 36. Varsken (Armenian Vazgen) had martyred his Christian wife Shushanik in 475, cf. Toumanoff, *op. cit.*, 262; an account of her martyrdom was probably produced a few years later, cf. Martin-Hisard, 'Le roi géorgien', 210–11. It is possible that Peroz succeeded in enlisting some Iberians for his campaigns in the east (presumably in the 460s or 470s), cf. Toumanoff, *op. cit.*, 366–7 and Martin-Hisard, *art. cit.*, 214 (following *HVG* 188–95).

[22] Toumanoff, *Studies*, 365, Chaumont, *EIr*, II, 430 and *EIr* III, 579, Lazar, 217–40 [157–78]; also Christensen, *L'Iran*, 295 and Frye, *Ancient Iran*, 322.

Kavadh had no opportunity to deal with the region until the opening of the sixth century, there was ample opportunity for Roman influence to make itself felt in the newly autonomous kingdoms. Thus, probably around the time of the peace of Balash, Roman links with the Iberians were cemented by a marriage alliance between Vakhtang and a relative of Zeno; territorial adjustments were also made, which may have restored Roman power in Abkhazia. At the same time Iberian influence was allowed to extend southwestwards into Cholarzene, just to the east of the region inhabited by the Tzani. Also around 485 Zeno's brother Longinus campaigned here and established a fortress (*fossatum Longini*) in eastern Tzanic territory. Clearly Roman interest in the area remained undiminished, but Leo wisely decided that more was to be gained by diplomacy at this point, and therefore accepted the extension of the Iberian kingdom.[23]

These developments paved the way for the defection to the Roman camp of both Lazica and Iberia in the 520s, when Persian pressure on the region became intolerable. For Kavadh was only gradually able to regain control of the Transcaucasus. Some efforts were made in the 490s to revive Zoroastrianism in Persarmenia, but as usual they sparked an uprising. Kavadh was unable to suppress the revolt before his expulsion at the hands of Zamasp, and upon his return he offered to allow the Armenians their religious freedom if they would join his expedition against the Romans.[24] Before invading Roman territory, Kavadh undertook an attack on the Iberians, in the course of which Vakhtang was mortally wounded. While Iberia was not at once restored to Sasanian control by this campaign, the division of the kingdom upon Vakhtang's

---

[23] *HVG* 177 on the territorial changes (with Toumanoff, *Studies*, 462 n.113 and van Esbroeck, 'Lazique', 207); cf. Hewsen's map in Thomson, *Rewriting Caucasian History*, liv (Klarjet'i = Cholarzene) and Martin-Hisard, 'Le roi géorgien', 226, from which the proximity of Cholarzene to Tzanica emerges most clearly. Martin-Hisard, *art. cit.*, 225–7, notes how Vakhtang's territorial aspirations coincide with the area where Georgian or related languages are spoken; the boundaries referred to by *HVG* may therefore have more to do with the situation in the ninth century (when the work was probably composed, see above ch.4 n.28) than the fifth.

On the marriage of Vakhtang, see Toumanoff, *op. cit.*, 367 and n.40 (with *HVG* 198, Thomson, *op. cit.*, 216 n.25 and van Esbroeck, *art. cit.*, 203). Longinus' campaign against the Tzani is referred to by Proc. at *Aed.* III.6.23; the location of the fort named after him is unknown, but clearly lay in the eastern part of Tzanica. *PLRE* II, Longinus 6 places the campaign in 485, when he was *magister militum praesentalis*; Braund, *Georgia*, 289 n.88 puts it c.488.

[24] Josh. Styl. §§21, 25 with Christensen, *L'Iran*, 352 and Grousset, *Histoire*, 231.

death must have weakened it considerably.[25] During the Anastasian war Kavadh was again forced to look north: the Sabir Huns had invaded, very probably encouraged by the Iberians seeking to maintain their independence.[26] Not long afterwards the Sabir king, Ambazuces, offered to hand over control of the Caspian Gates (here clearly the Dariel pass) to the Romans in return for an adequate payment. Anastasius refused the offer, calculating that it would benefit the Romans little to shoulder the burden of defending this strategic defile; since all the Transcaucasian kingdoms remained at least nominally attached to the Sasanians, invading Huns were more likely to harm Persian territory than Roman.[27] But the Romans continued to be involved in the region, spurred on by a Tzanic raid in 505. The task of subjugating these refractory highlanders may well have been started under Anastasius, and

---

[25] *HVG* 200–4 with Toumanoff, *Studies*, 367–8 and Thomson, *Rewriting Caucasian History*, 222 n.38. The mention of Zeno's accession here is a later interpolation (cf. Toumanoff, *op. cit.*, 367 n.40) and that of a change of Roman ruler may be doubted. Thomson follows Toumanoff in his belief that Vakhtang should be identified with Proc.'s Gourgenes (on whom see below); since Gourgenes defected to the Romans in the 520s, both believe that *HVG*'s account here is extremely condensed. *Contra* Lordkipanidse–Brakmann, 'Iberia II', 37, the identification has generally been discredited: cf. Braund, *Georgia*, 283 and Martin-Hisard, 'Le roi géorgien', 210 and n.36. *HVG* dates Vakhtang's death to his sixtieth year (200); Braund, having mistakenly placed the king's birth c.431, dates his death to 491, relying on a misinterpretation of a Syriac source, the life of Grigor. *Contra* Braund, *loc. cit.*, it does not refer to a war in the Transcaucasus in 491; the war mentioned there (Hoffmann, *Auszüge*, 80) happened after the thirtieth year of Kavadh's reign (*ibid.*, 79), i.e. after 518 at the very earliest.

If Vakhtang was born c.440 (see above n.14), then Kavadh's attack took place c.500, just before his attack on Roman territory (so Toumanoff, 'New light', 166 and van Esbroeck, 'Lazique', 207–9); the reference in the *HVG* to the accession of a new Persian king just before the attack must therefore refer to the restoration of Kavadh in 498/9 (*contra* Thomson, *op. cit.*, 218 n.32). *HVG* calls the new king Khuasro, but this is the name applied by the history to nearly every Persian ruler (as noted by Toumanoff, *op. cit.*, 366 n.35). On the division of the kingdom see *HVG* 204–5 with Toumanoff, *op. cit.*, 463.

[26] Proc. I.8.19 on the invasion, cf. also 9.24, 10.15, and *Aed.* II.1.5. See Christensen, *L'Iran*, 352 and Marquart, *Eranšahr*, 63 n.4, on Kavadh's war against the (Sabir) Huns, who irrupted again, however, around 515–16. *Contra* the views of (e.g.) Whitby, 'Defences', 717, Kavadh's war was not against the Hephthalites, see above ch.5 n.104. Proc. places the invaders to the north of Kavadh's kingdom (I.8.19); elsewhere (II.29.15), in a rather confused description, this appears to be where he locates the Sabirs.

[27] Proc. I.10.10–12. On Ambazuces, *PLRE* II, Ambazuces. Howorth, 'The Sabiri', 614–15, believed Ambazuces to be a Sabir, and dates his offer to Anastasius c.508; cf. also Isaac, *Limits*, 230. Proc. fails to date the episode, but the termini are obviously 506 (the end of the Anastasian war) and 518 (the death of Anastasius).

was eventually completed by Sittas in the early 520s. Henceforth the Romans had a secure foothold on the borders of both Lazica and Iberia.[28]

Whether or not he was aware of Ambazuces' offer, Kavadh now concentrated his efforts on the Transcaucasus. In 513/14 he suppressed a minor uprising among the Armenians, partly by confirming their religious freedom; elsewhere, however, he was evidently enforcing adherence to Zoroastrianism. Hence when the Lazic king Damnazes died in 521/2, his successor Tzath was expected to take part in Zoroastrian coronation ceremonies. Fortifications were installed at various points to defend against invaders from north of the Caucasus, and the Dariel pass was wrested from the sons of Ambazuces. Perhaps as a consequence of this, Kavadh may have been able to deflect into Roman territory the raid by Sabir Huns in 515, which therefore reached Cappadocia and Armenia. He also strengthened the Persian grip on Albania, constructing a new capital at Partaw, as well as installing a *marzban* at Mtskheta in Iberia around 520. All his efforts were soon nearly brought to nothing.[29]

iii) The early years of Justin's reign (518–c.525)

The accession of Justin in July 518 was not accompanied by any perceptible change in Roman-Persian relations. The new emperor doubtless apprised the Persian king of the change in ruler, and Kavadh will probably have responded with another request for money. Not for the

---

[28] Proc. I.15.24, with *Aed.* III.6–7, clearly puts Sittas' victory before the outbreak of full-scale war *contra* Stein II, 291, Braund, *Georgia*, 289 and *PLRE* III, Sittas 1; Howard-Johnston, 'Citharizon', 218, argues that the subjugation of the Tzani began early, pointing out that it would be unfeasible to attempt to reduce this hardy tribe in wartime (in the late 520s). Seibt, 'Westgeorgien', 140, rightly stresses the impact which the subdual of the Tzani had on the whole region. On the Tzanic raid of 505, Theod. Lect. *HE* 466, Stein II, 105. It was not until the late 550s that the Tzani challenged Roman control, Stein II, 516.

[29] On Persian building work in the Caucasus, see Kramer, 'The military colonization', 613. Stein II, 105, Bury, *HLRE* I, 434 and n.5 and Trombley, 'The decline' 69 and 83 n.28 for the Sabir raid of 515. On the fortification of Partaw, see Hübschmann, *Orts-namen*, 273 n.2, Marquart, *Eranšahr*, 118, M.-L. Chaumont, *EIr* I, 809; on Mtskheta and the Armenian revolt, Toumanoff, *CMH* IV, 601 and Grousset, *Histoire*, 233. Frye puts the installation of a *marzban* at Mtskheta slightly later than Toumanoff, in 522/3, *Ancient Iran*, 322. Stein II, 105, notes that the revolt also affected Roman Armenia, cf. *Chron. 724*, a.824 (115, 21), Mich. Syr. IX.11 (167). Proc. I.10.12 on Kavadh's seizure of the Caspian Gates. Toumanoff, *CMH* IV, 601 plausibly infers a Zoroastrianising policy by Kavadh and cf. e.g. *CP* 613 on the Zoroastrian rituals required of Tzath.

first time, the demand, if made, was backed up with a raid by the Lakhmid Arabs, in 519 or 520.[30] It was possibly in the course of this *razzia* that two Roman commanders, Timostratus and John, were captured by the Lakhmid king. Diplomatic activity continued nevertheless, and their release was soon negotiated by the presbyter Abraham, son of the diplomat Euphrasius. If there is any substance to the statement of Cedrenus that a peace treaty was agreed in the third year of Justin's reign (521/2), it might have had something to do with the success of Abraham's mission.[31]

A casual observer in Mesopotamia or Syria would have had reason to think that the peaceful days of the fifth century had returned. Roman fortifications were now strong enough to deter a Persian invasion, and Lakhmid incursions represented only an occasional menace. But troublesome signs will quickly have dissipated any such optimism. A huge comet, described as bearded, was seen in the east, 'and [people] were afraid'. As in 499 and 500, their fears proved justified. The 520s were marked by a series of violent earthquakes, which caused extensive destruction at cities such as Anazarbus, Corinth and Antioch; and Edessa suffered a devastating flood in 525.[32] For opponents of the Council of Chalcedon the comet also presaged persecution. Anti-Chalcedonian monks, bishops and priests were ejected from their cities and monasteries, sometimes by imperial forces, 'who oppressed them everywhere and mercilessly drove them from one place to another'. Although John of Ephesus' description of the persecutions must be

---

[30] Zach. VIII.5 (206) implies that Kavadh made several requests for Roman payments. On the raid of the Lakhmid king al-Mundhir, *Chron. 724*, a. 830 (111, 11), Elias Nis. a.831, Gregory p.73 and Mich. Syr. IX.16 (178). The last two sources place the raid in Osrhoene (they refer to the rivers Balikh [= Balissus] and Khabur); Gregory's next notice concerns the appearance of a remarkable woman of Cilicia, placed by Mal. (412) c.518/19. Hence although Stein II, 266, hesitates as to whether the raid was in 519 or 520, *PLRE* II, Alamundarus 2, is probably right to opt for 519. Vasiliev, *Justin I*, 277, inexplicably places it in 523. Shahîd, *Martyrs*, 241, and *BASIC* I, 43, prefers to attribute two raids to al-Mundhir in successive years.

[31] On the peace treaty of 521, see Shahîd, *Martyrs*, 241 and n.4 and *BASIC* I, 43; if his dating of the persecutions at Najran to 518 (rather than 523, see below Appendix n.10) is accepted, it follows that the two commanders were released in 520/1 rather than 524 (*contra* e.g. Stein II, 266 and *PLRE* II, Timostratus and Alamundarus 2). Cedrenus I.638 for the peace treaty in 521/2; since the war begun in 502 was only concluded in 532, Cedrenus' treaty can at most have been a renewal of the truce agreed in 506.

[32] Mal. 411.11–13 and *CP* 612.15–18 on the comet (in 519, cf. *CPW* 105 n.329). Mal. 417–19 on the other natural calamities, with Stein II, 241–2 and Vasiliev, *Justin I*, 349–50 (noting other sources).

treated with caution, the 520s clearly witnessed considerable disruption
throughout the diocese of Oriens, as successive patriarchs of Antioch
sought to regain control of the bishoprics and monasteries in their
territory.[33]

Meanwhile, further afield, a significant shift of alignments was
taking place, which was to rekindle hostilities between the two powers.
Several states in the Transcaucasus would try during the 520s to sever
their links with the Persians and enter into friendship with the Romans.
The defection of the Lazic king in 521/2 took place at a time when
relations between the two sides were still good, and was marked only
by diplomatic protestations on Kavadh's part. But by the time the king
of Iberia defected a few years later, the climate of relations between the
two powers had deteriorated. Iberia had long been in the Sasanian orbit,
and the Persians swiftly resorted to military intervention to retain their
control of the kingdom. Once the Romans had in turn despatched an
army to the region, the likelihood increased that war would engulf the
whole eastern frontier.[34]

As has been seen, Roman influence in the Transcaucasus had been
growing steadily from the late fifth century. The decision of the Lazic
king Tzath, upon the death of his father Damnazes, to reject a Zoroastrian coronation and to have his accession validated by Justin rather
than Kavadh was therefore a welcome, but not wholly unexpected,
development. When Tzath presented himself in the imperial capital, in
521 or 522, he was accorded a lavish welcome: he was baptised, given
a high-ranking Roman wife, and his investiture was marked by the gift
of magnificent regalia.[35] That the Romans perceived Tzath's defection

[33] Ps. Dion. II, 19–20 for anti-Chalcedonian perceptions of the comet. *Ibid.* 21 for the
      quotation (tr. Witakowski, 22), cf. 22–44. The involvement of troops in the perse-
      cutions cannot have improved relations with the provincials, but Ps. Dion.'s refer-
      ences to this also prove that there were now soldiers stationed at Amida (II, 37, 41).
      Whitby, *Maurice*, 213 and n.29, cautions against excessive reliance on John; Justin's
      persecution of anti-Chalcedonians was certainly not consistent, cf. Vasiliev, *Justin I*,
      221–41 (a detailed account, stressing that frontier provinces were initially less af-
      fected) and Stein II, 231–2.
[34] Braund, *Georgia*, 261, on the long-standing Sasanian control of Iberia; Lazica, by
      contrast, was a comparatively new acquisition, cf. e.g. *ibid.* 273 (post-470) and
      Lordkipanidse–Brakmann, 'Iberia II', 84–5; see also above n.18.
[35] *CP* 613–14, Mal. 412–13, Joh. Nik. 90.35–38; Theoph. A.M. 6015 (168–9) puts the
      defection in 522/3, but, as Mango–Scott note, 254 n.1, his chronology here is unreli-
      able. They prefer *CP*'s date of 522, while *CPW* 106 n.330 argues for 521, following
      Mal.'s implied chronology. Cf. also Braund, *Georgia*, 276–7 (c.522), Vasiliev, 260

as an important event is clear not only from the magnificence of his reception but also from the relationship which was established between the empire and the Lazic kingdom. For the Lazi, although nominally now subject to the Romans, paid no tribute to the empire, and contributed no forces; they themselves guarded the Transcaucasus for the Romans, and their new kings were merely ratified by the emperor.[36] Justin's actions were deplored by the Persians, who despatched an embassy to protest; Kavadh claimed, rather speciously, that Lazica had been subject to him 'from eternity' and noted that the developing good relations between the two powers had been damaged by the incident. The emperor in his reply endeavoured to reduce the tension by insisting that the initiative had come from the Lazi and that he could not refuse a request from one who wished to become a Christian.[37]

Under other circumstances, such a response might have proved intolerable to the Persians. But two factors served to diminish any desire the Sasanians might have cherished for a renewed offensive. First, Justin had skilfully turned a recent diplomatic disappointment to his own advantage. He had obtained an alliance with Zilgibis, a Hunnic king whose realm was north of the Caucasus and whose army could be used to attack Persian territories in the Transcaucasus and beyond. This coup, however, was brought to nothing when Zilgibis allied himself with Kavadh, having already received many gifts from the emperor. Once Justin heard of this development, he took advantage of the good relations which still existed between himself and Kavadh: he told the king about his earlier dealings with Zilgibis, warning that the Hunnic king would betray the Persians to the Romans, and urged that the two powers should cooperate against such barbarians rather than compete for their support. Kavadh, discovering that Zilgibis had indeed received payments from the Romans, immediately ordered his execution and

<hr>

(522), Stein II, 267 (522) and *PLRE* II, Ztathius (noting other chronicle sources which report his defection).

[36] Proc. II.15.2–4 with Vasiliev, *Justin I*, 258–9, Braund, *Georgia*, 280–81 and Lordkipanidse–Brakmann, 'Iberia II', 84. The Lazic kingdom itself, it should be noted, was far from poor, despite Proc. II.15 (see Braund, 'Procopius on the economy of Lazica', 221–5). The outbreak of war in the Transcaucasus in the late 520s led to Roman encroachments on Lazic autonomy, however.

[37] Mal. 413–14, *CP* 614–15, Joh. Nik. 90.39–41. See Engelhardt, *Mission*, 80–90, on Roman missionary work in the region during this period. Vasiliev, *Justin I*, 261–2, notes that Lazica had long been Christian by the sixth century, and suggests that Tzath wished to be baptised to confirm his adherence to Christianity (and opposition to Kavadh's Zoroastrianism).

destroyed his army. 'And thereafter Koades [Kavadh] decided, he says, to speak about terms of peace or rather friendship, declaring it to Justin the Roman emperor by means of an ambassador, Broeus.'[38]

The second, more general, factor favouring continued cooperation between the two powers was the enduring instability of Kavadh's position. In 499 he had regained his throne only with Hephthalite help, after losing it because of his unpopular radical measures.[39] Although by the 520s Kavadh had apparently abjured the revolutionary views which he had once espoused, their influence remained: the Mazdakite movement had gained a great following in the kingdom, to the extent that his eldest son Kaoses was an adherent. The position of the Mazda-kites was strong, and Kavadh, at least seventy years old in 522,[40] realised that he might be unable to eliminate them in his lifetime; more-over, if they were not to gain control of the kingdom at his death, an outcome he was keen to prevent, he would have to ensure that Kaoses did not succeed him. So he determined that another son, Khusro, would be his successor. Although it was the prerogative of the king to nominate his successor, Khusro's position might be vulnerable in the face of opposition from his elder brother.[41] In view of such uncertainty

---

[38] *CP* 615–16 (quotation, 616.6–8, tr. *CPW*, 107), Mal. 414–15 (naming the ambassador as Labroeus, cf. *PLRE* II, Labroius), with *CPW* 107 n.331, Vasiliev, *Justin I*, 264–5 (placing the episode in 522). Rubin, *ZI*, 259, suggests that Labroeus was involved in preparing the ground for Kavadh's proposal that Justin adopt Khusro, on which see below. The efficiency of Roman diplomats in this incident should be noted (cf. Lee, *Information*, 46–8); the chronicles are likely to be relying, directly or indirectly, on their reports stored in Constantinople, *ibid.* 35–40.

[39] It remains a matter of dispute whether it was his support for the Mazdakite sect that lost him the throne in 496; most scholars believe so, e.g. Christensen, *Le règne*, 95–106, Schippmann, *Grundzüge*, 49, but cf. Crone, 'Kavad's heresy', 22–3, who argues that Kavadh was introducing other radical measures in the 490s.

[40] Cf. *PLRE* II, Cavades I; Mal. 471, on his age in 531. Crone, 'Kavad's heresy', 30 and n.211, has argued that Kavadh was considerably younger than is attested. But both Mal. and Firdausi, VI, 155 state that he died an octogenarian. The oriental sources which she cites (n.210), e.g. Nöldeke, *Tabari*, 138–9, are completely inconsistent, cf. *ibid.* 138 n.4 and 139 n.1: at one moment Kavadh is an old man, at another a child. Christensen too, *Le règne*, 93 n.3, is dismissive of the tradition concerning the youth of Kavadh on his accession. Since Kavadh did not command any campaigns towards the end of his life, he can hardly have died in the field (*contra* Crone), and so arguments relating to his physical condition are irrelevant.

[41] Christensen, *L'Iran*, 353 on Kavadh's right to nominate his successor, cf. *ibid.* 263 on earlier Sasanian practice. As Christensen notes, *op. cit.*, 353, Proc.'s Kaoses is to be identified with Theoph.'s Phthasuarsan (the prince of Padhishkhvar), cf. Mango–Scott, *Theophanes* 261 n.7. On his allegiance to Mazdakism, Christensen, *loc. cit.* and Crone, 'Kavad's heresy', 31.

within his own kingdom, Kavadh looked beyond its frontiers. Having apparently recently consulted the royal archives concerning Lazica's role in Roman-Persian relations, he may have come across an allusion to the adoption of the young Theodosius II by his own predecessor Yazdgerd I. At any rate his next move was to propose to Justin that the latter adopt Khusro as his son, thereby guaranteeing his succession.[42]

The only source to report in detail Kavadh's request and the consequent negotiations is Procopius. According to him, Justin and his nephew Justinian were elated at the offer, and were inclined to accept it immediately. Their enthusiasm was quenched by the *quaestor* Proculus, who asserted that a written adoption would entitle Khusro to inherit the Roman empire. The *quaestor* recommended instead that the adoption be 'by arms', a method hitherto employed for barbarian kings.[43] Diplomats from both sides assembled on the border of the two empires

---

Whether the Mazdakites were extinguished before or after Kavadh's death is uncertain: Christensen, *Le règne*, 124 and Schippmann, *Grundzüge*, 51, place the massacre of the Mazdakites in 528/9, probably rightly (following Nöldeke, *Tabari*, 465–6, who countenanced the idea that a second strike may have been made against them at Khusro's accession). Crone, *art. cit.*, 32, places their destruction at the outset of Khusro's reign, rejecting the chronology of Mal. and Theoph.

[42] On the guardianship of Yazdgerd I over Theodosius II, see above ch.2 p.13 and Bardill–Greatrex, 'Antiochus'. See above p.133 on Kavadh's assertion of the long-standing Persian control of Lazica (even if it is incorrect); cf. Mal. 449–50 for Kavadh consulting written records. It is probable that the story of Yazdgerd's guardianship was known in some form in Persia, given the record of it in the Annals of Hamza, cf. Daudpota, 'The Annals', 71–2: according to Hamza, a delegate chosen by Yazdgerd, Sharwin Barmiyan, ruled the Roman empire for twenty years until the Roman emperor came of age.

Zach. IX.7 (230) claims that it was the Roman ambassador Rufinus who suggested that Kavadh's youngest son (Khusro) succeed him; but although Kavadh held Rufinus in high esteem (cf. Proc. I.11.24), it is unlikely that Rufinus did more than confirm to Kavadh the precedent of Theodosius and Yazdgerd. *PLRE* II (Rufinus 13) oddly states that during the mission reported by Procopius (I.11.24–30) Rufinus persuaded Kavadh to appoint Khusro to succeed him, even though the purpose of the embassy was to conduct negotiations regarding the request already made by Kavadh that Justin adopt Khusro.

[43] Proc. I.11.7–30. Rubin, *ZI*, 259–60, and 484 n.745 with Pieler, 'L'aspect politique', 421–32 on Proculus' (unjustified) fears over the adoption. Dewing, in his translation, 91 n.1, mistakenly considers that adoption 'by arms' means 'by force'. Stein II, 269, gives the parallels of Theodoric and Eutharic, the latter of whom was adopted by Justin himself; Jordanes, *Getica* 289, describes Zeno's adoption of Theodoric thus: *[Zeno] in arma sibi eum filium adoptavit*, clearly referring to the same procedure as was now offered to Kavadh and Khusro, cf. Cassiod. *Variae*, VIII.1.3, *factus est per arma filius* (Eutharic). There are no grounds for doubting the historicity of the event; it is accepted by Pieler, 'L'aspect politique', 400–7, Vasiliev, *Justin I*, 266–8 and Rubin, *ZI*, 259–61.

in Mesopotamia, while Khusro stationed himself on the Tigris near
Nisibis. Clearly hopes were high for a successful conclusion, notwithstanding the manner of adoption.[44] The Roman negotiators were both
veterans of the Anastasian war: Hypatius, despite his ignominious role
in the war, currently held the post of *magister militum per Orientem*,
and the diplomat Rufinus was well known to Kavadh.[45] The Persian
emissaries, Seoses (Siyavush) and the *magister* Mebodes (Mahbodh),
were no less distinguished. Seoses was second in power to Kavadh
himself, while Mebodes occupied another major position in the Persian
court, most probably the office of *spahbadh*.[46]

Despite the presence of such high-ranking dignitaries from either
side — or perhaps because of it — the negotiations quickly broke
down. For although Justin and Kavadh seem to have harboured a
genuine desire for peace, their attitude was not shared by all their
ministers. Thus Seoses, in the course of the discussions, brought up the
matter of Lazica, complaining that the Romans had seized it unjustly;
whereupon the Romans effectively terminated the negotiations by
making it clear that adoption by arms was an inferior method, reserved
for the use of barbarians.[47] It was now quite evident that, even if the
adoption went ahead, the Romans would do little or nothing to ensure
the succession of Khusro. 'The two parties therefore separated and
departed homeward, and Khusro with nothing accomplished was off to

---

[44] Proc. I.11.27 on Khusro's location; 11.22 on the use of adoption by arms for barbarians. The Persians will hardly have been aware of the different types of Roman
adoption.

[45] Proc. I.11.24 on the Roman envoys and Kavadh's friendship with Rufinus; according
to Proc., Kavadh and Rufinus knew one another through their fathers (Peroz and Silvanus respectively), cf. *PLRE* II, Silvanus 7 and I.16.1. Hypatius' appointment is
remarkable, although Justin and Justinian never broke with the nephews of Anastasius. It is possible, however, as is suggested by Rubin (*ZI*, 260–61), that he was
sent out as a potential scapegoat, should the negotiations fail (cf. Proc. I.11.38–9).

[46] Proc. I.11.25 on the Persian ambassadors. Seoses held the office of *adrastaran
salanes* (*arteshtaran salar*), Proc. I.6.18 (although he was not the first to hold it,
contra Proc.). Cf. Christensen, *L'Iran*, 131–2 and *EIr* II, 662 on the post; on the
identification of Seoses and Siyavush, Christensen, *Le règne*, 94. Mebodes is referred
to by Proc. as a *magister* (*officiorum*), most likely an allusion to the Persian office of
spahbadh, but possibly to that of *astabadh*: see above ch.5 n.86 and *PLRE* III,
Mebodes 1.

[47] Proc. I.11.28–30. According to Proc. 11.31 Seoses was accused of broaching the
subject of Lazica in order to sabotage the discussions; a similar suspicion surrounded
Hypatius, 11.31, 39. See also Greatrex, 'Hypatius', 140, on his role.

his father, deeply injured at what had taken place and vowing
vengeance on the Romans for their insult to him.'[48]

So far no date has been proposed for these negotiations. Procopius
does not provide one, and that put forward by Theophanes cannot be
trusted.[49] On the evidence of Procopius the negotiations must have
taken place after 521/2, the date of the defection of Lazica, and before
the death of Justin in 527. Further precision is possible: Hypatius must
have been dismissed from his post as *magister militum per Orientem*
some time before 527, since between April and August that year he was
reappointed to his old command.[50] Unfortunately the identity of his
successor before his reappointment is unknown, as is his length of
tenure. But a date of 524/5 at the latest for the negotiations may be
suggested, based on one further shred of evidence: the Iberian king
Gourgenes defected to the Romans at some point during Justin's reign,
after the adoption attempt, but before Justinian was raised to the purple.
His transference of allegiance can be dated tentatively to c.525, and so
can provide a *terminus ante quem* for the negotiations.[51]

One more piece of evidence remains to be examined. Zachariah of
Mytilene records unsuccessful talks between a Persian *spahbadh* and
two Roman envoys, Hypatius and Pharesmanes, around this time.
Many have sought to connect this episode with that related by Procopius, but the supposition is fraught with difficulties. First, there is the

---

[48] Quotation from Proc. I.11.30 (tr. Dewing). Khusro's disappointment implies that an
adoption by arms would have been acceptable; it would certainly have strengthened
his position, since potential rivals would not know that the Romans were unlikely to
intervene following such an adoption.

[49] Theoph. A.M. 6013 (167) places the talks in 520/1, following the Zilgibis episode
earlier the same year, but before Tzath's defection (put in 6015). Clearly no store can
be set by his chronology, cf. Mango–Scott, *Theophanes*, 254 n.1 (*contra ibid.*, 255
n.5). It is just possible that he had access to another source apart from Proc., for he
refers to a debate in the Senate unmentioned by Proc; see Pieler, 'L'aspect politique',
407 and Bardill–Greatrex, 'Antiochus', n.33.

[50] Cf. *PLRE* II, Hypatius 6 (Mal. 423); he was dismissed from the office for the last time
in 529 (Mal. 445).

[51] Proc. I.11.39 on Hypatius' first dismissal. Bury's suggestion, *HLRE* II, 81 n.3, that
11.31–9 is a digression referring to a later period, is unnecessary. Vasiliev, *Justin I*,
265, dates the negotiations to 522, immediately after the Zilgibis episode; Pieler,
'L'aspect politique', 400, prefers 522/4 and Schippmann, *Grundzüge*, 51, opts for
522/3. Stein II, 269, puts the adoption attempt in 525 (cf. *PLRE* II, Cavades, 525/6).
Despite *PLRE* II, Libelarius and Hypatius 6, Hypatius' successor was not Libelarius,
as I shall argue elsewhere; dates relying on Zach.'s evidence (and his references to
Liberius/Libelarius) are not reliable, cf. Stein II, 269 n.3. The date of Gourgenes'
defection (Proc. I.12.4–13) will be discussed below.

obvious difference in the composition of the Roman delegation between the two sources; both Procopius and Zachariah are well informed
concerning Pharesmanes and Rufinus, and are unlikely either to have
mistaken one for the other or to have omitted to mention such an important member of an embassy. Second, the negotiations reported by
both sources seem to have taken place at different times. The chapter in
which Zachariah describes the negotiations deals with events occurring
up to the early 530s, although the talks are placed between the earthquake at Antioch of May 526 and al-Mundhir's raid of 529; they also
follow an account of some Roman raids on Arzanene and Nisibis. It
seems likely therefore that Zachariah's notice refers to talks held very
close to the end of Justin's reign, when relations between the two sides
were more tense, probably after Hypatius had been reappointed *magister militum per Orientem* by Justin and Justinian (i.e. between 1 April
and 1 August 527).[52]

The failure of the talks described by Procopius did not make the
renewal of hostilities inevitable, but it did create a climate of mistrust
and suspicion, in which the slightest possible provocation might be
interpreted as a hostile act. In the event, the defection of the Iberian
king shortly after the negotiations led the Persians to begin military
operations in the Transcaucasus. It was nonetheless some years before
large-scale campaigning resumed in Mesopotamia, for reasons which
will be explored in the next chapter.

---

[52] Zach. VIII.5 (206) for the talks; VIII.4 (205) on the earthquake at Antioch (Bury,
HLRE II, 36 for its date). The negotiations must also have preceded Libelarius' raid
of mid-527, on which see below ch.7.i.c. Proc. refers to Pharesmanes at I.8.3; Zach.
recounts his deeds in the Anastasian war in detail. Both authors have numerous references to Rufinus; note esp. Zach. IX.7 (230) on his influence over Kavadh. Vasiliev,
Justin I, 168 n.20, takes Zach. as referring to the same negotiations as Procopius.
PLRE II, however, Hypatius 6 and Pharesmanes 3, separates the negotiations in the
two sources, cf. Stein II, 283, who dates Zach.'s episode to 527; see also Rubin, *ZI*,
486 n.757 (527 or 531) and Stein in *RE* X (1919), 1325, s.v. Iustinus 1 (527).

   At I.16.7 Procopius has Kavadh allude to Persian demands made before 528 (the
Minduos campaign), which could refer to these negotiations.

VII
The renewal of conflict (525–529)

Outright hostilities between Rome and Persia did not break out overnight after the failure of the negotiations for Khusro's adoption.
Kavadh still had to contend with the powerful Mazdakite sect in his
kingdom, and a war against Rome would do nothing to strengthen his
position or that of Khusro. Developments in the Transcaucasus, however, soon necessitated a Persian response. At first the two powers
avoided direct involvement in the region, but gradually both were
drawn into committing their own forces. At the same time as Roman
and Persian armies finally faced one another in Lazica, hostilities were
breaking out in Armenia and Mesopotamia. The conflict had entered its
final stage.

As had become traditional, Mesopotamia was the main theatre of
war, with some campaigning also in Armenia. But since it was events
in the Transcaucasus that precipitated the conflict, they have the prior
claim to be considered.

i) The reign of Justin

a) The build-up to war in the Transcaucasus

Even as discussions about adoption were taking place on the frontier in
524/5 the Persian king was tightening his grip on the Transcaucasus.
Efforts to ensure loyalty to the Sasanian throne may be supposed to
have been redoubled in the wake of Tzath's defection just a few years
earlier. But Kavadh's measures, requiring a strict adherence to Zoroastrianism, were scarcely calculated to keep in check the fiercely
Christian Iberians.[1] As a result, shortly after the adoption negotiations

---

[1] Proc. I.12.4 states, rather implausibly, that Kavadh only set about enforcing Zoroastrianism in Iberia after the breakdown in negotiations. But see above ch.6 p.130 on
earlier Persian activity in the region and Tzath's dissatisfaction with Zoroastrian
rituals; see also Toumanoff, review of Stein II, 483–4, arguing against Proc.'s

were broken off, the Iberian king Gourgenes made contact with the Roman emperor Justin, seeking assurances of his support against the Persians. The king's caution is understandable in light of the failure of previous Iberian revolts and the presence of a Persian *marzban* at Mtskheta.[2]

The only source to report Gourgenes' defection to the Romans is Procopius. The king himself is not attested elsewhere; even the Georgian annals have no record of him. While this should not call into doubt the historicity of Procopius' narrative — who, it will be recalled, campaigned in Italy alongside the eldest son of Gourgenes, Peranius — it does raise certain difficulties of chronology.[3] In a brief passage Procopius covers a whole series of events, starting with the contacts between Gourgenes and Justin (I.12.5). In response to Gourgenes' appeal, Justin first despatches Probus to recruit Huns for the defence of Iberia (12.6). When this proves unsuccessful, he sends his former secretary Peter and some Huns to Lazica to assist Gourgenes (12.9). Kavadh's response is to appoint a certain Boes to command a substantial force in Iberia, which succeeds in expelling Gourgenes and the Romans from the kingdom (12.11). Across the border in Lazica the Romans and the exiled Iberian nobility make a stand; the Persians are then brought to a halt, impeded by the difficult terrain (12.12). The focus of operations shifts to Lazica, now threatened by the large Persian force operating in neighbouring Iberia. The Iberian royal family seek refuge in Constantinople. Perhaps as a result of the news they bear of the failed campaign to defend their kingdom, Peter is recalled to Constantinople and

---

apparent chronology here. Proc. I.12.3 on the firm adherence to Christianity of the Iberians, on which see also above ch.6 p.124. According to Proc. I.12.4, Kavadh insisted that the Iberians follow Persian burial customs, i.e. expose their dead. This was an obvious method of revealing Christians, who were disgusted by the practice. It clearly remained an issue for Christians living under Persian rule, cf. Menander frg.6.1.405–7 (the terms of the peace treaty of 561/2), stipulating that Christians in Persia should be allowed to inter their dead.

2   Proc. I.12.5 on Gourgenes' approach; see above ch.6 n.29 on the *marzban*.

3   Cf. *PLRE* II, Gurgenes, which unfortunately follows the dubious identification of Gourgenes with Vakhtang Gorgasal (on which see above ch.6 n.25), and Braund, *Georgia*, 282–3. According to the Georgian annals, the king at this time was Bakur II (*HVG* 206 with Grousset, *Histoire*, 233 n.6, who notes the suggestion of Brosset, *Additions*, 85, that Gourgenes may have been 'un simple gouverneur ou *éristhaw* de quelque province, peut-être du Somkheth'). He might have had some connection with Mirdat, the son of Vakhtang by his Roman wife, cf. *HVG* 205 and Braund, *Georgia*, 284. *PLRE* III, Peranius, on the career of Gourgenes' son; Proc.'s text at I.12.11 is ambiguous: Peranius could be the eldest brother of Gourgenes, although this is unlikely.

ordered to return and defend Lazica at all costs. To accomplish this he is provided with an army and a fellow commander, Irenaeus (12.14). Procopius' interest in operations in Lazica fades at this point: he merely notes that the two forts on the border between Lazica and Iberia were occupied by the Roman troops, who however soon withdrew because of supply difficulties. In consequence, the Persians were able to take control of the forts with ease (12.19).

Clearly all these events must have taken place over several years, and some may even have occurred in the reign of Justinian, although his accession is reported by Procopius only at I.13.1. Procopius fails to name the βασιλεύς (emperor) who ordered the defence of Lazica by Peter and Irenaeus (12.14); that emperor could therefore be Justinian. Once the war moved to Lazica, it attracted the interest of the chroniclers. Hence our exclusive reliance on Procopius comes to an end, and some chronological indicators become available. The chroniclers are unanimous in assigning a campaign in Lazica to the year 528: they report that three *magistri militum* were despatched to Lazica to protect Tzath from the Persians. While the chroniclers are also in general accord as to the course of the campaign — initial heavy losses for the Romans due to their divided command followed by a Roman withdrawal — they vary considerably as to the identity of the Roman commanders. The *Chronicon Paschale* records the presence of Belisarius, Cerycus and Irenaeus, as does John of Nikiu. On the other hand, Malalas prefers Gilderich, Cerycus and Irenaeus, while Theophanes opts for Belisarius, Cerycus and Peter (perhaps trying to combine Malalas and Procopius).[4]

One further independent source, the life of Grigor, a high-ranking Persian convert to Christianity, sheds a little light on these events. Grigor, originally called Pirangushnasp according to the hagiography, was a member of the noble Mihran house. Kavadh put him in charge of a large army in Albania and Iberia, where, it seems, he was converted around 520. After three years of imprisonment Grigor was restored to his previous command. When war broke out with the Romans in the area, he was captured in battle and taken to the emperor. He was given a high rank by Justin, but after some years returned to Persia, having

---

[4] *CP* 618, Joh. Nik. 90.52–53, Mal. 427, Theoph. A.M. 6020 (175). On Irenaeus, cf. *PLRE* II, Irenaeus 7; on Cerycus, Gilderich and Belisarius, *PLRE* III, 184 (rejecting Belisarius' participation in the Lazic campaign), Cerycus (placing the campaign in 527/8) and Gilderich. See below nn.20–21 on the commanders involved.

become disillusioned with what he saw as the heretical views of the emperor.[5]

Hitherto the general approach to these various accounts of the war in Lazica and Iberia has been to distinguish the events recorded in Procopius from the notices of the chroniclers.[6] It seems more probable, however, that they should be integrated, even if this means supposing that Procopius is extending his account into Justinian's reign; for it is standard Procopian practice to subordinate chronology to geography.[7] Since Procopius fails to report the details of the defection of the Lazi, of which he was clearly aware, it may reasonably be supposed that he has likewise omitted the names of commanders other than Peter and Irenaeus as well as any reference to their engagements.[8] With these points in mind, the following chronological sequence may be proposed:

1) Kavadh starts to impose Zoroastrianism on Iberia in the early 520s, perhaps following Tzath's shift of allegiance in 521/2. Around the same time Grigor announces his conversion to Christianity and is imprisoned. A few years later the negotiations for the adoption of Khusro take place, closely followed by Gourgenes' appeal to Justin. In view of the number of developments which occurred between the appeal and the campaign of 528, an earlier date for the appeal, 524/5, is preferable to the more traditional c.526.[9]

---

[5]   Hoffmann, *Auszüge*, 78–81, where various dates are to be found (by the regnal year of Kavadh); on this life of Grigor (*BHO* 353), see J.M. Fiey, *DHGE* XXII (1987), 26–7. As a convert to the Nestorian church, Grigor will naturally have been dissatisfied with the views of the Chalcedonian Justin and Justinian.

[6]   So Stein II, 271, 283 and Kirchner, *Bemerkungen*, 9; Braund, *Georgia*, omits them entirely. Rubin, *ZI*, 266, does combine them. On the chronological problems here, cf. *CPW*, 109 n.337.

[7]   Cf. his excursus on southern Arabia, I.19–20, covering a long period. The structure of *Wars* I-VII, dealing with different fronts separately, operates in the same way. The annalistic historian Tacitus similarly felt obliged to treat together events which occurred in one region over several years, e.g. at *Annals* XII.40.

[8]   Proc. I.11.19 for Seoses' allusion to the defection of the Lazi (during the negotiations). Given that Proc. appears to omit precisely those matters which the chroniclers treat in detail, it may be suggested that he did so deliberately, conscious that his readers could read or hear of them elsewhere (such as in the first edition of Malalas, published early in Justinian's reign, cf. Croke, 'Malalas', 17–19).

[9]   For the 526 dating, see Braund, *Georgia*, 282 and *PLRE* II, Gurgenes. Rubin, *ZI*, 263, tends towards an earlier date, since he thinks Peter was removed from his command in 526. Toumanoff prefers 522 for Gourgenes' appeal, review of Stein II, 483, but largely so as to justify the identification of Gourgenes with Vakhtang Gorgasal.
     Hoffmann, *Auszüge*, 79–80, on Grigor's conversion, dated to year 30 of Kavadh's reign; since Khusro is said to have acceded to the throne in year 40 (not of the peace,

2) Justin, while readily agreeing to support Gourgenes, declined to offer direct aid. Instead, Probus, a nephew of the Emperor Anastasius, was despatched to recruit barbarian forces as allies of the Iberians. The same tactic had been attempted by the Iberians themselves during their uprising in the 480s, when they took advantage of their control of the Dariel Pass.[10] Probus' mission was only partly successful. His opposition to the Council of Chalcedon, as well as the riches he brought with him, did much to further the cause of Christianity in this already Monophysite region, from the Crimea to the Caucasus. But he was unable to enlist any actual forces to help counter the Persians in Iberia, and so returned to Constantinople.[11]

There are several possible reasons for Justin's decision to try to help the Iberians by means of Hunnic rather than Roman forces. First, as has been seen, it had long been the custom of both powers to engage the assistance of the Huns to gain an advantage in the Transcaucasus. Thus only a few years after Probus' mission, a certain Queen Boa led an army of Sabir Huns to victory over another Hunnic force allied to the Persians.[12] Second, as later became evident, the deployment of Roman forces in the region was no easy task; since none were stationed in Lazica, soldiers had to be brought in from Armenia or further afield.[13]

---

as Hoffmann inserts, but clearly of Kavadh's reign), this falls in 521. Kavadh's reign opened in 488 (or perhaps 484), but Zamasp's interregnum must be considered in calculating his regnal years: cf. Göbl, *Sasanian Numismatics*, table X, recording 43 regnal years of Kavadh from his coinage.

[10] Lazar 172 [118] on Vakhtang's promise to gain the assistance of the Huns against the Persians.

[11] Rubin, *ZI*, 261–2, notes the advantages of using of an anti-Chalcedonian for this mission, cf. Engelhardt, *Mission und Politik*, 80–90 and Vasiliev, *Justin I*, 250–52. On the anti-Chalcedonian stance of the Iberians and Armenians, see Toumanoff, 'Christian Caucasia', 172: this had been made clear at the First Council of Dvin in 505/6. It was not until the early seventh century that the Persians tried to exploit the divisions between supporters and opponents of Chalcedon, cf. Whitby, *Maurice*, 214.

Probus may also have succeeded in laying the groundwork for the Crimean king Grod, who was baptised in Constantinople in 528: Proc. I.12.6 on his visit to Bosporus (Kertch), cf. Mal. 431–2, Joh. Nik. 90.66–9, Mich. Syr. IX.21 (192), *PLRE* III, Grod, with Engelhardt, *op. cit.*, 85–7 and Rubin, *ZI*, 267.

[12] Mal. 430–31, Joh. Nik. 90.61–5, Theoph. A.M. 6020 (175) with *PLRE* III, Boa, and Stein II, 283; her victory is placed in 528 by the chroniclers. Rubin, *ZI*, 268, noting the improbably large army said to have been destroyed by Boa, suggests that the chroniclers are here reflecting imperial propaganda designed to encourage the Romans and intimidate the Persians. Note also the case of Zilgibis in the early 520s (on which see above ch.6 pp.133–4).

[13] See above ch.6 p.133. There were no Roman forces stationed in Armenia Interior, the nearest province in the empire, see above ch.5 n.25. Proc. I.12.15–19 on the problems

Third, and perhaps most importantly, the use of Roman forces would have serious diplomatic repercussions: it would be perceived by the Persians as a clear sign that the Romans were seeking to establish direct control of Iberia. Neither Justin nor Justinian appears to have wished for a resumption of all-out war, and so they preferred to assist the Iberians without escalating the tension that had already arisen in Roman-Persian relations. The use of Huns was a convenient, indirect form of intervention, which allowed Justin to disclaim responsibility for any attacks they might make on Persian forces.[14]

Probus must have spent at least several months in the region, especially since his first port of call was the Crimea. The most likely date for his mission is 526, based partly on calculating back from the battles which took place in Lazica in 528; for, as will become clear, several other events occurred between his return to Constantinople and the campaign of 528.[15]

3) Both sides continued to try to secure control of Iberia. Kavadh appointed the general Boes to direct operations, while Justin, still refusing to commit Roman soldiers to the area, instead sent his former secretary Peter with some Hunnic forces. In this phase of the war, the Romans failed to prevent the Persians from taking over the whole kingdom, and many Iberian nobles were forced to flee to the Lazic frontier. These events may be assigned to the period 526/7: time must be allowed for Probus to return to Constantinople, and for Peter then to reach Iberia and withdraw to the Lazic frontier.[16] It is unclear whether

---

of Roman soldiers stationed in eastern Lazica (with Braund, 'Procopius on the economy of Lazica', 221–5 on likely exaggerations by Proc.). Cf. also the difficulties experienced by Roman forces trying to campaign against the Lazi in the 450s, Priscus frg.33.1 with Kazanski, 'Contribution', 491 n.8.

[14] On the reluctance of the emperors to resume hostilities, see sections iii and iv below.

[15] Zach. XII.7 (330) also mentions Probus' mission. *PLRE* II, Probus 8, places it in c.526 and identifies it with the account in Zach., Whitby and Whitby in 527, *CPW*, 107 n.337, Stein II, 270–71, in 525/6. Zach.'s chronology is at odds with Proc.'s, in that he says that Probus met prisoners in the region who had been captured during the Anastasian war, and had lived there for 34 years; since the war began in 502, this would mean 536 at the earliest for Probus' visit. Despite this, he and Proc. are almost certainly referring to the same event, as has generally been accepted. Both remark on the wealth brought by Probus: Zach. describes his distribution of it among the Christianised peoples, Proc. refers to his going ξὺν χρήμασι πολλοῖς (I.12.7).

[16] Proc. I.12.9–13 with *PLRE* II, Petrus 27, dating Peter's despatch to 526/7, cf. Stein II, 271 (526). Braund, *Georgia*, 282 n.52, rightly argues that Proc. is probably exaggerating in stating that all the members of the Iberian aristocracy fled: there were usually supporters of the Sasanians among the nobility. Boes should not be identified with the Bawi of Joshua (§59), who almost certainly died before the end of the

Gourgenes himself got to the imperial capital; his son Peranius, however, enjoyed a lengthy career in the Roman army. Their flight marked
the end of the monarchy in Iberia.[17]

4) The Iberian refugees proceeded to Constantinople, and Peter was
recalled from Lazica. Again, time must be allowed for Peter to make
his way to the capital, then to return to Lazica with more troops; according to Procopius he was accompanied by another commander,
Irenaeus. Since both these men are reported by the chroniclers to have
campaigned in Lazica in 528, it can safely be assumed that all are
referring to the same events. Peter will have been present in Constantinople in late 527, following his failure to defend Iberia during that
year, and back to retrieve the situation in the following year.[18]

When our various sources have been integrated in this way, it becomes
possible to expand Procopius' narrative both from the chroniclers and
from the life of Grigor.[19] In one engagement in 528 both sides suffered
heavy losses, an outcome which vexed the emperor and was attributed
to the divided Roman command; for three generals, Cerycus, Irenaeus
and Gilderich had been placed in joint charge of the forces.[20] In

---

Anastasian war (§95). He is described as a *varizes* by Proc. (I.12.10), on which rank
see Blau, 'Altarabische Sprachstudien', 313 and n.2 and Justi, *IN*, 340, Wahrič no.3.
M.-L. Chaumont in *EIr* IV, 318, Boes, curiously places his mission to Iberia in 523.

[17] Proc.'s assertion (II.28.20) that the departure of Gourgenes and his entourage ended
the Iberian monarchy is usually accepted, cf. Stein II, 294 and Braund, *Georgia*, 283;
but Toumanoff, review of Stein II, 487–8, is more sceptical.

[18] Proc. I.12.14. In light of Proc.'s failure to specify the name of the emperor and the
ἔπειτα δέ there, it is likely that the events narrated thereafter took place in the reign
of Justinian, rather than Justin. There is no doubt that the same Peter is referred to by
Proc. and the chroniclers, cf. *PLRE* II, Petrus 27; it is surprising, however, that while
according to Proc. he had been the *notarius* of Justin (II.15.8), *CP*, 618 and Theoph.
A.M. 6020 (174.25) refer to him as the former *notarius* of the emperor — who in 528
was Justinian. Unless he served both men in the same capacity, a certain blurring of
the two emperors seems to have occurred in the chroniclers. This Peter had been
captured by Justin a quarter of a century earlier in Arzanene, see above ch.5 n.72.

[19] Bury, *HLRE* II, 80 n.5 suggested identifying the chroniclers' account with Proc.
I.12.20–22 (the incursion by Belisarius and Sittas into Persarmenia). But, since their
expedition took place before Justinian became emperor (cf. 12.21), i.e. before April
527, his proposal should be rejected.

[20] Despite the statements of some chroniclers, Belisarius is highly unlikely to have taken
part in this campaign, since by 528 he had been appointed *dux Mesopotamiae*, cf.
PLRE III, 184, although it places the engagement in Justin's reign; also Hofmann,
Zur Kritik, 21–2 (placing it in 527). Whitby, *CPW*, 109 n.337 notes that *CP* was using
Mal. here, not very attentively; accordingly its mention of Belisarius, followed by
later chronicles, does not carry much weight. Substitution of a well-known name for a
less familiar one is a common mistake in ancient sources: the other commanders

consequence, Peter was then given overall authority, and withdrew the army from the area; he may even have succeeded in inflicting a defeat on the Persians.[21] But, in spite of Justin's promises to Gourgenes, Iberia had clearly been abandoned.[22] The Romans were content to retain control of Lazica, though part even of this kingdom slipped from their control. Peter was unable to hold the two forts, Sarapanis and Scanda, which lay on the border next to Iberia, despite replacing their usual Lazic garrison with Roman soldiers. Whether because of difficulties in supplying the new garrison, or because of Lazic reluctance to cooperate with the occupying force, the Romans were obliged to withdraw even before the Persians arrived.[23]

No further fighting took place in the Transcaucasus during this war. The Persians, having regained control of Iberia and taken possession of the two nearest Lazic forts, made no further attempt to wrest Lazica from the Romans. Although the two sides chose to conduct their main campaigns elsewhere, neither had lost interest in the region. During the negotiations which led to the Eternal Peace Justinian was initially prepared to concede the two forts to the Persians, but when he changed his mind and insisted that they be restored to Roman control, Khusro refused to continue the discussions. Only after ceding two Armenian strongholds to the Persians did Justinian succeed in securing the return

---

involved were probably Cerycus and Gilderich, as Mal. relates, cf. *PLRE* III, Cerycus and Gilderich, and see above n.4. It is unclear whether Peter was also present at this defeat.

[21] A victory is attributed to Peter by *CP*, 618 and Theoph. A.M. 6020 (174), but it is not reported by Mal. (427), who merely states that the Romans withdrew from the area (probably the border region between Lazica and Iberia, cf. Proc. I.12.19). It may be a patriotic invention of later chroniclers, although the life of Grigor (Hoffmann, *Auszüge*, 80) says that he was captured by the Romans after being defeated. Mal.'s reference elsewhere (441) to Persian forces in Persarmenia and Lazica in 528 under a Peroz, said to be a son of Kavadh, presumably refers to the same campaign; Justi, *IN*, 248, Peroč 21 and 335, Usan 7, identifies this Peroz with Kaoses, as does *PLRE* II, Caoses. Given Kaoses' links with the Mazdakites (see above ch.6 p.134 and n.41), such an identification is unconvincing.

[22] Proc. I.12.5–6 for Justin's guarantee that he would not yield Iberia to the Persians.

[23] Proc. lays great stress on the difficulties of supplying the forces in this (as he claims) barren country (I.12.13, 17, cf. VIII.13.5), although Sarapanis, situated on the river Phasis, can be supplied with ease. See Braund, *Georgia*, 287–8 on the forts and Proc.'s exaggerations (with *idem*, 'Procopius on the economy of Lazica', 221–5). Proc. I.12.15 and II.15.1–3 on the Lazi guarding their own territory and 15.6 on the friction which resulted from the deployment of Romans in Lazica, exacerbated (according to Proc.) by the insolent behaviour of Peter.

of the Lazic forts.[24] The importance of the Transcaucasus should not
then be underestimated: it was developments here that had led to the
resumption of war, even if most of the campaigning took place well to
the south. A little over a decade later, the region again played a significant role in fostering strife between the two sides: complaints about
the occupation of Lazica by Roman forces probably helped persuade
Khusro to break the Eternal Peace and invade the kingdom in 541.
Thenceforth the two powers were actively engaged in warfare there for
two decades.[25]

b) Skirmishes in Armenia

While Justin was seeking to bring aid to the embattled Iberians, two
young Roman commanders led a couple of bold plundering expeditions
into Persarmenia. The Roman leaders, Belisarius and Sittas, destined to
become Justinian's most prominent generals, enjoyed mixed fortunes.
They seized large quantities of booty in their first raid, but were
brought to battle and defeated in the second by the Armenian generals
Narses and Aratius. Once again the only source for these events is
Procopius, who fails to provide any explicit date; however a close
examination of his account yields some chronological clues.

First, since Procopius describes the two commanders as 'bodyguards
of the general Justinian, who later shared the empire with his uncle
Justin', it follows that the expeditions must have taken place before 1
April 527, when Justinian became co-emperor. Given the severity and
duration of the Armenian winter, it is unlikely that the raids could have
been in January–March 527, so they must have taken place in 526 at
the latest. Furthermore, if they are dated any earlier than 526, their
context becomes inexplicable: in 524/5 negotiations about the adoption
of Khusro were in progress, and Sittas was probably still occupied in

---

[24] Proc. I.22.3–18 with Braund, *Georgia*, 290–91. Roman interest in the region is
attested by the preface to *Nov*.28 (cited by Braund, *loc. cit.*), specifically alluding to
the two forts, and Proc. II.15.27–30, where the Lazi claim that the Persians will be
able to launch seaborne attacks on Constantinople from their kingdom. On Persian
interest, cf. Proc. II.28.24–30 and Braund, *op. cit.*, 273–5.

[25] Proc. II.15.12–30 on the defection of the Lazi in 541, cf. the complaints of the
Armenians at II.3.28–57. Cf. Braund, *Georgia*, 292 on tension in the Transcaucasus
triggering campaigns in Mesopotamia. As he notes, 'Transcaucasia could not be invaded easily without support among the Lazi', which helps to explain why no Persian
attacks took place between 529 and the Eternal Peace: the Lazi were still loyal to their
new masters. Braund, *op. cit.*, 295–311, on the conflict from 541.

pacifying Tzanica.[26] The target of the Roman raids in Persarmenia is
not specified by Procopius, nor is their motivation. Persian Armenia,
situated on the northern part of Rome's frontier with Persia, covered a
wide area. Procopius locates it next to Iberia, and places the Persarmenians on the other side of the mountains from the Lazi. The incursions were probably therefore linked with the struggle taking place
in Lazica and Iberia: Belisarius and Sittas were seeking to relieve the
Iberians by forcing the Persians to divert forces southwards.[27]

c) Tensions in Mesopotamia and Syria

Before 527 virtually no information is available on what was happening
in the southernmost sector of the frontier. Zachariah refers vaguely to
raids by the Lakhmid king al-Mundhir and to Roman attacks on
Arzanene and the area around Nisibis; the latter may have been a reaction to the former. That Arab raids had taken place is confirmed by
Malalas, who reports that Justin and Justinian in 527 reappointed Hypatius to his eastern command in order to 'protect the eastern regions
from Saracen incursions'. These incidents can most plausibly be dated
to late 525 or 526. They were followed by negotiations held between
April and June 527, which failed, however, to reach any conclusion.[28]

The Roman reaction to the breakdown of the talks was to launch an
immediate attack on Persian territory. The *dux* of Mesopotamia Libelarius led his men, presumably mainly, if not exclusively, *limitanei*,
towards Nisibis, but they were unable to capture the city and pressed on

---

[26] Proc. I.12.20–22, 12.21 for the quotation (tr. Dewing). See above ch.6.iii on the
negotiations, n.28 on Sittas' campaigns in Tzanica. On the conditions for campaigning in Armenia, see Whitby, *Maurice*, 202 and above ch.2 n.65. The raids are
dated by Hartmann, *RE* III (1899), 210, s.v. Belisarius, and Clinton, *Fasti* I, 745, to
526; by Stein II, 271–2, during the reign of Justin; by *PLRE* III, 182 and Sittas 1, in
527, as also by Howard-Johnston, 'Citharizon', 218.
    It may tentatively be suggested that Sittas, having completed the subjugation of the
Tzani, occupied the post of *dux* of Tzanica at the time of the raids. The seat of the *dux*
was Horonon: see Proc. *Aed.* III.6.15–18, where it is noted that Horonon bounded the
territory of the Tzani, the Roman empire, and Persarmenia. The post was probably
created immediately after the pacification of the tribe and the construction of the fort,
cf. Howard-Johnston, 'Citharizon', 220.

[27] On the position of Persarmenia, Proc. VIII.2.20, cf. I.10.1 (mention of the Lazi and
Iberians) and 15.20; Proc. *Aed.* III.3.3 puts Persarmenia to the north of Sophanene.
See also Adontz, *Armenia*, 168–79.

[28] Zach. VIII.5 (206) and see above ch.6 n.52 for the dating of the talks. On Hypatius'
re-appointment, Mal. 423.13–15 with *PLRE* II, Hypatius 6; Theoph.'s date (A.M.
6016 [171] = A.D. 523/4) results from his cavalier repositioning of Mal.'s entries, cf.
Mango–Scott, *Theophanes*, 261 nn.10–11. Translation from Jeffreys–Scott, 243.

to Thebetha, which they also failed to take. Suffering in the summer heat, the remnants of the army withdrew with difficulty to Dara, with the loss of much infantry.[29] Justinian, unimpressed by Libelarius' performance, ordered that he be replaced by his own bodyguard Belisarius; the newly appointed *dux* thereupon chose Procopius as his *assessor.*[30]

The Roman invasion of 527 may be interpreted in several ways. It has been viewed as part of a general resurgence in Roman ambitions in the east, an opening shot in a 'long delayed war of revenge'.[31] If so, the timing of the emperors is curious. Antioch was still recovering from an earthquake. Edessa, closer to the frontier, had just suffered a devastating flood. Furthermore, there were virtually no Roman forces stationed in Armenia, and rebuilding work was incomplete at many important border forts. Libelarius' unimpressive foray, far from giving the appearance of a well-thought-out first blow in a concerted Roman assault on the Persian empire, seems rather to be a hasty defensive reaction. If this interpretation is correct, the Romans, conscious of the weakness of the Mesopotamian frontier, and particularly of the fortress at Dara, were probably seeking to preempt any attempt to disrupt their building work. In similar fashion, just over half a century later, the Persians invaded Roman territory shortly before the expiry of the truce

---

[29] Proc. I.12.23, Zach. IX.1 (222); the text has Timus (Hamilton-Brooks, n.2), which must refer to Timostratus; Rubin, *ZI*, 486 n.758 on Tebeth/Thebetha. Stein II, 272 n.2, places the episode in summer 527 (before the end of June, noting Zach.'s references to the summer heat), followed by *PLRE* II, Libelarius. Earlier Stein preferred to place the events in 526, *RE* X (1919), 1326, Iustinus, where he argued that Belisarius succeeded Libelarius as *dux* in 526. Nagl, *RE* XIII (1927), 14, s.v. Libelarius, seems to suggest 529/30 for the attack on Nisibis.

In general, cf. the difficulties experienced by the *magister militum per Orientem* Marcian in early 573: he too failed to take either Nisibis or Thebetha, and was dismissed by the emperor (Justin II) soon afterwards, cf. Whitby, *Maurice*, 256–7 and *PLRE* III, Marcianus 7.

[30] Proc. I.12.24. Needless confusion has arisen over Libelarius' dismissal and Beliarius' appointment. As *PLRE* III, 183, notes, Proc. is here designating Belisarius as *dux* rather than *magister militum per Orientem*, and he is unlikely to have made a mistake as to his predecessor. Zach.'s mention of Timostratus in connection with the raid is merely by way of a chronological indicator; he had no part in the attack, and died soon afterwards. He is described by Zach. as a *dux stratelates*, which I take to refer to the post of *magister militum*, whether *vacans* or *per Orientem* (in which position he could have preceded Hypatius), cf. *PLRE* II, Timostratus. Shahîd, *BASIC* I, 174, emends Zach.'s text to deny him the position of *stratelates*, though he accepts that he might have held the rank of *magister militum vacans* (n.4). Zach. is mistaken in making Belisarius the successor of Timostratus, cf. Greatrex, 'Dukes'.

[31] Howard-Johnston, 'Citharizon', 220.

agreed in 575; they too were in a weak position, being aware that the emperor Tiberius had succeeded in raising numerous troops for the new campaigning season, while their own north-eastern frontier may have been coming under pressure from the Turks.[32]

Libelarius' invasion was accompanied by two equally unsuccessful ventures elsewhere on the frontier. To the south, an attempt was made by Thomas of Aphphadna (Apadna), a *silentiarius*, to construct a fort at Thannuris; according to Zachariah, Justin had been informed that the place would make a good base from which to repel Arab raids, and he will no doubt also have been aware that it had been the site of a Roman fort in the past. Little progress was made there, however, before the builders were driven off by marauding Arabs and Kadishaye from Singara and Thebetha, and their work demolished.[33] To the north, another fort-building project was undertaken in the region of Melabasa. The Melabasa mountains are situated downstream from Amida on the Tigris, on the north side of the Tur Abdin, threatening Arzanene from the southwest.[34] But the Persians were able to check this enterprise too through the intervention of Gadar the Kadisene, a trusted commander stationed in Arzanene.[35]

---

[32] See above ch.6 p.131 on the disasters which struck the east in the 520s. Rebuilding work was still going on at Dara at this time, cf. Whitby, 'Dara', 758. Whitby, *Maurice*, 268–9, on the Persian strike in 578 and the suggestion that it was prompted by weakness.

[33] Zach. IX.2 (222–3); Zach.'s text actually has 'during the lifetime of Justinian the king', but Brooks (surely rightly) argues that Justin must be meant. Cf. Vasiliev, *Justin I*, 275–6.
    On the utility of a fort at Thannuris, clearly eventually built by Justinian, cf. Proc. *Aed.* II.6.14–16, where it is also stated that it was designed to ward off Saracen intruders; see above ch.6 n.7 for the possibility that Anastasius also carried out work at Thannuris. *PLRE* II, Thomas 11, wrongly states that Thomas was sent to build a city at Apadna. On Thannuris, see also Kennedy-Riley, *Desert Frontier*, figs.68 and 69 and pp.118–21. This building attempt must have been in June-July 527, around the time of Libelarius' raid: see Zach. IX.2 (223).

[34] Zach. IX.5 (226–7). On the location of Melabasa, see Dillemann, *Mésopotamie*, 316–18. Honigmann, *Ostgrenze*, 17–18, places Biddon (his name for the projected Roman fort, see next note) on the left bank of the Tigris by Mt Melabaš. Whitby, *History*, map 4, places the Melabas mountains to the southeast of the Tur Abdin; but the intervention of Gadar, based in Arzanene, favours Dillemann's siting; see also Dillemann, *op. cit.*, 34, arguing (against Honigmann, *loc. cit.*) that the Melabasa mountains extended over both sides of the Tigris.

[35] Zach. IX.5 (226–7) explicitly dates the episode to 527, after the thwarting of the attempt to build a fort at Thannuris, i.e. August 527 (since the new indiction year began on 1 September). A textual uncertainty has led to this episode being frequently identified with Belisarius' attempt to fortify Minduos (Proc. I.13.1–8): Zach.'s text reads *bidhwin*, which, if correct, must be a place name. But Nöldeke long ago argued

ii) The opening of Justinian's reign (527–9)

a) The Lakhmid threat

Upon becoming sole emperor in August 527 Justinian soon took thought for the eastern provinces, and particularly for their vulnerability to Lakhmid raids. A new *comes Orientis*, Patricius, was appointed in October and instructed to rebuild the city of Palmyra in Phoenicia Libanensis. He was further ordered to transfer a *numerus* of regular soldiers (*comitatenses*) there, who were to assist the *limitanei* in defending the region. In addition, one of the *duces* of Phoenicia was to move his base forward from Emesa to Palmyra.[36] Even in late 527 Justinian evidently felt more concern about the raids of al-Mundhir than the possibility of a Persian invasion. His interest in Arab affairs proved quite justified.

In early 528 a quarrel arose between the *dux* of Palaestina Prima Diomedes and the Kindite chieftain al-Harith, which undid the alliance sealed during the reign of Anastasius. Little is known of the activities of this al-Harith (not to be confused with his Ghassanid homonym)

---

that the word should be emended to *badgun* ('therefore'), 'Zwei Völker', 159 n.1, accepted by Hamilton-Brooks, 226 n.5, though apparently subsequently rejected by Brooks in his Latin translation, p.66 and n.5 (cf. the Syriac text, p.96, where he has inserted a full stop after *bidhwin*). Since there are no good reasons for identifying Proc.'s campaign with Zach.'s (which took place while Belisarius was *dux*, though it is not stated that he commanded the mission), Nöldeke's emendation should be accepted. *PLRE* III, 183–4, however, accepts the reading *bidhwin*, and because it wishes to associate Belisarius with the operation, rejects Zach.'s dating; it places the operation in early 528, before the battle at Minduos/Thannuris (on which see below ii.c).

Cf. also Dillemann, *Mésopotamie*, 316–18 and fig.40, rightly arguing against any identification of Proc.'s Minduos and Zach.'s Melabasa (*contra* e.g. Rubin, *ZI*, 487 n.777). As he notes, operations at Melabasa would more likely have been undertaken by a commander from Martyropolis (or Amida) than Dara.

[36] Mal. 425–6, cf. Theoph. A.M. 6020 (174) with Mango–Scott, *Theophanes*, 268 n.3, Shahîd, *BASIC* I, 172–3 and Stein II, 289. On the archaeological remains of Justinian's work at Palmyra see Seyrig, 'Antiquités syriennes', 239–42 and Starcky–Gawlikowski, *Palmyre*, 70–71. Treadgold, *Army*, 97 n.35 is needlessly sceptical about the existence of two *duces* in Phoenicia Libanensis. Shahîd, *op. cit.*, 171–2, notes the report of *Chron. 1234*, 151 (cf. Mich. Syr. IX.20 [189] and Barhebraeus, 73) that Justinian visited the east during Justin's reign; but his concern for protecting the eastern provinces and Jerusalem is explicable without accepting this poorly attested episode.

Contra Howard-Johnston, 'Citharizon', 220, the strengthening of Palmyra was in no way threatening to the Persians, as is clear from Proc. *Aed.* II.11.10–12. The attempt to fortify Thannuris is another example of a measure aimed more against Lakhmids than Sasanians.

since the agreement of 502, but it appears that in the mid-520s he
seized control of the Lakhmid capital, Hira, for several years. He must
then have headed westwards, where he became the phylarch of Palaestina Prima. Having quarrelled with the local *dux*, al-Harith fled east
into the desert, where he was slain by al-Mundhir.[37] The emperor's
reaction was swift: he wrote personally to the *duces* of Phoenicia,
Arabia and Mesopotamia, as well as to several phylarchs, ordering
them to avenge al-Harith's death. The Roman force failed to locate al-
Mundhir, but exacted vengeance through the capture of his camp and
several Persian forts; according to Malalas the army returned trium-
phantly to Roman territory in April 528.[38] The sacking of four Persian
forts by a joint Roman-Ghassanid force will have further increased
tensions, but the emperor was clearly determined to respond vigorously
to the Lakhmids, presumably in the hope of deterring them from further
raids. If this was his object, he was to be sorely disappointed. In spring
529 al-Mundhir riposted with his most devastating and wide-ranging
raid to date, penetrating as far as the fringes of Antiochene territory,
having advanced by way of Emesa and Apamea. According to
Zachariah, four hundred virgins were seized by him en route and sacrificed to the goddess al-'Uzza. By the time a Roman force could be put
in the field to oppose him, he had withdrawn into the desert once
more.[39] Again Justinian sought to avenge the blow, and reinforcements,

---

[37] Mal. 434–5, Theoph. A.M. 6021 (179). Mal.'s reference to the 'inner *limes*' desig-
nates the inner recesses of the Arabian peninsula, cf. Mayerson, 'A note', 181–3 *contra* Bowersock, '*Limes Arabicus*', 228; see also the comments of Shahîd, *BASIC* I,
150–51 and Mango–Scott, *Theophanes*, 272 n.9 (on Theoph.'s use of the term).
Theoph. wrongly puts this episode after events of 529 (178), cf. Mango–Scott, *op.
cit.*, 273 n.17. Mal. reports that al-Mundhir led an army of 30,000 against al-Harith
(the Kindite), a remarkable figure, if accurate (it is accepted by Sartre, *Trois études*,
166). See above ch.5.ii on the alliance of 502.   On al-Harith's career, cf. Shahîd, *op.
cit.* 41, 46, 149, Olinder, *Kings of Kinda*, 64–6, Rothstein, *Die Dynastie*, 87–92
(noting that the Kindite interregnum may instead have occurred during the Anastasian
war). *PLRE* II, Arethas, oddly places the interregnum after al-Harith's flight in 528. It
has recently been suggested that Mal.'s Arethas here may not have been a Kindite:
see Whittow, 'Rome and the Jafnids', text to nn.13–14.

[38] Mal. 435 (the Bonn edition omits the date, cf. Bury 'Johannes Malalas', 229 and
Mango–Scott, *Theophanes* 273 n.17) and Theoph. A.M. 6021 (179) with *PLRE* III,
Arethas (the Ghassanid), Dionysius 1, Gnouphas, Ioannes 6, Naaman 1, Sebastianus
1. Shahîd, *BASIC* I, 70–76, draws attention to the emperor's unusual step in writing to
the commanders directly. He also considers the provenance of the phylarchs in detail,
and argues that the camp sacked by the Romans was not Hira, al-Mundhir's capital
(74); cf. also Sartre, *Trois études*, 166–8.

[39] Mal. 445, Theoph. A.M. 6021 (179), who is more detailed here and places the raid in
March 529, cf. Zach. VIII.5 (206–7), who mentions Apamea and Emesa. Joh. Nik.

including an infantry detachment from Phrygia known as the Lyco-cranitae, were sent to the east. They arrived in Antioch in April, and then set off for Lakhmid and Persian territory; but no more is heard of them and it is likely that they accomplished little. More pressing business soon arose for the Roman forces in the east.[40]

b) The reorganisation of Armenia

In 528 the emperor's sights turned also to the main eastern frontier. Perhaps on account of the escalation of hostilities in Lazica, he decided to implement significant changes to the Roman defences of Armenia. The vulnerability of both Armenia Interior and the former Armenian satrapies had been amply demonstrated by Kavadh's invasion of 502, and little had been done by Anastasius to remedy the situation.[41] The recent setback suffered by Belisarius and Sittas in Persarmenia may have further prompted Justinian to take steps to protect the region. The emperor's measures were wide-ranging. He sought to deal with the defence of the area as a whole, but did not neglect the fortification of particular bases. At the strategic level, he created a unified command

---

90.79–80 adds that al-Mundhir burnt Chalcis. Feissel, 'Remarques', 326–7, stresses that al-Mundhir probably only just reached the *territorium* of Antioch, Theoph.'s Litargon referring to Litarba, in the plain of Chalcis; hence Stein II, 284 and n.2 perhaps overstates the range of the raid. The reports of Mich. Syr. IX.16 (178) and Barhebraeus 73, partly following Zach. VIII.5, probably allude to both the 519/20 raid and that of 529, see above ch.6 n.30. Whitby, *Maurice*, 199 n.2, gives 527 as the date for the first raid, cf. Shahîd, *BASIC* I, 45–6, 79–80 and *PLRE* II, Alamundarus, who put Zach.'s raid in 527 and the chroniclers' in 529. I prefer (with Stein, *loc. cit.*) to identify Zach.'s raid with that of the chroniclers, and place it in 529; but Zach.'s report at VIII.5 (206–7) is hard to place chronologically, and may allude to more than one incursion (as Shahîd notes, *op. cit.*, 43).

    On the sacrifice of the virgins (perhaps at Emesa), see Shahîd, *op. cit.*, 732–3, who suggests that Zach. is here referring to a convent at Emisa (in Syria).

[40] Mal. 445, Theoph. A.M. 6021 (178) with Shahîd, *BASIC*, 79–80 and Rubin, *ZI*, 495–6 n.836 on the Lycocranitae. In *Nov.*24.1.37 (535), the Lycocranitae appear as highland robbers, not perhaps the most suitable choice of forces for desert-warfare (cf. the poor performance of the Lycaonians, neighbours of the Lycocranitae, at the battle of Callinicum, Proc. I.18.38–40). For a good map of the Pisidian and Phrygian highlands see Mitchell, *Anatolia* I.1, map 5 (270–71).

    Trombley, 'War and Society', II, notes building work in the territories of Antioch and Apamea (e.g. at Androna and il-Burdj) in the late 520s, probably occasioned by these raids.

[41] Howard-Johnston, 'Citharizon', 219, stresses that some work may have been started under Anastasius, but if so, it was brought to completion only under Justin and Justinian, cf. Whitby, 'Development', 727. However Anastasius had certainly carried out some improvements at Theodosiopolis and Melitene, see above ch.6 n.8.

for the whole eastern frontier extending from the former satrapies to Lazica; not only did this indicate the importance attached to this front by the emperor, but it also gave a freer hand to the *magister militum per Orientem* to counter the Persians in the principal field of conflict, Mesopotamia. Sittas, newly appointed *magister militum per Armeniam et Pontum Polemoniacum et gentes*, was put in charge of all the *duces* who held commands in the region. The Armenians were compensated for the loss of their remaining autonomy by the recruitment of staff and soldiers from their midst, and, to stiffen the forces newly enlisted and the *limitanei* of the *duces*, four *numeri* were transferred to the new command from the *magister militum per Orientem*. Whereas in 502 the only Roman forces available to defend Armenia had been those under the *dux Armeniae* at Melitene, by 529 there were six *duces* (at Tzanzakon, Horonon, Artaleson, Citharizon, Martyropolis and Melitene) and the *magister militum* (based at Theodosiopolis).[42]

The bases of these various commanders were also attended to by the emperor. Fortifications were completed or strengthened along the frontier, for instance at Citharizon and Theodosiopolis. Although this work is impossible to date either from archaeological evidence or from Procopius' *De Aedificiis*, Malalas does report rebuilding work at Martyropolis in 528. Hence it may reasonably be supposed that work elsewhere along the frontier in Armenia was undertaken around the same time.[43]

---

[42] Mal. 429–30 with *C.J.* I.29.5 (undated) and Proc. *Aed.* III.2.1, 3.7–8, 3.14, 5.12, 6.17, 6.26, discussed in detail by Adontz, *Armenia*, 107–13; cf. Stein II, 290–91 and 289 n.5 on the date, and Whitby, 'Development', 727–8. Howard-Johnston, 'Citharizon', 219–20 with 227 nn.23–4, (rightly) argues that the ducates were created piecemeal rather than all being established at the same time as the new post of *magister militum*; the connection he draws between the reorganisation and the defeat of the Roman armies in Lazica in 528 is less convincing, since the changes must have been planned before the campaign of 528. In any case the new commander had little to do with Lazica initially. At least 10,000 troops were stationed in the region, cf. Adontz, *op. cit.*, 110–11 for some estimates; note also the transfer of Bulgar prisoners, enrolled in *numeri*, to Lazica and Armenia in 529, reported only in Theoph. A.M. 6032 (219), cf. Mal. 451 (giving the date).

 The satraps and the *comes Armeniae* were abolished by this reform. Further modifications to the government of the region were to follow in 536: see Adontz, *op. cit.*, ch.7.

[43] Mal. 427 on Martyropolis, renamed Justinianoupolis by the emperor (although Stein II, 290 n.1, argues that Martyropolis has been confused with Bazanis here). See also Adontz, *Armenia*, 114, Whitby, 'Martyropolis', 179–82, and Howard-Johnston, 'Citharizon', 220.

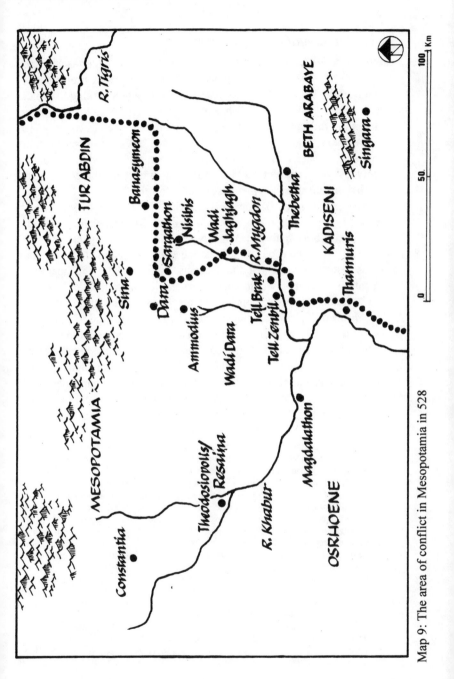

Map 9: The area of conflict in Mesopotamia in 528

c) Mesopotamia and Osrhoene

Further south, a major fort-building expedition was undertaken by the new *dux* of Mesopotamia, Belisarius. The location of the projected fort is uncertain, but clearly the Romans were once again seeking to protect their territory by the establishment of bases very close to the border. Given the difficulty of erecting such forts in the face of active Persian intervention, Justinian may not have expected Belisarius to succeed; his campaign would, however, like the unsuccessful undertakings of the previous year, prevent the Persians from hindering the work being carried out at Dara and other bases on the frontier.[44]

The campaign of Belisarius is described by several sources, which do not agree on all points. Procopius reports that Justinian ordered the *dux* to construct a fort at Minduos, 'which is over against the very boundary of Persia, on the left as one goes to Nisibis.' The builders made good progress, but the Persians, concerned by the operation, threatened that they would soon intervene if the Romans did not halt construction. Justinian, apprised of the Persian warning, ordered the two *duces* of Phoenicia, Coutzes and Bouzes, to bring aid to Belisarius. A battle ensued at the construction site, in which the Romans were defeated; thus the Persians gained control of the site and razed it to the ground.[45] Zachariah, on the other hand, tells of a campaign 'into the desert of Thannuris'. Here Belisarius and his fellow commanders were tricked by a Persian ruse — the use of concealed trenches — and heavily defeated.[46] Malalas describes an invasion of Mesopotamia by a

---

[44] See above n.43 for the work going on at Martyropolis; n.32 for that at Dara. The construction of Dara in the first place had been facilitated by Kavadh's absence from the vicinity and the presence of a large Roman army, see above ch.6.i; even so, Anastasius had also made payments to Kavadh to ensure that operations were not interrupted. The rebuilding work carried out at Circesium (in Osrhoene) and the installation of a *dux* probably took place later, in the 540s, see below ch.9 n.11. On the considerable effort required to construct a new fort, see Whitby, *Maurice*, 212–13 and *Strategikon* X.4 (346–50). Whitby notes that 'the whole processs ... could only be contemplated if the side organizing the construction had a decisive superiority in the field and could prevent enemy harassment'. This was not true in 527 or 528, which strengthens the suspicion that the campaigns were diversionary tactics.

[45] I.13.1–8; quotation from 13.2, ἐν ἀριστερᾷ ἐς Νίσιβιν ἰόντι. Although the texts of Veh, Haury-Wirth and Dewing *ad loc.* all read Μίνδουος, the Bonn edition reads Μίνδουος, which Dillemann preferred (*Mésopotamie*, 316 n.2); other scholars have likewise insisted on using the form Mindon, cf. e.g. Whitby, *Maurice*, 210, 'Dara' 758. Proc. may be wrong in describing Coutzes as a *dux* of Phoenicia: he seems to have been replaced by Proclianus by the time of the battle, see below n.47.

[46] Zach. IX.2 (223–4). Belisarius' fellow commanders are named as Coutzes, Basil, Vincent and Atafar (to be identified with Mal.'s Tapharas and with Jabala, father of

force of 30,000 under the command of 'a Meran' and Xerxes; the latter
is referred to as a son of Kavadh, while the former is clearly a misunderstanding of the Persian name Mihran. The incursion took place
around the time that Xerxes' elder brother Peroz is said to have been
operating in Lazica and Persarmenia. Against the invaders a Roman
force set out under Coutzes, the former *dux* at Damascus according to
Malalas; with him were Sebastian, some Isaurians, Proclianus, *dux* of
Phoenicia, the *comes* Basil, Belisarius and the phylarch Tapharas. In
the battle Tapharas and Proclianus were killed, and Sebastian and Basil
captured; Coutzes fell into Persian hands after being wounded, while
Belisarius managed to escape. The Persians too suffered heavy losses,
and soon returned to their own territory.[47]

While the campaign can confidently be dated to 528, the site of
Belisarius' defeat is still disputed.[48] Malalas merely refers generally to
Mesopotamia, but Zachariah specifies that the battle was fought in the
vicinity of Thannuris; the operation follows a reference to possible
Persian fortification work there. Procopius, as has been seen, locates
the battle site at Minduos, apparently to the north of Nisibis. Since
Thannuris lies some 80 km south of Nisibis, there seems to be a significant discrepancy between our two most detailed sources. Several
solutions have been proposed. Although none are entirely satisfactory,
some at least can be rejected as implausible.

---

al-Harith, according to Shahîd, *BASIC* I, 63–6 with his note on Zach.'s text at 174–5;
but see now Whittow, 'Rome and the Jafnids', text to nn.15–17, for doubts on this
identification). See also *PLRE* III, Buzes (inferring that he was the *dux* at Palmyra at
this point), Cutzes (former *dux* at Damascus, see above n.45, below n.47), Basilius 2,
Tapharas, Vincentius. Rance, *Tactics*, 195–6, suggests that Zach. may be referring to
trenches surrounding the Persian camp.

[47] Mal. 441–2. Cf. *PLRE* III, Proclianus (accepting him as *dux*, although under Cutzes it
asserts that Bouzes and Coutzes were the *duces* of Phoenicia Libanensis), Sebastianus
1 (suggesting that he may have been the *tribunus* of a unit of Isaurians). Malalas'
figure of 30,000 is suspiciously large; see below ch.8 n.20 on his inflation of the size
of the Persian army at Dara in 530. For the mistaking of the Persian name Mihran for
an office, see Christensen, *L'Iran*, 105 n.3; the general is presumably the same as
Proc.'s Peroz (described as a *mirranes*), I.13.16, cf. *PLRE* III, Perozes. A son of
Kavadh by the name of Xerxes is unattested elsewhere: Nöldeke, *Tabari*, 147 n.1, is
sceptical of Mal.'s accuracy on this point.

[48] Mal. dates the episode to 528, when the struggle for control of Lazica was at its
height; it is also clear from the position of the entry that 528 must be the correct date.
Cf. Sotiriadis, 'Zur Kritik', 115, placing the campaign in spring or summer 528, accepted by Bury, *HLRE* II, 81. Shahîd, *BASIC* I, 76 dates the operation to summer 528,
following the expedition against al-Mundhir (see above ii.a); this is preferable to
PLRE III's 'early 528', Tapharas and cf. 184. Evans, *Justinian*, 116, inexplicably
places the campaign in 527.

One option is to discount the testimony of Zachariah. Minduos is usually placed to the northeast of Dara, and the attempt to fortify it regarded as a Roman attempt to encircle Nisibis; hence the determination of the Persians to frustrate the operation. Dillemann suggested that the name Minduos is linked to the river Mygdon, and therefore located the projected base between the forts at Sina and Banasymeon, mentioned in the *De Aedificiis*. The great drawback with this view is that it involves dismissing Zachariah's reference to Thannuris altogether.[49] Alternatively, it is possible that Procopius' Minduos is a reference to Sargathon, a fortress situated between Dara and Nisibis and described by Dillemann as a Persian fortification in the Byzantine style. The site is nevertheless some distance from Thannuris and, given that Belisarius did not succeed in constructing anything at Minduos, the remains found there add no weight to the identification.[50] A final option is to reappraise Procopius' reference to Nisibis: it could be suggested that 'on the left as one goes to Nisibis' does not specify the route from Dara. For if Nisibis were approached from the south, from around the area of Thannuris, then the two authors' accounts could perhaps be reconciled, and Minduos situated where the Mygdon (thus accepting Dillemann's link of Minduos and Mygdon) bends to the west near Tell Brak, having flowed south from Nisibis until this point. One point in favour of this hypothesis is the provenance of the Roman commanders involved in the battle: Coutzes and Bouzes came from Phoenicia Libanensis, whereas if Minduos were to the north of Dara, one might expect reinforcements from the region of Amida and Martyropolis. However this must remain a tentative proposal, for the most natural reading of Procopius would be to consider the route to Nisibis as originating in Dara.[51]

---

[49] See fig.40 in Dillemann, *Mésopotamie*, 317; Proc. *Aed.* II.4.14 for Sina and Banasymeon. Whitby, *Maurice*, map 12, 255, appears to place 'Mindon' (see above n.45) much further to the northeast of Nisibis than Dillemann; in 'Dara', 758, he places it in the Tur Abdin. Cf. also Sinclair, *Eastern Turkey*, III, 340–41, for a map of the area and some other potential sites between Dara and Nisibis (e.g. Deir Kürk).

[50] de' Maffei, 'Fortificazioni', 237–41, for the argument that Minduos can be identified with Sargathon, cf. Dillemann, *Mésopotamie*, 228, for his description — which clearly could be applied to a Roman fort.

[51] Dillemann, *Mésopotamie*, 174 and fig.31, 227, notes archaeological finds at Tell Brak, which he identifies with Sihinnus, found on itineraries. Cf. Kennedy–Riley, *Desert Frontier*, 187–9, who report Poidebard's belief (*Trace*, 144) that the remains were Justinianic. There was another fort nearby at Tell Zenbil, Kennedy–Riley, *op. cit.*, 155–6. An excellent map of this region is to be found in van Liere and Lauffray, 'Nouvelle prospection'. *PLRE* III, Buzes, places the battle by Thannuris, rather than

The site of Minduos eludes final resolution. Of the three proposals discussed, the third is perhaps the most satisfactory, since it comes closest to reconciling Zachariah and Procopius. Wherever Belisarius' campaign took place, much work had been completed on fortifications elsewhere in 528. But the emperor, aware that a Persian invasion of Mesopotamia was increasingly likely, realised that his border fortresses remained vulnerable to Persian attack, which would leave the provinces beyond exposed to a plundering expedition. To ensure that the Persians could not penetrate far into Roman territory, even if frontier bases were captured, several senators were sent out from Constantinople to the east. They were instructed to garrison cities there, such as Amida, Edessa, and Constantia, which had come under attack during the Anastasian war.[52] Their forces were supplemented by regular units probably drawn from the armies of the *magistri militum praesentales* and the Balkans, placed under the command of Hypatius' brother Pompey.[53]

It was not the presence of these reinforcements, however, that brought temporary peace to the frontier late in 528. An unusually severe winter, which heightened the suffering of the victims of the earthquake at Antioch in November, persuaded the two sides to suspend hostilities.[54]

Minduos, as does Shahîd, *BASIC* I, 76. The ruins at Tell Brak and Tell Zenbil cannot of course be connected with Belisarius' failed campaign, but they do identify these places as favoured sites for forts.

[52] Mal. 442.8–13. Sura and Beroea also received garrisons. The Senate was in Justinian's reign a very restricted body, and so the senators sent out (some of them described as patricians) were among the highest ranking people in the capital, cf. *PLRE* II, Alexander 19 (with *PLRE* III, Plato 1 and Theodorus 4) and Jones, *LRE*, 529. *PLRE* suggests that they may have been made *magistri militum (vacantes)* for their mission. Given the relatively small number of senators, it is possible that both Plato and Theodore are the ex-city prefects of that name, *PLRE* II, Plato 3 (? = *PLRE* III, Plato 3) and Theodorus *qui et* Teganistes 52: city prefects might be expected to have men upon whom they could call in cases of need. Evidently, despite Leo's legislation on the subject, certain senators possessed forces of their own, presumably *bucellarii* of some kind, cf. Whitby, 'Recruitment', 117, noting mention of such forces again during the Nika riot.

[53] Mal. 442.13–16, specifying that Illyrians, Scythians, Isaurians and Thracians served in Pompey's force. See also *PLRE* II, Pompeius.

[54] Mal. 442.16–17 on the truce, 442–3 on the earthquake; cf. Ps. Dion. II, 73, on the snow and 'harshness of the winter frost' at Antioch (tr. Witakowski, *Chronicle*, 68). Stein II, 420, on the date of the earthquake (29 November 528).

iii) Negotiations for peace (529)

However aggressively the Romans may have acted in 528, they can have had little appetite for a resumption of warfare the following spring. To take only the eastern provinces, Antioch lay in ruins, Laodicea was struck by an earthquake on 2 January, while later in the year Amasea and Myra, in Helenopontus and Lycia respectively, both suffered the same fate.[55] Then in March came the raid of al-Mundhir, further terrorising the citizens of Oriens. Under such circumstances Justinian's decision to seek a conclusion to hostilities is quite comprehensible. It will have been only a little after al-Mundhir's raid that the emperor despatched his *magister officiorum* Hermogenes to the Persian court, for on 12 May he arrived in Antioch.[56] Around the same time two further important measures for the defence of the east were implemented. The Ghassanid chief al-Harith, the son of Jabala, was granted 'the dignity of king' (ἀξίωμα βασιλέως): he became, in effect, a supreme phylarch, exercising control over not only his own phylarchate in Arabia, but also those of other phylarchs in other provinces. By this measure the emperor hoped to make the Ghassanid ruler the equal of his Lakhmid foe, since hitherto the various Roman phylarchs had found difficulty in coordinating their responses to al-Mundhir's raids. In addition, the ineffectual *magister militum per Orientem* Hypatius was dismissed, having utterly failed to deter Lakhmid attacks. He was replaced by Belisarius, who was ordered to prepare for war against the Persians.[57] Evidently Justinian was far from confident of the success of Hermogenes' mission — rightly so, as it turned out.

Hermogenes arrived at Kavadh's court in July 529, bearing gifts for the king, and formally announced to him the accession of Justinian. The delay in making the announcement was unfortunate. Even as Hermogenes was making his way to Kavadh a bloody insurrection was breaking out in Palestine; it had begun in the spring as a riot in Scythopolis

[55] Stein II, 420, assembles the evidence.
[56] Mal. 445.17–19, Theoph. A.M. 6021 (178.19–22), the latter providing the date of 12 May. Cf. Scott, 'Diplomacy', 160.
[57] On al-Harith's elevation, see the exhaustive discussion of Shahîd, *BASIC* I, 95–124, which supersedes his earlier articles 'The Patriciate', 'Arethas' and 'Procopius and Arethas'; also Sartre, *Trois études*, 170–72. Shahîd, *op. cit.*, 108–9, dates it to late 529, although at 124, discussing the Usays inscription, he appears to place it earlier in the year; cf. *PLRE* III, Arethas (dating it to 528/9).

On Hypatius' dismissal and Belisarius' appointment, Mal. 445.13–17, Theoph. A.M. 6021 (178.18–19), placing Belisarius' appointment in April 529, with *PLRE* III, 184. Lee, *Information*, 115, strangely puts it in 530.

in which Samaritans were involved in fighting with Jews and
Christians. The origins of the rebellion probably lay in Justinian's
recent intolerant legislation against non-Christians. Samaritan restive-
ness may have received further encouragement from the success of al-
Mundhir's raid earlier in 529. The riot in Scythopolis escalated into a
major uprising when it became clear that Justinian intended to take
measures against the Samaritans; they proceeded to inflict much
damage on the countryside, and their leader, Julian, seized control of
Neapolis. An imperial force was mustered by the *dux* of Palestine
Theodore the snub-nosed (Simus), comprising both Romans and Ghassanids. Julian abandoned Neapolis, but nonetheless his forces were
swiftly brought to battle and heavily defeated. News of Julian's actions
in Neapolis reached the emperor at the same time as his severed head.[58]

By July it is highly likely that Kavadh had been told of the revolt.
Nor will the earthquake at Antioch have escaped his notice: al-Mundhir
had been able to see its impact at first hand earlier that year.[59] Furthermore, by the time that Hermogenes reached the Persian court, Kavadh's
position as king was probably more secure than it had been for a long
time, since (according to Malalas) the powerful Mazdakite sect had
finally been suppressed in 528/9.[60] It is not surprising therefore that the

---

[58] Mal. 445–7 with frg.44, *CP* 619–20 (with *CPW* 111 n.343); also Theoph. A.M. 6021
(178) and Cyr. Scyth. *V. Sabae*, 171–4 (dating the start of the revolt to April 529); on
the other chronicle sources see Jeffreys-Scott, *Malalas*, 260. Zach. IX.8 (231–2)
attributes the revolt to Samaritan knowledge of Persian attacks on Roman territory,
cf. Rabello, *Giustiniano*, 417. Justinian's legislation: *C.J.* I.5.12, dated to 527 (with
Vasiliev, *Justin I*, 244, 247). For a detailed account of the uprising see Winkler, 'Die
Samariter', 435–457, Crown, 'The Samaritans', 132–3, Holum, 'Caesarea', 68–9;
also Shahîd, *BASIC* I, 82–3, 89–91 and *PLRE* III, Theodorus 5, Ioannes 8, *PLRE* II,
Irenaeus 7. The danger posed by a Samaritan revolt is illustrated by the fact that in
555 the *magister militum per Orientem* took the field against them in person, cf. Mal.
487 and *PLRE* III, Amantius 2.

It is uncertain which Ghassanid chief, al-Harith or his brother Abu Karib, took part
in the suppression of the Samaritans; Shahîd, *op. cit.*, 83–6, favours al-Harith but
accepts that Abu Karib may have been involved. Paret, 'Note', 259–60 and Sartre,
Trois études, 168–70 note that the two phylarchs mentioned by Malalas need not be
the same person. See also now Sartre, 'Deux phylarques', 152.

[59] Theoph. A.M. 6021 (179) dates the rejection of Hermogenes' overtures to 529, but
his chronology here is clearly awry: he places the battle of Dara in this year and puts
Khusro rather than Kavadh on the Persian throne. As Mango–Scott, *Theophanes*, 273
n.14, argue, he has simply reordered Mal.'s material (455–6). Cf. also *PLRE* III,
Hermogenes 1 and Winkler, 'Die Samariter', 447–8. On Persian knowledge (and ex-
ploitation) of Roman difficulties, see Lee, *Information*, 109–112 (esp.110).

[60] Mal. 444 (and Theoph. A.M. 6016 [169–70]) with Mango–Scott, *Theophanes*, 261
n.5 and Nöldeke, *Tabari*, 465–6 (rejecting Theoph.'s placing of the episode in 523/4);

letter which Kavadh gave Hermogenes to bear to Justinian was uncompromising:

> Koades, Emperor of Emperors, of the rising sun, to Flavius Justinian Caesar, of the setting moon. We have found it written in our ancient records that we are brothers of one another and that if one of us should stand in need of men or money, the other should provide them. From that time to the present we have remained constant in this. Whenever nations have risen against us, against some we have been compelled to fight, whilst others we have persuaded by gifts of money to submit to us, so it is clear that everything in our treasury has been spent. We informed the emperors Anastasius and Justin of this, but we achieved nothing. Thus we have been compelled to mobilize for war, and having become neighbours of Roman territory we have been compelled to destroy the peoples in between on the pretext of their disobedience, even though they had done nothing wrong. But, as pious Christians, spare lives and bodies and give us some of your gold. If you do not do this, prepare yourselves for war. For this you have a whole year's notice, so that we should not be thought to have stolen our victory or to have won the war by trickery.[61]

As in 502 (and 518/19), Kavadh's prime concern is his still depleted treasury. He makes no mention of the various clashes in Mesopotamia, nor does he complain of Roman fortifications at Dara or elsewhere. He alludes to the fighting in the Transcaucasus, clearly the region where the Persians 'had become neighbours of Roman territory', and implicitly blames the Romans for the sufferings of the Iberians. Since the Romans were almost certainly aware of the state of Persian mobilisation, Kavadh was hardly revealing any secrets by giving advance notice of an invasion, should the Romans refuse to make a payment; his line of attack, however, would be much harder to ascertain.[62] Clearly Roman activity on the frontier had not provoked the Persians to war: a contribution of gold would suffice to avert any Persian attack. Kavadh's hope that Justinian would pay up, unlike his predecessors,

---

see above ch.6 n.41. Vasiliev, *Justin I*, 256 n.3, rightly connected the destruction of the Mazdakites with a revival in Persian military activity, although he dated this change to 523.

[61] Mal. 449–50, tr. Jeffreys-Scott, *Malalas*, 263–4. It is generally accepted that Mal. reflects the text of Kavadh's letter fairly accurately, cf. e.g. Scott, 'Diplomacy', 160 (noting a stylistic difference from the rest of Mal.) and (more generally) Lee, *Information*, 37–8.

[62] See above ch.5.ii on Kavadh's request in 502 and ch.6.iii on that of 518/19. Lee, *Information*, 113, notes how Justinian was aware in the preceding year of Khusro's plans for an invasion in 540; as he argues, it was almost impossible for either power to conceal preparations for a major campaign, *ibid.* 118–20.

was not unreasonable. For although the emperor refused Kavadh's request in 529, only three years later he did consent to make a substantial payment to the Persian treasury.[63]

Late in 529 Justinian will have received Kavadh's reply. The Persian demand for money, while unsurprising, can hardly have been welcome. Natural disasters and imperial liberality had by now taken their toll on the Roman treasury, previously so well provided for.[64] Prevarication seems to have been the preferred response. In the spring Hermogenes set off once more, accompanied this time by Rufinus, an ambassador well chosen to mollify the Persian king. By March they were in Antioch.[65] From there they proceeded to Dara, where they signalled their presence to Kavadh, expecting to be summoned for an audience. But by this point, June 530, the king had mustered his forces and was determined not to let the opportunity slip; it will also have been clear to him that the ambassadors had returned to the front empty-handed. The stage was set for a full-scale confrontation.[66]

iv) Conclusion

Although it is frequently assumed that full-scale war broke out anew between the two powers in 527, it has become clear that no major operation was carried out before 530 (with the possible exception of the fighting in Lazica in 528).[67] The absence in our sources of any large

---

[63] It seems probable that Kavadh was sincere in implying that he would not invade if the Romans paid him the gold, given that discussions were still going on in 530 (Proc. I.13.11). The continuation of negotiations after the battles of Dara and Satala also implies a desire for peace.

[64] Stein II, 422, on Justinian's expenses, e.g. his consular largesse in 528 (presumably more than the 4000 lbs. of gold he spent as consul in 521, cf. Marc. com. a.521) and building work in Constantinople and elsewhere. 200 lbs. of gold was contributed towards the rebuilding of Antioch, Seleucia and Laodicea, and their taxes remitted for three years (Mal. 444). See also Stein II, 306–7, on the 10,000 solidi ransom paid in 528 to the Bulgars for the Roman general Constantiolus. Joh. Lyd. de Mag. III.54 (145.1–4) emphasises the general shortage of money.

[65] Mal. 452 and Theoph. A.M. 6022 (180) (more detailed) with Scott, 'Diplomacy', 161. On Rufinus' connections with Kavadh, see above ch.6 n.45.

[66] Mal. 452 and Theoph. A.M. 6022 (180). Hermogenes and Rufinus would have made it known to the king if they had brought any moneys with them, cf. Rufinus' embassies in 502 (Josh. Styl. §50) and 532 (Proc. I.22.10–14). As has been noted (ch.3.ii), the Persian army was difficult to mobilise; hence Kavadh will have been unwilling to let the campaigning season pass by without making use of it, if the Romans proved unforthcoming.

[67] Solari, 'La politica', 359, places the resumption of war as early as 525; Howard-Johnston, 'Citharizon', 218, dates it to 527, Stein II, 271, to 526.

Roman force, not to mention the *magister militum per Orientem* Hypatius, is surely significant; the hasty despatch of Pompey and the senators in 528 further implies that no attempt had yet been made to assemble the field army of the east.[68] The various fort-building campaigns and raids which took place between 526 and 529 were minor affairs, and had no conclusive result. They were therefore no obstacle to the resumption of negotiations in 529, which only foundered (temporarily) when no money was forthcoming from the Romans.[69]

Neither power had anything to gain from a resumption of hostilities. The Roman empire had been hit by a succession of natural disasters, notably the flood at Edessa in 525, followed by the earthquakes at Antioch in 526 and 528; Kavadh, meanwhile, was engaged in suppressing the Mazdakites in his kingdom and trying to maintain his grip on the Transcaucasus.[70] A costly large-scale campaign, which would probably lead to corresponding retaliation by the enemy, was therefore a most unattractive prospect. Hence, despite Justinian's building activity and administrative changes in the east, there is little sign of a Persian reaction until 530. By then Kavadh was in a stronger position, having assembled a large force near the Mesopotamian frontier with a second army ready in Persarmenia.[71] Yet he now faced a Roman empire more capable of defending itself than at any point hitherto: not only had new forts been built and old ones repaired (even if everything had not been completed by 530), but the army of the *magister militum per Orientem* was stationed outside Dara, ready to contest any invasion of Roman territory. The king had therefore been content to demand money from the emperor, hoping to spare himself a bloody confrontation, which might bring scant gain even in the event of victory.[72] Justinian, on the other hand, had little gold to spare; having spent much effort and money on strengthening the frontier defences, and with his field army positioned outside Dara, he was naturally reluctant to yield to Kavadh's demands.

---

[68]   It was probably only with Belisarius' appointment to succeed Hypatius in 529 that the field army was mustered and moved to Dara.

[69]   Kavadh's subsequent insistence on the danger posed by the construction of Minduos (Proc. I.16.7) comes during a later phase of the negotiations in a clearly rhetorical context.

[70]   See above nn.55 and 60.

[71]   Note, however, that negotiations were still underway in 530, and that Belisarius was surprised to hear that Kavadh's army was moving against him (Proc. I.13.12).

[72]   Mal. 450.10–12 for Kavadh's exhortation to the Romans, as Christians, to spare their own lives and hand over the money he requested.

Thus full-scale war broke out again in 530, the Persians once more invading Roman territory to back up their demands for Roman payments. But this time Kavadh's forces were to make little progress in their assault; and in August, only two months after the battle of Dara, Rufinus and a fellow ambassador, Alexander, were invited to resume negotiations.[73]

---

[73]   Mal. 453 and Theoph. A.M. 6022 (181); see below ch.8.iv.

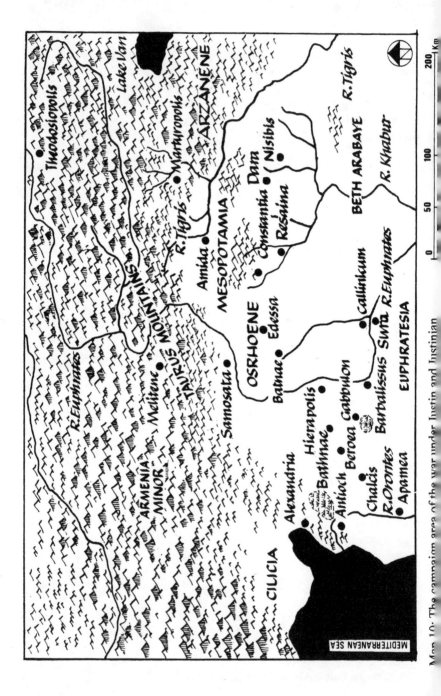

Map 10: The campaign area of the war under Justin and Justinian

Map 11: The eastern provinces of
the empire, A.D. 529

167

VIII
The campaigns of 530

Fulfilling his threat of the previous year, Kavadh launched his attack on Roman territory in the summer of 530. Having largely given up the advantage of surprise, so often exploited by the Persians, the king tried to compensate for it by two means. First, he divided his forces and attacked on two fronts: one army was directed against the troublesome fortress at Dara, while the other was to invade Roman Armenia, hitherto such an easy target for Persian invasions. Second, his armies attacked before the promised year's grace had expired. Hermogenes had arrived at Kavadh's court in July 529. This, then, was the earliest date at which the king's promise could have been made. But Persian forces advanced on Dara in June 530. The timing of the strike against Dara therefore took Belisarius and the Roman ambassadors by surprise, since they believed that they still had at least one month before Kavadh would invade.[1]

i) Sources

For the events of 530 we are almost exclusively reliant on Procopius. As an eye-witness, he gives a detailed account of the battle of Dara which is of the highest value; concerning the campaign in Armenia he appears to be well informed, but offers fewer details. The chroniclers add nothing of substance to Procopius, save Theophanes, who dates the battle of Dara to June of the eighth indiction (530). Zachariah, the only other independent source of any worth, confirms the important role played by the Heruls in the battle; and, like Procopius, he emphasises the confidence of the Persians in their attack on Belisarius' forces.[2]

---

[1] Note the ἄφνω at Proc. I.13.12 (implying that the Persian advance was unexpected). Lee, *Information*, 115–16, 119, classifies the invasions of 530 among those undertaken without any attempt to exploit or create an advantage. Cf. the Persian attack in 578, 30 to 40 days before the truce of 575 was due to expire (Whitby, *Maurice*, 268–9).

[2] Proc. I.13.9–I.15, Mal. 452–3, Theoph. A.M. 6022 (180–81), Zach. IX.3 (224–5), who makes no mention of Belisarius, however. Lee, *Information*, 115–16, is rightly

ii) The battle of Dara

In 530 Roman hopes were high that negotiations with Kavadh might yet produce a peaceful outcome. In March that year Hermogenes and Rufinus were at Antioch; from here they set off for the frontier. Rufinus halted in Hierapolis, where he awaited a summons from the Persian king, while Hermogenes proceeded to Dara.[3] But Justinian was well aware that Rufinus' mission might fail, and he had taken steps to deal with the possibility of a Persian invasion. An army of 25,000 men had been mustered at Dara during the preceding year, and placed under the command of the *magister militum per Orientem* Belisarius; the *magister officiorum* Hermogenes was later instructed to act as joint commander.[4]

Whatever the emperor's intentions in assembling such a substantial force at Dara, the Persians did not regard it favourably. 'When they discovered that the Romans were encamped outside Dara, the Persians divided their forces into three commands and attacked with 70,000 men.' Of course the Roman army had not been gathered overnight, any more than that of the Persians. But by June it will have become clear to Kavadh and his generals that no subsidies were forthcoming from the Romans; and it was rather for this reason that the king refused to summon the ambassadors, and then ordered his forces to attack the

---

prepared to accept Proc.'s accuracy in his reporting of these campaigns; cf. also Cameron, *Procopius*, 146. Mal. 455–6 adds some information to Proc. I.15 on the Armenian campaign, despite Rubin, *PvK* 369.

Proc.'s source for events in Armenia in 530 may have been a member of Sittas' entourage; he provides no information on events there after Sittas moved south to Samosata in 531 (Mal. 465), on which see below ch.9.

3   Mal. 452.15–22 and Theoph. A.M. 6022 (180.21–7) place both Rufinus and Hermogenes at Dara, but Proc.'s assertion that Rufinus remained at Hierapolis (I.13.11) should be preferred. His role as an ambassador would have been compromised (as Hermogenes' was, see below n.4) if he had joined the Roman army stationed at the frontier. As *PLRE* II, Rufinus 13, notes, Mal. is probably mistaken to refer to him as a *stratelates* (i.e. *magister militum*) here; but *PLRE*, *loc. cit.*, is itself inaccurate in stating that both Rufinus and Hermogenes remained at Hierapolis. It is possible, of course, that Rufinus initially went as far as Dara, but was later ordered back to Hierapolis by Justinian.

4   On the functions of the *magister officiorum*, see Jones, *LRE* 368–9 and above ch.5 n.98. Like Celer, Hermogenes no doubt had a part in coordinating the Roman command: in 531 he had difficulty reconciling Belisarius and the *dux* Sunicas, cf. Mal. 462 with *PLRE* III, Hermogenes 1. But unlike Celer, he does not seem to have played any role in determining campaign strategy. Hermogenes' participation in the battle at Dara seems to have precluded him from negotiations, at least temporarily: Rufinus, when visiting Kavadh in August 530, was accompanied by the *comes* Alexander rather than Hermogenes.

Roman army at Dara.[5] Since by this point both armies had faced one another across the frontier for some months, the Persian advance did not catch the Romans unprepared. It was probably only the timing of the operation that occasioned some surprise since, as has been suggested, it still seemed as though there was room for diplomacy.[6] The chroniclers' reference to Belisarius' army encamped outside Dara is significant. Why should the army have been stationed outside, rather than inside, the city? It is highly likely that the fortifications of the city were still being strengthened at this time, an undertaking which may have been going on since the accession of Justinian, when relations between the two powers had begun seriously to deteriorate. If this hypothesis is correct, it would explain why the *magister militum* based himself outside the city, and chose not to accept a siege despite the uncertain quality of his troops.[7]

As the Persian soldiers crossed the frontier in June 530, their spirits will have been high. Given the outcome of nearly all their most recent engagements against the Romans, they had good grounds for optimism. In any case their objectives can have been only very limited. The optimum result of their invasion would be a defeat of the Romans in the field and the capture of Dara. This would put Kavadh in a commanding position in the ensuing negotiations, and enable him to ask a considerable sum for handing back the city, either wholly destroyed or dismantled to some extent.[8] Perhaps in part to demonstrate his confidence, the Persian general Peroz chose the most obvious invasion route. From Nisibis he followed the main highway westwards, towards Constantia, but at Ammodius he halted and set up camp. Here he was only twenty stades (7.7 km) south of Dara.[9]

---

[5] Mal. 452.22–453.2, tr. Jeffreys-Scott, 265, cf. Theoph. A.M. 6022 (180.28–181.2).

[6] See above n.1.

[7] Whitby, 'Dara', 758–9 (with nn.34–5), dates Justinian's work on Dara to the period between the defeat at Thannuris and 532, on the grounds that it could not have been carried out after the Eternal Peace without provoking the Persians to war. The morale of Belisarius' forces cannot have been high, given their earlier defeats and the length of time since any Roman army had beaten the Persians (cf. Proc. I.14.21–2, 54). Some troops were quartered in Dara: see below n.25.

[8] Proc. probably overemphasises the hubris of the Persians, cf. esp. I.14.12 (Peroz orders the Romans to prepare a bath for him in Dara); but note Zach. IX.3 (224), who remarks that the Persians were confident because of the losses they had inflicted on the Romans earlier. Proc. I.16.6–8 (a speech of Kavadh to Rufinus) lays great stress on Persian annoyance at the fortress of Dara and the king's desire to remove it.

[9] For the road, see Dillemann, *Mésopotamie*, 'route 1', 155–62, fig.12 (the Peutinger table), p.134/5, and figs.18 (p.149) and 20 (p.156) for a modern map. Dillemann, *op.*

As soon as he heard of the Persian advance, Belisarius set about preparing the ground for battle. Since the opposing army would be approaching Dara from the south, it was on this side that he concentrated his efforts. Perhaps taking advantage of the presence of builders at the city, he organised the construction of a sophisticated trench system not far from the south gate. The soil here was suited to the enterprise, and the ditches used in the battle may subsequently have been integrated into the defences of the city.[10] The trench system devised by Belisarius was to play a key role in the Roman victory outside Dara. Its purpose was not so much to catch impetuous enemy cavalry unawares — like the ditch used so effectively by the Hephthalites in 484 — as to prevent enemy cavalry from engaging the unreliable Roman infantry. The need to shield the infantry from cavalry is readily observable in the *Epitedeuma* of Urbicius, who advocated the planting of sharp stakes in the ground to break cavalry charges.[11] In addition, the trench helped to neutralise the Persian advantage in numbers, since it allowed the Romans to station their best forces on the flanks, while minimising the danger of being defeated in the centre. A similar technique had been employed to offset a numerical inferiority by Sulla at Chaeronea, and by Caesar against the Belgae; in these cases, however, the trenches were on the flanks, to prevent envelopment by enemy cavalry. A closer parallel to Belisarius' trench might be found in the

---

cit., 228, for the figure of 7.7 km; as he notes, there is a problem concerning the measurement of Proc.'s stade here. Cf. Theoph. Sim. V.4.4, where the distance between Ammodius and Dara is given as 14 (no unit): Whitby, in his note (*History*, 136 n.17), suggests that Theophylact, or his source, originally had 40 stades (which Whitby calculates to be the equivalent distance in stades between the two places).

[10] Proc. I.13.13, placing the trenches a stone's throw away from the gate opposite Nisibis (*contra* Evans, *Justinian*, 117, who puts the battle 3.5 km from the city). This gate is presumably the one facing Ammodius referred to at *Aed.* II.1.26, and therefore on the south side of the city. Whitby places the gate between the easternmost of four towers in the southern section of the wall and the water gate (see the plan of Dara in 'Dara', 740, fig.41.2, and his placing of the gate on p.742). The Persians are known to have advanced from Ammodius (Proc. I.13.15, cf. Zach. IX.3 [224]), i.e. from the south; see also Proc. *Aed.* II.1.26–7 on the earthworks situated here, later removed by the emperor. *Ibid.* II.1.24–5 on the moat later incorporated into the city's defences and the softness of the soil; cf. Whitby, 'Dara', 761. Alternatively, Belisarius may have adapted the trenches already under construction to his own use.

[11] On the Hephthalite tactics, Proc. I.4.7–8, noted too by Maurice, *Strategikon* IV.3 (194), and numerous oriental sources on which see e.g. Cameron, 'Agathias on the Sassanians', 154 (though she is unnecessarily sceptical of the ruse). On the quality of the Roman infantry, see above ch.2 p.38, and note the speech of Principius and Tarmutus, Proc. V.28.23–7 (with Grosse, *Militärgeschichte*, 279). On Urbicius' suggestion and the protection from cavalry, *Epitedeuma*, 370.

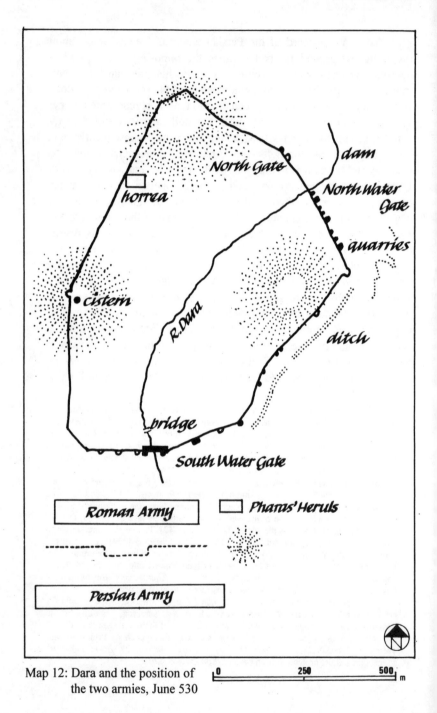

Map 12: Dara and the position of
the two armies, June 530

stakes of the English longbowmen at Agincourt, which successfully frustrated the charges of the French horsemen.[12]

Once the ditches had been prepared, the commander had to order his line of battle. Procopius provides a detailed account of the disposition of Roman forces, although he frequently fails to specify the size of the units serving under the various officers. The total strength of the Roman army was 25,000 men, among whom there were 300 Heruls and at least 1200 Huns.[13] Beyond this there is no indication of how strong the flanks or the centre were, or what proportion of the force the infantry made up. The troops on the wings may have been stronger than usual, considering that the centre was protected by the ditch; but the fact that five commanders (John, son of Nicetas, Cyril, Marcellus, Germanus and Dorotheus) are named on the right, while Bouzes alone is mentioned on the left (apart from the Heruls), need not imply that there

[12] Frontinus, *Strategemata*, II.3.17 on Sulla; on Caesar, *Bellum Gallicum*, II.8, with Goldsworthy, *Roman Army*, 133; English archers, Keegan, *Face of Battle*, 90 where he adduces other parallels. Cf. also *Peri Strategias* 35 (with Elton, *Warfare*, 251) on the placing of cavalry on the flanks. Elton, *op. cit.*, 252, notes the use of trenches in fourth century warfare; Socr. *HE* VII.20.3 mentions a ditch constructed by the Romans in the war of 421–22.

The precise form of the trench remains unclear (Proc. I.13.13–14). The problem is whether the shorter straight stretch of trench in the middle lay forward from, or to the rear of, the other longer straight sections. Plans of the battle in accordance with both interpretations have been drawn up without addressing the issue (in Dewing's translation, p.106; Oman, *Art of War*, 29, Rubin, *ZI*, Karte 1 and Haury, 'Procopiana (2)', 12). Belisarius' intention was evidently to ensure that the infantry played as little part as possible in the fighting; with the trench blocking any possible cavalry charge by the Persians, they would be free to discharge their missiles. It is slightly more likely that the central section of the trench lay to the fore of the rest, since this would allow the cavalry detachments of Sunicas and Simmas to come to the aid of the main cavalry wings without having to traverse the trench; but this is not a decisive argument, since Proc. specifically states that there were many passages across it (13.13). I have therefore followed the plans of Dewing (and to some extent Haury) in my diagram of the battle; the alternative version is given by Oman and Rubin.

[13] I.13.23 for 25,000; 13.20, 21 for two detachments of 600 Huns (Massagetae) and one of 300 Heruls. Each Hunnic detachment was commanded by two leaders, who may each therefore have held charge of 300 men, cf. the Gothic leader Sarus in the early fifth century, 'a heroic man and invincible in battle', who was accompanied by two or three hundred followers, Olympiodorus frg.6.10–14 (tr. Blockley). The 300 men under each leader would then have constituted a *numerus*, cf. Grosse, *Militärgeschichte*, 274 and Treadgold, *Army*, 94. If Zach.'s terms are at all accurate, one of the two commanders on each flank may have been subordinate: Sunicas is described by him as a *rish hila*, i.e. a commander (IX.3, ed. Brooks 94.11), while Simuth/Simmas is termed a *chiliarchos* (ed. Brooks 94.12 with n.5), a title associated with the command of several *numeri*, cf. Ravegnani, *Soldati*, 62 and 76 n.8.

was any major difference in numbers between the two flanks.[14] Behind
the infantry in the centre were positioned the forces of Belisarius and
Hermogenes; for the most part these will have been the *bucellarii* of the
two men, comprising an élite force ready to intervene at any point
where the Roman forces might experience difficulties.[15]

One of the most important contingents at the battle was that of the
Heruls, under the command of Pharas. In Procopius' account he and his
men play a critical role, and this receives some confirmation from
Zachariah. Justinian made much use of the Heruls in his wars; a part of
the tribe had been given territory in the Roman empire during the reign
of Anastasius, and Justinian moved them to better lands in Pannonia. It
is likely therefore that Pharas' men were serving the empire as
foederati rather than as *symmachoi*.[16]

The commanders of the Huns were, like Pharas, regular companions
of Belisarius (though relations between him and one of them, Sunicas,
grew tense later the following year). Of the four Hunnic commanders
named by Procopius, Aigan, Ascan, Simmas and Sunicas, only Ascan

[14] Comparison with the expedition against the Vandals in 533 is instructive. 5000
cavalry took part in the campaign against Gelimer, accompanied by 10,000 infantry,
Proc. III.11.2; it may be inferred therefore that there were no fewer than 5000 cavalry
present at Dara, and probably closer to 8000 (assuming the same 2:1 ratio).
Treadgold, *Army*, 47 (cf. 50–51), puts the army of the *magister militum* at 20,000,
including 5000 cavalry; this figure fits well with Proc.'s, since the forces of the local
duces (comprising more cavalry) should be added to the field army.

On the Roman commanders, see *PLRE* III, Buzes, Cyrillus 2, Dorotheus 1, Germanus 1, Ioannes 32, Marcellus 2. Most of these seem to have been commanders of
numeri (e.g. of *foederati*), but given that the *duces* of Mesopotamia and Osrhoene can
be expected to have participated in the battle, it is likely that Bouzes was the former
(in 531 he is found in Amida and Martyropolis) and John the latter (he was still
serving on the eastern front in 541). Despite *PLRE* III, Sunicas may have been a *dux*
(as Mal. states, 453.9), perhaps of Euphratesia, where he played a leading role in
harrying the Persians in the following year (see below ch.9 n.15); however the term
can also be applied to a commander of several *numeri*, cf. Ravegnani, *Soldati*, 62.

Shahîd, *BASIC* I, 131–4, argues for al-Harith's participation in the battle, on the
grounds that he had recently been promoted by Justinian; but Proc.'s failure to
mention the Ghassanids cannot be so lightly dismissed.

[15] Proc. I.13.22. The position of the infantry behind the central trench must be inferred
from Proc.'s description, cf. Ravegnani, *Soldati*, 66–7.

[16] On the (eastern) Heruls in this period, see Rappaport in *RE* VIII (1912), 1160–63;
Proc. VI.14 for a history of the tribe, and see above ch.2 n.93. Proc. expresses his dislike for the Heruls in general at IV.4.30 (though he excludes Pharas and his men).
Zach. IX.3 (225) for their role at Dara. As Whitby, 'Recruitment', 108 and n.217
notes, the Heruls apparently served both as *symmachoi* and as *foederati* (cf. Proc.
VII.33.13). Pharas and his men are distinguished from *symmachoi* in the list of forces
sent to North Africa (Proc. III.11.11), which implies that they at least were *foederati*.

is heard of again in the *Persian Wars*, at the battle of Callinicum, while Aigan took part in the Vandalic expedition. It is known from Malalas, however, that both Sunicas and Simmas were present at Callinicum, and the Apskal mentioned in the same context most probably represents Procopius' Ascan. These Hunnic *symmachoi* were almost certainly composed entirely of horse-archers, and were used to maximum effect by Belisarius.[17] Clearly confident in their ability, Belisarius entrusted them with a pivotal role in his troop dispositions, positioning them on the other side of the ditch in front of the infantry, next to each flank. His judgement was vindicated, since during the engagement Sunicas was able to break off from the fighting on the Roman left to take an active part in the rout of the Persian left; such a manoeuvre in the midst of a battle requires great discipline. Belisarius' plan had the further advantage of covering every eventuality. For if the Roman cavalry on the wings proved victorious, then the Huns could be thrown in to turn the victory into a rout. Alternatively, as in fact happened, if the Roman cavalry should be forced back, then the Huns could assail the enemy forces in the flank and throw them into confusion.[18]

Procopius' description of the Persian deployment is brief, but is confirmed by the slightly later *Strategikon*, where the Persian tendency to divide their line into three is noted, as well as that of keeping the front of their formation even and dense.[19] Since Kavadh, by now an octogenarian, did not take part in the campaigns of 530 or 531, the

---

[17] Proc. I.13.20, 21 on the Hunnic leaders (that the Massagetae are to be equated with Huns is clear from III.11.9; cf. e.g. Maenchen-Helfen, *World of the Huns*, 5–9 on the term Massagetae). Mal. 462–5 on Callinicum; Proc. I.18.38 for Ascan's presence at the battle. Zach. IX.3 (224) mentions Huns called Sunica and Simuth, the second of whom may be identified with Procopius' Simmas, cf. Hamilton-Brooks, 224 n.4. Cf. *PLRE* III, Aigan, Ascan, Simmas (accepting that Simmas is Simuth, although mistakenly supposing Zach. IX.3 to refer to an attack by the Persians on Dara in 527, in which he defended the city) and Sunicas. On the identification of Mal.'s Apskal with Ascan, see below ch.9 n.25. Aigan was part of Belisarius' household in 533 (Proc. III.11.7), but may have been enlisted among them only after his campaigns in the east: see Grosse, *Militärgeschichte*, 289 and *PLRE* III, Aigan. On the status of Huns as *symmachoi*, see above ch.2 n.94.
      Proc. describes the Hunnic contingent destined for North Africa as consisting exclusively of horse-archers (III.11.12), and so it may be inferred that the forces present at Dara were of a similar nature.
[18] The relative vulnerability of the Persian flanks and rear is noted in the *Strategikon*, XI.1 (358–60). Proc. I.13.19–21 on the position of the Huns; 14.44 on the battle on the right.
[19] *Strategikon* XI.1 (354–6); cf. Mal. 453 for the three-fold division of the Persian army here.

chief command was entrusted to Peroz. He had with him a force of
40,000 men, supplemented before the battle by a further 10,000 from
Nisibis.[20] He was a member of the Mihran house, which traditionally
had control of the army. Indeed, so often had the Romans come across
Persian generals of that name that they had inferred that 'Mihran' was
actually the name of an office.[21] Peroz took charge of the Persian centre
in the battle, and assigned Pityaxes to command his right wing and
Baresmanas the left. Nothing further is known about these men, and in
any case their names probably represent Persian titles.[22]

On what was expected to be the day of the battle Belisarius deployed his forces at dawn in the formation described. The Persians,
advancing from Ammodius, refrained from engaging immediately;
Procopius says they were daunted at the unusual discipline of the Roman army. The *Strategikon* describes the same tactic, noting that the
Persians frequently deferred combat when it was clear that their

---

[20]   Proc. I.13.23 for 40,000, 14.1 for the extra 10,000. This is a more credible figure than
       Mal.'s 70,000 (453), since Proc. had no motive for diminishing Persian numbers.
       Many of the 50,000, if the Persian army was as large as that (cf. Proc.'s inflation of
       Gothic troop numbers in the *Gothic Wars*, noted by Evans, *Justinian*, 141), will have
       been infantry, who played scarcely any part in the battle. See Kirchner, *Bemerkungen*,
       11 on the two figures, and for accepting those of Proc.

[21]   Christensen, *L'Iran*, 109, on the large number of army commanders from the Mihran
       (and Suren) families, though it is not proven that the supreme command was ex-
       clusively in their hands; also *ibid.* 105 n.3 on the confusion of Roman authors, cf.
       Stein II, 288 n.3 on Proc.'s mistake. Rubin, *ZI*, 486 n.765, distinguishes this Peroz
       from the Peroz fighting in Lazica in 528 (Mal. 441), since Mal. refers on the same
       page to a 'Meran' in Mesopotamia, who is more likely to be the commander at Dara
       in 530; see above ch.7 n.21. Mal. also states that a son of Kavadh was present. He is
       probably referring to Xerxes, who had taken part in the battle against Belisarius in
       528 (Mal. 441), though Mal. is the only source to refer to a son of Kavadh by this
       name, see above ch.7 n.47. Mal. 452 for the commanders at Dara: the Greek text
       surely refers to Mihran *and* the son of Kavadh, though the Latin translation seems to
       run them together, *Meram, primarius Persarum filius*, and the Jeffreys translation
       (265) is ambiguous. Theoph. clearly distinguishes the two, A.M. 6022 (181.6).

[22]   On Pityaxes, cf. Justi, *IN*, 254, Πιτιάζης, Christensen, *L'Iran*, 102, *PLRE* III,
       Pityaxes. It is probably a rendering of the Persian title *petiaxes*, the Armenian
       bdeashkh. Cf. Ammianus' *vitaxa* (XXIII.6.14), whom he regards as a governor of a
       province, a *magister equitum*; Nöldeke suggested identifying him with Hormizd, the
       governor of Arzanene (Zach. IX.6 [228]), 'Zwei Völker', 159 n.2. On the position of
       bdeashkh, ruler of a border province, see Toumanoff, *Studies*, 184 and Garsoïan, *Epic
       Histories*, 516–17, Frye, *Ancient Iran*, 295 (noting the antiquity of the title) and
       Sundermann's entry in *EIr* IV, 'bidaxš', 242–4.

       The name Baresmanas could be a rendering of the Persian *marzban*, as Rubin
       suggests, *PvK* 368; cf. also *PLRE* III, Baresmanas, and *CP* 732.21 with *CPW* 188
       n.490.

opponents were well prepared for battle.[23] Eventually, late in the afternoon, Peroz despatched a squadron of cavalry from his right wing in
order to test the Romans' mettle. The squadron was thrown back by the
forces of Bouzes and Pharas, who employed the Scythian technique of
suddenly wheeling about to face their pursuers, having initially given
ground. It was a particularly bold tactic, since the *Strategikon* specifically discourages the use of such a manoeuvre against the Persians, on
account of their good discipline.[24]

By the time that the Persian forces had been thrown back, a full-
scale battle was unlikely. But there was sufficient time for a display of
arms of a type usually associated with heroic times, but not unknown in
late antiquity — a duel of champions: in the war of 421–22 the *comes
foederatorum* Areobindus is said to have defeated the Persian Arda-
zanes in single combat, and less than a century afterwards remarkable
feats of martial prowess are attributed to the Emperor Heraclius in his
campaigns against the Persians. Procopius provides a vivid description
of two duels fought by a bath attendant of Bouzes, named Andreas,
both times in response to challenges from Persian soldiers. On the
second occasion Andreas went forth to do battle in defiance of the
orders of Hermogenes, who had strictly forbidden him to take part in
any further such engagements. From both duels Andreas emerged
victorious, to the delight of the Roman soldiers observing the
proceedings from the walls of the city. After the second fight the
Persian army withdrew to Ammodius, and the Romans retired to their
camp.[25]

---

[23] Proc. I.13.24; *Strategikon* XI.1 (354–6). Cf. Goldsworthy, *Roman Army*, 144–5, on
stand-offs occurring when 'one or both armies had adopted a very strong position':
Belisarius' trenches did not permit him to attack, while the Persians were aware of the
Roman defences (see below n.27).

[24] Proc. I.13.25–7. *Strategikon*, XI.1 (358–60) on not using the tactic against the
Persians; XI.2 (364), on the Scythian technique. The author does on the other hand
recommend charging the Persians, so as to minimise Roman losses from Persian
archery, XI.1 (358).

[25] Mal. 364 for Areobindus' victory; for a similar description of a single combat before
battle, cf. Proc. VIII.31.11–16, where Coccas is defeated by the Armenian Anzalas
before the battle at Busta Gallorum. See Chapot, *La frontière*, 208 and n.2, Rance,
Tactics, 254, with Glück, 'Reviling and Monomachy' (considering an earlier period),
on the phenomenon of individual combat; cf. also Olympiodorus' description of
Boniface's prowess, frg.40.1–3 with Blockley, *FCH* II, 219 n.76. On Heraclius' feats
in battle in Cilicia see Bury, *HLRE*[1] II, 236. Holum, *Theodosian Empresses*, 166,
notes the tough reputation of bath attendants in connection with the disturbances
during the council of Ephesus: see (e.g.) *ACO* I.1.3.50 (a letter from Cyril) on the

No fighting took place on the following day. While the Persians at Ammodius received 10,000 reinforcements from Nisibis, Belisarius and Hermogenes sought to persuade Peroz to withdraw from Roman territory and to reopen negotiations. The Persian general refused their proposal, claiming that he no longer had any confidence in Roman promises; he may be presumed to have been alluding to the failure of the Romans to make any payment to Kavadh, despite the king's repeated requests. After a further exchange of letters, the two sides concluded that battle was inevitable and made their preparations accordingly. The Romans, in order to show the justice of their cause, affixed the letters to the tops of their standards; according to both Procopius and Tabari, the same procedure had been employed by the Hephthalite Huns in their overwhelming victory over King Peroz in 484.[26]

On the next day Peroz addressed his army at dawn — a time of special significance to Zoroastrians, when they were accustomed to do obeisance to the rising sun. Procopius attributes a lengthy speech to the commander, filled with the *topoi* which readers of classicising history would expect to find in such an address; he likewise reports a speech of Belisarius and Hermogenes, to which greater credence may be given. Both serve to highlight the anxiety felt by the Roman commanders about the strength of the Persians and the unimpressive record of the Roman forces in earlier engagements.[27]

---

criticisms levelled against those who had accompanied him from Alexandria ἐκ τοῦ βαλανείου.

On Andreas' victories, Proc. I.13.29–39. Hermogenes was presumably concerned about the potentially adverse affect on Roman morale if Andreas was defeated. The περίβολος into which the Romans withdrew (13.38) was that of Dara, cf. 14.12.

[26] Proc. I.14.1–12 for the letters. For a speech similar in tone to the letters of Belisarius, cf. Menander, frg.26.1.112–32, where Zachariah, addressing the Persian Andigan, ends by referring to Persian treachery (cf. Proc. I.14.5–6 for Peroz's accusation of Roman faithlessness); this whole fragment (26.1), on events on the eastern frontier near Dara in 580–81, including speeches exchanged between Romans and Persians, has many similarities to Proc. here. The complaints of Peroz (Proc. I.14.5–6) are similar to those later made by Kavadh, I.16.4–8.

Proc. I.4.9 for the Hephthalite king affixing to his standard the salt used by Peroz in swearing his oath, cf. Nöldeke, *Tabari*, 126, where Peroz's letter is hung from the king's lance.

[27] The opening words of Peroz's speech echo the sentiment of Catiline in Sallust, *Bellum Catilinae*, 58.1–3; likewise the theme of the inexperience of the Romans (14.14) recalls the inexperience of the Syracusans in Gylippus' speech at Thuc. VII.66.1 and 66.4 (cf. also 14.21 — the disadvantage of numerical superiority — with Thuc. VII.67.3). On Proc.'s awareness of earlier classical writers see e.g. Greatrex,

Dara

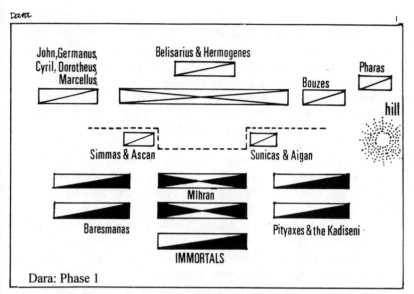

Dara: Phase 1

Once their address was completed, Belisarius and Hermogenes ordered their troops into position (phase 1). The Persian general, having moved his army up from Ammodius, was faced with the problem of how to exploit his significant numerical advantage. For the proximity of the city of Dara, to the rear of the Roman army, prevented the Persians from attempting to threaten the Romans' rear. Peroz's solution was to allow his troops to fight in rotation, a procedure requiring good coordination between units. The élite corps of Immortals, however, he held in reserve.[28] While both sides were still deploying their forces, the Herul commander Pharas suggested to Belisarius that he place himself behind a hill; here, he pointed out, he and his men could climb up and emerge to hit the Persians in the rear, throwing them into confusion. Belisarius accepted the proposal, and Pharas stationed his men accordingly.[29]

'The Classical Past'. Worthy of note is Peroz's mention of the Roman trench, of which he was evidently aware (14.15), as well as the Roman commanders' dismissive description of the Persian infantry (14.25), on which see above ch.3 pp.54–5. For some perceptive general comments on such addresses by commanders, questioning the likelihood that the entire army could have been present, see Goldsworthy, *Roman Army*, 145–7; Hansen, 'The battle exhortation', is highly sceptical of the whole genre of pre-battle speeches as reported by classical historians.

[28] Proc. I.14.28–32. On the Immortals see above ch.3 n.48. For units fighting in rotation, cf. the Persian tactics at Thermopylae, Hdt. VII.210.

[29] Proc. I.14.33. Proc., while praising Belisarius' qualities at VII.1.6–16, makes no mention of his readiness to take advice; it was, however, traditional for Roman generals in

The Persians drew up their army in its customary three-fold formation, but did not attack at once. Such delays on their part were sufficiently typical to be remarked on by the author of the *Strategikon*,
who attributes it to their ability to tolerate heat. In this case they
attempted to gain an advantage over the Romans by striking them just
when they were accustomed to have their mid-day meal; the Persians
usually did not eat until late afternoon. Their tactic was hardly novel: it
was used to better effect by the Persian general Nabedes outside Nisibis
only eleven years later, while Ammianus mentions the hunger and
thirst of the Roman troops at the battle of Adrianople waiting to fight in
the August heat.[30] The Persian attack opened with the discharge of
volleys of arrows; the Romans responded in kind, but were at a
disadvantage, since not only did the Persians have a more rapid rate of
fire, but they could also use different archers in rotation. Furthermore,
the constant shifting of Persian detachments made it difficult for the
Romans to interpret their enemy's movements. The situation might
have resulted in severe losses for the Roman army, forcing them either
to charge the Persians or withdraw altogether, had not a favourable
wind greatly reduced the impact of the Persian arrows.[31]

Following the exchange of fire, the two armies met in close combat.
No fighting in the centre is referred to by Procopius, and it may be

---

earlier times to solicit and accept advice from commanders, cf. Goldsworthy, *Roman
Army*, 131–2. Belisarius was likewise prevailed upon to fight at Callinicum in the
following year, contrary to his better judgement. Cf. Proc. V.28.28–9 for another
instance of his acceding to a request; and at II.19.45 he accepts the advice of John,
son of Nicetas (in 541).

It is not unlikely that the hill behind which Pharas hid was the 'great mound of
earth', later removed by Justinian to protect the city from mining operations (*Aed.*
II.1.26–7).

[30] Proc. I.14.34, with *Strategikon* XI.1 (356), on Persian delaying; Ravegnani, *Soldati*,
67 on the Roman mid-day meal. Proc. II.18.17–18 on Nabedes catching the Roman
commanders Peter and John by surprise in 541. Cf. the Spartan victory at
Aegospotami, Xenophon, *Hellenica* II.1.22–7; Hypatius and Patricius in the
Anastasian war had also been surprised by the Persians while having their lunch,
Proc. I.8.14–15. Ammianus XXXI.12.13 on Roman hunger and thirst at Adrianople,
while the Goths deferred the battle. See also Keegan, *Face of Battle*, 88–9, on the
discomfiture of the troops at Agincourt during a four-hour wait before battle.

[31] Proc. I.14.35–6. This was the typical opening of a battle in late antiquity, cf. Elton,
Warfare, 254, 256. See above ch.2 n.121 on Roman and Persian archery; it is
discussed more fully by Proc. at 18.32–34, where he contrasts the rapid rate of
Persian fire unfavourably with the more penetrating firepower of the Romans. Cf.
Strategikon XI.1 (358) on the need to charge, and Proc.'s praise of contemporary
Roman archery at I.1.15. The impact of the wind should not be underestimated: Zach.
IX.4 (226) notes that at the battle of Callinicum the wind was against the Romans.

assumed that the trench effectively confined the mêlée to the two flanks. It was Bouzes' forces on the Roman left who suffered most in the early stages of the battle. For although the Romans could expect to have the advantage over Persians in close combat, they instead here found themselves up against the Kadishaye (Kadiseni), a warlike people from Beth Arabaye.[32] But the success of the Kadishaye was short-lived. As Bouzes' men withdrew in disorder, the cavalry of Sunicas and Aigan charged into the attackers' left flank; and at the same time Pharas and his Heruls emerged from the hill to hit the Kadishaye in the rear (phase 2). The Persians and Kadishaye were thrown back in disorder, and their cavalry sought the shelter of the infantry phalanx. The Romans maintained their discipline and formed up opposite the phalanx, rather than recklessly continuing their pursuit.[33]

Peroz had yet to deploy his best forces, the Immortals. He decided to attempt to break the Roman right wing by secretly strengthening his own left wing with the entire contingent of Immortals. But Belisarius and Hermogenes, observing the battle from the rear, perceived his manoeuvre, and were able to take effective counter-measures. They ordered Sunicas and Aigan to transfer from the left wing to the right, so as to reinforce the forces of Simmas and Ascan. Sunicas' men were able to pass through the Roman lines and take up their new position in time to meet the Persian advance — an indication of their great speed

---

[32] Proc. I.14.38 on the success of the Kadishaye against Bouzes' forces. *Strategikon* XI.1 (356) on the Persians' inferiority in close combat. The Kadiseni/Kadishaye were probably natives of the area around Thebetha and Singara, rather than a branch of Huns (as is sometimes asserted). John of Antioch is the only ancient author to refer to them as Huns, frg.214, *FHG* IV, 28, referring to Kavadh fleeing to the Kadiseni. This is almost certainly a mistake for Kidarites, since in 496Kavadh fled northeast, where the Kidarites had earlier been situated (cf. Nöldeke, 'Zwei Völker', 158 n.3). See above ch.5.ii on the trouble caused by the Kadishaye to Kavadh in 502; they may also have rebelled in 506, see above ch.6 p.111. They are clearly not to be identified with Strabo's Kadousioi (XI.7.1) near the Caspian Sea, and it is doubtful whether they were related to the Cadusii attested in Shapur I's time. Procopius would probably have referred to them as Καδισηνοὶ καλούμενοι Οὖννοι if they were Huns, and they are never attested north of Arzanene, and so it seems more likely that they were a powerful local tribe, as Nöldeke argued, *ibid.*, 161; Maenchen-Helfen, *World of the Huns*, 440, likewise accepts that they had no connection with the Huns. See also Brunner, 'Geographical and administrative divisions', 761 and Dillemann, *Mésopotamie*, 97–8; Christensen, *L'Iran*, 347 n.4, and Marquart, *Eranšahr*, 77 n.2, nonetheless describe them as a branch of the Hephthalites.

[33] Proc. I.14.39–43. Proc. refers to both Persians and Kadishaye among the forces routed by Sunicas and Pharas.

and discipline. 1200 Huns were now protecting the Roman centre and
right wing, which were further strengthened by the deployment behind

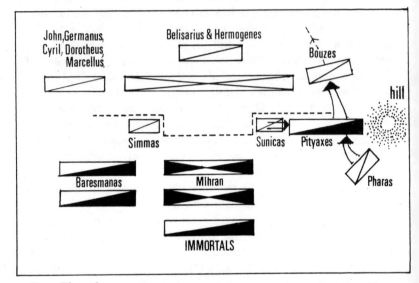

Dara: Phase 2

them of contingents drawn from Belisarius' own forces. Thus the same
technique which had led to the Persian defeat on the left was successfully repeated on the right; for while the Persians threw more forces, in
particular the Immortals, into this attack, the Romans had
correspondingly more cavalry to pit against the flank of the advancing
attacker (phase 3).[34]

---

[34] Proc. I.14.44–5. Cf. Goldsworthy, *Roman Army*, 150–53, on the advantages for a
      general of remaining to the rear of the battle — especially that of being able to react
      to developments.

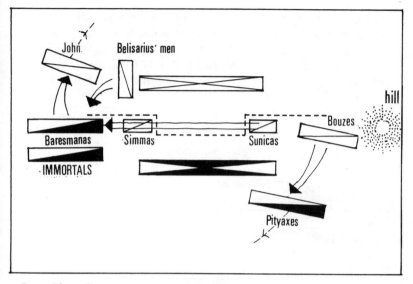

Dara: Phase 3

The Persian left wing, under the command of the one-eyed 'Bares-manas', then proceeded to charge the Roman right. The forces of John and his fellow commanders were unable to withstand the shock. They quickly fell back in disarray, as Belisarius had anticipated. But the attackers' own formation will itself have become disrupted in the charge, and hence was all the more vulnerable to the Roman stroke which followed. The Huns, probably in conjunction with Belisarius' men, suddenly drove into the right flank of the advancing Persians, creating a wedge in the middle of the attacking forces (phase 4). The bulk of the Persians were cut off behind the Huns, while others, including the standard-bearer of Baresmanas, remained closer to the main Persian lines. The ensuing mêlée naturally favoured the Romans, as the Persians who were cut off tried to wheel around and protect their rear. First the Persian standard-bearer Sagus was slain by Sunicas; the Immortals and Baresmanas hastened to recover the standard, but the Roman forces stood firm, and Baresmanas himself fell in the field, another victim of Sunicas. The Persians then took flight, in the course of which many more were killed. The infantry, who might have attempted to cover the retreat of the cavalry, as seems to have happened initially on the Persian right, instead themselves turned to flee, and suffered heavy losses: Bouzes and the Heruls are said to have inflicted

large casualties on the infantry to the east of the city. Belisarius and
Hermogenes restrained the Romans from pursuing the enemy too far,
aware that, should the Persian troops rally, victory might be thrown
into jeopardy: the Roman army was extremely vulnerable in the disorder following a victory, as Procopius remarks of the battle at Tricamerum in December 533.[35]

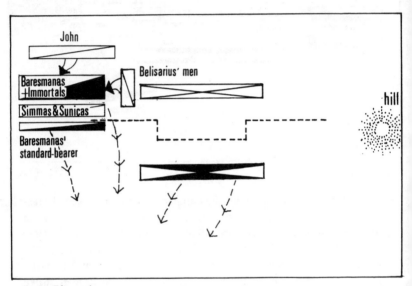

Dara: Phase 4

The success of the Romans in the field was their first in the east
since the war of 421–22. It was a remarkable triumph, and one which
would never again be matched during Justinian's reign. Procopius
claims that the Persians lost half their army in the battle, though some

---

[35] Proc. I.14.46–53. Mal. 453.8–10 for Sunicas' slaying of Sagus, presumably to be
identified with Baresmanas' standard-bearer. Zach. IX.3 (224–5) confirms Sunicas'
feats, describing how he and Simuth (Simas), with only twenty men, drove back the
Persians, 'passing boldly and vigorously from one part of the field to another, and
cutting men down right and left with the lance.' He too reports the death of two Persian leaders, doubtless Sagus and Baresmanas, as well as the havoc wreaked by
Bouzes and the Heruls on the eastern side of the city. Chapot, *La frontière*, 58–9,
considers Persian discipline to have been flawed by excessive dependence on their
commander: cf. Proc. I.14.50 for Persian horror at the death of Baresmanas. Proc.
IV.4.1–3 for the disorder of the Roman army after Tricamerum.

allowance must be made for exaggeration.[36] Such was the general pride in the achievement that a bronze statue of the emperor on horseback was erected in the hippodrome to commemorate it. Two inscriptions survive from the statue, alluding to the defeat of both Persians and Bulgars in the same year.[37] In spite of this reverse, the Persians refused to abandon the Mesopotamian front altogether: clashes took place further south, where their forces sought to lay waste Osrhoene.[38]

iii) The battle of Satala

Meanwhile, to the north, a Persian force consisting mainly of barbarian allies moved against the *magister militum praesentalis* Sittas and the *magister militum per Armeniam* Dorotheus.[39] The Persian offensive here is better viewed as connected with operations in the Transcaucasus than with the campaign in Mesopotamia: by this point the Persians had taken control of the forts on the Lazic border with Iberia, and had perhaps pushed even further towards the Black Sea. Hence this invasion was probably also aimed at the Black Sea, in an attempt to cut off the Lazi and the newly subjugated Tzani from the Romans.[40]

The general chosen by Kavadh to lead the rather motley invasion

---

[36] Proc. I.17.26 on Persian losses (over 25,000), also emphasising Kavadh's annoyance with Peroz, 17.26–8; his assertion cannot be dismissed out of hand, since a rout can result in a great disparity in losses, cf. e.g. Elton, *Warfare*, 256 (on the battle of Strasbourg: 247 Romans killed, 6000 to 8000 Alamanni).

[37] *Anth. Gr.* XVI.62–3 (= *Anth. Pl.*) for the epigrams, with Cameron, 'Some prefects', 42–6, arguing that they were both inscribed on the same statue, one by the praetorian prefect Julian (*PLRE* III, Iulianus 4), the other by the city prefect Eustathius (*PLRE* III, Eustathius 1). The statue is mentioned in the *Patria* (*Parastaseis Syntomoi Chronikai* §61 with Cameron–Herrin's notes, 251) but should not be identified with that set up in the Augustaeum (Proc. *Aed.* I.2.1–12), which also depicted the emperor triumphing over Persians. See also Mango, *Art*, 117–18 on the epigrams and Croke, 'Justinian's Bulgar Victory Celebration', 192–4 (who identifies the Scythians of the epigram with the Bulgars beaten by Mundus).

[38] Proc. I.14.54–5 with Zach. IX.3 (225). Proc. I.16.1 says that the Persian army remained outside Dara until negotiations recommenced, but this is highly unlikely, see below, iv.

[39] On the commanders, *PLRE* III, Dorotheus 2 and Sittas 1. Exactly when in 530 the campaign took place is unclear. It was probably roughly at the same time as that in Mesopotamia or a little later; the dust-clouds thrown up at Satala (Proc. I.15.12) imply that the battle took place in high summer, and negotiations restarted in August, presumably after news of the defeat reached Kavadh (Theoph. A.M. 6022 [181]), see below, iv. Whitby, *Maurice*, 202 (citing Menander frg.18.6.22–5) notes that the Persians did not usually campaign in the region until August; but, as in 576, they may have invaded earlier than usual to gain the initiative.

[40] So Veh, *Perserkriege*, 472.

force into Armenia was Mermeroes (Mihr-Mihroe). He became a specialist in Transcaucasian warfare, going on to serve in the region for almost a quarter of a century, and on the whole proving himself a redoubtable foe to the Romans.[41] According to Procopius, Mihr-Mihroe's army was composed entirely of Persian allies or subjects rather than actual Persians. The multiplicity of operations against the Romans had evidently begun to place a considerable strain on Persian manpower: some 50,000 men were involved in the battle of Dara, and Boes' force deployed in Iberia is described by Procopius as being very large. Here, moreover, the Persians could find allies more easily than elsewhere. The Persarmenians had already taken part in the war, having repelled an incursion by Sittas and Belisarius some years previously.[42] Another group serving in the Persian army was the Sunitae, a people otherwise unattested in any western source, but known to the Armenians as the Siwnik. Their country was on the edge of Armenia, and was considered by some to be separate from Persarmenia.[43] The Sabirs, three thousand of whom are said to have served in Mihr-Mihroes' army, were often employed by both Persians and Romans as allies in the sixth century, until their disappearance around 575; they are described by Procopius as 'a most warlike race'. They had come to occupy the Kuban steppes as far as the Volga in the mid-fifth century, having been pushed eastwards by the Avars, and in turn displacing westwards the Saraguri, Urogi and Unoguri. The chroniclers preserve details of the attempts made by the two great powers to enlist Sabir

[41] Mihr-Mihroe may be referred to at Zach. IX.6 (228) as Mihr Girowi, who is employed by Hormizd the *bdeashkh* to recruit Huns for the war in Arzanene and Sophanene. Cf. Justi, *IN* 203, Ahrens-Krüger, *Kirchengeschichte*, 173 n.3; the only difficulty with the identification is that Mihr Girowi seems to be a less important official in Zach. than Mihr-Mihroe in Proc. Cf. also *PLRE* III, Mermeroes, which does not connect him with Mihr Girowi.

[42] Proc. I.15.1–2 on Mihr-Mihroe's force; I.12.10 on Boes' army, 12.20–22 on the defeat of Belisarius and Sittas. See Adontz, *Armenia*, ch.10, esp. 218–19, on Armenians in Persian service.

[43] Proc. I.15.1 on the Sunitae. It is unclear what location Proc. has in mind for them, since his geography of the region is confused; it appears that they lay to the east of the Tzani, north of the Persarmenians, with the Alans to their northeast. Proc.'s geography is particularly obscure because of his confusion of the Boas and Phasis rivers, cf. I.15.20–21, II.29.14–19, though VIII.2.6–9 seems to refer only to the Boas and not to equate it with the Phasis. Proc.'s Sunitae are identified with Zachariah's Sisakan (XII.7 [328]) by Adontz, *Armenia*, 171–2, who notes that their territory was usually incorporated in Persarmenia; cf. Garsoïan, *Epic Histories*, 490–91 and Hewsen, *Geography*, 189 n.189. Both Marquart (*Eranšahr*, 122) and Hübschmann (*Ortsnamen*, 237 n.2) prefer the reading Ἀλβανοῖς at Proc. I.15.1 to Haury's Ἀλανοῖς.

support during the 520s, but the Sabirs were quite capable of launching unsolicited attacks, as they had in 515.[44]

Opposing these forces were the newly reorganised *duces* and the *magister militum* of Armenia. Dorotheus, the second *magister militum per Armeniam* since the creation of the post only two years previously, was probably based at Theodosiopolis. He was supported there by his predecessor Sittas, now a *magister militum praesentalis*, creating a type of dual command similar to that wielded by Belisarius and Hermogenes, Sittas, unlike Hermogenes, had the primary role in strategic decisions; his recent marriage to Theodora's sister Comito had established him as a dependable agent of the imperial family.[45] The commanders, hearing of the Persian preparations, sent out two bodyguards to find out more details. Although one was captured by some Huns, the other was able to give an accurate report to the Roman generals of the size and position of the Persian army. As a result, Dorotheus and Sittas were able to lead a swift strike against the assembled Persian troops. Their surprise attack was completely effective, but failed to avert the Persian invasion; it is likely that they defeated only part of the Persian army, while Mihr-Mihroe was elsewhere with the bulk of his forces.[46]

It was therefore just a short time later that Mihr-Mihroe's army, 30,000 strong, invaded Roman territory. He may have followed the

[44] On the Sabirs, cf. Howorth, 'The Sabiri', who assembles most of the ancient evidence; also Haussig, 'Theophylakts Exkurs', 364 and n.342, Maenchen-Helfen, *World of the Huns*, 432 and 440, and *CHEIA*, 259–60. They are placed in the Caucasus region by Proc., beyond the Alans, i.e. to the north of the Caspian Gates (here, the Dariel Pass), II.29.15, VIII.3.5; their divided loyalties to Rome and Persia, VIII.11.22–5.

[45] Proc. I.15.3 on the Roman generals, cf. Mal. 465, 469, 472 (from 531). Dorotheus, presumably no stranger to the region, had perhaps recently served as a *dux* at one of the newly built forts in Armenia, such as Citharizon or Artaleson. Adontz, *Armenia*, 109, believes that Dorotheus was still a *dux* at this stage, though Proc.'s text is hardly ambiguous, cf. Stein II, 289 and n.5 and Durliat, 'Le titre', 318–19; he died during the Vandalic war. *Contra* Stein II, 291, Sittas' promotion was not due to his subjugation of the Tzani (accomplished some years previously, see above ch.6 n.28), but probably to his marriage (in 528). Cf. *PLRE* III, Sittas 1 and Dorotheus 2.

[46] Proc. I.15.4–8; 15.9 on the location of most of Mihr-Mihroe's army. The two spies are described as *doryphoroi*, who were apparently senior to *hypaspistai* among *bucellarii*, and often entrusted with important tasks, cf. Grosse, *Militärgeschichte*, 290, Lee, *Information*, 116, 172–3, and see above ch.2 n.118. Proc.'s information may have come from one of them, Dagaris, later described in very complimentary terms at I.22.19, when he was returned to the Romans in exchange for a high-ranking Persian. Cf. also *PLRE* III, Dagaris. See below ch.9 n.47 on spies in general.

Euphrates westwards, skirting the much improved defences of Theodosiopolis, and trying to force the two *magistri militum* into battle by penetrating deep into Roman territory; another possible route would be along the Boas river, past Pharangium and Bayburt.[47] At Satala, a nodal point for east-west routes in eastern Anatolia, the Romans decided to make a stand; here Sittas could use the terrain to greatest effect. Leaving most of his forces in Satala, he led a thousand men behind one of the surrounding hills, in order to attack the Persians from the rear while they were encircling the city.[48] The enemy's numerical superiority left him little choice but to rely on outwitting the Persians; most of the Roman army was deployed in Mesopotamia, and he had fewer than 15,000 men. On the next day, the Persians advanced from their camp at Octava, and set about investing the city. As they were doing so, Sittas' men emerged from the hill nearby, charging down against the besiegers; the clouds of dust kicked up by the cavalry gave an impression of a substantial force. The Persian army immediately withdrew from the walls.[49] Since their forces had been dispersed all round the city, they attempted to regroup and form up in dense formation to meet the attackers. Sittas perceived their intention, however, and foiled the manoeuvre by dividing his force into two, separating the Persian army into two parts. Witnessing these developments, the defenders in Satala rushed out to join in the attack, and a fierce cavalry mêlée ensued, with both sides practising the Scythian tactic of feigning flight, and then wheeling about against the pursuer. Although the Persians were under attack from both sides, the

---

[47] Proc. I.15.9; 15.11 for the size of the Persian army. His mention of Octava would be useful if it could be located; it is not to be found in Bryer–Winfield, *Pontus*. 56 stades should be the equivalent of about 22 km, but Procopius does not say whether the Persians encamped to the east or the north of the city. It would have taken the Roman commanders only about four days to reach Satala from Theodosiopolis, once they knew the route of the invading army, cf. Bryer–Winfield, *op. cit.*, 37–8 and n.193. On the strength of Theodosiopolis' defences (forty years later), see Menander frg.18.6.180–85 with Whitby, *Maurice*, 201. Lee, *Information*, 116 n.25, rightly emphasises that the Romans were not taken by surprise by Mihr-Mihroe's attack; it was only at Satala that he was able to bring the Roman forces to battle.

[48] Whitby, 'Notes', 101–2, suggests that Sittas decided to fight outside the city because the city's defences were in need of repair; clearly, however, they were adequate to give some protection for Dorotheus' men. Proc. *Aed.* III.4.2–3 on the repairs. For a plan of Satala and the surrounding mountains see Mitford, 'Bilotti's Excavations', 229 fig.8; on the importance of its position, *idem*, 'Some inscriptions', 165–8.

[49] Proc. I.15.11–12. Belisarius successfully exploited this effect of dust clouds in 558 against Zabergan's Kotrigurs, Agath. V.19.9.

Romans finally assured themselves of victory only through the capture of Mihr-Mihroe's standard.[50]

The Persian forces then retreated to their camp. From there they returned homewards, unmolested by the Romans. Sittas will have been deterred from pursuing the invaders by their still substantial numbers, as well as by the unpredictable nature of campaigning in Armenia. Furthermore, he will have been aware that the Persian defeat would in itself have an effect on the loyalty of her allies in the region. And indeed the victory at Satala soon brought substantial diplomatic gains to the Romans: not only did they acquire the border forts of Pharangium and Bolum, but three Armenian chiefs defected to their cause.[51] The first to abandon the Persians were Narses and Aratius, who had defeated Belisarius and Sittas only a few years previously; together with their mother, they crossed the border and were generously received by the *cubicularius* Narses, a fellow Persarmenian. News of the gifts presented to his two brothers was enough to persuade Isaac, the youngest of the three, to follow suit; it was he who handed over the fortress of Bolum to the Romans.[52]

The loss of Pharangium was a particularly heavy blow to the Persians, since it lay in gold-mining territory and had supplied the Persian king with important revenues. The controller of the mine, Symeon, exploited the waning of Persian fortunes astutely, refusing to pay any further gold to Kavadh, but making no contribution to the Romans either, thereby maximising his profits. The Romans were nonetheless content to accept the situation, conscious of the loss to the

---

[50] Proc. I.15.12–16. The ξυμμορία at 15.13 must have comprised 500 men, if Sittas' 1000 cavalry divided themselves into two such units; this fits with Grosse's estimate of 500 (*Militärgeschichte*, 274) as the size of a *numerus*. See above p.177 on the 'Scythian' tactics. Their use here perhaps has more to do with the number of Hunnic allies on either side than Roman or Persian proficiency in them. By the time of the *Strategikon* (XI.1 [360]), the Romans themselves could employ such tactics, though the Persians apparently could not (XI.1 [356]). The importance of the standards to the Persians and their allies is clearly illustrated by the battles of Satala and Dara.

[51] Proc. I.15.17–19, 26–33. Whitby, *Maurice*, 202, on the dangers of campaigning in Armenia. The location of Bolum is uncertain: it is generally identified with the Armenian Bolberd, to the east of Theodosiopolis, see Adontz, *Armenia*, 22; Thomson also identifies Bolberd with Bolum, *Lazar*, 294, cf. Hewsen, *Geography*, 209 n.252. See below n.53 on Pharangium.

[52] Proc. I.15.31–3 with *PLRE* III, Narses 1, Narses 2, Aratius, Isaaces 1. Stein II, 292 n.1, notes Adontz's suggestion that they were members of the Kamsarakan family.

Persian treasury already inflicted by Symeon's gesture.[53] The reduction of the Tzani and Sittas' victory had thus done much to extend Roman power in the region. Roman influence now advanced up the fertile Boas valley, part of which had hitherto been in Persian hands. Kavadh never succeeded in recapturing either Pharangium or Bolum by force; instead, Justinian was able to use them as bargaining chips in the negotiations of 532, exchanging them for the two Lazic forts, Sarapanis and Scanda, which had fallen to the Persians.[54]

iv) Negotiations

The Persians did not hurry to reopen negotiations after the battle of Dara: Kavadh no doubt hoped for a victory in Armenia to improve his bargaining position. Eventually, however, Rufinus and the *comes* Alexander were summoned to the king's court, where they arrived in August 530.[55] While Theophanes merely reports that 'after much discussion, [the ambassadors] established the terms of peace and departed peacefully',[56] a more elaborate account of the embassy is furnished by Procopius. According to him, Kavadh was still concerned at the failure of the Romans to make any contributions to the defence of the Caspian Gates; he was also unhappy with the erection of the fortress of Dara, which, he claimed, obliged him to maintain a standing

---

[53] Proc. I.15.26–30; Symeon did hand over Pharangium itself to the Romans, however. Pharangium is generally identified with modern Ispir and Strabo's Syspiritis (XI.14.9), cf. Adontz, *Armenia*, 22–3 and Bryer–Winfield, *Pontus*, 56 and n.393; its gold is also mentioned by Mal. 455–6 (though Stein II, 292 n.3, thinks Mal. is referring to other gold mines), but his passage is confused. He states that the gold reserves were only discovered in Anastasius' time (unlikely, given Strabo's mention of them), yet implies that before Anastasius all the revenues from the mines had been divided between Rome and Persia, and thereafter had gone only to the Romans. It is possible that in Anastasius' reign the Romans had managed to get possession of some of the gold-producing region. The subjugation of the Tzani (recounted by Proc. here, at I.15.19–25) will have placed Pharangium still more in the Roman orbit. The versions of Proc. and Mal. cannot be reconciled completely; all that is certain is that Pharangium lay in territory disputed by the two sides, and that both laid claim to the revenues from the gold. Socr. *HE* VII.18 reports a similar dispute over claims to gold-mines at the start of the 421–22 war, which could be a reference to the same area; cf. the mention of gold mines in Lazar and Thomson's note in his translation, 170 [117] n.3.

[54] Proc. I.15.26 on the Boas valley, cf. Bryer–Winfield, *Pontus*, 7; also Adontz, *Armenia*, 24. Proc. I.22.18 for the exchange.

[55] Mal. 453, Theoph. A.M. 6022 [181], cf. Proc. I.16.1–8, with Scott, 'Diplomacy', 161. According to Proc. I.16.1 the Persians did not leave Dara until Rufinus' embassy to Kavadh. More probably, the Persian force remained inside Roman territory, at Ammodius, until Rufinus was summoned.

[56] Theoph. A.M. 6022 [181.10–11], tr. Mango-Scott, 275, cf. Mal. 454.11–13.

army nearby to protect his territories. He therefore reiterated his demand that the Romans should either dismantle Dara or share the burden
of the defence of the Caspian Gates. In case the ambassadors failed to
grasp the implication of his complaints, he hinted to them as they
departed that he would desist from further attacks if he received an
adequate payment from the Romans. Rufinus and Alexander were back
in Constantinople in the autumn, where they were joined by
Hermogenes.[57]

The emperor was 'filled with joy' upon hearing the report of the
ambassadors, just as he had rejoiced at Kavadh's request that his uncle
adopt Khusro. Now at last it seemed as though peace with Persia was
within his grasp. He composed a letter to the Persian king and entrusted
it to Rufinus, who set out once again for Persian territory at the end of
530 or in early 531. By the time he approached the frontier, however,
he discovered that Kavadh was already making plans to renew his
offensive.[58] Clearly the king had had a change of heart since his discussions with Rufinus and Alexander in August, and it is possible to
divine the reasons for this. First, news of the seriousness of the Samaritan uprising had reached him by way of emissaries and refugees
from the rebellion. They assured the king of their readiness to assist
him in capturing Jerusalem with the 50,000 people who had already
joined the revolt. In the event, nothing came of the proposed
collaboration. Some of the Samaritan leaders who had negotiated with
Kavadh were captured by Belisarius and revealed what had taken place,
and the rebellion had in any case all but been crushed in 529. Yet

---

[57] Proc. I.16.1–10, where Rufinus interestingly addresses the king as the brother of
Justinian (on which term see Helm, 'Untersuchungen', 385, Whitby, *Maurice*, 205–6
and Scott, 'Diplomacy', 163 with Ammianus XVII.5.3 and *de Cer.* I.89; Kavadh himself says that the two kings are brothers in his letter to Justinian of 529, Mal. 449, cf.
415.8–9); see above ch.2 n.53. Since the points raised by Kavadh in his speech tally
so well with earlier demands noted by other sources, Proc.'s general accuracy here
should not be doubted.
   Proc. 1.16.10 notes Hermogenes' arrival in Constantinople; Mal. 454.11 puts the
ambassadors' return to the capital at the end of September, Theoph. (A.M. 6022
[181.11]) at the end of November, cf. Scott, 'Diplomacy', 161.

[58] Mal. 454–5 (454.14 for the quotation), Theoph. A.M. 6023 (181), cf. Proc. I.11.10 on
Justinian's joy at Kavadh's adoption proposal. Sotiriadis, 'Zur Kritik', 119–20, demonstrates that the letter in Mal. is almost certainly Justinian's, not Kavadh's, despite
appearances; see also Scott, 'Diplomacy', 161. The content (e.g. the urgent need to
make peace, references to 'the Lord God' [454.19], and an apparent allusion to the
age of the [Persian] king) (455.5–6) certainly suits Justinian better; indeed this may
be the letter which the emperor tried to send to Kavadh through Rufinus.

Kavadh was not to know that the Samaritans' news was both exaggerated and belated, and it was partly at least on the basis of their mission that he determined to invade Roman territory once more.[59] Secondly, the Persian grip on the Transcaucasus had been dangerously shaken by the defeat at Satala. The defection of Narses, Aratius and Isaac and the insubordination of Symeon provided dangerous precedents for others to follow, while the loss of Pharangium and Bolum gave the Romans the upper hand in any negotiations to arrange peace terms. The loss of revenue from the gold mine at Pharangium, and perhaps from others elsewhere in the vicinity, must have further inclined Kavadh to continue hostilities, since his wars with Rome were invariably chiefly motivated by financial considerations. Engaging in diplomacy in 531 would therefore have presented an appearance of weakness, which might encourage other Armenian princes to defect; and the Persian treasury would be in no better condition, even if the gold mines were returned, and actually worse if they were not.[60]

---

[59] Mal. 456 for the capture of the Samaritan envoys, cf. Theoph. A.M. 6021 (179), placing their capture in 529, with Mal. 455. But see Winkler, 'Die Samariter', 447–8, rightly preferring 530; Rabello, *Giustiniano*, 421–2, suggests that there may be some exaggeration in the references to the proposed Persian-Samaritan co-operation. See above ch.7 pp.160–61 on the course of the uprising.

[60] Mal. 455–6 and Theoph. A.M. 6021 (179) present the loss of Pharangium (and perhaps other gold-bearing areas) as a mere pretext for the king's abandonment of negotiations. It is clear, however, that the repercussions of Satala were an important factor in the breakdown of talks.

IX
The final campaign

For his final assault on the Roman empire, Kavadh learnt from the failures of the previous year. As a result of the reorganisation of the Roman frontier and the presence of adequate forces nearby, direct invasions were no longer effective. In order to gain any plunder, a way of circumventing the border defences had to be found; and it is not impossible that, as Procopius relates, it was the phylarch al-Mundhir, who suggested that the Persians accomplish this by invading Syria and Euphratesia along the river Euphrates. Al-Mundhir will at any rate have had the opportunity to observe the comparative unpreparedness of this area during his raid of March 529.[1] It was a move which the Romans might have anticipated, had they looked back to earlier centuries: in 354 the Persian general Nohodares had unsuccessfully attempted to penetrate Osrhoene, judging Mesopotamia to be too well guarded, while in 252 the Euphrates route appears to have been employed by Shapur I in his second devastating incursion into Roman territory.[2] But these precedents had quickly been forgotten, and the army sent by Kavadh made good progress in the early stages of the invasion; only

---

[1] Proc. I.17.30–39 on al-Mundhir's suggestion. See above ch.7 p.152 on his raid in March 529. Zach. IX.4 (225) explicitly notes the Persian change of tactics in response to their failures against Dara.

[2] On Nohodares see Ammianus XIV.3.2 (who, like Proc. [I.17.2], stresses the novelty of such an attack). Millar, *Near East*, 159–60 on Shapur I's invasion in 252. It is likely that a predecessor and namesake of al-Mundhir approached Antioch by a similar route in 421, but he was overwhelmingly defeated by the Roman general Vitianus, cf. Socr. *HE* VII.18 and *PLRE* II, Alamundarus 1. The Euphrates route was successfully employed again in 573, cf. Whitby, *Maurice*, 258; on the dangers it presented for the Persians, see *ibid.* 199.

   Although al-Mundhir had raided as far as Antioch as recently as 529, this would hardly have alerted the Romans to the danger of a Persian invasion here; his route had lain well to the south of the Euphrates, following the Orontes northwards along the line Emesa-Apamea-Antioch.

the swift reaction of Belisarius prevented further damage to the prosperous countryside of northern Syria.[3]

i) Sources

Right from the start, the battle of Callinicum aroused controversy; even the campaign leading up to it witnessed divisions among the Roman leaders. The defeat of Belisarius was bound to have repercussions, coming so soon after the string of Roman successes in the preceding year. Some regarded the *magister militum* as having failed to protect the provinces adequately and accused him of abandoning the field of battle precipitately. Others, such as Procopius, endeavoured to defend his reputation, arguing that he was forced to fight against his will by the ill-discipline of his own men. Once Hermogenes had reported the defeat to Justinian, the emperor set up a commission of enquiry to investigate what had happened; in charge of the enquiry was the former *dux* of Moesia, Constantiolus. Having consulted the generals involved in the battle, as well as the *magister officiorum*, he reported back to Justinian. There can be little doubt that he found in favour of the detractors of Belisarius, who was immediately removed from his command and ordered back to the capital.[4] Despite the justified scepticism which surrounds the working of such enquiries nowadays, the verdict of Constantiolus' commission has been accepted with remarkable ease.[5] In fact, it is far more likely that Constantiolus' verdict reflects his own and other commanders' dislike for their superior, an attitude which was to plague Belisarius for the rest of his career. For this reason Malalas' version should be regarded with as much circumspection as that of Procopius: his account is not necessarily any less partisan than

---

[3]   On the prosperity of north Syria at this time, see Tate, 'Le problème', 333–4; also Algaze, 'Preliminary report', 205–6 and 233 fig.26, on the density of settlement near Zeugma, just to the north of the area hit by the Persians.

[4]   Proc. I.18.24–56 for his version of the battle. Mal. 462–5 on the battle, 465–6 on Constantiolus' enquiry. See Kirchner, *Zur Beurteilung*, 14, on Mal.'s use of Hermogenes' report; also Bury, *HLRE* II, 87 n.2, Jeffreys, 'Malalas' sources', 209–10, and Scott, 'Diplomacy', 165.

[5]   *PLRE* III, 186 is singularly trenchant: 'The account in Malalas is to be preferred, since Procopius clearly conceals Belisarius' responsibility for the disaster as shown by his silence about the enquiry of Constantiolus and his version of the recall and dismissal of Belisarius'; cf. Cameron, *Procopius*, 158 and Shahîd, *BASIC* I, 136–9 and esp. 141 — 'Malalas had no axe to grind ...'. Sotiriadis, 'Zur Kritik', 122, also prefers Mal., but cf. Kirchner, *Zur Beurteilung*, 16 and Rubin, *ZI*, 500–1 n.882, for a different view.

that of Belisarius' *assessor* simply because he is reporting the results of an official enquiry.[6]

Procopius and Malalas give by far the most detailed narratives of the events of 531; the latter probably had access not only to Constantiolus' report, but also to one by Hermogenes concerning events later in the year. Some useful information can be gleaned from Zachariah in particular, and many chroniclers preserve at least a notice of the Roman defeat at Callinicum.[7]

ii) The Callinicum campaign

Early in 531, 'at the opening of spring' according to Procopius, a Persian army, 15,000 strong, crossed into Roman territory by Circesium; it was accompanied by a detachment of Lakhmid Arabs, which probably brought its total strength to around 20,000 men. It was the traditional time for starting campaigns, when supplies were most readily available and movement was easy. Since therefore the timing of the invasion would not take the Romans by surprise, the Persians had to hope that its direction would.[8] Their force was not large, but it

---

[6] Constantiolus' own career hitherto had been brief but checkered, cf. *PLRE* III, Constantiolus; after an initial success, he had been captured by the Bulgars, but was ransomed for a substantial sum by Justinian. He may therefore have owed his appointment as head of the commission more to imperial favour than to ability. The Hunnic leader Sunicas had quarrelled with Belisarius during the campaign (Mal. 462), so it is unsurprising that Mal. (465) says he was one of the most valiant commanders at the battle. If *PLRE* III, Constantinus 3, is correct in accepting that the general Constantine took over the command of Belisarius' army in the east after his dismissal (Zach. IX.6 [228]), and if it is supposed that he was already acquainted with Belisarius at the time, then the evidence of another enemy of the *magister militum* will have been taken into account: Constantine later tried to assassinate Belisarius during the siege of Rome in 538.

 More realistic assessments of Constantiolus' verdict may be found in Rubin, *ZI*, 289 (stressing potential hostility to Belisarius in the east) and Bury, *HLRE* II, 87 n.3. Belisarius' dismissal may reflect the emperor's desire to defuse tensions in the high command rather than any loss of confidence in him (he was soon to be re-employed).

[7] Mal. 468.10–11 on Hermogenes' report, which appears to have taken up where Constantiolus' enquiry left off (466.13). Theoph. chooses to omit the events of 531 altogether, as Mango–Scott note, *Theophanes*, 276 n.5: he moves the Eternal Peace forward, placing it just after the battle of Dara. Zach. IX.4 (225–6) for his version. Numerous modern accounts of the campaign are available: Kirchner, *Zur Beurteilung*, 14–16, Rubin *ZI*, 285–8, Stein II, 292, Sotiriadis, 'Zur Kritik', 121–4, Bury *HLRE* II, 86–7 (though his figures are wrong, cf. Stein II, 292 n.2), and now Shahîd, *BASIC* I, 134–42.

[8] Proc. I.17.1 on the opening of spring. Lee, *Information*, 91–2 on campaigns in the spring, cf. Whitby, *Maurice*, 200. Since the battle of Callinicum was fought on 19

consisted entirely of cavalry, and could therefore expect to inflict great damage before withdrawing at high speed. According to Procopius, the Persian commander was called Azarethes, although this is probably a misunderstanding of the title *hazaraft*; al-Mundhir acted as guide to the expedition with a considerable force of his own, which was destined to play an important role in the campaign.[9]

Realising that a Persian invasion was imminent, Justinian had sent Hermogenes, the *magister officiorum*, back to the east. At the point when Hermogenes reached Antioch, Azarethes had probably passed Callinicum in his advance up the north bank of the Euphrates. Certainly by the time the *magister officiorum* had arrived at Hierapolis the Persians had crossed the river and penetrated as far as Gabbulon.[10] Meanwhile Belisarius, the *magister militum*, had not been inactive. It was apparently not until Azarethes' force was spotted at Callinicum that he was apprised of the invaders' route. What Roman forts there were along the Euphrates here, such as Circesium and Zenobia, were in bad condition and poorly guarded. 'And so it was possible for the Persians freely, whenever they wished, to get into the middle of Roman territory before the Romans had word of the hostile inroad' says Procopius in the *De Aedificiis*, clearly referring to this invasion; perceiving the vulnerability of the region, the emperor subsequently devoted himself to upgrading the forts of Osrhoene along the Euphrates.[11] As

---

April, the invasion must have begun in March. Note Mal. 461.8–12 for Roman knowledge of the impending attack.

[9] Proc. I.18.1 on Azarethes, cf. Mal. 461.10 (Exarath); on the name, see Justi, *IN* 88, Exarath, who strangely dates his period of leadership to 529, and *PLRE* III, Azarethes; *Chron. 724*, a.840 (115, 21), gives his name as Zuraq. See also Nöldeke, *Tabari*, 76 n.2, Stein II, 292 n.2, Rubin, *ZI*, 498–9 n.865 and Christensen, *L'Iran*, 409. Proc. I.17.1 and 18.1 on al-Mundhir's forces, cf. Mal. 461.13.

[10] Mal. 461–2 on Hermogenes' and Azarethes' movements, implying (by the mention of Circesium and Callinicum) a route north of the Euphrates. Note that, *contra* Jones, *LRE*, 1486, Callinicum is in Osrhoene (as Mal. states), not Euphratesia.

[11] Proc. *Aed.* II.8.10 for the quotation (about improvements made at Zenobia). The upgrading of defences along the Euphrates clearly took place after Khusro's attacks in the 540s: note Proc. *Aed.* II.9.1–2 (on Sura) and *Wars* II.21.30–31 (on Callinicum, being rebuilt in 542, cf. Whitby, 'Notes', 93–4). The case of Circesium is less certain: Whitby, 'Development', 727 and Stein II, 289, noting that Khusro avoided it in 540 (Proc. II.5.2–3), argue that it was strengthened by Justinian early in his reign; but Proc.'s report also states that the city was protected by the rivers Aborras (Khabur) and Euphrates on two sides, and by a wall on the other, whereas after its refortification by Justinian it was wholly enclosed by a wall (*Aed.* II.6.7–9). Since no other forts along the Euphrates had been fortified by 531, and in view of Proc. *Aed.* II.8.10 (quoted above), it is highly unlikely that any work had yet been carried out at Circesium. Given Mal.'s mention of Circesium (461.14), there seems no need to posit

soon as he heard the news, Belisarius set off westwards, but since he did not know whether Azarethes' invasion was merely a feint, he left a considerable portion of his army at Dara.[12] It was therefore with only 3000 men, as well as 5000 Ghassanid allies under the phylarch al-Harith, that Belisarius marched off to confront the invaders; the small size of his force was probably compensated for by its mobility, since he will have detached only cavalry units to accompany him.[13]

Within two weeks the Persian advance had almost ground to a halt. By a series of forced marches Belisarius had overtaken the invaders and reached Chalcis, barring their way westwards. Meanwhile the Persians had been occupied in laying siege to the town of Gabbulon and plundering the surrounding area.[14] Near Gabbulon they constructed a camp, defended by a system of ditches, which failed, however, to protect them from the Romans. The *dux* Sunicas, with 4000 men, launched an assault on the Persians and Lakhmids who were scattered around the neighbouring villages. But in doing so he contravened the orders of the *magister militum*, who was unwilling to engage the enemy, at least until the Roman forces were united.[15] By now

---

a route of Singara-Thannuris-desert-Sura-Barbalissus-Gabbulon for Azarethes, as does Rubin, *ZI*, 498 n.865.

[12] Belisarius' caution may well have been vindicated by an attempt to capture Dara by 'the Mihran': Proc. *Aed.* II.2.19 refers to a siege undertaken by the Persians during Kavadh's reign, which can hardly be the battle of 530, and may therefore be a failed attempt in the following year. The difficulty with this is that 'the Mihran' (Peroz) was dismissed after the battle of Dara (Proc. I.17.26), i.e. probably before spring 531; but, as *PLRE* III, Perozes, notes, this Mihran might be a different commander.

[13] Mal. 461.16–18 with Stein II, 292 n.2. Mal. clearly includes al-Harith's men among Belisarius', although one might expect the *magister militum* to have been able to muster more than 3000 men for the expedition. However, some of the *duces* who had fought at Dara (e.g. Sunicas), may have resumed posts elsewhere after the battle, and hence have joined Belisarius later; Bouzes, who was ill, remained at Amida (with at least some forces, see below p.207) during the whole campaign, cf. *PLRE* III. Proc. I.18.6 states that the cavalry commanders in the campaign were those who had served at Dara, while different infantry officers are named, and so probably only cavalry had hastened westwards with the *magister militum*.

[14] Proc. I.18.8 for Belisarius at Chalcis and the Persians at Gabbulon (cf. Mal. 462), roughly 48 km apart (Rubin, *ZI*, 498 n.865). Rubin, *ZI*, 286, proposed that Belisarius marched westwards from Dara via Samosata and Zeugma, but a more direct route would be Dara-Constantia-Edessa-Hierapolis, for which see *TAVO* B VI 14. By this route it is approx. 300 km from Dara to Chalcis. An unencumbered Roman force could cover 30 km in a day, and within the empire supplies for such a small force will not have been hard to obtain; see Elton, *Warfare*, 245 on marching speeds.

[15] Mal. 462 on the Persian camp and Sunicas' attack (he may have been the *dux* of Euphratesia) and Belisarius' anger at him. Mal.'s description of trenches filled with caltrops around the Persian camp, is confirmed by Zach. IX.2 (223), describing a very

Hermogenes had arrived in Hierapolis, accompanied by 4000 men and the commanders Apskal (Ascan), Stephanus and Simmas. When told of the location of the Persians he proceeded southwards to Barbalissus, perhaps following the west bank of the Euphrates, skirting the Persians to the west; here, some two hundred and thirty years earlier, the soldier-martyrs Sergius and Bacchus had been taken for judgement by the *dux* of Euphratesia, Antiochus. But Azarethes, aware that the way directly westwards was now barred, had turned north, towards Bathnae. This allowed Belisarius to advance to the Euphrates, as far as Barbalissus. It was here, then, that the Roman army assembled, and the *magister officiorum* Hermogenes sought to reconcile the *magister militum* Belisarius with his *duces*.[16]

Despite Hermogenes' efforts, the Roman high command remained divided. On the one hand, Belisarius, displaying his characteristic caution, believed that he had fulfilled his objectives: the Persians were being forced back, and could be followed at a safe distance until they had left Roman territory. The Romans, he reasoned, had nothing to gain by offering battle, and much to lose. But other commanders, probably including the *magister officiorum* himself, thought it necessary to exact vengeance on the invaders: Euphratesia and Syria had suffered at their hands, as well having borne the brunt of earlier Lakhmid raids. The citizens of Antioch in particular, who had fled their city upon hearing of the capture of Gabbulon, and had just been obliged to pay a huge ransom to secure the return of captives seized by al-Mundhir in 529, will hardly have had much sympathy for the apparent hesitation of Belisarius. Furthermore, the victories of the previous year had boosted Roman confidence, and for that reason many will have felt that the enemy should not be allowed to escape unscathed.[17]

---

similar system used in 528 (the battle of Minduos/Thannuris); cf. *Strategikon* XI.1 (354). See Rance, *Tactics*, 196, on Persian camps and their use of trenches.

[16] Mal. 462. Rubin, *ZI*, 498 n.865, noting that there is no conflict between Proc.'s placing of Belisarius at Chalcis and Mal.'s reference to Barbalissus: the Persians spent some time (one to two weeks, he suggests) in the vicinity of Gabbulon. 'Passio Antiquior', 384–5, on the arrival of the two martyrs in Barbalissus, cf. *PLRE* I, Antiochus 2 (dating the episode to 303/5). Sergius and Bacchus were especially venerated by the troops of Syria; see e.g. *IGLS* V, 2155 (an inscription of 524/5 from Garion/Ghour).

[17] Proc. I.18.11–12 on Belisarius' views (and their unpopularity in the army); also 18.17–23, justifying his tactics. Cf. his similar approach in 541, Proc. II.21. Note the caution of *Peri Strategias* 33 when faced with a numerically equal or superior enemy (and referring to Belisarius in the same chapter); also *Strategikon* VIII.2.86 (296). Mal. 460–61 for the ransoming of al-Mundhir's captives (with Shahîd, *BASIC* I, 81),

At the instigation of Hermogenes, the Roman army, now 20,000 strong, moved to follow the Persians. The Persians had pressed only a little north of Gabbulon, reaching the villages of Bathnae and Beselathon; there the Roman army made contact with them and pushed them south, back towards Gabbulon. This time the Persians besieged the town in earnest and succeeded in capturing it.[18] It appears that Belisarius' army, setting forth from Barbalissus, had somehow managed to position itself north of the Persian force, and was driving the invaders back southwards. Azarethes, now confronted by a substantial Roman force deep in hostile territory, realised that he was in a dangerous position. The capture of Gabbulon and nearby villages was his last act of aggression before withdrawing to the southeast. To cover his retreat from Gabbulon, the Persian commander gave the Romans the impression that he was preparing for battle; then his army stole away from the town under cover of night, taking its plunder with it. As soon as Belisarius learned what had happened, he pursued the invaders, always remaining one day's march behind them.[19] The Persians retreated by the route they had used for their invasion, following the Euphrates through Euphratesia, this time keeping to the south of the river, past Barbalissus then Sura. Belisarius continued to shadow them, while discontent increased among his men. Eventually, on 18 April 531, Good Friday, the Persians encamped opposite the city of Callinicum. Just when they were about to depart on the following day, Belisarius' men came upon them, having set off that morning from Sura. Once the Persians proceeded beyond Callinicum, they would be

---

462–3 for the flight of the Antiochenes. Mal. 463.1–2 on Roman commanders being keen to fight the invaders. The troops of the *duces*, drawn from the regions affected by Lakhmid raids, will have been particularly dismayed by Belisarius' strategy; see also Rubin, *ZI*, 500 n.882 on hostility towards Belisarius in the east.

[18] Honigmann, *Topographie*, 23 and map 1 places Beselathon a little southeast of Bathnae, northeast of Gabbulon, accepted by Dussaud, *Topographie*, 475 and n.5. The Bathnae in Syria should be distinguished from the more important Batnae in Osrhoene, attacked during the Anastasian war, cf. Benzinger, *RE* III (1899), 124, s.v. Bathnae, Rubin, *ZI*, 499 n.867 and Petersen, 'A Roman prefect', 278–9; Julian had visited Syrian Bathnae during his advance in March 363: see Cumont, *Études Syriennes*, 20–21 and Bowersock, *Julian*, 108–9. Proc. I.18.5 for the size of the Roman force, with Mal. 461–2, referring to 16,000 troops altogether, but not providing an overall figure, cf. Stein II, 292 n.2.

[19] Mal. 463.3–6, Proc. I.18.11. Proc. (18.9) emphasises the danger of Azarethes' position (cf. Whitby, *Maurice*, 199) in terms similar to Socrates' description of the Saracens' fear in 421 when they encountered a Roman army in the same region (*HE* VII.18), on which see Shahîd, *BAFIC*, 29 and n.29.

entering uninhabited territory, as inhospitable to pursuers as pursued; only a few dilapidated Roman forts would be left between Azarethes and the Sasanian kingdom. The Roman soldiers and officers, aware that this was their last chance to engage the enemy, demanded that battle be joined with the Persians; but both Belisarius and Hermogenes refused them.[20]

iii) The battle of Callinicum

The insistence of the two *magistri* was unavailing. Not for the first time the impetuousness of the Roman soldiery forced its leaders into a change of heart, and, as on previous occasions, it proved to be a disastrous mistake. Just under two hundred years earlier the young Emperor Constantius had been similarly unable to rein back his forces when the Persians were attacking Singara. The Roman infantry had insisted on giving chase to the Persian cavalry as it retreated in the late afternoon, and had experienced some initial success. But the lengthy pursuit left the Romans exhausted and thirsty, and they quickly fell victim to a Persian counter-attack. Likewise in 531 Belisarius' men were seriously disadvantaged, having marched all the way from Sura on an empty stomach, as part of their fast for Easter Sunday.[21] So hostile was the reception which greeted Belisarius' speech in defence of his strategy that he gave in to the clamours of the soldiers; he must have feared that some of his commanders would in any case engage the enemy in defiance of his orders, which could only lead to the piecemeal destruction of the Roman army. It is also possible that Hermogenes broke ranks

---

[20] Proc. I.18.13–16, followed by Belisarius' speech to his troops, 18.17–23. Lauffray, *Halabiyya*, 32 on Persian influence in eastern Euphratesia; *ibid.* 52–6 on the prosperity of the area around Callinicum compared with further southeast, with Ammianus XIV.3.4 and Proc. *Aed.* II.6.12–16 and *Wars* I.18.12 (stating that the Persians were about to enter an utterly uninhabited region). See also above ch.2 n.60.

[21] On the battle of Singara, see the accounts of Libanius, *Or.*59.99–120 and Julian, *Or.*1, 22D–25B, both translated in Dodgeon–Lieu, *Eastern Frontier*, 181–90 (with other briefer notices; see the notes on p.386); cf. also Lightfoot, *Eastern Frontier*, 43–4 on the battle. It probably took place in 344, see most recently Burgess, *Cont. Ant.* a.344 and note. Cf. also the eagerness of the Roman troops to engage the Alamanni at Strasbourg in 357, despite a lengthy march and Julian's fears, Ammianus XVI.12.8– 19 (esp. 14–15, the men's confidence and their desire to engage the enemy before he dispersed), with Elton, *Warfare*, 216; on this occasion their enthusiasm was crowned with success. Other instances may easily be found, e.g. Tacitus, *Historiae* II.18 (Vestricius Spurinna in A.D. 69) and Corippus, *Iohannis* VI.478–505, on John Troglita's reluctance to engage the Moors in 547; his troops insisted and were heavily defeated, cf. *PLRE* III, Ioannes *qui et* Troglita 36.

with the *magister militum* and agreed to the demands, thereby obliging
his fellow commander to follow suit. In the afternoon of 19 April 531
the Romans arranged their forces in battle formation, while Azarethes
did likewise.[22]

Belisarius drew up his forces at right angles to the Euphrates.[23] At
the southernmost end, on rising ground, he stationed al-Harith and his
5000 Ghassanid allies. Next to them he placed a contingent of Lycaonians, poorly trained highland infantry from Phrygia, under the
leadership of Stephanacius, Dorotheus and Mamas (or Mamantius).[24]
Adjacent to the Lycaonians lay the formidable cavalry of Ascan, in a
position similar to the one they had occupied at Dara.[25] In the centre
Belisarius took his stand with his own men, while on his left he positioned the Huns of Sunicas and Simmas; his left flank, adjoining the
Euphrates, was held by the Roman infantry under the command of

---

[22] Proc. I.18.24–6 for Belisarius' change of heart, cf. Mal. 463 (who fails to note any
      division within the Roman army). Zach. IX.4 (225–6) reports that the Persian
      commander, whom he calls Asthebid (on which title see above, ch.5 n.86) actually
      asked Belisarius not to attack during the fast before Easter, to which he agreed; if this
      is true it will reflect Persian reluctance to do battle and will have reinforced the
      Roman soldiers' belief that the Persians were too weak to resist attack. Zach. also
      confirms the army's discontent with Belisarius' cautious policy. Proc. II.18.16–26 for
      the sort of divided attack which the *magister militum* wanted to avoid (two
      commanders in 541 approach closer to Nisibis than the rest of the army and are
      therefore driven back before the rest of Belisarius' forces can intervene).

[23] Proc. I.18.26–7 is the clearest source concerning Belisarius' dispositions, but Mal.
      463 adds important details. Like Proc., Mal. puts the Romans on the south side of the
      Euphrates, but places the river behind rather than beside them. Cf. Bury, *HLRE* II,
      86–7 and 87 n.1, and Rubin, *ZI*, 499 n.872.

[24] Mal. 463.11–13 (Dorotheus and Mamas) with Proc. I.18.7 (Longinus and Stepha-
      nacius, the latter mentioned by Mal. at 463.23); they may have been tribunes of the
      newly raised *numeri*, as *PLRE* III, Dorotheus 3, suggests. Cf. the Lycocranitae raised
      to fight the Lakhmids, ch.7 n.40. Mal.'s Dorotheus might be identical with the
      commander on the right wing at Dara (= *PLRE* III, Dorotheus 1), but *PLRE* is
      probably right to distinguish them, while Mamas is an uncertain reading, cf. *PLRE*
      III, Mamas. Proc. I.18.38–40 on the poor quality of the Lycaonian troops, described
      as Isaurians, but evidently much inferior; Rubin, *ZI*, 500 n.882, argues convincingly
      that Mal.'s distinction of Phrygians and 'Isaurians' is mistaken, though it is accepted
      by *PLRE* III, Dorotheus 3.

[25] As Rubin, *ZI*, 500–1 n.882, remarks, there can be no doubting that Malalas' Aspcal
      and Procopius' Ascan are identical. *PLRE* III nonetheless separates Ascan and
      Apskal, as did Bury, *HLRE* II, 87. Since Mal. has already named two Lycaonian
      commanders (and Proc. two others), he is probably mistaken in stating that Apskal
      was the leader of the Phrygians (464.1–4). The confusion may have arisen because
      Apskal/Ascan and his men were positioned next to the Lycaonians.

Peter, a bodyguard of Justinian.[26] Although our picture of the Roman order of battle for Callinicum is less clear than that for Dara, it appears that Belisarius was reversing the tactics he had used in the previous year. Then he had refused a battle in the centre, concentrating his strength on the flanks; now he preferred to leave the infantry on the wings, with his best cavalry in the centre. He could anticipate that the infantry might turn to flight, and that the Ghassanids might abandon their position, but he could hope nonetheless to keep his main force intact and undivided.[27] For his part, Azarethes entrusted his left flank to al-Mundhir, while deploying his own cavalry in the centre, and his infantry on the right, opposite that of the Romans (phase 1).[28]

The battle began with the customary exchange of missiles. On this occasion the Romans had the worst of it, largely on account of a strong westerly wind, which increased the power and penetration of the already more numerous arrows of the Persians.[29] By mid-afternoon neither side had gained the advantage in the skirmishing and discharge of missiles that had been taking place; Scythian-type tactics appear to have been attempted against Sunicas and Simmas, but without success.[30] The attacks in the north may have been purely diversionary, for then came the decisive stroke: the best Persian troops were shifted to the left wing and, in concert with al-Mundhir's men, shattered the Roman right. Most of al-Harith's forces melted away, leaving the Lycaonians and Ascan to defend the Roman position, and giving the

[26] On Peter, Proc. I.18.6, not to be confused with Petrus 27 in *PLRE* II, who campaigned in Lazica: he is Petrus 2, *PLRE* III. Proc.'s positioning of Peter and the infantry on the left should be combined with Mal.'s statement (463.13–14) that Sunicas and Simmas were stationed there.

[27] *Peri Strategias* 35 on the usual positioning of cavalry on the flanks; 35.8 for the occasional inversion of this procedure.

[28] Proc. I.18.26.

[29] Proc. I.18.32–4 insists that the Persians were at a disadvantage in the exchange of arrows. The author of the *Strategikon*, however, while aware of both Roman and Persian techniques with the bow (I.1 [74–6]), advises the Romans to come to close quarters with the Persians as soon as they are within bowshot (XI.1 [358]). Zach. IX.4 (226) on the wind against the Romans; the coldness of the day which he also notes will have harmed both sides.

[30] Proc. I.18.35 on two-thirds of the day having passed, 18.31 on skirmishes; the Romans cannot have reached the Persian camp until late morning, having set off from Sura the same day. Coulston, 'Tactical developments', 67, notes that battles were seldom decided by archery. Mal. 463.15–17 on the Persians attacking Sunicas and Simmas, then retreating hurriedly.

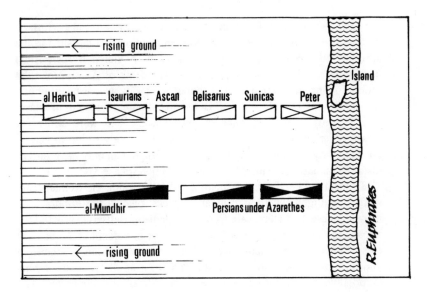

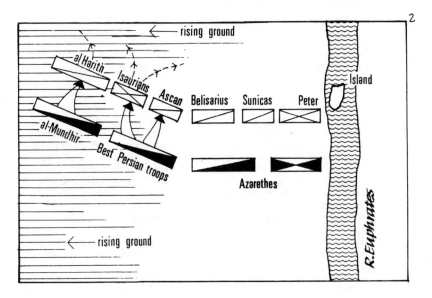

Callinicum: Phases 1 and 2

Persians command of the higher ground (phase 2).[31] Ascan performed notable feats in his defence of the Roman position, but perished in the struggle; other Roman casualties included the phylarch Abrus ('Amr) and the Lycaonian leader Stephanacius. The death of Ascan broke the morale of the inexperienced Lycaonian troops, who had been among the most vociferous critics of Belisarius. Some remained in place, offering only token resistance to the attackers, and were easily cut down; others apparently fled northwards, desperately trying to escape the enemy by crossing the Euphrates. Their flight can only have further disrupted an already imperilled Roman position (phase 3).[32]

To meet the Persian attack coming from the south, the Roman army shifted its alignment through ninety degrees, placing the Euphrates to its rear (phase 4).[33] Here, safe from encirclement, Belisarius ordered the remaining cavalry to dismount and join Peter in defending the bank in close formation. His tactics were clearly the best means available to him of minimising further casualties and ensuring that as many troops as possible reached safety on the other side of the Euphrates. The formation described by Procopius resembles the *foulkon* presented in the *Strategikon*, a dense mass of infantry in which the shields of the front rank interlock, while those of the second rank are placed above the heads of the leading ranks. While it is unlikely that Belisarius' troops would have kept hold of their lances to fend off the Persian horse, as the *Strategikon* recommends, the bowmen protected by the

---

[31] Proc. I.18.35–6, Mal. 463.17–464.7. Both Proc. and Mal. mention rumours that al-Harith's men had betrayed the Romans, but neither endorses them, despite the accusations of partiality levelled at Proc. by Shahîd, *BASIC* I, 134–6; it is not clear that Proc.'s ξυμφρονήσαντες (18.35) refers to an agreement between al-Harith and the best Persian forces rather than just among the élite troops themselves. Allegations of treachery, it should be remembered, would serve the interests of all Roman leaders forced to explain their conduct in the battle. Shahîd, *ibid.* 136–41 (with 178–9), is largely successful in rebutting the accusations of treachery (countenanced by Rubin, *ZI*, 287), suggesting rather that some (non-Ghassanid) phylarchs may have abandoned al-Harith out of anger at his recent promotion. As Shahîd, *ibid.* 142, notes, al-Harith's role in the field later the same year demonstrates that he at least was not viewed as a traitor; Mal.'s statement that al-Harith and some of his men remained in the field of battle should therefore be believed (and is not incompatible with Proc., who merely implies that all the Arabs fled).

[32] Proc. I.18.38–40 with Mal. 463.23–464.9 (noting the flight of the 'Isaurians' — to be identified with the Lycaonians — northwards). Mal.'s placing of contingents here in relation to the Euphrates seems awry, as elsewhere. On Abrus, see *PLRE* III, Abrus and Shahîd, *BASIC* I, 137 (suggesting that he was a relative of al-Harith).

[33] Proc. I.18.44, cf. Mal. 463.9–10 (wrongly stating that the river was at the Romans' rear at the outset of the battle).

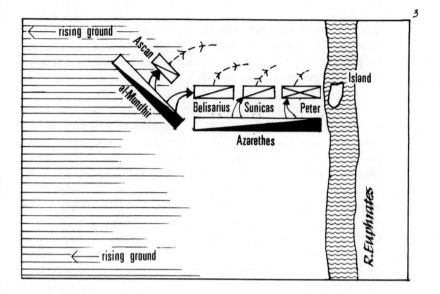

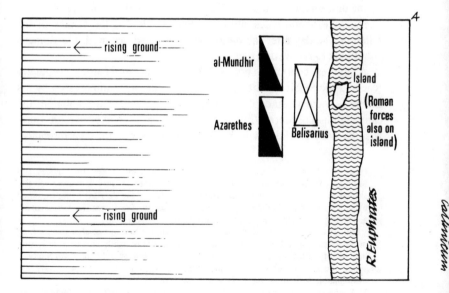

Callinicum: Phases 3 and 4

shield wall will have been able to inflict considerable damage on the
attackers. The discipline of the infantry which remained on the south
bank is attested by their steadfastness in the face of enemy charges; to
counter the Persian cavalry they took to clashing their shields, a well-
known horse-scaring tactic.[34]

There is a remarkable divergence between the two principal sources
for the aftermath of the engagement. According to Procopius, the Romans arrived at Callinicum only on the day after the battle, having
passed the night on the island on which they had sought refuge.
Malalas, still highlighting the role of Sunicas and Simmas, asserts that
the Romans arrived at Callinicum on the day of the battle, having
pursued the Persians for two miles. He follows up this unlikely account
with the report that it was the Romans, including the citizens of
Callinicum, who on the next day — Easter Sunday — despoiled the
Persian corpses left on the field of battle. It appears that the 'official'
version departed further from the truth in the final stages of the engagement than in any other part, transforming the Roman defeat and withdrawal across the river into a victory parade by the two *duces* followed
by the despoliation of a battlefield still in the hands of the enemy. More
likely, as Procopius describes, the Persians looted the bodies of the
fallen on the day after the battle; once they had departed, the Romans
could look to recovering their dead.[35]

Azarethes continued his withdrawal after the battle, eventually
reaching the Persian court. Kavadh, it appears, was unimpressed by his
general's victory: since the largest place captured was Gabbulon, the
campaign had produced little booty, and casualties had been high. Likewise by May Justinian will have learnt of his general's performance,

---

[34] Proc. I.18.41–8; cf. Mal. 464.15–18 (an infantry battle fought by Sunicas and
Simmas). *Strategikon* XII B 16 (442–4) for the close infantry formation (clearly
similar to the earlier Roman *testudo*), cf. XI.I (356) on the Persians being disturbed
by a close infantry formation, and *Peri Strategias* 36. See Rance, *Tactics*, 218–27,
and Ravegnani, *Soldati*, 59–60, 64, on this tactic.

    Mal. 464.10–14 states that Belisarius was among the first to flee after the crushing
of the Roman right. He has seldom been believed, and is rightly viewed as reflecting
the hostility of his source, which prefers to exalt the bravery of Sunicas and Simmas.
While the exploits of the Huns are passed over by Proc., they are clearly not
incompatible with his account. On Mal.'s bias here, see above section i.

[35] Mal. 464.14–465.6, cf. Proc. I.18.49–50 (noting that the fighting continued until
nightfall). Mal. 465.1–3 on the pursuit of the Persians towards evening and the arrival
of the *duces* in Callinicum (on the other side of the Euphrates) is singularly obscure.
Kirchner, *Zur Beurteilung*, 15, points out the implausibility of Mal.'s version; Rubin,
ZI, 286, argues that both sides plundered the battlefield in turn on the Easter Sunday.

and an enquiry was quickly set up; it did not take long to bring about the dismissal of the *magister militum per Orientem*.[36]

iv) The aftermath of Callinicum

Immediately after the battle Hermogenes went to the Persian court to reopen negotiations, but found the king unreceptive; Kavadh still wished to gain the advantage over the Romans before ceasing hostilities. He had therefore ordered a force to invade Osrhoene, which attacked the fort of Abgersaton. Bouzes, who had remained at Amida during the campaign because of illness, sent his nephew Domnentiolus to defend the fort; but in spite of the efforts of the defenders, and the losses they inflicted on the Persians, Abgersaton was eventually stormed by the besiegers.[37] The victorious Persians then withdrew to their own territory. Meanwhile Belisarius and his commanders apparently remained inactive, awaiting the results of Constantiolus' enquiry. In May or June the report was handed to the emperor, who thereupon relieved Belisarius of his command and ordered him back to the capital. His successor, according to Malalas, was Mundus, hitherto the *magister militum per Illyricum*; a certain Constantine may have taken over immediate command of Belisarius' army.[38]

Justinian now took further measures to bring the war to a close. On the one hand he ordered Sittas to move south and take charge of the defence of the east; he also sent a financial contribution to the east, in

---

[36] Proc. I.18.50–56 for the poor reception of Azarethes (perhaps exaggerated) and the large number of casualties. Mal. 463–4 notes the deaths of Naaman (al-Nu'man), a son of al-Mundhir (perhaps the eldest, cf. Shahîd, *BASIC* I, 137), the 'tribune' Andrazes and several exarchs; one, Amerdach, was captured after being wounded by Sunicas. Rubin, *ZI*, 288, rightly refers to the battle as a 'Pyrrhussieg'. Mal. 465 for Hermogenes' report to the emperor and the setting up of the enquiry.

[37] Mal. 465–6, apparently shortly after the battle of Callinicum, with Zach. IX.4 (226) and *PLRE* III, Domnentiolus. The location of Abgersaton is unknown.

[38] Mal. 466.13–18 on Constantiolus' report and the appointment of Mundus; see above n.6 on Constantine. The accession of Mundus is open to doubt: he had been appointed *magister militum per Illyricum* only in 529, and when he was present in Constantinople in January 532 he held the same post (Proc. I.24.40). There is no other evidence that he ever served east of Constantinople. His appointment, if genuine, may therefore have been purely honorary; or Mal. may be mistaken, and the post have been left vacant until Belisarius regained it in 532/3 (*PLRE* III, 187). Alternatively, Proc. I.21.3 might imply that the eastern command was given to Sittas. Stein II, 293, accepts Mundus' appointment, as does *PLRE* III, Mundus; Rubin, *ZI*, 289, thinks his appointment unlikely, but proposes no alternative.

the hands of the former praetorian prefect Demosthenes, to ensure that all the cities were provided with adequate supplies for a siege.[39] At the same time diplomatic pressure on Kavadh was stepped up. An attempt by al-Mundhir to enter into negotiations through a deacon called Sergius was rebuffed, although the deacon was sent back to the Lakhmid chief with gifts from the emperor. Justinian replied directly to Kavadh in the wake of al-Mundhir's initiative, sending Rufinus to him to urge that he come to terms, and stating that 'it is honourable and glorious to make the two states [...] live in peace. If you do not do this, I shall seize the Persian land for myself.'[40] Although the threat was unrealistic, it was well chosen: for Kavadh, who was around eighty years old, will have been anxious to avoid compounding the difficulties facing the accession of his designated successor, Khusro. Later in the year Rufinus was sent to Kavadh again, this time accompanied by Strategius; they brought gifts from both the emperor and the empress for the Persian king and his wife. But they got no further than Edessa, since the king deferred receiving them until he had launched one further invasion of Roman territory.[41]

The remaining operations of the war all took place further north, where the campaigning season began only in summer. While the Persians made a final attempt at seizing a Roman base (at Martyropolis), the *magister militum per Armeniam* Dorotheus went on the offensive in Persarmenia, where he gained control of several important Persian

---

[39] Proc. I.21.3 on Sittas. Mal. 467.19–22 on Demosthenes, perhaps the same man who had governed Osrhoene under Anastasius, cf. *PLRE* II, Demosthenes 3 and 4. In July he reached Edessa, *Chron. Ede.* 103. Josh. Styl. §81 notes the establishment of depots throughout the cities of the East in 504/5.

[40] Mal. 466.18–467.6 (quotation from Jeffreys-Scott, 272) and cf. Scott, 'Diplomacy', 163–4. Shahîd, *BASIC* I, 142–3, argues that Sergius was the bishop of Sergiopolis, who had taken part in the conference of Ramla (in 519); he rightly sees al-Mundhir's move as inspired by the Persian king, and Justinian's despatch of gifts as an attempt to entice the Lakhmid chief away from his allegiance to Persia.

[41] Mal. 467.8–14. Scott, 'Diplomacy', 164, suggests that Mal. may be in error when he states that Kavadh was married to his own sister: he may have misinterpreted an attempt by the empress to claim the Persian queen as her sister, just as their husbands called one another brothers. See also Proc. *Anecd.* 30.24 on Theodora's unprecedented role in contacts with the Persian court. *PLRE* II, Rufinus 13, places the embassy of Rufinus and Strategius after the battle of Callinicum but fails to mention the letter delivered by Rufinus to Kavadh, apparently before this mission. The tone of the two embassies is too different for them to be identified. Rufinus' first mission was in June, after al-Mundhir's approach to Justinian (Mal. 466.18), and he need not have returned to the capital after conveying the message; this would allow time for his second (unsuccessful) mission, perhaps in August 531.

fortresses.[42] Kavadh was spurred to make the attempt on Martyropolis by events which had taken place earlier that summer on the frontier between Sophanene and Arzanene. Gadar the Kadisene, who helped guard Arzanene for the king, had invaded Sophanene with a small force, plundering the lands around Attachas. The *dux* based at Martyropolis, Bessas, had therefore sallied out to drive off the invaders, but his first engagement proved inconclusive. The Romans had then in-flicted a serious defeat on the Persians at Beth Helte, to the southeast of Attachas, in a second battle; once again, Scythian tactics were em-ployed to good effect, inducing the Persians to break ranks. Gadar fell in the battle, and Yazdgerd, the nephew of the governor of Arzanene, Hormizd, was captured by the Romans. The *dux* had followed up his success by ravaging Arzanene, thereby offering a personal insult to the Persian king, to whom the lands belonged.[43]

The Persian campaign against Martyropolis was conducted by Aspebedus, Mihr-Mihroe and Khanaranges, their army consisting at least partly of Huns recruited by Mihr-Girowi. They first invaded Roman Mesopotamia, then turned north, passing through the Tur Abdin and crossing the Tigris into Sophanene.[44] Even without Bessas' recent

[42] Mal. 469 is the only source to report Dorotheus' successes, including the capture of a mountain fort filled with the goods of Persian traders (in summer 531). Mal. does not identify the fort, but his description of it is similar to Proc.'s of Anglon, near Doubios (Dvin), II.25.1–9, also a trading centre, and attacked by the Romans in 543. If this identification is correct, Dorotheus had made substantial inroads into Persarmenia.

[43] Zach. IX.5 (227), IX.6 (227–8), with Whitby, 'Arzanene', 207, on Arzanene as Persian crown property and Kavadh's determination to avenge Bessas' raid. Cf. Mal. 468–9, an account of Hermogenes' report to the emperor, which describes the two battles; Hermogenes might well have inflated the numbers (Mal. speaks of 6000 invaders, of whom 2000 were killed), and so Zach.'s figures (700 Persian cavalry, accompanied by some infantry; 500 Roman cavalry) cannot simply be dismissed. Zach. explicitly places the events in the summer of 531. Despite the note of Hamilton-Brooks (227 n.4), Attachas is not as far from Martyropolis as Proc. believes (I.21.9, 100 stades): the actual distance is 20 km, which is closer to Zach.'s four stades. Cf. Dillemann, *Mésopotamie*, 235–6 and Georg. Cypr. 938 (with Honigmann's note, p.65). For the location of Beth Helte, see Honigmann, *Ostgrenze*, 17 and map 1; he notes that Zach.'s reference to a battle by the Tigris must refer to the Nymphius (Batman Su) rather than the Tigris itself. Cf. also *PLRE* II, Bessas (though it wrongly places Martyropolis in Mesopotamia).

There was another Attachas further south, near Amida, cf. Proc. *Aed.* II.4.14, but it is unlikely to be the one referred to by either Proc. or Zach.

[44] On Aspebedus, see above ch.5 n.126, on Mermeroes, ch.8 n.41; Khanaranges is probably another misunderstanding of a title as a name, cf. Proc. I.5.4. The route of the invaders is uncertain: Proc. refers to Mesopotamia (I.21.4), from which I infer a route north through the Tur Abdin. An approach through Arzanene is also possible.

successes, the city had long been a thorn in the Persian side, 'for it acts as an ambush and a place of refuge for a Roman army, enabling it to ravage Arzanene.' The renovations carried out there by Justinian in 528 rendered it still more menacing. By September 531 the Persian army had encamped outside and started to lay siege to it; the defenders, caught unprepared for an attack so late in the year, had few supplies, and feared that they would not be able to hold out for long. The Persians, under orders from Kavadh not to return until Martyropolis had fallen, used every method possible to capture it. Mines were dug, a mound built against the wall, scaling-ladders erected, and even a wooden siege-tower constructed. But their efforts were no more successful than those of their predecessors at Amida in the autumn of 502: the defenders of Martyropolis proved equally resourceful, and one person in particular devised a clever counter-measure to the Persian siege-tower. A taller tower was constructed within the walls, which allowed the defenders to fire down on the attackers, rendering their tower useless; from their own tower the Romans then used a machine to drop stones on the besiegers, crushing men and matériel beneath it.[45]

Unfortunately for the Persians, the defenders of Martyropolis enjoyed several advantages not shared by the Amidenes in 502. First, there were among them 'Bouzes and a Roman force of no small size', presumably including the *numerus* placed there by Justinian in 528.[46] Second, and even more important, help was close at hand. Sittas mustered a large Roman force, joined up with al-Harith and Hermogenes, and arrived in Amida in October or November. From there the army proceeded to Attachas, only 20 km to the north of the besiegers. By this point — November or December — there was no longer any need for them to intervene. The cold climate and the rumour of the approach of the Roman army would probably have been enough in themselves to

---

[45] Quotation from Zach. IX.6 (228), tr. Hamilton-Brooks. On the fortifications of Martyropolis, see Howard-Johnston, 'Citharizon', 220 and Mal. 427. Whitby, 'Martyropolis', 182, prefers Proc.'s account in *Aed.* (III.2) to that in the *Wars* (I.21.7–8); the latter may exaggerate the weakness of the city so as to underline the fragility of the Roman position after the removal of Belisarius, cf. Rubin, *PvK* 378 (and note e.g. Proc. I.21.23). Zach. IX.6 (228) states that the besiegers only arrived in September (the start of year ten). Proc. I.21.7–8 on the siege; more details in Mal. 469–70 (presumably from a report of Hermogenes). The defenders' machine recalls the ballista at Amida known as 'the crusher' (see above ch.5 p.89 with n.48). On the siege techniques employed in general, cf. e.g. Elton, *Warfare*, 260–62.

[46] Zach. IX.6 (228), cf. Proc. I.21.5, adding that Bessas was present, and mentioning a garrison; Mal. 427 on the *numerus*.

induce the Persians to retreat; but when the besieging generals also heard that their king had just died and that a Roman-allied Hunnic army was marching in their direction, they hesitated no longer. The Romans, eager to hasten the withdrawal of the invaders, promptly handed over two hostages, and the Persian army departed.[47]

Once on the throne, Khusro moved quickly to come to terms with the Romans. An envoy was despatched to the Roman ambassadors, presumably Rufinus and Strategius, summoning them to the Persian court; but they refused his invitation, explaining that their mandate did not extend to discussions with the new king. Khusro therefore sent a message to the emperor through Hermogenes, and requested that the imperial ambassadors be allowed to approach him. Justinian, however, declined the king's request outright, and refused to acknowledge him as Kavadh's successor. The emperor perceived that he now held the advantage, and was determined to exploit it: by not recognising Khusro he could hope to destabilise the new king's position, which was far from secure. But despite Justinian's efforts, Khusro was able to overcome the opponents of his accession, and the emperor soon abandoned his intransigent stance. A renewed Persian request, this time for a truce of three months, was favourably received and hostages exchanged; meanwhile the Roman ambassadors were recalled to the capital to consult with the emperor.[48]

The inhabitants of the Roman east had one more invasion to endure before peace was at last concluded. Ironically, it was inflicted not by Romans or Persians, but by Sabir Huns. Earlier in the year the Persians had made efforts to recruit Sabirs for their campaigns against the

---

[47] Proc. I.21.9–27, including an interesting account of the defection of a Persian spy, who then persuaded the Persian commanders that the Hunnic force was going to attack them (rather than the Romans); see also Zach. IX.6 (229) on the suffering of the Persians, Mal. 470 on their concern over the approach of Sittas' force. Proc. stresses the hesitation of Sittas and Hermogenes, but it is clear that there was no need for them to intervene. Kavadh died on 13 September 531, cf. *PLRE* II, Cavades and Stein II, 294 n.2; news of his death will probably not have reached the besiegers until October.

On the κατάσκοποι (spies) mentioned by Proc., cf. *Strategikon*, II.11 (130), IX.5 (330–34). For this episode see Rubin, *ZI*, 502 n.909; on Roman/Persian intelligence in general, Lee, 'Embassies', 455–61 and *Information*, 170–77, esp. 177 n.26 on Persian spies.

[48] On Justinian's manoeuvrings, Mal. 471–2 (who also notes the internal problems facing Khusro). On Khusro's accession, Proc. I.21.17–22 with Stein II, 294 n.2: he may have been crowned a month before his father's death. Also Christensen, *L'Iran*, 361–2 on the opposition of Kaoses, the king's brother, and see above ch.6 pp.134–5.

Romans. Some had served in the siege of Martyropolis, and more were still on their way at the time the siege was abandoned. Arriving to find that they were no longer required, but nothing daunted, they proceeded to ravage Roman territory, raiding as far south as Cilicia, Euphratesia and the environs of Cyrrhus. They encountered little resistance, no doubt taking many people by surprise through the timing of their raid (December 531). Only as they withdrew were counter-operations mounted: the *duces* at Martyropolis and Citharizon and the *magister militum per Armeniam* Dorotheus succeeded in defeating detachments of the invaders and recovering some of their spoils.[49]

Although at first the Romans suspected that the Sabirs had been operating at the instigation of the Persians, an enquiry conducted by Rufinus cleared the Persians of complicity. There was no longer any obstacle to negotiations, and the moment was propitious for peace: both monarchs, as Procopius describes in successive chapters of his *Wars*, were soon to find their régimes seriously threatened. A costly and inconclusive foreign war was desirable for neither.[50]

---

[49] Mal. 472–3, Proc. I.21.28 (playing down the Sabir raid), Zach. IX.6 (229), noting the forays of the *duces*; also Zach. VIII.5 (212) on some Huns who reached the Tur Abdin. The line of their retreat northwards can be traced by these defeats: see Howard-Johnston and Ryan, *Scholar*, 56. On the date of the incursion, see also *Chron. 724*, a.843 (111, 14; the text has 'Indians', which has been emended to 'Huns') and *Chron. Edess.* 103 (December 531) with Stein II, 293 and n.2. Trombley, 'War and Society', text to nn.44–5 on the impact of the raids evident in the epigraphical record.

[50] Proc. I.23 (esp. 23.4–6) on the plot against Khusro by his younger brother Zames (of uncertain date, cf. *PLRE* II, Zames, and Christensen, *L'Iran*, 381–2). Proc. I.24 on the Nika riot of January 532, which came close to unseating Justinian; see Bury, 'Nika riot', Evans, *Justinian*, 119–25 and Greatrex, 'Nika riot'. The fact that Rufinus' enquiry absolved the Persians of blame for the raid need not imply that they were not responsible: the Roman desire for peace was such that they might have been prepared to overlook evidence of Persian involvement.

X
The Eternal Peace (532–540)

i) Negotiations

As soon as Rufinus had established in his enquiry that the raid of the Sabir Huns had not been inspired by the Persians, he led an embassy to Khusro's court. Alexander, Thomas, Hermogenes and Rufinus — a remarkably high-level delegation — met Khusro at a location on the Tigris, probably in February or March 532. They were empowered to arrange peace terms with the king and spared no effort in fulfilling their mission. According to Procopius, the envoys were excessively submissive; whether or not his accusation is justified, their approach was initially successful, and Khusro set forth his terms.[1]

The king's demands, it turned out, were simple and for the most part acceptable to the Romans. Khusro agreed to a peace of indefinite duration, in return for which Justinian was to make him a one-off payment of 110 *centenaria* as a subsidy for the defence of the Caspian Gates; the headquarters of the *dux* of Mesopotamia was to be moved from Dara back to Constantia; he, Khusro, would maintain control over Sarapanis and Scanda, the two Lazic forts captured during his father's reign, and the emperor would return to him the Armenian forts of Pharangium and Bolum.[2] The ambassadors were initially prepared to accept all these demands, apart from the restoration of the Armenian forts. This they had no authority to concede, and Rufinus was despatched to the capital to consult with the emperor; the negotiations

---

[1] Proc. I.22.1–2, cf. Mal. 477.4–6 (mentioning only Rufinus), with Scott, 'Diplomacy', 165, dating Rufinus' mission to after February 532 (note Proc.'s αὐτίκα at 22.1, following the Sabir raid). *PLRE* II, Rufinus 13 (cf. *PLRE* III, Alexander 1) dates the embassy to late 531; *PLRE*'s dates are all too early here, based on a mistaken dating of the Sabir raid (to October, rather than December, 531; see above ch.9 n.49). See also *PLRE* III, Hermogenes 1 and Thomas 4 on the other ambassadors.

[2] Proc. I.22.3–5.

were therefore suspended for seventy days, a period judged sufficient
for a return trip to Constantinople.[3]

By April or May 532 Rufinus had returned to the frontier, where he
found that tension had risen once again: rumours (no doubt inspired by
the Nika riot) had reached Khusro that Justinian had executed his chief
ambassador, and these had prompted the king to move his forces
towards Roman territory. Rufinus was able to defuse the situation,
however, and reported to Khusro that the emperor had consented to his
terms. While Khusro and Rufinus put the final touches to the peace, the
other ambassadors set about conveying the money across the frontier to
Nisibis. At this point the whole process was thrown into disarray:
Justinian, in a characteristic change of heart, suddenly ordered the
ambassadors to reject Persian retention of the two Lazic forts. Already
a substantial sum of money had been brought to Nisibis, which placed
Rufinus, the leading advocate of a settlement, in a dangerous position.
Only by humbly beseeching the Persian king was he able to persuade
him to return the gold and to defer hostilities for the moment. The
Roman envoys thereupon went back to Dara with the gold, while
Khusro withdrew his forces from the frontier. Rufinus' colleagues,
suspicious of his success in dealing with Khusro, reported him to the
emperor; but nothing came of their accusations.[4]

Only a few months later, probably in September 532, Hermogenes
and Rufinus again visited the Persian court. Contacts had no doubt
continued during the intervening period, for the two sides now had little
difficulty in settling the remaining points of dispute.[5]

---

[3] *PLRE* is wrong to identify Mal.'s three-month truce (472.13) with Proc.'s seventy-
day deadline for Rufinus' return to the negotiations (I.22.7): the truce was earlier (see
above ch.9 p.211), and in any case Proc.'s seventy days are not described as a truce.
   The caution of the Roman delegation was justified: Justin II was greatly angered
when the ambassador John exceeded his powers in his dealings with Khusro in 567/8,
cf. Menander, frg.9.1–2, *PLRE* III, Ioannes 81 and Lee, 'Embassies', 458–9. On the
time allowed for Rufinus' return, see Whitby, *Maurice*, 256 n.9, who suggests that
news from the eastern front might reach the imperial capital in ten days by the
imperial post; see also above ch.5 n.67.

[4] Proc. I.22.9–15 with *PLRE* II, Rufinus 13. Zach. IX.7 (230–31) reports that Rufinus
had supported Khusro's claims as the successor of Kavadh, which is accepted by Lee,
Information, 47; if true, it would help to account for his influence with Khusro. On
the procedure for the hand-over of payments, see Iluk, 'The export of gold', 84–5.

[5] There is still some dispute as to the precise date of the treaty. Proc. explicitly puts it
in the sixth year of Justinian's reign (April 532–March 533, I.22.17). Mal. 477.13–22
implies a date late in 532: the notice of the peace follows one on the restoration of
John the Cappadocian to his post as praetorian prefect, which had taken place by
October that year (cf. *PLRE* III, Ioannes 11). *Chr. Edess.* 104 dates the conclusion of

ii) The treaty

The Eternal Peace signed by the two sides differed little from the agreement nearly reached earlier the same year. Justinian undertook to pay the sum of 110 *centenaria* to Khusro, the equivalent of 11,000 lbs. of gold. Both sides agreed to hand back the forts they had captured during the war, and so the Armenian forts of Pharangium and Bolum were returned to the Persians, while the Romans recovered the Lazic forts at Sarapanis and Scanda, as Justinian had wanted. Iberia remained in Persian hands; the only concession to those who had defected to the Roman cause was that they were allowed to choose whether to remain at Justinian's court or return to their homeland.[6] All captives and hostages taken by either side were returned. Finally, Khusro and Justinian specifically acknowledged one another as brothers, and agreed that each would bear assistance, military or financial, to the other, should he stand in need of it.[7]

The treaty arranged by Hermogenes, Rufinus and Khusro was ratified by both sides. After thirty years of war, the two powers were at peace once more. The terms of the treaty testify to the desire of both sides for peace. Khusro was prepared to return the Lazic forts to Justinian and did not insist upon the removal of the fortress at Dara. The Romans for their part consented to transfer the base of the *dux* of

---

the peace to September 532, while Zach. IX.7 (231) places it in year 11 (September 532–August 533), adding that it was in summertime. Marc. *com.* places it in 533, though it should be remembered that he also places the fall of Amida in the wrong year. For September 532 see Stein II, 295 n.1, followed by Cameron, *Mediterranean World*, 110; Stein oddly believed that the treaty only came into effect in 533, however.

[6] See above ch.7 n.17 on the disappearance of the Iberian royal family; Toumanoff, 'Caucasia and Byzantium', 120 and n.34 on the cession of Iberia in 532. Theoph. A.M. 6027 (216) reports the arrival of an Iberian dynast, Zamanarzus, in Constantinople in 534/5, who was cordially received by the emperor and sent back to his kingdom. He may have been a ruler of (part of) Iberia, with whom the emperor sought to gain influence; but attempts to identify him either with Gourgenes (Stein II, 295 n.1) or another member of the royal house of Iberia (Toumanoff, *Studies*, 385 n.8, cf. 371–2) are highly speculative. See also Mango–Scott, *Theophanes*, 313 n.1, for a discussion of the episode.

The sum of 11,000 lbs. of gold refers to 11,000 Roman lbs., the equivalent of 7934 modern lbs. (taking one Roman lb. as 327.45g, cf. *OCD*[3], 1621; Jones, *LRE*, xv, puts the Roman lb. at 321g).

[7] Proc. I.22.16–18 (noting in particular the return of the Hunnic spy Dagaris, on whom see *PLRE* III, Dagaris). Mal. 477.16–22, noting the mutual assistance treaty. Cf. also Stein II, 294–5, Bury, *HLRE* II, 88, Rubin, *ZI*, 297 and Güterbock, *Byzanz*, 43–5 on the terms of the treaty in general. On the *centenarion*, the unit of payment, see Dagron–Morrisson, 'Le *kentènarion*'.

Mesopotamia from Dara to Constantia.[8] Justinian made a substantial
monetary contribution to the Persians, but avoided the ignominy of
annual subsidies, which might have given the impression that the Romans were tributaries of the Sasanians. The size of the Roman payment
should not be exaggerated. It certainly did not represent an excessive
blow to the Roman treasury, as a few earlier examples of expenditure
may demonstrate. In 443 Attila had forced Theodosius II not only to
make annual payments to the Huns of 2100 lbs. of gold, but also to pay
an outstanding sum of 6000 lbs. of gold. A quarter of a century later,
the Emperor Leo had launched a huge expedition to reconquer North
Africa from the Vandal king Geiseric; the attempt failed disastrously,
and is reported to have cost the treasury 1300 *centenaria* (130,000 lbs.
of gold). Furthermore, it has been calculated that in the sixth century
the annual income to the treasury from Egypt, the richest province of
the eastern empire, was 20,000 lbs. of gold. Even with the rebuilding
necessary in the capital after the Nika riot, and the continuing reconstruction of Antioch, the imperial treasury was quite capable of
sustaining such a single donation.[9] For the Persians, on the other hand,
it represented the largest Roman contribution ever made to their
treasury. That their need for funds had not diminished since the
Anastasian war is clear from Kavadh's repeated demands for money
right up to his death; the donation will have greatly relieved the
pressure on Sasanian finances, while at the same time boosting the

---

[8] Proc. I.22.16, cf. Stein II, 294. Mal. puts the length of the war at thirty-one years
(478.2), but he will have been counting inclusively (from October 502).

[9] Priscus, frg.9.3.1–10, for the payments to Attila, with Iluk, 'The export of gold', 87;
Priscus, frg.52.1–3 on Leo's expedition of 468 (under Basiliscus), with Blockley,
FCH II, 399 n.184 (for comparably large figures from other sources); see also Elton,
Warfare, 118 and n.2. For the revenue of Egypt, Jones, *LRE*, 463 and n.126. Jones,
loc. cit., suggests an annual income in gold of only 400 *centenaria* for the eastern
empire (40,000 lbs.), based on *Anecd.* 19.8; however he overlooks Proc.'s statement
there that this sum was raised illegally, and hence excludes all the legitimate income
of the government. On later payments to the Persians, usually made in several,
smaller, instalments, see Whitby, *Maurice*, 208; the ransoms extorted by Khusro in
the 540s were considerably less, cf. table IV in Iluk, 'The export of gold', 92.
  The insignificance to the Roman treasury of the sum paid is stressed by Rubin,
'Diplomacy and war', 684, cf. Isaac, 'The Army', 129–32, and Moorhead, *Justinian*,
24, noting what good value the payments were; *contra*, Stein II, 295, on the large
scale of the expenditure, though his view that it was linked to Roman payments owed
since 363 is not justifiable (even if the sum bears a certain numerical relation to
earlier demands by Kavadh, e.g. Zach. VIII.5 [206], 500 lbs., cf. Mich. Syr. IX.16
[178], 5500 *centenaria*, presumably a mistake for lbs. of gold).

reputation of the king who had secured the deal.[10] The agreement to assist the other power may merely have ratified an earlier agreement on the same lines noted by Joshua the Stylite and Malalas, which had not prevented previous Roman emperors from refusing aid to the Persians on several occasions. It was nevertheless a dangerous undertaking, since it could easily furnish Khusro with a pretext for war, should he make further demands for payments.[11]

Never before had Rome and Persia agreed to an eternal peace. It was to last, according to Malalas, 'for the duration of both their [i.e. Rome's and Persia's] lives'.[12] Earlier treaties had been made for one hundred years, perhaps one hundred and twenty; and the eastern frontier had even known periods of peace during which the two sides were technically at war. But the optimism of both parties, and perhaps particularly of Justinian, in proclaiming an indefinite peace, proved to be unwarranted, and later in his reign the emperor preferred to make more limited payments in return for fixed periods of peace.[13] It should not be doubted, however, that the peace actually was proclaimed as 'eternal': Justinian specifically refers to the treaty in the second edition of the *Codex Justinianus*, where he notes *pacem cum Persis in aeternum*

---

[10] In 244 the Emperor Philip the Arab had paid 500,000 *denarii* (here to be equated with *aurei*, cf. Guey, 'Autour des *Res Gestae*', 262 and Pekánen, 'Le tribut', 277), as Shapur I himself boasted in his *Res Gestae*: see Maricq, '*Res Gestae*', 308–9, lines 9–10, also in Dodgeon–Lieu, *Eastern Frontier*, 45 with 358 n.25. The weight of the *aureus* decreased substantially through the third century; under Philip it averaged 4.52g (cf. Bland, 'The development', 83 table 2 and 97 fig.13), which is comparable to the *solidus* of Constantine and corresponds to 72 *aurei* to the (Roman) lb. Philip's payment is thus the equivalent of slightly less than 7000 lbs. of gold, 'somme considérable, certes, mais non démesurée', according to Loriot, 'De Maximin', 774. See also King, 'The role of gold', 446–7, on the devaluation of the *aureus*, and Potter, *Prophecy and history*, 221–5 on the treaty generally.

[11] See above ch.2 pp.15–16 and cf. Iluk, 'The export of gold', 83–4. Güterbock, *Byzanz*, 45 is sceptical of Mal.'s information concerning the agreement.

[12] Mal. 477.15–16, tr. Jeffreys–Scott, 282; but note the uncertainty of the text here, most easily resolved by postulating that 'of the two states' was accidentally copied twice by a scribe. So Festugière, 'Notabilia II', 236–7; *contra*, Jeffreys–Scott, 282.
    Gold coins of Severus Alexander survive (from 222–28) bearing the slogan *pax aeterna* and connected with the eastern frontier; if the emperor had ever made such a peace with the Parthians, it was in any case soon swept aside by the Sasanians. Cf. *RIC* IV.2, 67, 83 (no.164) and 93 (no.291) with Winter, *Friedensverträge*, 61.

[13] Soz. IX.4.1 on a 100-year peace in 408/9, cf. 120 years in Josh. Styl. (§7), although this treaty is probably an invention. Stein II, 502, 510 and Iluk, 'The export of gold', 90–91, on Justinian's later payments.

confirmavimus. Neither side was permitted to attack the other under
any circumstances, unless the terms of the peace were breached.[14]

iii) The aftermath

Just as the opening of the war had been presaged by a spear in the
heavens, so now 'a great shower of stars from dusk to dawn' marked its
conclusion. At Hierapolis a limestone block was inscribed with praises
of the emperor for bringing an end to the war; on one side it proudly
declared 'There is peace between Romans and Persians with (the help
of) God the holy; the money has been given and ...'.[15] The 530s indeed
provided a welcome respite to inhabitants of the eastern provinces, save
for the most zealous opponents of the Council of Chalcedon. Perhaps
the best illustration of the peaceful climate on the frontier comes from a
life of the anti-Chalcedonian John of Tella, martyred in 538. Ephraem,
the patriarch of Antioch, was eager to capture John, but discovered that
he was to be found in Persian territory. He therefore secured the
assistance of the *marzban* stationed in Nisibis in tracking John down, in
return for a payment of money. In winter 536–7, the *marzban*'s men
succeeded in apprehending John and bringing him to Nisibis. There,
before he was handed over to Ephraem's men, he was questioned by
the *marzban* through interpreters. The Persian complained that John
had intruded on Persian territory without obtaining permission; but the
bishop replied that 'today, as there is such profound peace between
these two states, I did not know one state from the other.' 'The two
kings are brothers in love,' he went on, and that was the reason why he
had no difficulty in crossing the border. Having been imprisoned in
Nisibis for a month, John was handed over to Ephraem's men and
taken to Dara, then Antioch, where he finally met his end.[16]

---

[14] *C.J.* I.27.2 pr. for the quotation (cf. Proc. I.22.17 for the term 'eternal'). The intended
   infinite duration of the peace must be stressed in light of the arguments of Higgins,
   'International relations', 286 n.22, followed by Toumanoff, *Studies*, 371 n.57; they
   interpret the treaty as having had no terminus, and oddly infer that it allowed either
   party to break the peace at its convenience. See also Moorhead, *Justinian*, 24 n.17.

[15] Mal. 477.10–12 on the shooting stars, tr. Jeffreys–Scott, 282, cf. Zach. IX.7 (231) and
   Ps. Dion. II, 53. On the inscription, see Roussel, 'Un monument', 367–8; quotation
   from IV (which breaks off before the end). See Greatrex–Lieu, *Eastern frontier*, for a
   translation of all four parts.

[16] *Vit. Ioh. ep. Tel.* 42–59, esp. 42–6 (quotations from 46, 72 of the Syriac text). Cf. Lee,
   Information, 59 on the episode and see above ch.2 n.70. *PLRE* III, Cometas 2, dates
   John's arrest to 1 February 537; cf. Zach. X.1 (297–300) on the sufferings of the anti-
   Chalcedonians (including John).

Shortly before John's arrest, a threat to the tranquillity of the border region had narrowly been avoided. A severe winter in 535–6 was followed by an exceptionally dry summer, both perhaps part of the same climatic crisis. A group of 15,000 Arabs, possibly Kindites, were driven out of the desert by the drought, presumably in the late summer of 536; denied pasturage in Persian territory by al-Mundhir, they pushed into Euphratesia, probably in the area around Zenobia and Sergiopolis, south of the Euphrates. Conflict was averted, however, by the *dux* Batzas, who evidently managed to satisfy the needs of the tribesmen. John of Tella's views on the concordant great-power relationship appeared to be well grounded.[17]

But the longer the peace continued, the more fragile it became. Justinian, who apparently shared John of Tella's optimistic assessment of Roman-Persian relations, did not hesitate to make drastic reductions in the defences of the eastern provinces. Above all, a great quantity of manpower was diverted first to North Africa, then to Italy; a glance at the contingents involved in the Vandalic and Gothic wars reveals just how many units which had fought in the east were subsequently transferred westwards. Batzas may in fact have had little option but to bribe the invading Arabs to leave, even if he was careful not to show his weakness. More seriously, those troops which remained were demoralised and paid infrequently. For the first few years of the peace the pay of the *limitanei* was allowed to fall in arrears, and it was finally cancelled when it appeared that their services were no longer required. Even if they still received sufficient income from their lands, such treatment could only be deleterious to morale. Field army troops were little better off. Throughout the empire pay was often slow to arrive, sparking disturbances or mutinies in both North Africa and Italy.[18] An

---

[17] Marc. *com.* 536.11, on which see Shahîd, *BASIC* I, 194–6 with 206–8 (noting the absence of the Ghassanids) and *PLRE* II, Alamundarus 2, *PLRE* III, Chabus, Hezidus, Batzas 1. Croke, *Chronicle*, 130, suggests that the harsh winter and summer were caused by a volcanic eruption in the southern hemisphere; Farquharson, 'Byzantium, Planet Earth and the Solar system', 266–7, tentatively proposes the impact of a comet as the reason for the peculiar conditions; cf. also Koder, 'Climatic Change', 276.

[18] Proc. III.11 on the troops sent to North Africa in 533, V.5.1–7 on those sent to Italy (fewer in number). Proc. *Anecd.* 24.12–14 on Justinian's cut-backs to the *limitanei* generally, often regarded as referring to the aftermath of the truce of 545, cf. Casey, 'Justinian and the *limitanei*', 215 and Bury, *HLRE* II, 358 n.4, but which could also refer to the Eternal Peace, cf. Ravegnani, *Soldati*, 96. Casey, *art. cit.*, 221–2, argues from numismatic evidence that in Palestine at least the removal of pay from the *limitanei* did not occur until the 540s; but cf. Jones, *LRE*, 677, suggesting that the

incident at Dara in 537 may be connected with this issue. A certain John, known as Cottistis, attempted to seize control of the city, but was foiled by the prompt action of the inhabitants. Ominously, John secured the help of the bodyguards of the commander at Dara for his enterprise, an indication that discontent among the troops was widespread; *bucellarii* were likewise among those who revolted against Solomon in North Africa in 536.[19] Fortifications too were allowed to deteriorate. Those close to the frontier, having recently been strengthened, required less attention in the first place, but in northern Syria, Osrhoene and Euphratesia others were either left untouched or repaired at a very slow pace. The incursions of Khusro in the early 540s quickly revealed not only the inadequate state of the city walls of this region, but also the unwillingness or inability of the troops stationed there to resist attack.[20]

As Procopius notes, the Romans were fortunate that the Persians made no attempt to exploit the uprising in Dara. Only two years later a dispute was to arise between the two Arab chiefs, Lakhmid and Ghassanid, which would embroil the great powers in another lengthy war. It is highly probable, furthermore, that the quarrel — over grazing lands — was deliberately manufactured by al-Mundhir at Khusro's instigation, to provide a pretext for war; even when efforts were made to resolve the issue, Khusro was quick to make further allegations. Whatever the immediate underlying causes of the king's decision to invade Roman territory in 540, the effects of the eight years of the Eternal Peace proved significant: the label 'eternal' had induced the emperor to neglect his eastern defences unduly, which in turn encouraged the Persians to take advantage of the situation. Not for the last time in

---

garrison of Beroea which defected to Khusro in 540 consisted of unpaid *limitanei* (Proc. II.7.37).

Whitby, 'Recruitment', 111–13, plays down the impact of the cancellation of pay, cf. Treadgold, *Army*, 204–5; also Jones, *op. cit.*, 661–3. On the mutinies over pay, see Treadgold, *op. cit.*, 203–4 and Kaegi, *Military Unrest*, 47–55. On the revolts in Africa, Proc. IV.14 (against Solomon); IV.18 (against Germanus, hence 536/9).

[19] On John's revolt, see Proc. I.26.5–12 with Zach. X.1 (299), Elias Nis. [a.852] and Marc. *com.* 537.4 with *PLRE* III, Ioannes Cottistis 24, Kaegi, *Military Unrest*, 65 and Croke, *Chronicle*, 131. Proc. refers to bodyguards (*doryphoroi*, i.e. *bucellarii*) at 26.9; I presume that these belonged to the commander of Dara, and had defected to John. If they were John's from the outset, however, then the revolt was equally serious, since it was led by such a senior commander.

[20] Whitby, 'Development', 728–9, cites various examples of the poor defences of the region, e.g. Beroea, Antioch, Chalcis; at Callinicum the city walls were still undergoing repairs in 542 (Proc. II.21.30–31).

history had the seeds of a new war been sown by the peace terms of the last.[21]

---

[21] Proc. I.26.9 on the potentially disastrous effects of the coup at Dara. On the *strata* dispute between al-Harith and al-Mundhir, see Proc. II.1 with Shahîd, *BASIC* I, 209–16, Stein II, 485–6 and Whitby, *Maurice*, 208. The quarrel probably arose in 539, see Shahîd, *op. cit.*, 210; Justinian was aware of Khusro's plans already in 539, as Lee, *Information*, 113, notes (from Proc. II.4.14).

The Persian War under Justin and Justinian: a chronology

Background

505	Construction of Dara begun; Theodosiopolis strengthened
	Raid of Tzani
513	Armenian revolt
515	Raid of Sabir Huns
519/20	Al-Mundhir raids Roman territory
521/2	Defection of Lazic king Tzath to the Romans
524/5	Appeal of Iberian king Gourgenes to Justin
c.525	Negotiations over adoption of Khusro by Justin
526	Mission of Probus to the Crimea and the Caucasus

The course of the war

526/7		Peter sent to Iberia with Huns
		Sittas and Belisarius raid Persarmenia
527	spring	Justinian associated with Justin as emperor
	summmer	Failure of Roman assaults on Nisibis and Thebetha
		Belisarius succeeds Libelarius as *dux* at Dara
		Hypatius becomes *magister militum per Orientem*
	1 August	Justinian becomes sole emperor
		Failed attempts to construct forts at Thannuris and Melabasa
		Peter fails to prevent the Persians from overrunning Iberia
528	spring	Al-Harith the Kindite killed by al-Mundhir
		Roman reprisal raid captures some Persian forts
	spring/summer	Battles between Romans and Persians in the Transcaucasus
		Belisarius defeated while attempting to defend the fortification work at Minduos
		Sittas appointed *magister militum per Armeniam*
		Senators despatched to defend eastern cities

528 (*cont.*)	winter	Hostilities suspended on account of harsh weather conditions
529	spring	Al-Mundhir's raid towards Antioch, followed by a Roman reprisal strike
		Belisarius succeeds Hypatius as *magister militum per Orientem*
	summer	Hermogenes visits the Persian court to negotiate
		Outbreak of Samaritan revolt
530	June	Persians defeated by Belisarius outside Dara
	summer	Sittas repulses the Persian attack on Satala
		Romans gain control of Pharangium and Bolum
		Rufinus' negotiations with Kavadh
	autumn	Negotiations suspended
531	spring	Azarethes' invasion along the Euphrates
	19 April	Persian victory over Belisarius at Callinicum
		Belisarius dismissed as *magister militum per Orientem*
		Fall of Abgersaton to the Persians
	summer	Bessas beats off the first Persian attempt on Martyropolis
	autumn	Kavadh dies (13 September)
		Second siege of Martyropolis abandoned
	winter	Raid of Sabir Huns on Roman provinces
532	spring	First round of peace talks with Khusro, broken off following a disagreement over the Lazic forts
	summer	Final negotiations, culminating in the Eternal Peace

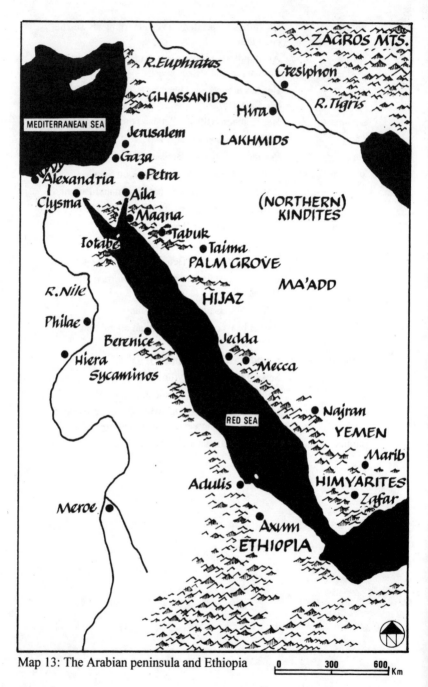

Map 13: The Arabian peninsula and Ethiopia

| 0 | 300 | 600 | Km |

224

Appendix
The Roman initiative in southern Arabia

Roman and Persian armies never clashed south of Lower Mesopotamia in the sixth century. But both powers were directly involved in the Red Sea area at different times: the Romans played an important role there at the start of the century, while later, in the 570s, the south-western part of the Arabian peninsula was actually annexed by Khusro I. During the war of 502–532 Justinian tried to enlist the support of Roman allies in the region against the Persians. Although his efforts produced almost no tangible result, they nonetheless merit consideration. It was chiefly economic factors that led the emperor to turn his attention southwards. Throughout his reign Justinian had found it hard to raise sufficient funds for his wars; for, as Cicero remarked, 'money [is] the sinews of war'. The substantial reserves accumulated during the reign of Anastasius were rapidly depleted by his successors through lavish spectacles and generous donations to cities struck by natural disasters. Writing somewhat later in Justinian's reign, John the Lydian paints a gloomy picture of the lack of available resources: 'there was need of money: nothing of what needed doing could be done without it.' What was worse, leaving aside the issue of the Caspian Gates, the Romans actually contributed, albeit indirectly, to the pay of Persian soldiers. This they did by importing all their silk through Persian intermediaries, who consequently made a healthy profit on what they had purchased earlier from Chinese merchants in Sri Lanka and elsewhere. Had Justinian's attempt to break the Persian monopoly on this precious material succeeded, he would at one stroke have reduced the expenditure of the Roman treasury and deprived the Persians of a lucrative trade.[1]

---

[1]   Cicero, *Philippic* V.5 (*nervos belli, pecuniam infinitam*). Joh. Lyd. *de Mag.* III.54 (143.3–4), cited by Vasiliev, *Justin I*, 256; see above ch.6 p.131 on the natural disasters and Stein II, 243–4, on the large expenditure of Justin and Justinian. Proc. I.20.9 on Justinian's desire to put an end to Roman payments to Persians for silk (on which see below). It may safely be supposed that the Sasanian state participated in the profits of its silk merchants, cf. Lukonin, 'Taxes and trade', 741, Garsoïan, 'Byzantium and the Sasanians', 571 (on customs posts) and Evans, *Justinian*, 234.

i) Background

Both Romans and Sasanians had long been interested in the Arabian peninsula. In the fourth century the Persian king Shapur II campaigned in Bahrain and the Hijaz, while a Lakhmid chief, Imru' al-Qays, undertook campaigns against both Himyarites (in modern-day Yemen) and the Ma'add tribe (in the centre of the peninsula).[2] The conversion of the Roman empire to Christianity provided a further stimulus to contacts with the region. Under Constantius II missionaries were sent to Ethiopia and Himyar. At first they enjoyed only limited success, but by the early fifth century the new religion was gaining ground in southern Arabia, an area hitherto dominated by pagans and Jews. The centre of the emergent Christian community was Najran. Here in 467 the Christian Azqir was imprisoned, and then sent to the Himyarite king, Sharakb'il Yakkuf, at whose court he proceeded to dispute with Jews; but on the advice of the king's counsellors he was soon sent back to Najran to be martyred.[3] The Christians of Himyar had close links with their co-religionists across the Red Sea in Ethiopia: it is through Ethiopian sources that the martyrdom of Azqir is known. Confirmation of these contacts comes from the opening of the sixth century; an inscription attests the presence of Ethiopian merchants at the Himyarite capital Zafar, and it appears that the Himyarite king at this time, Martad'ilan Yanuf, was himself Christian.[4]

That previous Roman emperors had been prepared to tolerate the flow of money to an enemy should not occasion surprise: in the seventeenth century the Spanish would employ the Dutch to transport naval stores to Spain from the Baltic, and the money they paid would help fund Dutch forces defending their territory against Spanish attacks (cf. Howard, *War*, 44).

[2] On Shapur II's campaigns and the career of Imru' al-Qays (known from the famous inscription found at Nemara dating from A.D. 328, tr. by Bellamy, 'A new reading', 46), see Shahîd, *BAFIC*, 39–41 and 61–62 with Nöldeke, *Tabari*, 53–6; also Sartre, *Trois études*, 136–9 and Matthews, *Ammianus*, 350 and 532 n.87. It is clear that Imru' al-Qays ended up an ally of the Romans.

[3] Cf. Müller, 'Himyar', 311, Rubin, 'Byzantium', 387–8, Christides, 'The Himyarite-Ethiopian War', 128, and Beeston, 'The martyrdom of Azqir', 5–8. On Christianity in the region in the fifth century see also Shahîd, *BAFIC*, 360–81 and 511. For a history of events before the fifth century, Rubin, *ZI*, 297–304, Letsios, *Erythra Thalassa*, 147–90, Pigulewskaja, *Byzanz*, 198–214 and Fowden, *Empire*, 109–13.

[4] Müller, 'Himyar', 312. The inscription dates from 619 of the Himyarite era, which corresponds to A.D. 504, following Loundine, 'Sur les rapports', 314–17 and Rubin, 'Byzantium', 392–3 (who place the beginning of the Himyarite era in 115 B.C.). So also Müller, 'Himyar', Pigulewskaja, *Byzanz*, 180 and now Nieskens, 'Vers le Zéro-tage', 98–103. Contrary views on the start of the Himyarite era range from 109 to 118 B.C., cf. Ryckmans, *La persécution*, 11 (109 B.C.) and Smith, 'Events', 452 (118 B.C.).

At just this time Roman influence in the Red Sea underwent a revival. The nadir of Roman fortunes in the region had been reached in the 470s, at roughly the same point at which Lazica too had slipped from imperial control: in 473 the island of Iotabe was wrested from the Romans by the Arab chief Imru' al-Qays, and his annexation was subsequently ratified by Leo.[5] But in 498 the *dux* of Palestine Romanus recaptured Iotabe from the Arabs, and handed it over to Roman traders 'to inhabit under its own laws, to import goods from the Indies and to bring the assessed tax to the emperor.' It was an important development, for the island was a major commercial centre, strategically located at the mouth of the Gulf of Aqaba. Its wealth in the 470s is alluded to by Malchus, while Choricius notes the large revenues derived from the trade with India.[6] Without the recovery of Iotabe Justinian could not have hoped to bypass the Persian middlemen of the silk trade.

At the southern end of the Red Sea, however, a reaction against the spread of Christianity — and Roman influence — was gaining ground. A Himyarite king called Dimion or Dimnos executed Roman traders and confiscated their goods. The Ethiopians were quick to respond. Their king, whose name is variously given as Aidug, Andas or Addad, overthrew the Himyarite king, thus avenging the merchants, and then adopted Christianity in fulfilment of a vow.[7] A Christian still occupied

---

[5]   Malchus, frg.1 (who calls him Amorcesus) with Sartre, *Trois études*, 155 on the seizure of the island. Letsios, 'The case of Amorkesos', 530, notes the importance of the island for the empire's trade, cf. Rubin, 'Byzantium', 388; see also Shahîd, *BAFIC*, 61–90. Despite Rubin, *loc. cit.* and Isaac, *Limits*, 247 n.170, Iotabe should probably be identified with the modern Tiran, cf. Abel, 'L'île de Jotabé', 513 and Sartre, *IGLS* XIII, 116 n.4; Proc. I.19.4 places the island 1000 stades from Aelas, and states that beyond it the sea opens out. Mayerson, 'A note', 34, prefers to place the port on the Arabian coast, near the Gulf of Aqaba. See above ch.6.ii on the waning of Roman fortunes in the Transcaucasus.

[6]   Malchus frg.1 on the island's wealth, cf. Choricius *Or.* 3.67 and Sartre, *IGLS* XIII, 117 n.1. Quotation from Theoph. A.M. 5990 (141.16–17), tr. Mango–Scott, 217. The island also held a substantial Jewish population: Choricius, *Or.* 3.66–78, describes operations conducted by the Roman commanders Aratius and Stephanus against Jewish raiders some time in the 530s. Cf. Abel, 'L'île de Jotabé', 529–32 (suggesting that the raiders came from Maqnā) and Litsas, *Choricius*, 75, 268. *PLRE* III, Aratius, offers no date for the campaigns, but they must postdate his defection to the Romans in 530 and predate Choricius' oration (placed in 535/6). See Rubin, 'Byzantium', 400, on the importance of the renewed contact with the Red Sea; also Mayerson, 'The port of Clysma', 122–4, on the wealth of Clysma, another prosperous Roman port on the Red Sea.

[7]   Mal. 433–4 (placing the episode probably in 527/8), Theoph. A.M. 6035 (223, dating it to 542/3, having moved it forward by one indiction cycle, cf. Mango–Scott, *Theophanes*, 324 n.1) and Ps. Dion. II, 54–6. The Ethiopian king during Justin and

the throne of Himyar in 516, when an inscription records a campaign
waged by king M'adikarib Y'afur in central Arabia against the
Lakhmid ruler al-Mundhir.[8] In the following year, however, M'adikarib
died unexpectedly, and his place was taken by a Jewish leader, Dhu
Nuwas. His rule was at once challenged by the Ethiopian king Ella
Asbeha (also known as Kaleb), who despatched an army under a certain Hywn' to remove him. The new Himyarite king appeared at first to
submit to the invaders, but once the Ethiopian army had dispersed to
garrison various towns, he counter-attacked and defeated the enemy
detachments piecemeal. Over the winter of 517–18 he entered into
contact with al-Mundhir and the Sasanians, hoping to secure their
support. Thus 'what had been a trivial squabble between two neighbouring south Semitic peoples had become part of a world conflict.'[9]

The attempt of Dhu Nuwas to widen the conflict was not a success.
While early in Justin's reign the Romans scored several diplomatic
successes in the Transcaucasus, Kavadh was still dealing with the
Mazdakite sect; and al-Mundhir, some at least of whose followers were
Christians, was to prove unwilling to offer support to a persecutor as

---

Justinian's reign was Ella Asbeha (on whom see below), who was also a Christian
before he invaded Himyar, and so Aidug must predate him. The most convincing
interpretation is given by Rubin, 'Byzantium', 390–92, who places the episode in the
late fifth century, cf. Harmatta, 'The struggle', 101–2. Dimion should not be
identified with Dhu Nuwas (on whom see below), despite Shahîd, *Martyrs*, 265 and
Christides, 'The Himyarite-Ethiopian War', 141–2. Cf. also Engelhardt, *Mission und
Politik*, 141–2.

Rubin further suggests, *art. cit.*, 394–5, that the name of the Ethopian king may refer to a prince of Adulis who seized power in Ethiopia, and converted to Christianity
when he won. Harmatta proposes, *art. cit.*, 103, that Dimnos may be a rendering of a
Himyarite king called Dhu Ma'ahir, cf. Rubin, *art. cit.*, 397–8.

Resentment of foreign Christian influence persisted nonetheless: Beeston,
'Martyrdom of Azqir', 7 (cf. Harmatta, 'The struggle', 103) stresses the anti-Roman
element in the actions of the Himyarite king Dhu Nuwas only a few years later;
Shahîd, 'Byzantino-Arabica', 123–5, suggests that Dhu Nuwas' zeal for persecution
was inspired partly by hostility to foreign (Ethiopian) Christians, and partly by
Christian (Roman) persecution of Jews.

[8]   Cf. Müller, 'Himyar', 312–13 (suggesting that M'adikarib was backed by Ethiopian
troops), Harmatta, 'The struggle', 104, Rubin, 'Byzantium', 399–400 and n.63.

[9]   Müller, 'Himyar', 313 on Dhu Nuwas' tactics and Hywn''s expedition, with
Christides, 'The Himyarite-Ethiopian War', 118, on the destruction of the garrison at
Zafar; also Harmatta, 'The struggle', 104 and Drewes, 'Kaleb and Himyar', 27–30, a
reference I owe to Prof. A.F.L. Beeston. On Dhu Nuwas' appeal see Letsios, *Erythra
Thalassa*, 252, Harmatta, *art. cit.*, 103. The quotation is from Robert Browning,
Justinian and Theodora, 30. On the many names of the Ethiopian ruler Ella Asbeha
see Shahîd, *Martyrs*, 252–60, Müller, 'Himyar', 316 and *PLRE* II, Elesboas; on the
names of Dhu Nuwas, Rubin, 'Byzantium', 390 and Shahîd, *op. cit.*, 260–68.

fanatical as Dhu Nuwas. Undaunted, the Himyarite ruler campaigned to the north-east of Najran in the summer of 518, before turning his attention to the city itself. In November that year thousands of Christians there were martyred, among them St Arethas, whose life, composed in the 530s, is a valuable source for these events. News of the atrocities spread rapidly across the peninsula. Two versions of a letter of Symeon of Beth Arsham describing the massacre survive; further details are provided by the 'Book of the Himyarites'.[10]

In the wake of the martyrdoms at Najran a conference was held at Ramla, near the Lakhmid capital Hira, in February 519. The involvement of both powers in the affairs of the peninsula emerges clearly from the list of those who attended: among the participants was Abraham, father of Nonnosus, who had concluded the treaty with the Ghassanids and Kindites in 502, as well as representatives of various Persian churches, al-Mundhir himself and envoys from Dhu Nuwas.[11] Reports of the persecution of the Christians in Himyar did not assist the Himyarite ruler. Although Symeon of Beth Arsham was abused by Ma'add tribesmen on his way to the conference, Abraham was able to secure the release of two Roman generals held by the Lakhmids; and al-Mundhir was dissuaded from providing any succour to Dhu Nuwas.[12]

---

[10]   Müller, 'Himyar', 314, on Dhu Nuwas' campaigns and the martyrdom; also Rubin, 'Byzantium', 392–3 and Beeston, 'Two Bi'r Hima inscriptions', 49–50, with *idem*, 'The chain', 6. On the *Mart. Ar.* see Pigulewskaja, *Byzanz*, 194–6 (196 for the dating), Shahîd, *Martyrs*, 181–231 and Huxley, 'On the Greek *martyrium*', 41; it actually places the martyrdom of Arethas in late 523, a date still favoured by some (e.g. Letsios, *op. cit.*, 250–51, Shitomi, 'De la chronologie', 35–40, *idem*, 'Notes', 316–19), but Devos, 'Quelques aspects' 114–16, provides powerful arguments against the later date; cf. also Shahîd, *Martyrs*, 235–42, and Rubin, 'Byzantium', 410 n.46, for an earlier dating.
   Müller, 'Himyar', 315 on the letter concerning the martyrs; Pigulewskaja, *Byzanz*, 186–94, Smith, 'Events', 452–3, Shahîd, *Martyrs*, 114–58 and Shitomi 'De la chronologie', 34–5 on the letter and the 'Book of the Himyarites' (questioning its reliability). Ryckmans, 'A Confrontation', 120–30 (cf. 'Les rapports') regards the Book as derived from the *Mart. Ar.*, a view rejected by Shahîd, 'Further reflections', 164–5.
[11]   Shahîd, 'Byzantino-Arabica' 115–18 (on the participants), but placing the conference in 524 (120). *Idem, Martyrs*, 235–42 revises the dating, arguing instead for 519, cf. *BASIC* I, 40; see also Rubin, *ZI*, 310. Müller, 'Himyar', 315 and Devos, 'Quelques aspects', 114–16 also place the conference in 519. Those who place the martyrdoms at Najran in 523 naturally place the conference in 524; cf. e.g. Shitomi, 'De la chronologie', 35–40, for an alternative chronology.
[12]   Abuse of Simeon, Zach. VIII.3 (193), cf. Ps. Dion. II, 58; Zach. VIII.3 (198), cf. Ps. Dion. II, 62–3, on opposition to persecution by Christians among al-Mundhir's men,

The wide circulation of accounts of the massacres at Najran sowed
the seeds for the downfall of the persecutor; and tangible evidence of
his deeds further aroused his opponents. A half-burnt copy of the bible
was brought to the Ethiopian king, Ella Asbeha, and his aid was in-
voked. He in turn passed on the item to the Emperor Justin, asking him
to provide transport for his forces across to southern Arabia.[13] While
the Romans prepared a fleet and the Ethiopians mustered their forces,
Dhu Nuwas was experiencing difficulties in his own camp. Some
Himyarites, apparently disillusioned with his régime, crossed over to
Ethiopia; among them was a certain Sumyaf'a Ashw'a (Procopius'
Esimiphaeus), a kinsman of Dhu Nuwas.[14] In the early 520s the merchant Cosmas Indicopleustes observed Ethiopian preparations for their
retaliatory expedition; but it was not until 525 that Ella Asbeha was at
last able to confront Dhu Nuwas.[15]

Soon after Pentecost 525 some seventy ships gathered at Gabaza, the
port of Adulis, and set off for the opposite coast. The Roman contribution was significant: the port of Aelas provided fifteen ships, that of
Clysma twenty, and Iotabe a further seven. The Ethiopian force attacked at two points and triumphed over the Himyarites. Ella Asbeha

with Shahîd, 'Byzantino-Arabica', 127. On the release of the generals, John and
Timostratus, see Shahîd, *BASIC* I, 40–42 and above ch.6 p.131.

[13] Nöldeke, *Tabari*, 188–90 with Vasiliev, *Justin I*, 293–4 and n.67. See also Huxley,
'On the Greek *martyrium*', 49, on the presence of Roman clerics among the Najran
martyrs, a further reason for Justin's intervention. Justin also promised to send troops,
though they apparently never took part in the campaign (Huxley, *art. cit.*, 49–50).

[14] For the identification of Sumyaf'a Ashw'a and Esimiphaeus, see Loundine, 'Sur les
rapports', 319 n.23, Shahîd, *Martyrs*, 228, Rubin, 'Byzantium', 411 n.47 and *PLRE*
III, Esimiphaeus; Huxley, 'On the Greek *martyrium*', 53, is more sceptical. On his
relationship to Dhu Nuwas, Christides, 'The Himyarite-Ethiopian War', 128 and
Shahîd, *op. cit.*, 224. Letsios, *Erythra Thalassa*, 258, on his defection to the
Ethiopians and conversion to Christianity.

[15] Cosmas Indicopleustes, *Topogr.* II.56 (369), usually dated to c.522 at the latest, cf.
Pigulewskaja, *Byzanz*, 182 on the preparations; Huxley, 'On the Greek *martyrium*',
47, argues that Cosmas' reference to the start of Justin's reign must mean 518 or 519.
The preparations probably represent an earlier (unsuccessful) attempt to remove Dhu
Nuwas, cf. Rubin, 'Byzantium', 400.

Rubin, *loc. cit.*, rebuts the view that the interval between the massacre and the
counter-strike is too long (it is sometimes used to argue that the persecutions must
have occurred in 523), cf. Smith, 'Events', 455, pointing out the shortage of vessels
available to the Ethiopians. See also Shahîd, *Martyrs*, 220–22, on a failed initial
attack of the Ethiopians in which 15,000 soldiers perished, and the possible landing of
Sumyaf'a Ashw'a before Ella Asbeha's invasion around Hisn al-Ghurab (where an
inscription attesting Sumyaf'a building a fort has been discovered from 525); Smith,
loc. cit., gives a translation of the inscription (with a different interpretation).

commanded the section which landed to the north and advanced on the capital Zafar; Dhu Nuwas was defeated while opposing the landing of the other Ethiopian army to the south.[16] No allies came to the assistance of the embattled Dhu Nuwas: it is likely that around this time al-Mundhir lost his capital to the Kindites, and it may be doubted in any case whether the Christians among his followers would have countenanced him giving aid to such a notorious persecutor.[17] At Zafar Ella Asbeha constructed churches, as also at Marib. Sumyaf'a Ashw'a was installed as king, and St Gregentius sent to take up the post of archbishop of southern Arabia; Ella Asbeha returned to Ethiopia, having remained in Himyar for seven months.[18]

ii) Justinian and southern Arabia: the aims

Sumyaf'a Ashw'a ruled Himyar on behalf of the Ethiopians for about five years. In 530 or 531 a revolt took place among the Ethiopian forces left to garrison the country, in the course of which Sumyaf'a was imprisoned. In his stead a certain Abraha, who had once been the slave of a Roman merchant of Adulis, was elevated to the throne.[19] Abraha went on to rule Himyar and to extend his authority northwards until perhaps

---

[16] On the campaign, *Mart. Ar.* VII.33–IX.38, (749–58), Shahîd, *Martyrs*, 222–6, Rubin, *ZI*, 312–13, Vasiliev, *Justin I*, 296–7; also Nöldeke, *Tabari*, 194–5 and Huxley, 'On the Greek *martyrium*', 50–51. For the provenance of the ships, *Mart. Ar.* VII.29 (747) with Vasiliev, *op. cit.*, 295 and Letsios, *Erythra Thalassa*, 257.

[17] Harmatta, 'The struggle', 104, on the occupation of Hira; and see above ch.7 n.37.

[18] Müller, 'Himyar', 317–19, Harmatta, 'The struggle', 104; Christides, 'The Himyarite-Ethiopian War', 115, on the appointment of Gregentius, and 134 on his 'Acts'. Proc. I.20.1 on the installation of Sumyaf'a Ashw'a, note also above p.xiv.

On Ella Asbeha's stay in Himyar, see Vasiliev, *Justin I*, 298, Christides, 'The Himyarite-Ethiopian War', 122, Shahîd, 'Byzantium in Southern Arabia', 62 and Huxley, 'On the Greek *martyrium*', 52. On the appointment of Sumyaf'a Ashw'a, see Shahîd, *Martyrs*, 228–30, where he suggests that he took the name Abraha upon converting to Christianity (and consequently escaped mention in some sources through sharing the name of his successor); see below n.20.

[19] Proc. I.20.2–4 on Abraha. On the garrison left with Sumyaf'a Ashw'a see Rubin, 'Byzantium', 401 and n.62. Smith, 'Events', 450 and 456 and Ryckmans, *La persécution*, 6–7 for various arguments on the date of Abraha's coup and of the Hisn al-Ghurab inscription, *CIS* IV.3, no.621; also Huxley, 'On the Greek *martyrium*', 53. Those who prefer an earlier start of the Himyarite era prefer a later date for Abraha's seizure of power: Smith, 'Events', 463, puts it c.533, and Pigulewskaja, *Byzanz*, 255, in 531 or 532. It is far more likely to have been in 530/1, however, cf. Müller, 'Himyar', 318, Harmatta, 'The struggle', 105 and Letsios, *Erythra Thalassa*, 259. Ryckmans, *loc. cit.*, draws attention to the fact that Masudi (a tenth-century source, cf. Nöldeke, *Tabari*, xxvi) refers to Abraha opposing Ella Asbeha while Kavadh was still alive (i.e. before September 531), a useful *terminus ante quem* if correct.

as late as 569/70, the so-called 'Year of the Elephant'. Much more is known of him than of his predecessor, who in some sources is passed over altogether.[20] At first Ella Asbeha sought to challenge the usurper, and at least one Ethiopian expedition was mounted to re-establish control. A relative of the Ethiopian king, perhaps the Ariat of the Arab tradition, was placed in command of an expeditionary force. Once in Himyar, however, he achieved little. According to one Arabic source, his treatment of the poor made him unpopular; Procopius reports that his forces fraternised with those of Abraha and slipped from his control.[21] Ella Asbeha may have been so vexed at his relative's failure that he undertook a second expedition; if such an attack took place, it had no more success than the previous one. Probably in the late 530s the Ethiopian king died, and Abraha was left to rule Himyar unmolested.[22]

---

[20] Cf. Smith's chronological table, 'Events', 465; the 'Year of the Elephant' is generally put in 569/70, but Kister, 'The campaign of Huluban', 428, has argued that the expedition of the Elephant took place in 552. *PLRE* III is ungenerous regarding the length of Abraha's rule, placing its terminus in ?547. On Abraha cf. also *EI²* I, 102–3.
       Some sources make Abraha the successor of Dhu Nuwas, cf. Ryckmans, *La persécution*, 6–7 on the Arab tradition; also Nöldeke, *Tabari*, 194–204 for two Arab versions, one making Abraha the direct successor of Dhu Nuwas, while the other brings in another ruler, Ariat. Christides, 'The Himyarite-Ethiopian War', 129, suggests that Sumyaf'a Ashw'a was omitted because he was of no interest to the hagiographical sources; cf. Letsios, *Erythra Thalassa*, 259. If Shahîd is correct about Sumyaf'a's change of name (see above n.18), it would provide another possible explanation for the elimination of Sumyaf'a from the record.
[21] Proc. I.20.5–8 on the expeditions, with Smith, 'Events', 451 and Nöldeke, *Tabari*, 215 on Sumyaf'a's hostility to the poor. Proc. puts the Ethiopian force at 3000 men, while Tabari (Waqidi) gives a figure of 4000. The Arab tradition implies that Ariat had exercised control in Himyar for some time before being ousted by Abraha, while Proc. represents him as being despatched in response to Abraha's seizure of power; this discrepancy may be resolved by supposing that Ariat campaigned for some time unsuccessfully against the usurper, and that during this period his troops were suborned by Abraha.
       Ariat has also been identified with the Anganes of Mal. (457–9) and the Arethas of Theoph. A.M. 6064 (244–5), though Theoph.'s entry is misplaced in 571/2, cf. Jeffreys, 'A lacuna', 273–4 and Mango–Scott, *Theophanes*, 363 n.7 (offering a different explanation); Nöldeke, *Tabari*, 190 n.3, for the identification, and note that Anganes (Mal. 457) is referred to as a relative of Ella Asbeha. Cf. also Smith, 'Events', 449–51, stating that 'Ariat … corresponds in description though not in name to the Anganes of Malalas' (451), with Carpentier, *De SS Aretha et Ruma*, §126, 698–9. Nöldeke, *Tabari*, 200 n.4, and Carpentier, *loc. cit.*, for the suggestion that Ariat is the commander referred to in Proc.
[22] The Arab versions agree with Proc. (I.20.7) concerning the rage of Ella Asbeha, cf. Nöldeke, *Tabari*, 196–9. But it appears that he eventually forgave the usurper, once he had given pledges of allegiance. Smith, 'Events', 465, puts Ella Asbeha's death

Since Abraha came to power only towards the end of the war of 502–532, it was his predecessor, Sumyaf'a Ashw'a, whom Justinian invited to support his war against Persia, at the same time also sending an embassy to the Ethiopian king.[23] The emperor wished both kingdoms to play a part in opposing Sasanian interests. Procopius describes his intentions thus:

> [F]or he purposed that the Ethiopians, by purchasing silk from India and selling it among the Romans, might themselves gain much money, while causing the Romans to profit in only one way, namely, that they be no longer compelled to pay over their money to their enemy ... As for the Homeritae (Himyarites), it was desired that they should establish Caïsus (Qays), the fugitive, as captain over the Maddeni (Ma'add), and with a great army of their own people and of the Maddene Saracens make an invasion into the land of the Persians.[24]

The arrangement proposed to the Ethiopians comprised the more important part of the imperial design. The silk trade was of great significance to the Roman empire and was subject to strict regulations: only the *comes commerciorum* was allowed to purchase the product from barbarians. Demand had grown in the late empire, as Ammianus notes in the fourth century, [*sericum*] *nunc etiam infimorum sine ulla discretione proficiens* ('nowadays [silk is] available even to the lowest without any distinction'). Since at this time silk could only be obtained from the Far East, the Persians, through whose territory the product would have to travel, held an effective monopoly on the supply to the Roman empire. While in peace time such a situation could be tolerated, it became far less acceptable during war; the Persians may even have attempted to capitalise still further on their advantage by charging higher prices.[25]

---

c.536. Altheim–Stiehl, *Die Araber*, 391, note a story that Ella Asbeha abdicated to become a monk, cf. *PLRE* II, Elesboas.

[23] The embassy to Himyar and Ethiopia took place in 530 or 531; its precise chronology will be discussed below.

[24] Proc. I.20.9, tr. Dewing, 193.

[25] *C.J.* IV.40.2 on the *comes commerciorum*; see Oikonomides, 'Silk trade', 33, and Jones, *LRE*, 826, on the monopoly of the silk trade in the Roman empire under Justinian. Ammianus XXIII.6.67 on silk in the fourth century, tr. Rolfe. Proc. *Anecd.* 25.13–26 on the increase in prices (undated). On the silk trade, see esp. Pigulewskaja, *Byzanz*, 158–71, Harmatta, 'The struggle', 98–9 and Winter, 'Handel und Wirtschaft', 62; on this episode and the trade disputes with Persia going back to the fourth century, Pigulewskaja, *op. cit.*, 197 and 214–15. Also Rubin, 'Byzantium',

If, therefore, the Persian intermediaries could be cut out, serious losses could be inflicted on the enemy's finances. The Red Sea route had long been used for the import of goods from the east, bringing considerable prosperity to ports such as Iotabe and Aelas.[26] The Ethiopians, as fellow Christians who had recently received Roman aid, were well disposed to cooperate with the emperor; and their country was ideally positioned for their merchants to supplant the Persians as middle-men.[27] But when Ella Asbeha endeavoured to put Justinian's plan into practice, it soon became clear that the emperor had underestimated the extent of Sasanian trading power. The Ethiopian merchants who travelled to ports in India and Sri Lanka discovered that Persian dealers were in the habit of purchasing all the silk that arrived from the east, thus making it impossible to avoid buying the commodity from them. The imperial initiative therefore came to nothing; but even had it proved successful, it is likely that the war would have finished before the Sasanian treasury was in any way harmed by the loss of revenue.[28]

384, and Smith, 'Events', 426–8 (with Cosmas, *Topogr.* II.45–6, 351–3) on the silk trade in Justinian's time.

Later in Justinian's reign, two monks brought eggs of *bombyx mori* to Constantinople, allowing the production of silk to begin within the empire: Proc. VIII.17, discussed by Pigulewskaja and Evans, *Justinian*, 235. On trading relations between Rome and Persia generally, see Winter, *art. cit.*, 46–74.

[26] See above n.6 on the revenues accruing to Iotabe from goods from 'India' (a vague term, cf. e.g. Salles, 'Fines Indiae', 171). The prosperity of Aelas is noted by the sixth century pilgrim Antoninus of Placentia's *Itinerarium*, §40 (p.185) = *PL* 72.912 (where it is called Abela); cf. Gutwein, *Third Palestine*, 139. The Edict of Anastasius laid down that the *dux* of Palestine (i.e. Palaestina III, presumably) was to be paid from the revenues of Clysma rather than from the public treasury, which points to a significant income from trade, cf. Sartre, *IGLS* XIII, 112–17 and Mayerson, 'The port of Clysma', 123. See also Rubin, 'Byzantium', 384, on the advantages to the Romans of the Red Sea route for silk, with Harmatta, 'The struggle', 96–7 and Pigulewskaja, *Byzanz*, 218.

[27] Although the Ethiopians were anti-Chalcedonians, the common bond of Christianity outweighed internal Christian disputes over doctrine, cf. e.g. Engelhardt, *Mission und Politik*, 36–7, Rubin, *ZI*, 317, Vasiliev, *Justin I*, 252–3. On the two factors motivating Roman policy, politics/religion and trade, see Letsios, *Erythra Thalassa*, 269–72, Rubin, 'Byzantium', 383–5 and Shahîd, *BASIC* I, 145–6.

[28] Whitehouse–Williamson, 'Sasanian maritime trade', 29 and 44 on Sasanian dominance of seaborne trade with the east, confirmed by archaeological finds in Sri Lanka, cf. Carswell, 'The Port of Mantai', 199; see also Rubin, 'Byzantium', 401 and Rubin, *ZI*, 315–16 on the failure of the Roman initiative. Shahîd, *BASIC* I, 145–6, argues unconvincingly that the venture 'had some success'. Salles, 'Fines Indiae', 173–4, notes the evidence of the Roman merchant Cosmas, who does not appear to have

The other part of Justinian's plan, involving the Himyarites, was at least more direct. In conjunction with the Ma'add, Sumyaf'a Ashw'a was to undertake a campaign against the Persians. The emperor is unlikely to have envisaged that forces from southern Arabia could actually reach a Persian army, but, perhaps through Roman contact with the Kindites, he may well have been aware of earlier conflicts between the Himyarites and the Lakhmids. As has been noted, the Himyarite king M'adikarib Y'afur had campaigned in 516 against al-Mundhir in central Arabia; if therefore Sumyaf'a Ashw'a had been persuaded to follow the example of his predecessor, then it is just possible that al-Mundhir might have been prevented from guiding the Persian invasion of Syria in 531. But Justinian's request probably surpassed the abilities of Sumyaf'a, who was heavily dependent on Ethiopian backing to maintain his position, and the disturbances which culminated in the elevation of Abraha may already have started by this point. A further obstacle to the proposed invasion lay in the turmoil which had embroiled the central Arabian confederations of the Ma'add and Kindites. The Kindite king Qays, who had succeeded al-Harith in 528, and who also ruled over the Ma'add, had murdered a relative of Sumyaf'a Ashw'a, and was therefore living as an exile. Apparently seizing the opportunity, the Ma'add had decided to break free of the Kindite confederation. Hence Justinian had to ask Sumyaf'a not only to mount an expedition but also to resolve the chaos in central Arabia by re-installing Qays, notwithstanding the murder he had committed.[29]

---

travelled beyond the Red Sea himself, but is aware of the plentiful traffic with the Indian Ocean.

[29] See above n.8 on M'adikarib Y'afur's campaign. On the Ma'add, see Shahîd, *BASIC* I, 146–8, 160–66; they eventually fell under Lakhmid control, cf. Shahîd, *op. cit.*, 165 and Rubin, *ZI*, 305. On Himyarite links with Kinda see Nöldeke, *Tabari*, 148 (where the Himyarites order al-Harith the Kindite to attack Hira). Qays may have been restored to his position in charge of the Kindites, but probably not until after the downfall of Sumyaf'a Ashw'a. Shahîd, *op. cit.*, 147, 164–5, argues that a campaign was undertaken by Qays in accordance with Justinian's desire (although the sources he cites provide no dates). Another Qays was placed in charge of the Ma'add by Abraha during his campaign in the north (probably in the late 540s, and perhaps alluded to by Proc. I.20.13), cf. Smith, 'Events', 437, Nöldeke, *Tabari*, 203–4 and Bosworth, 'Iran and the Arabs', 605–6.

The identity of Proc.'s (and Nonnosus') Qays is disputed. Some identify him with the poet Imru' al-Qays (so Stein II, 298–9, Sartre, *Trois études*, 174–6, Aigrain, 'Arabie', 1198), but cf. the objections of Olinder, *Kings of Kinda*, 114–16 and Shahîd, 'Byzantium and Kinda', 59 and appendix 1. Whether or not he is to be identified with the poet, he was a grandson of al-Harith (the Kindite).

iii) Justinian and southern Arabia: the methods

It remains to consider the timing and context of the Roman embassies to southern Arabia. An unusual wealth of sources is available for this burst of diplomatic activity, including not only Procopius and Malalas, but also the brief fragments of the work of Nonnosus.[30] Nonnosus records three embassies (A-C below) to the region, two undertaken by his father, Abraham, and one by himself; the difficulty arises in working out the relationship between these three missions and those reported by Malalas and Procopius. A list of the embassies is given below, each designated by a letter for ease of reference:

A. Abraham's first mission to Qays, who is described as φύλαρχος δὲ τῶν Σαρακηνῶν ἐχρημάτιζε Κάϊσος ἀπόγονος ᾿Αρέθα ('Caisus, the grandson of Arethas,[31] held the position of phylarch of the Saracens') and as having control over the Kindites and Ma‘add tribe. Abraham made a treaty with him, and brought back his son Mavia to Constantinople as a hostage.

B. Nonnosus' mission to Qays and Ella Asbeha: his brief was to persuade Qays to come to the emperor (Justinian, according to the preface to Nonnosus' fragment), which he failed to do, and to visit Ella Asbeha and the Himyarites.

C. Abraham's second mission to Qays, when he succeeded in persuading him to come to Constantinople, leaving his kingdom to his two brothers, Ambrus ('Amr) and Yezid.[32] Qays then received the phylarchate of Palestine (the Greek actually has 'Palestine' in the plural), bringing with him many followers.[33]

D. Julian's mission, reported by Procopius, and dated by him to between 527 and 531 certainly, and most probably to 530 or 531. He was instructed to persuade Sumyaf‘a to restore Qays to his rule

---

[30] Nonnosus' fragments are in *FHG* IV, 178–81, esp.179.

[31] Although ἀπόγονος usually means simply 'descendant', it is clear that in this context it should be translated as 'grandson', cf. *PLRE* III, Caisus, and Shahîd, *BASIC* I, 154.

[32] On whom cf. *PLRE* III, Ambrus 1 and Iezidus 1 with Shahîd, *BASIC* I, 158.

[33] Nonnosus' use of the plural is important, since it probably implies some sort of honorary appointment to a phylarchate rather than a formal position as phylarch of Palestine. He is thus unlikely to have displaced the Ghassanid phylarch of Palestine, Abu Karib, whose tenure of the post is therefore irrelevant to the chronology of this mission (despite Pigulewskaja, *Byzanz*, 262 and Sartre, *Trois études*, 175). So Shahîd, 'Byzantium and Kinda', 68, Aigrain, 'Arabie', 1199–200. *PLRE* III, Caisus, suggests the plural may refer to a phylarchate of Palaestina I and II, cf. Shahîd, *BASIC* I, 158–60.

over the Ma'add and to urge greater commercial cooperation between Constantinople and the Ethiopians.[34]

E. Finally there is the embassy reported by Malalas, conducted by an
    ambassador named by Theophanes as Julian. The chroniclers re-
    port a successful Roman request to an 'Indian' ruler (Anganes and
    Ella Asbeha are both named) to launch an attack upon the
    Persians.[35]

The sequence of these embassies has been considered most recently by
Irfan Shahîd. He puts A soon after al-Harith the Kindite's death in 528,
arguing that Qays succeeded to the phylarchate held by his grandfather,
and that Abraham renewed the *foedus* concluded with the Kindites in
502. He then wants to link B and D, viewing them as part of the same
mission: Nonnosus was the junior partner of Julian, and had to inform
his superior whether he had been successful in persuading Qays to
come to Constantinople. He places this second two-pronged embassy
around 530, followed closely by C, despatched after the Roman defeat
at Callinicum. The chroniclers' account (E) represents Julian's report,
according to his analysis.[36] However, such an interpretation unduly
telescopes the various embassies. This can be seen most clearly in the
differing accounts of Qays' circumstances: initially, at the time of A, he
is a powerful chieftain, but then in 530/1 he is a wandering renegade
(D), finally emerging again in a strong position (C). Such a fluctuation

---

[34] Proc. I.20.9–11; note esp. the τότε at 20.9, apparently placing the embassy just after
      the defeat at Callinicum, where the digression began. Cf. Shahîd, *BASIC* I, 157 and
      n.487.
[35] Mal. 457–9, cf. Theoph. A.M. 6064 (244–5). The episode is placed by Mal. in 530,
      during the negotiations which followed the battle of Dara; cf. Shahîd, *BASIC* I, 157.
      D and E clearly refer to the same mission.
[36] 'Byzantium and Kinda', 60–67; cf. *BASIC* I, 155–60 for a restatement of his views.
      Smith, 'Events', 435, argues that Abraham visited Qays twice before 530, and that
      Nonnosus visited him after his restoration, thus rearranging the order of embassies
      reported by Nonnosus. Note that Proc.'s text (I.20.11) strongly implies that Qays was
      not restored by Sumyaf'a, although it has often been assumed that he was (cf. Shahîd,
      BASIC I, 147 and Rubin, *ZI*, 315); see also above n.29. Pigulewskaja, *Byzanz*, 198,
      262–3, offers other possible datings, apparently internally inconsistent. *PLRE* III,
      Iulianus 8, Caisus and Nonnosus, accepts the views of Shahîd. Smith, 'Events', 449,
      also linking B and E, proposes that Nonnosus was Julian's interpreter or that Julian
      was the author of the fragments attributed to Nonnosus.
      Pigulewskaja, *Byzanz*, 182, argues that Mal. derived his information from Nonnosus
      on the grounds that he uses the same term to refer to the Himyarites, Ἀμερῖται. But,
      as Shahîd points out, 'Byzantium and Kinda', 63, Julian may also have written an
      account of his embassy, which could then have been used by Mal.; the coincidence of
      the form of the word need not be significant.

of fortunes in so short a space of time appears improbable. Furthermore, the aims of missions B and D are not strictly compatible: according to Nonnosus, his brief was to persuade Qays to come to Constantinople, while Procopius reports that Julian was to attempt to have
him appointed to the command of the Ma'add.[37]

Shahîd's proposed chronology for the embassies is based at least in
part on a distrust of the evidence of Procopius: he doubts whether Qays
had actually murdered a relative of Sumyaf'a Ashw'a and whether he
was a fugitive. But an alternative analysis of the embassies is possible,
one which does not call into doubt Procopius' account.[38] There is no
need to suppose that the embassies of Nonnosus and Julian were
simultaneous. Once this linkage is removed, all three of the missions
reported by Nonnosus may be placed after D/E, over the course of the
530s, which would explain why his account contains no mention of
Persia (a notable omission). It would be preferable for B to occur
sooner rather than later in the 530s, since Ella Asbeha is mentioned in it
as king of Ethiopia, but beyond that the dating must remain imprecise.
The rationale behind A, B and C would then be connected more to the
situation in southern Arabia than to relations with Persia: confirmation
that diplomatic contacts were maintained with the region may be found
in the Marib dam inscription, dating from 542, which attests the
presence at Abraha's court of embassies from Constantinople and
Persia, as well as from Lakhmids and Ghassanids. The identification of
D and E need not be challenged: both are clearly dated to 530/1.[39]

---

[37] If B and D are supposed to refer to the same mission, it is also becomes unclear as to
why Qays should be unwilling to abandon his life as a fugitive to go to the imperial
capital. All Nonnosus' fragments refer to events which took place when Justinian was
on the throne, i.e. in 527 or later; Shahîd places A in 528, following the death of al-
Harith the Kindite and the Roman reprisal raid against al-Mundhir. As a *terminus
ante quem* he offers the elevation of al-Harith the Ghassanid to the status of chief
phylarch, after which, he argues, Qays would have been less amenable to Roman
diplomacy; clearly this is not a firm *terminus*, however.

[38] 'Procopius and Kinda', *passim*, esp. 76, for Shahîd's doubts (less pronounced in
BASIC I, 158, where he accepts the murder and the exile, though 'as an expression of
his [Proc.'s] *Kaiserkritik*'). Cf. Beeston, 'The martyrdom of Azqir', 9, for a more
positive assessment of Proc.'s worth on Arabian affairs.

[39] On the dates of D and E, see above nn.34–5. *CIS* IV.2, no.541 (278–96) for the Marib
dam inscription, on which see Letsios, *Erythra Thalassa*, 290, Smith, 'Events', 440–
41 and Beeston, 'Judaism and Christianity', 274. On the death (or retirement) of Ella
Asbeha, see above n.22. Embassy A could still be placed in 528 and linked to the
renewal of the treaty with the Kindites, as Shahîd proposes.

iv) Conclusion

In both southern Arabia and the Transcaucasus Roman influence was in the ascendant in the early sixth century, a development closely linked to the spread of Christianity. But Ethiopia and Himyar were never likely to play as significant a part in wars between Rome and Persia as the more centrally located kingdoms of Armenia, Iberia and Lazica. Nevertheless, sources such as Procopius, Nonnosus, the Martyrium of Arethas and Cosmas Indicopleustes reveal a growing interest in the Red Sea area, as does the epigraphic record. Justinian's decision to seek to exploit Roman contacts with the Christian countries there should be seen in this context. If he had been able to bypass the Persian silk merchants, he would undoubtedly have inflicted a blow to the Persian treasury; but he could not have known of the extent to which Persian traders dominated commerce in the Indian Ocean. And if Sumyaf'a Ashw'a had undertaken a campaign against the Lakhmids late in 530, then the Persian invasion of Syria and Euphratesia might have been deferred or avoided altogether: when Abraha attacked the Lakhmids in the late 540s, al-Mundhir was obliged to despatch his nephew 'Amr to repel the Himyarites.[40]

Despite the apparently negative assessment of Procopius, the emperor's embassies to southern Arabia could have had an impact on the war: in the early ninth century the chronicler Theophanes thought the region important enough for him to redate the embassy of Julian (in Malalas) to 571/2, so as to make it a cause for the outbreak of war between Rome and Persia under Justin II. That Justinian's embassies did not produce any tangible result was due in part to the overambitious nature of his plan, and in part to the swift conclusion of the war.[41]

---

[40] Fowden, *Empire*, ch.5 on the role of Christianity in the Transcaucasus and southern Arabia (and elsewhere); see also above n.27. See above ch.4 on the sources; above, p.229 on the composition of the Martyrium of Arethas (in the 530s). Cosmas was writing in the mid-sixth century, cf. *PLRE* III, Cosmas 2. See above n.29 on the campaign of Abraha in the late 540s; see Smith, 'Events', 436–7, and Shahîd, 'Procopius and Arethas', 376, on the role of 'Amr (not reported by *PLRE* III, Ambrus 2).

[41] Theoph. A.M. 6064 (244–5) with Mango–Scott, 363 n.7 (and see above n.21), for the suggestion of Theoph.'s motivation.

Events in southern Arabia: a chronology

467	Azqir imprisoned in Najran, then martyred
473	Imru' al-Qays (Amorcesus) gains control of Iotabe
498	Romanus recaptures Iotabe
504	Ethiopian traders attested in Himyar
?	Murder of Roman traders by Dimion; Ethiopian invasion t Aidug overthrows Dimion; Aidug converts to Christianity
516	M'adikarib Y'afur campaigns against al-Mundhir in Centr Arabia
517	Death of M'adikarib Y'afur; Dhu Nuwas seizes power
517/8	Dhu Nuwas in contact with al-Mundhir and the Persians
518	(summer) Dhu Nuwas campaigns northeast of Najran
518	(autumn) Dhu Nuwas martyrs the Christians of Najran
519	The Conference at Ramla; the two letters concerning t massacre at Najran written
c.522	Cosmas Indicopleustes observes Ethiopian preparations for war
c.524/8	Kindite interregnum in Hira
525	Ella Asbeha's expedition to recapture Himyar
c.530	Embassy of Julian to Sumyaf'a Ashw'a
c.530/1	Abraha overthrows Sumyaf'a Ashw'a
530s	Expeditions of Ella Asbeha to oust Abraha
542	Marib dam inscription
547	Abraha's campaign in Central Arabia
570/575	Khusro I takes over Himyar

Bibliography

Abbreviations

Abbreviations not listed here are as given in *The Oxford Dictionary of Byzantium*. Abbreviations of ancient classical and non-classical sources will be found under Primary Sources, below.

Arabian Studies	*Arabian Studies in honour of Mahmoud Ghul. Symposium at Yarmouk University, December 8–11, 1984*, ed. M. M. Ibrahim (Wiesbaden, 1989).
ARB	*L'armée romaine et les barbares du IIIe au VIIe siècle*, edd. F. Vallet and M. Kazanski (Paris, 1993).
ASS	*Acta Sanctorum*, 71 vols. (Paris, 1863–1940).
BSO	*Byzantium and the Semitic Orient before the Rise of Islam*, I. Shahîd (London, 1988).
Byzantine Diplomacy	*Byzantine Diplomacy*, edd. J. Shepard and S. Franklin (Aldershot, 1992).
Caucaso	*Il Caucaso: Cerniera fra culture dal Mediterraneo alla Persia* in *Settimane di Studio del centro Italiano di studi sull' alto medioevo* 43 (1996), 2 vols.
CHEIA	*The Cambridge History of Early Inner Asia*, ed. D. Sinor (Cambridge, 1990).
CHIr	*Cambridge History of Iran*, vol. III.1–2, ed. E. Yarshater (Cambridge, 1983).
CIS	*Corpus Inscriptionum Semiticarum*, vol.4 (*Corpus Inscriptionum Himyariticarum*), tomes 1–3 (Paris, 1889–1929).
DRBE	*The Defence of the Roman and Byzantine East*, edd. P. Freeman and D. Kennedy, BAR International Series 297 (Oxford, 1986).
EFRE	*The Eastern Frontier of the Roman Empire*, edd. D. H. French and C. S. Lightfoot, BAR International Series 553 (Oxford, 1989).

EI²	*The Encyclopaedia of Islam*, 2nd ed. (London–Leiden, 1960–).
EIr	*Encyclopaedia Iranica*, ed. E. Yarshater (London, 1985–).
FCH	*The Fragmentary Classicising Historians of the Later Roman Empire*, 2 vols, ed. and tr. R. C. Blockley (Liverpool, 1981–3).
FHG	*Fragmenta Historicorum Graecorum*, ed. C. Müller, vol.4 (Paris, 1851), vol.5 (Paris, 1870).
Hinterland	*Constantinople and its Hinterland*, edd. C. Mango and G. Dagron with G. Greatrex (Aldershot, 1995).
HVG	Juansher, *The History of Vakhtang Gorgasal*, tr. R. W. Thomson, *Rewriting Caucasian History* (Oxford, 1996), 153–251.
JRA	*Journal of Roman Archaeology*.
LRE	A. H. M. Jones, *The Later Roman Empire* (Oxford, 1964).
OCD³	*The Oxford Classical Dictionary*, third edition, edd. S. Hornblower and A. Spawforth (Oxford, 1996).
ODB	*The Oxford Dictionary of Byzantium*, ed. A. Kazhdan, 3 vols. (Oxford, 1991).
PLRE	*Prosopography of the Later Roman Empire*, edd. J. Martindale *et al.*, 3 vols. (Cambridge, 1971–92).
RAE	*The Roman Army in the East*, ed. D. L. Kennedy (Ann Arbor, Michigan, 1996).
RBAE	*The Roman and Byzantine Army in the East*, ed. E. Dabrowa (Cracow, 1994).
RIC	*The Roman Imperial Coinage*, edd. H. Mattingly, C. H. V. Sutherland, R. A. G. Carson *et al.*, 10 vols. (London, 1923–94).
Shifting Frontiers	*Shifting Frontiers in Late Antiquity*, edd. H. Sivan and R. W. Mathisen (Aldershot, 1996).
SRA	*The Byzantine and Early Islamic Near East. States, Resources, Armies*, Studies in Late Antiquity and Early Islam, vol.3, ed. A. Cameron (Princeton, 1995).
Studi Etiopici	*IV Congresso Internazionale di Studi Etiopici*, vol.1 (Rome, 1974).
Studies in Malalas	*Studies in Malalas*, edd. E. Jeffreys, with B. Croke and R. Scott (Sydney, 1990).
TAVO	*Tübinger Atlas des Vorderen Orients* (Wiesbaden, 1977–).

Primary sources

Note: Armenian sources, such as Ełishe or Łazar P'arpec'i, are cited from the translations by R. W. Thomson. The first number refers to the page number in Thomson's translation, while that in square brackets refers to the page numbers of the text translated. References to Syriac and Arabic works are to the translations here listed (except where indicated).

Non-classical works

Agapius = Agapius, *Kitab al-'Unvan*, ed. and tr. A. A. Vasiliev, *PO* 8 (1912).

Ananias (of Širak), see Hewsen, *Ananias* (below).

Bal'ami = *Chronique de Tabari traduite sur la version persane*, 2 vols, tr. M. H. Zotenberg (Paris, 1869).

Barhebraeus = Gregory bar Hebraeus, *The Chronography of Gregory Abu'l Faraj (Bar Hebraeus)*, vol.1, tr. E. A. W. Budge (London, 1932).

Burkitt, *Euphemia* = *Euphemia and the Goth with the Acts of the Martyrdom of the confessors of Edessa*, ed., tr. and comm. F. C. Burkitt (London-Oxford, 1913).

Chr. Edess. = *Chronicon Edessenicum*, CSCO ser.3 tom.4 pt.1, *versio*, tr. I. Guidi (Paris, 1903); also in *Untersuchungen über die Edessenische Chronik*, ed. and tr. L. Hallier (Leipzig, 1892).

Chron. 724 = *Chronicon Miscellaneum ad A.D. 724 pertinens*, CSCO ser.3 tom.4 part 2, tr. J.-B. Chabot (Paris, 1903); partial translation in *The Seventh Century in the West-Syrian Chronicles* (see below), 14–23. (In footnotes the first number is that of the *CSCO* translation, the second is that of Palmer).

Chron. 819 = *Chronicon anonymum ad a.d. 819*, tr. J.-B. Chabot along with *Chron. 1234*, vol.1.

Chron. 846 = *Chronicon ad A.D. 846 pertinens*, CSCO ser.3 tom.4 part 2, tr. J.-B. Chabot (Louvain, 1904).

Chron. 1234 = *Chronicon anonymum ad a.c. 1234 pertinens*, CSCO ser.3 tom.14, tr. J.-B. Chabot (Louvain, 1937).

Chron. Arbela = *Die Chronik von Arbela — Ein Beitrag zur Kenntnis des ältesten Christentums im Orient*, tr. P. Kawerau, *CSCO* tom. 200 (Louvain, 1985).

Chron. Seert = Chronicle of Seert (= *Histoire nestorienne inédite*), ed. A. Scher, tr. l'abbé Pierre, *PO* 4 (1908), 5 (1910), 7 (1911) and 13 (1919).

Elias Nis. = Elias of Nisibis, *Eliae Metropolitae Nisibeni Opus Chronologicum*, pars prior, *CSCO* ser.3 vol.7, ed. and tr. E. W. Brooks (Rome-Paris-Leipzig, 1910).

Elishe = *Ełishē: History of Vardan and the Armenian War*, tr. R. W. Thomson (Cambridge, Mass., 1982).

Eutychius = Eutychius, *Annales*, tr. Pocock, *PG* 111 with M. Breydy, *Das Annalenwerk des Eutychios von Alexandrien, CSCO* tom. 471–2 (Louvain, 1985).

Firdausi = Firdausi, *Le livre des rois par Abou'lkasim Firdousi*, tr. J. Mohl, vols.5–6 (Paris, 1866–8).

Isaac of Antioch, Sermons = *S. Isaaci Antiocheni Opera Omnia*, ed. and tr. G. Bickell, vol.1 (Giessen, 1873).

Jac. Ede. *Chr.* = 'The Chronological Canon of James of Edessa', tr. E. W. Brooks, *ZDMG* 53 (1899), 261–327, also in *Chronicon Iacobi Edesseni, CSCO* ser.3 tom.4, part 3, tr. E. W. Brooks (Paris, 1903).

Jacob of Sarug, *Ep.* = *Iacobi Sarugensis epistulae quotquot supersunt*, ed. G. Olinder, *CSCO* tom.57 (Louvain, 1952).

Joh. Eph. *HE* = John of Ephesus, *Ecclesiastical History*, tr. R. Payne Smith, *The Third Part of the Ecclesiastical History of John of Ephesus* (Oxford, 1860); also *Historiae Ecclesiasticae Pars Tertia, CSCO* tom.55, tr. E. W. Brooks (Louvain, 1952).

Joh. Eph., *Lives* = John of Ephesus, 'Lives of the Eastern Saints', ed. and tr. E. W. Brooks, *PO* 17 (1923), 18 (1924) and 19 (1925).

Joh. Nik. = *Chronicle of John, bishop of Nikiu*, tr. R. H. Charles (London, 1916).

Josh. Styl. = Joshua the Stylite, *The Chronicle of Joshua the Stylite*, ed. and tr. W. Wright (Cambridge, 1882); also tr. J. Watt and F. Trombley (Liverpool, 1998).

Lazar = *The History of Łazar P'arpec'i*, tr. R. W. Thomson (Atlanta, Georgia, 1991).

Mari = Maris, Amri et Slibae, *De patriarchis Nestorianorum*, tr. H. Gismondi, vol.1 (Rome, 1899).

Mich. Syr. = Michael Syrus, *Chronique de Michel le Syrien, Patriarche Jacobite d'Antioche 1166–1199*, tr. J.-B. Chabot (Paris, 1900), vol.2 (cited by chapter and page number in Chabot's translation); also *Chronique de Michel le Grand tr. sur la version arménienne du prêtre Ischok*, V. Langlois (Venice-Paris, 1868).

Moberg, *Book* = A. Moberg, *The Book of the Himyarites* (Lund, 1924).

Moses = *Moses Khorenats'i, History of the Armenians*, tr. R. W. Thomson (Cambridge, Mass., 1978).

Movses = Movsēs Dasxuranci, *The History of the Caucasian Albanians*, tr. C. J. F. Dowsett (London, 1961).

Narrationes Variae = *Narrationes Variae*, in *Chronica Minora*, tr. E. W. Brooks and I. Guidi, *CSCO* ser.3 tom.4, part 3 (Paris, 1903).

P'awstos or *Epic Histories* = *The Epic Histories attributed to P'awstos Buzand (Buzandaran Patmut'iwnk')*, tr. and comm. N. G. Garsoïan (Cambridge, Mass., 1989).

Ps. Dion. II = *Chronicon pseudo-dionysianum vulgo dictum*, vol.2, ed. J.-B. Chabot, *CSCO* tom.104 (Paris, 1933), tr. R. Hespel, *CSCO* tom.213, vol.507 (Louvain, 1989). Partial tr. in W. Witakowski, *Pseudo-Dionysius of Tel-Mahre, Chronicle, known also as the Chronicle of Zuqnin. Part III* (Liverpool, 1996). The references in the text are to the pages of Chabot's edition, as given in Witakowski's translation.

Sebeos = *Histoire d'Héraclius par l'évèque Sebêos*, tr. F. Macler (Paris, 1904); a new translation by R. W. Thomson, with commentary by J. D. Howard-Johnston, is forthcoming.

Syn. Or. = *Synodicon Orientale*, ed. and tr. J.-B. Chabot (Paris, 1902).

Tabari = Tabari, *Geschichte der Perser und Araber zur Zeit der Sassaniden*, tr. T. Nöldeke (Leiden, 1879, repr. 1971).

al-Tha'alibi = al-Tha'alibi, *Histoire des rois des Perses par Al-Tha'alibi*, tr. and ed. H. Zotenberg (Paris, 1900).

V. Ioh. ep. Tell. = Elias of Nisibis, *Vitae Iohannis episcopi Tellae* in *Vitae Virorum apud Monophysitas celeberrimorum*, ed. and tr. E. W. Brooks, *CSCO* ser.3 tom.27 (Paris, 1907).

Zach. = J. F. Hamilton and E. W. Brooks, *The Syriac Chronicle known as that of Zachariah of Mitylene* (London, 1899), ed. and tr. E. W. Brooks, *Historia Ecclesiastica Zachariae Rhetori vulgo adscripta*, *CSCO* ser.3. tom.5, 2 vols. (tr.), 2 vols. (ed.) (Paris, 1924); and tr. and annot. K. Ahrens and G. Krüger, *Die sogennante Kirchengeschichte des Zacharias Rhetor* (Leipzig, 1899). (Footnotes provide page references to the translation of Hamilton–Brooks, in addition to chapter and book.)

Greek and Latin works

ACO = *Acta Conciliorum Oecumenicorum*, edd. E. Schwartz and J. Straub (Berlin, 1914–83).

Agath. = Agathias, *Historiae*, CFHB, ed. R. Keydell (Berlin, 1967), tr. J. D. Frendo (Berlin-New York, 1975).

Ammianus = Ammianus Marcellinus, *Rerum gestarum libri qui supersunt*, ed. and tr. J. C. Rolfe (London, 1935–9); and ed. W. Seyfarth (Leipzig, 1978).

Anth. Gr. = *Anthologia Graeca*, 4 vols., ed. H. Beckby (Munich, 1957–8).

Antoninus of Placentia = Antoninus of Placentia, *Itinerarium*, in *Itinera Hierosolymitana, saeculi IV–VIII*, ed. P. Geyer (Leipzig-Vienna-Prague, 1898, repr. New York-London, 1964), 159–91; also in *PL* 72, 897–918.

Caesar, *Bell. Gall.* = Caesar, *Bellum Gallicum* in *C. Iuli Caesaris Commentarii*, vol.1, ed. A. Klotz (Leipzig, 1952).

Cedr. = Cedrenus, *Compendium Historiarum*, ed. I. Bekker, 2 vols., CSHB (Bonn 1838–9).

Choricius = Choricius of Gaza, ed. R. Foerster and E. Richsteig, (Leipzig, 1929); tr. and comm. F. Litsas, *Choricius of Gaza: An approach to his work*, unpublished Ph.D. thesis (Chicago, 1980).

Cicero, *Philippic* = Cicero, *Philippics*, ed. and tr. D. R. Shackleton Bailey (Chapel Hill, N.C. and London, 1986).

CJ = *Codex Justinianus*, ed. P. Krueger, (Berlin, 1954).

Cont. Ant. = *Continuatio Antiochiensis Eusebii*, ed., tr. and comm. R. Burgess (forthcoming).

Corippus, *Ioh.* = *Flavii Cresconii Corippi Iohannidos Libri VIII*, edd. J. Diggle and F. R. D. Goodyear (Cambridge, 1970).

Cosmas, *Topogr.* = Cosmas Indicopleustes, *Topographie Chrétienne*, ed. and tr. W. Wolska-Conus (Paris, 1968–73).

CP = *Chronicon Paschale*, ed. L. Dindorf, CSHB (Bonn, 1832).

CPW = M. and M. Whitby (tr.), *Chronicon Paschale 284–628 AD* (Liverpool, 1989).

CTh = *Codex Theodosianus*, ed. T. Mommsen (Berlin, 1962), tr. C. Pharr (Princeton, 1952).

Cyr. Scyth. = Cyril of Scythopolis, ed. E. Schwartz, *Kyrillos von Skythopolis*, Texte u. Untersuchungen XLIX.2 (Leipzig, 1939); tr. and comm. A. J. Festugière, *Les moines d'Orient: Les moines de Palestine*, III.1–3 (Paris, 1962–3); and R. M. Price with J. Binns, *The Lives of the Monks of Palestine* (Kalamazoo, Mich., 1991).

Cyr. Scyth., *V. Ioh.* = *Vita S. Iohannis Hesychastae* in Schwartz (as above).

Cyr. Scyth., *V. Sab.* = *Vita Sabae* in Schwartz (as above).

De Cer. = Constantine Porphyrogenitus, *De Ceremoniis*, ed. J. J. Reiske, CSHB (Bonn, 1829).

Decret. Gelas. = *Das Decretum Gelasianum*, ed. E. von Dobschütz (Leipzig, 1912).

Eustath. = Eustathius of Epiphaneia, fragments, ed. C. Müller, *FHG* IV, 138–42.

Evagrius = Evagrius, *Ecclesiastical History*, edd. J. Bidez and L. Parmentier (London, 1898).

Expositio = *Expositio totius mundi et gentium*, ed. J. Rougé, SC 124 (Paris, 1966).

Frontinus, *Strategemata* = Frontinus, *Strategemata*, ed. M. B. McElwain, tr. C. E. Bennett (Cambridge, Mass., 1980).

George of Cyprus = *Le Synecdèmos d'Hiéroclès et l'opuscule géographique de Georges de Chypre*, ed. and comm. E. Honigmann, (Brussels, 1939).

Hdt. = Herodotus, *Historiae*, ed. C. Hude, third edition (Oxford, 1927).

Heliodorus, *Aethiopica* = Héliodore, *Les Éthiopiques*, edd. R. M. Rattenburg and T. W. Lumb, tr. J. Maillon, 3 vols. (Paris, 1935–43).

Hierocles, *Synekdemos* = *Le Synecdèmos d'Hiéroclès et l'opuscule géographique de Georges de Chypre*, ed. and comm. E. Honigmann (Brussels, 1939).

Joh. Ant. = John of Antioch, fragments, ed. C. Müller, *FHG* IV and V, 535–622 and 27–38 respectively.

Joh. Lyd. *de Mag.* = John Lydus, *De Magistratibus Populi Romani*, ed. R. Wuensch (Leipzig, 1903); also ed. and tr. A. C. Bandy (Philadelphia, Penn., 1983).

Jordanes, *Get.* = Jordanes, *Getica*, *MGH AA* V.1, ed. Th. Mommsen (Berlin, 1882); also, *Iordanis De origine actibusque Getarum*, edd. F. Giunta and A. Grillone (Rome, 1991).

Jordanes, *Rom.* = Jordanes, *Romana*, *MGH AA* V.1, ed. Th. Mommsen (Berlin, 1882).

Julian, *Or.* = Julian, *Orationes*, in *L'empereur Julien, oeuvres complètes* I.1, ed. J. Bidez (Paris, 1932).

Libanius, *Or.* = Libanius, *Orationes*, 7 vols., ed. R. Foerster (Leipzig, 1903–1913).

Lucian, *Quomodo Historia conscribenda sit* = Lucian, *Quomodo Historia conscribenda sit* (Πῶς δεῖ Ἱστορίαν συγγράφειν) in *Luciani Opera*, vol.3, ed. M. D. Macleod (Oxford, 1980), 287–319.

Mal. = Malalas, *Chronographia*, ed. L. Dindorf, CSHB (Bonn, 1831); tr. and annot. E. and M. Jeffreys and R. Scott (Melbourne, 1986).

Malchus = Malchus of Philadelphia, in *FCH* II, 402–54.

Marc. *com.* = *The Chronicle of Marcellinus*, ed. Th. Mommsen, tr. B. Croke (Sydney, 1995). Mommsen's original text in *MGH AA* XI (Berlin, 1894), 60–104.

Marc. *com. addit.* = *Additamentum* to *The Chronicle of Marcellinus* in Croke (above) and Mommsen (above), 104–8.

Mart. Ar. = *Martyrium S. Arethae et sociorum*, ed. E. Carpentier, *ASS* Oct. vol.10 (Brussels, 1866), 721–62.

Maurice, *Strategikon* = Maurice, *Strategikon*, ed. G. T. Dennis (Vienna, 1981); tr. G. T. Dennis (Philadelphia, 1988).

Menander = *The History of Menander the Guardsman*, ed. and tr. R. C. Blockley (Liverpool, 1985).

ND = *Notitia Dignitatum*, ed. O. Seeck (Berlin, 1876, repr. Frankfurt, 1962).

Nic. Call. = Nicephorus Callistus Xanthopulus, *Ecclesiasticae Historiae*, *PG* 145–7.

Nonnosus = Nonnosus, fragments, ed. C. Müller, *FHG* IV, 178–81.

Nov. = Justinian, *Novellae* in *Corpus Juris Civilis* vol.3, edd. R. Schoell and W. Kroll (Berlin, 1954).

NTh = *Theodosii II Leges Novellae* in *CTh* (above).

Olympiodorus = Olympiodorus of Thebes, in *FCH* II, 152–208.

Petr. Patr. = Peter the Patrician, fragments, in *FHG* IV, 180–91.

Parastaseis Syntomoi Chronikai = A. Cameron and J. Herrin, *Constantinople in the Early Eighth Century. The Parastaseis Syntomoi Chronikai* (Leiden, 1984).

'*Passio antiquior*' = '*Passio antiquior SS Sergii et Bacchi*', *AB* 14 (1895), 373–95; tr. J. Boswell, *The Marriage of Likeness* (London, 1995), 375–90.

Peri Strategias = Anon. (? Magister Syrianus) *Peri Strategias*, ed. and tr. G. T. Dennis in *Three Byzantine Military Treatises*, CFHB (Washington D.C., 1985).

Priscian, *Pan.* = Priscian of Caesarea, *De laude Anastasii imperatoris*, ed. E. Baehrens, in *Poetae Latini Minores*, vol.5 (Leipzig, 1883); also ed. and tr. A. Chauvot, *Procope de Gaza, Priscien de Césarée, Panégyriques de l'empereur Anastase 1er* (Bonn, 1986).

Priscus = Priscus of Panium, in *FCH* II, 222–376.

Proc. = Procopius, *Bella*, ed. J. Haury, rev. G. Wirth, 2 vols. (Leipzig, 1963); ed. and tr. H. B. Dewing, 5 vols. (Cambridge, Mass., 1914–28).

Proc. *Aed.* = Procopius, *De Aedificiis*, ed. J. Haury, rev. G. Wirth (Leipzig, 1964); ed. and tr. H. B. Dewing (Cambridge, Mass., 1940).

Proc. *Anecd.* = Procopius, *Anecdota*, ed. J. Haury, rev. G. Wirth (Leipzig, 1963); ed. and tr. H. B. Dewing (Cambridge, Mass., 1935).

Sallust, *Bellum Catilinae* = Sallust, *Bellum Catilinae*, ed. L. D. Reynolds (Oxford, 1991).

Socr. *HE* = Socrates, *Kirchengeschichte*, ed. G. C. Hansen, GCS (Berlin, 1995).

Soz. *HE* = Sozomen, *Kirchengeschichte*, ed. J. Bidez, rev. G. C. Hansen, second edition, GCS (Berlin, 1995).

Strabo = Strabo, *Geography*, ed. and tr. H. L. Jones (Cambridge, Mass., 1917–1932).

Suidas = Suidas, *Lexikon*, ed. A. Adler (Leipzig, 1928–38).

Tacitus, *Annals* = Tacitus, *Annales*, ed. E. Koestermann (Leipzig, 1965).

Tacitus, *Historiae* = Tacitus, *Historiae*, ed. E. Koestermann (Leipzig, 1969).

Theod. *HE* = Theodoret (of Cyrrhus), *Historia Ecclesiastica*, ed. L. Parmentier, GCS (Berlin, 1954).

Theod. Lect. *HE* = Theodore Anagnostes (= Theodore Lector), *Kirchengeschichte*, ed. G. C. Hansen, GCS (Berlin, 1971).

Theoph. = Theophanes, *Chronographia*, ed. C. de Boor (Leipzig, 1883), tr. C. Mango and R. Scott with G. Greatrex (Oxford, 1997).

Theoph. Byz. = Theophanes Byzantinus, fragments, ed. C. Müller, *FHG* IV, 270–1.

Theoph. Sim. = Theophylact Simocatta, *Historiae*, ed. C. de Boor, rev. P. Wirth (Stuttgart, 1962), tr. and annot. M. and M. Whitby (Oxford, 1986).

Thuc. = Thucydides, *Historiae*, ed. H. S. Jones, rev. J. E. Powell (Oxford, 1942).

'Tübingen Theosophy' = *Fragmente griechischer Theosophien*, ed. H. Erbse (Hamburg, 1941).

Urbicius, *Epitedeuma* = Urbicius, *Epitēdeuma* in *Arta Militară*, ed. H. Mihaescu (Bucharest, 1970), 368–72.

van den Ven, *V. Syméon Stylite* = P. van den Ven, *La vie ancienne de Syméon stylite le jeune*, Subsidia Hagiographica 32, 2 vols (Brussels, 1962–70).

Vegetius, *Epitoma* = Vegetius, *Epitoma Rei Militaris*, ed. C. Lang (Leipzig, 1885); tr. N. P. Milner, *Vegetius: Epitome of Military Science* (Liverpool, 1993).

Xenophon, *Hellenica* = Xenophon, *Hellenica*, ed. E. C. Marchant (Oxford, 1900).

Zon. = Zonaras, *Epitome Historiarum*, ed. L. Dindorf, vol.3 (Leipzig, 1870).

Zos. = *Zosime. Histoire Nouvelle*, ed. and tr. F. Paschoud, 3 vols (Paris, 1971–1989).

Secondary Sources

Abel, 'L'île de Jotabé' = F.-M. Abel, 'L'île de Jotabé', *RevBibl* 47 (1938), 510–38.

Adontz, *Armenia* = N. Adontz, *Armenia in the period of Justinian: The political conditions based on the 'Naxarar' system*, tr. and rev. N. G. Garsoïan (Lisbon, 1970).

Ahrens–Krüger, *Kirchengeschichte*, see Zach. in sources (non-classical), above.

Aigrain, 'Arabie' = R. Aigrain, 'Arabie', *DHGE* III (1924), 1158–1339.

Alexander, *Oracle* = P. J. Alexander, *The Oracle of Baalbek. The Tiburtine Sibyl in Greek Dress* (Washington D.C., 1967).

Algaze, 'Preliminary report' = G. Algaze, R. Breuninger, C. Lightfoot, M. Rosenberg, 'The Tigris-Euphrates Archaeological Project: A preliminary report of the 1989–1990 seasons', *Anatolica* 17 (1991), 175–240.

Allchin–Hammond, *Archaeology of Afghanistan* = F. R. Allchin and N. Hammond, *The Archaeology of Afghanistan from earliest times to the Timurid period* (London, 1978).

Allen, 'An early epitomator' = P. Allen, 'An early epitomator of Josephus: Eustathius of Epiphaneia', *BZ* 81 (1988), 1–11.

Allen, *Evagrius* = P. Allen, *Evagrius Scholasticus, the Church historian* (Louvain, 1981).

Allen, 'Zachariah Scholasticus' = P. Allen, 'Zachariah Scholasticus and the *Historia Ecclesiastica* of Evagrius Scholasticus', *JThSt* 31 (1980), 471–88.

Altheim–Stiehl, *Die Araber* = F. Altheim and R. Stiehl, *Die Araber in der alten Welt*, V.1 (Berlin, 1968).

Anderson, 'Alexander' = A. R. Anderson, 'Alexander at the Caspian Gates', *TAPA* 59 (1928), 130–63.

Arrignon–Duneau, 'La frontière' = J.-P. Arrignon and J.-F. Duneau, 'La frontière chez deux auteurs byzantins: Procope de Césarée et Constantin VII Porphyrogénète' in *Geographica Byzantina*, ed. H. Ahrweiler (Paris, 1981), 17–30.

Austin–Rankov, *Exploratio* = N. J. E. Austin and B. Rankov, *Exploratio. Military and political intelligence in the Roman world from the Second Punic War to the Battle of Adrianople* (London, 1995).

Bardill–Greatrex, 'Antiochus' = J. Bardill and G. Greatrex, 'Antiochus the *praepositus*: a Persian eunuch at the court of Theodosius II', *DOP* 50 (1996), 171–97.

Beeston, 'Judaism' = A. F. L. Beeston, 'Judaism and Christianity in pre-Islamic Yemen', *L'Arabie du Sud: Histoire et Civilisation*, ed. J. Chelhod, vol.1 (Paris, 1984), 271–8.

Beeston, 'The chain' = A. F. L. Beeston, 'The chain of al-Mandab' in *On both sides of al-Mandab. Ethiopian, South-Arabic and Islamic Studies presented to Oscar Löfgren on his ninetieth birthday, 13 May 1988 by colleagues and friends* (Istanbul, 1989), 1–6.

Beeston, 'The martyrdom' = A. F. L. Beeston, 'The martyrdom of Azqir', *Seminar for Arabian Studies* 15 (1985), 5–10.

Beeston, 'Two Bi'r Hima Inscriptions' = A. F. L. Beeston, 'Two Bi'r Himā Inscriptions Re-examined', *BSOAS* 48 (1985), 42–52.

Bellamy, 'A new reading' = J. A. Bellamy, 'A new reading of the Namārah Inscription', *JAOS* 105 (1985), 31–51.

van Berchem, 'Recherches' = D. van Berchem, 'Recherches sur la chronologie des enceintes de Syrie et de Mésopotamie', *Syria* 21 (1954), 254–70.

van Berchem–Strzygowski, *Amida* = M. van Berchem and J. Strzygowksi, *Amida* (Heidelberg, 1910).

Bivar, 'Cavalry Equipment' = A. D. H. Bivar, 'Cavalry Equipment and Tactics on the Euphrates Frontier', *DOP* 26 (1972), 273–91.

Bivar, 'The political history' = A. D. H. Bivar, 'The political history of Iran under the Arsacids', *CHIr* III.1, 21–99.

Bland, 'The development' = R. F. Bland, 'The development of gold and silver coin denominations' in *Coin Finds and Coin Use in the Roman World*, edd. C. E. King and D. G. Wigg (Berlin, 1996), 63–100.

Blau, 'Altarabische Sprachstudien' = O. Blau, 'Altarabische Sprachstudien II', *ZDMG* 27 (1873), 295–363.

Blockley, *ERFP* = R. C. Blockley, *East Roman Foreign Policy: Formation and Conduct from Diocletian to Anastasius* (Leeds, 1992).

Blockley, *Menander* = *The History of Menander the Guardsman*, ed. and tr. R. C. Blockley (Liverpool, 1985).

Blockley, 'Romano-Persian Peace treaties' = R. C. Blockley, 'The Romano-Persian Peace treaties of A.D. 299 and 363', *Florilegium* 6 (1984), 28–49.

Blockley, 'Subsidies and Diplomacy' = R. C. Blockley, 'Subsidies and Diplomacy: Rome and Persia in late antiquity', *Phoenix* 39 (1985), 62–74.

Blockley, 'The division' = R. C. Blockley, 'The division of Armenia between the Romans and the Persians', *Historia* 36 (1987), 222–34.

Boss, *Justinian's Wars* = R. Boss, *Justinian's Wars* (Stockport, 1993).

Bosworth, 'Iran and the Arabs' = C. E. Bosworth, 'Iran and the Arabs before Islam', *CHIr* III.1, 593–612.

Bowersock, *Julian* = G. Bowersock, *Julian the Apostate* (London, 1978).

Bowersock, '*Limes Arabicus*' = G. Bowersock, '*Limes Arabicus*', *HStClPhil* 80 (1976), 219–29.

Brandes, 'Anastasios' = W. Brandes, 'Anastasius ὁ δίκορος: Endzeiterwartung und Kaiserkritik in Byzanz um 500 n. Chr.', *BZ* 90 (1997), 24–63.

Braund, *Friendly King* = D. C. Braund, *Rome and the Friendly King* (London, 1984).

Braund, *Georgia* = D. C. Braund, *Georgia in Antiquity* (Oxford, 1994).

Braund, 'Procopius on the economy of Lazica' = D. C. Braund, 'Procopius on the economy of Lazica', *CQ* 41 (1991), 221–5.

Breydy, *Annalenwerk*, see Eutychius, in sources (non-classical), above.

Brock, 'The Conversations' = S. P. Brock, 'The Conversations with the Syrian Orthodox under Justinian', *OrChP* 47 (1981), 87–121.

Brock, 'Syriac historical writing' = S. P. Brock, 'Syriac historical writing: a survey of the main sources' in *Studies in Syriac Christianity* (Aldershot, 1992), I.

Brosset, *Additions* = M. Brosset, *Additions et Eclaircissements à l'histoire de la Géorgie jusqu'en 1469 de J.-C.* (St Petersburg, 1851).

Brückner, *Zur Beurteilung* = M. Brückner, *Zur Beurteilung des Geschichtsschreibers Procopius von Casearea* (Ansbach, 1896).

Brunner, 'Geographical and administrative divisions' = C. Brunner, 'Geographical and administrative divisions: settlements and economy', *CHIr* III.2, 747–77.

Bryer, 'Some notes (1)' = A. D. Bryer, 'Some notes on the Laz and Tzan (1)', *Bedi Kartlisa* 21–22 (1966), 174–95.

Bryer, 'Some notes (2)' = A. D. Bryer, 'Some notes on the Laz and Tzan (2)', *Bedi Kartlisa* 23–24 (1967), 161–8.

Bryer–Winfield, *Pontus* = A. Bryer and D. Winfield, *The Byzantine Monuments and Topography of the Pontos*, vol.1 (Washington D.C., 1985).

Burgess, 'A new reading' = R. W. Burgess, 'A new reading for Hydatius *Chronicle* 177 and the Defeat of the Huns in Italy', *Phoenix* 42 (1988), 357–63.

Burgess, *Cont. Ant.*, see *Cont. Ant.*, in sources (classical), above.

Burkitt, *Euphemia*, see in sources (non-classical), above.

Bury, *HLRE* = J. B. Bury, *History of the Later Roman Empire*, 2 vols. (London, 1923, repr. New York, 1958).

Bury, *HLRE*[1] = J. B. Bury, *A History of the Later Roman Empire*, 2 vols. (London, 1889).

Bury, 'Johannes Malalas' = J. B. Bury, 'Johannes Malalas: the text of the codex Baroccianus', *BZ* 6 (1897), 219–30.

Bury, 'Nika riot' = J. B. Bury, 'The Nika riot', *JHS* 17 (1897), 92–119.

Cameron, 'Some prefects' = A. D. E. Cameron, 'Some prefects called Julian', *Byzantion* 47 (1977), 42–64.

Cameron, 'The date' = A. D. E. Cameron, 'The date of Zosimus' New History', *Philologus* 13 (1969), 106–10.

Cameron, *Later Roman Empire* = A. Cameron, *The Later Roman Empire* (London, 1993).

Cameron, *Mediterranean World* = A. Cameron, *The Mediterranean World in Late Antiquity, A.D. 395–600* (London, 1993).

Cameron, *Procopius* = A. Cameron, *Procopius and the sixth century* (London, 1985).

Cameron, 'Sassanians' = A. Cameron, 'Agathias on the Sassanians', *DOP* 23–4 (1969–70), 69–183.

Cameron, 'The Sceptic' = A. Cameron, 'The Sceptic and the Shroud' in *Continuity and Change in Sixth-Century Byzantium* (London, 1981), V.

Capizzi, *Anastasio* = C. Capizzi, *L'imperatore Anastasio I* (Rome, 1969).

Carpentier, *De SS. Aretha et Ruma* = E. Carpentier, *De SS. Aretha et Ruma*, *ASS* Oct., vol.10 (Brussels, 1866), 661–721.

Carrié, 'L'Etat' = J.-M. Carrié, 'L'Etat à la recherche de nouveaux modes de financement des armées (Rome et Byzance, IVe – VIIIe siècles)', *SRA*, 27–60.

Carswell, 'The Port of Mantai' = J. Carswell, 'The Port of Mantai, Sri Lanka' in *Rome and India: The Ancient Sea Trade*, edd. V. Begley and R. D. De Puma (Wisconsin-London, 1991), 197–203.

Casey, 'Justinian and the *limitanei*' = P. J. Casey, 'Justinian, the *limitanei*, and Arab-Byzantine relations in the sixth century', *JRA* 9 (1996), 214–22.

Chapot, *La frontière* = V. Chapot, *La frontière de l'Euphrate de Pompée à la conquête Arabe* (Paris, 1907).

Chassin, *Bélisaire* = L. M. Chassin, *Bélisaire, Généralissime byzantin (504–565)* (Paris, 1957).

Chaumont, 'Conquêtes Sassanides' = M.-L. Chaumont, 'Conquêtes Sassanides et Propagande Mazdéenne', *Historia* 22 (1973), 664–710.

Chaumont, *Recherches* = M.-L. Chaumont, *Recherches sur l'histoire de l'Arménie de l'avènement des Sassanides à la conversion du royaume* (Paris, 1969).

Chaumont, 'Un Astabad' = M.-L. Chaumont, 'Un Astabad (*magister officiorum*) à la cour des Sassanides au IIIe siècle?', *Muséon* 81 (1968), 231–40.

Chekalova, 'Jesu Stilit' = A. Chekalova, 'Jesu Stilit ili Prokopij', *VizVrem* 42 (1981), 71–7.

Christensen, *Iranshahr* = P. Christensen, *The Decline of Iranshahr* (Copenhagen, 1993).

Christensen, *Le règne* = A. Christensen, *Le règne du roi Kawādh et le communisme Mazdakite* (Copenhagen, 1925).

Christensen, *L'Iran* = A. Christensen, *L'Iran sous les Sassanides*, second edition (Copenhagen, 1944).

Christides, 'The Himyarite-Ethiopian War' = V. Christides, 'The Himyarite-Ethiopian War and the Ethiopian occupation of South Arabia in the Acts of Gregentius (ca. 530 A.D.)', *Annales d'Éthiopie* 9 (1972), 115–46.

Chrysos, 'Byzantine Diplomacy' = E. K. Chrysos, 'Byzantine Diplomacy, 300–800' in *Byzantine Diplomacy*, 25–39.

Chrysos, 'Some Aspects' = E. K. Chrysos, 'Some Aspects of Roman-Persian Legal Relations', *Kleronomia* 8 (1976), 1–60.

Clauss, *Magister officiorum* = M. Clauss, *Der magister officiorum in der Spätantike (4.–6. Jahrhundert)* (Munich, 1980).

Clinton, *Fasti* = H. F. Clinton, *Fasti Romani*, 2 vols. (Oxford, 1845–50).

Coulston, 'Later Roman armour' = J. C. N. Coulston, 'Later Roman armour, 3rd–6th centuries AD', *Journal of Roman Military Equipment Studies* 1 (1990), 139–61.

Croke, *Chronicle*, see Marc. *com.*, in sources (classical), above.

Croke, 'Justinian's Bulgar Victory Celebration' = B. Croke, 'Justinian's Bulgar Victory Celebration', *BSl* 41 (1980), 188–95.

Croke, 'Malalas' = B. Croke, 'Malalas, the man and his work', *Studies in Malalas*, 3–25.

Croke, 'Marcellinus and Dara' = B. Croke, 'Marcellinus and Dara: a fragment of his lost *de temporum qualitatibus et positionibus locorum*', *Phoenix* 38 (1984), 77–88.

Croke and Crow, 'Procopius and Dara' = B. Croke and J. Crow 'Procopius and Dara', *JRS* 73 (1983), 143–59 (= XI in B. Croke, *Christian Chronicles and Byzantine History – Fifth-Sixth Centuries* [Aldershot, 1992]).

Crone, 'Kavad's heresy' = P. Crone, 'Kavād's heresy and Mazdak's revolt', *Iran* 29 (1991), 21–42.

Crow, 'Frontiers of Cappadocia' = J. G. Crow, 'A review of the physical remains of the frontiers of Cappadocia', *DRBE*, 77–91.

Crow, 'The Long Walls' = J. G. Crow, 'The Long Walls of Thrace', in *Hinterland*, 109–24.

Crown, 'The Samaritans' = A. D. Crown, 'The Samaritans in the Byzantine orbit', *Bulletin of the John Rylands Library* 69 (1986), 96–138.

Cumont, *Études Syriennes* = F. Cumont, *Études Syriennes* (Paris, 1917).

Dagron–Morrisson, 'Le *kentènarion*' = G. Dagron and C. Morrisson, 'Le *kentènarion* dans les sources byzantines', *RN* 17 (1975), 301–14.

Dain, 'Les stratégistes' = A. Dain, 'Les stratégistes byzantins', *TM* 2 (1967), 317–92.

Daniélou–Marrou, *The First Six Hundred Years* = J. Daniélou and H. Marrou, tr. V. Cronin, *The Christian Centuries*, vol.1, *The First Six Hundred Years* (London, 1964).

Daudpota, 'Annals' = U. M. Daudpota, 'The Annals of Hamzah al-Isfahāni, translated from the Arabic', *K. R. Cama Oriental Institute Journal* 22 (1932), 58–120.

Davis, 'The problem' = D. Davis, 'The problem of Firdawsî's sources', *JAOS* 116 (1996), 48–57.

Debevoise, *Parthia* = N.C. Debevoise, *A political history of Parthia* (Chicago, 1938).

Dédéyan, *Histoire* = G. Dédéyan, ed., *Histoire des Arméniens* (Paris, 1982).

Delbrück, *Barbarian Invasions* = H. Delbrück, *The Barbarian Invasions*, tr. W. J. Renfroe, Jr. (Lincoln, NE, 1980).

Demandt, *Spätantike* = A. Demandt, *Die Spätantike–Römische Geschichte von Diocletian bis Justinian* (Munich, 1989).

Devos, 'Quelques aspects' = P. Devos, 'Quelques aspects de la nouvelle lettre récemment découverte, de Simeon de Bêth Aršâm sur les martyrs Himyarites', *Studi Etiopici*, 107–16.

Devreesse, 'Arabes-Perses' = R. Devreesse, 'Arabes-Perses et Arabes-Romains, Lakhmides et Ghassanides', *RevBibl/Vivre et Penser* 51 (1942), 263–307.

Dillemann, *Mésopotamie* = L. Dillemann, *Haute Mésopotamie et pays adjacents* (Paris, 1962).

Dodgeon–Lieu, *Eastern frontier* = M. Dodgeon and S. N. C. Lieu, *The Roman Eastern Frontier and the Persian Wars, 226–363* (London, 1991).

Donner, 'The Role of Nomads' = F. M. Donner, 'The Role of Nomads in the Near East in Late Antiquity' in *Tradition and Innovation in Late Antiquity*, edd. F. M. Clover and R. S. Humphreys (Madison, 1989), 73–85.

Drewes, 'Kaleb and Himyar' = A. J. Drewes, 'Kaleb and Himyar: another reference to Hywn'?', *Raydan. Journal of Ancient Yemeni Antiquities and Epigraphy* 1 (1978), 27–30.

Durliat, 'Armée' = J. Durliat, 'Armée et société vers 600. Le problème des soldes', *ARB*, 31–8.

Dussaud, *Topographie* = R. Dussaud, *Topographie historique de la Syrie antique et médiévale* (Paris, 1927).

Eadie, 'Roman mailed cavalry' = J. W. Eadie, 'The development of Roman mailed cavalry', *JRS* 57 (1967), 161–73.

Eadie, 'The Transformation' = J. W. Eadie, 'The Transformation of the Eastern Frontiers', *Shifting Frontiers*, 72–82.

Elton, 'Defining Romans' = H. W. Elton, 'Defining Romans and barbarians', *Shifting Frontiers*, 126–35.

Elton, *Warfare* = H. W. Elton, *Warfare in Roman Europe A.D. 350–425* (Oxford, 1996).

Engelhardt, *Mission und Politik* = I. Engelhardt, *Mission und Politik in Byzanz. Ein Beitrag zur Strukturanalyse byzantinischer Mission zur Zeit Justins und Justinians*, Miscellanea Byzantina Monacensia 19 (Munich, 1984).

van Esbroeck, 'Lazique' = M. van Esbroeck, 'Lazique, Mingrélie, Svanéthie et Aphkhazie du IVᵉ au IXᵉ siècle', *Caucaso*, 195–218.

Evans, *Justinian* = J. A. S. Evans, *The Age of Justinian. The circumstances of imperial power* (London, 1996).

Farquharson, 'Byzantium, Planet Earth and the Solar system' = P. Farquharson, 'Byzantium, Planet Earth and the Solar system' in *The Sixth Century. End or Beginning?*, edd. E. Jeffreys and P. Allen (Brisbane, 1996), 263–9.

Feissel, 'Remarques' = D. Feissel, 'Remarques de toponymie syrienne d'après des inscriptions grecques chrétiennes trouvées hors de Syrie', *Syria* 59 (1982), 319–41.

Festugière, 'Notabilia II' = A. J. Festugière, 'Notabilia dans Malalas II', *RPhil* 53 (1979), 227–37.

Fiey, *Nisibe* = J.-M. Fiey, *Nisibe, métropole syriaque orientale et ses suffragants des origines à nos jours* (Louvain, 1977).

Fornara, 'Julian's Persian expedition' = C. W. Fornara, 'Julian's Persian expedition in Ammianus Marcellinus and Zosimus', *JHS* 111 (1991), 1–15.

Fornara, *The Nature of History* = C. W. Fornara, *The Nature of History in Ancient Greece and Rome* (Berkeley, 1983).

Foss, 'The Persians in Asia Minor' = C. Foss, 'The Persians in Asia Minor and the End of Antiquity', *EHR* 90 (1975), 721–47.

Fotiou, 'Recruitment shortages' = A. S. Fotiou, 'Recruitment shortages in sixth century Byzantium', *Byzantion* 58 (1988), 65–77.

Fowden, *Empire* = G. Fowden, *Empire to Commonwealth. Consequences of monotheism in late antiquity* (Princeton, 1993).

Frézouls, 'Les fluctuations' = E. Frézouls, 'Les fluctuations de la frontière orientale de l'empire romain' in *La Géographie administrative et politique d'Alexandre à Mahomet. Actes du Colloque de Strasbourg* (Leiden, 1981), 355–86.

Frye, *Ancient Iran* = R. N. Frye, *The History of Ancient Iran* (Munich, 1984).

Frye, 'Sasanian system' = R. N. Frye, 'The Sasanian system of walls for defense' in *Studies in Memory of Gaston Wiet*, ed. M. Rosen-Ayalon (Jerusalem, 1977), 7–15.

Frye, 'The political history' = R. N. Frye, 'The political history of Iran under the Sassanians', *CHIr* III.1, 116–80.

Gabriel, *Voyages* = A. Gabriel, *Voyages archéologiques dans la Turquie orientale* (Paris, 1940).

Garsoïan, 'Byzantium and the Sasanians' = N. G. Garsoïan, 'Byzantium and the Sasanians', *CHIr* III.1, 568–92.

Garsoïan, *Epic Histories*, see P'awstos, in sources (non-classical), above.

Gascou, 'L'institution des bucellaires' = J. Gascou, 'L'institution des bucellaires', *BIFAO* 76 (1976), 143–56.

Gentz, *Die Kirchengeschichte* = G. Gentz, *Die Kirchengeschichte des Nicephorus Callistus Xanthopulus und ihre Quellen* (Berlin, 1966).

Gibbon, *Decline* = E. Gibbon, *Decline and Fall of the Roman Empire*, ed. J. B. Bury, 7 vols. (London, 1897–1902).

Ginkel, *John of Ephesus* = J. J. van Ginkel, *John of Ephesus. A Monophysite Historian in Sixth-Century Byzantium*, diss. (Groningen, 1995).

Glück, 'Reviling and Monomachy' = J. J. Glück, 'Reviling and Monomachy as battle-preludes in ancient warfare', *Acta Classica* 7 (1964), 25–31.

Göbl, 'Sasanian coins' = R. Göbl, 'Sasanian coins', *CHIr* III.1, 322–39.

Göbl, *Sasanian Numismatics* = R. Göbl, *Sasanian Numismatics*, tr. P. Severin (Braunschweig, 1971).

Goubert, *Byzance* = P. Goubert, *Byzance avant l'Islam. I. Byzance et l'Orient sous les successeurs de Justinien. L'empereur Maurice* (Paris, 1951).

Goossens, *Hiérapolis* = G. Goossens, *Hiérapolis de Syrie* (Louvain, 1943).

Grant, *Historians* = M. Grant, *Greek and Roman Historians: Information and Misinformation* (London, 1995).

Gray, 'Eastern *limes*' = E. W. Gray, 'The Roman Eastern *limes* from Constantine to Justinian — Perspectives and Problems', *Proceedings of the African Classical Association* 12 (1973), 24–40.

Gray, *The Defense of Chalcedon* = P. T. R. Gray, *The Defense of Chalcedon in the East (451–553)* (Leiden, 1979).

Greatrex, 'The Classical Past' = G. Greatrex, 'The Classical Past in the classicising historians' in *The Reception of Classical Texts and Images*, edd. L. Hardwick and S. Ireland (Milton Keynes, 1996); accessible at http://www.open.ac.uk/OU/Academic/Arts/CC96/ccfrontpage.htm

Greatrex, 'Dukes' = G. Greatrex, 'Dukes of the eastern frontier', forthcoming.

Greatrex, 'Fifth-century wars' = G. Greatrex, 'The Two fifth century Wars between Rome and Persia', *Florilegium* 12 (1993), 1–14.

Greatrex, 'Hypatius' = G. Greatrex, 'Flavius Hypatius, *quem vidit validum Parthus sensitque timendum*', *Byzantion* 66 (1996), 120–42.

Greatrex, 'Lawyers and Historians' = G. Greatrex, 'Lawyers and Historians in Late Antiquity' in *The Transformation of Law and Society in Late Antiquity*, edd. R. Mathisen and H. Sivan (forthcoming).

Greatrex, 'Nika riot' = G. Greatrex, 'The Nika riot: a reassessment', *JHS* 117 (1997), 60–86.

Greatrex, *Procopius* = G. Greatrex, *Procopius and the Persian Wars*, D. Phil. thesis (Oxford, 1994).

Greatrex, 'Procopius and Agathias' = G. Greatrex, 'Procopius and Agathias on the defence of the Thracian Chersonese', *Hinterland*, 125–9.

Greatrex, 'Stephanus' = G. Greatrex, 'Stephanus, the father of Procopius of Caesarea?', *Medieval Prosopography* 17.1 (1996), 125–45.

Greatrex, 'The dates' = G. Greatrex, 'The dates of Procopius' works', *BMGS* 18 (1994), 101–14.

Greatrex, 'Ziatha' = G. and M. Greatrex, 'The Hunnic invasion of the East of 395 and the fortress of Ziatha', *Byzantion* 68 (1998), forthcoming.

Greatrex–Lieu, *Eastern Frontier* = G. Greatrex and S. N. C. Lieu, *The Eastern Roman Frontier and the Persian Wars, A.D. 363–628*, forthcoming.

Grierson, *Byzantine Coins* = P. Grierson, *Byzantine Coins* (London, 1982).

Grosse, 'Die Rangordnung' = R. Grosse, 'Die Rangordnung der römischen Armee des 4.–6. Jahrhunderts', *Klio* 15 (1918), 123–61.

Grosse, *Militärgeschichte* = R. Grosse, *Römische Militärgeschichte von Gallienus bis zum Beginn der byzantinischen Themenverfassung* (Berlin, 1920).

Grousset, *Histoire* = R. Grousset, *Histoire de l'Arménie* (Paris, 1947).

Grumel, *Chronologie* = V. Grumel, *La Chronologie*, Bibliothèque byzantine, Traité d'études byzantines, vol.1 (Paris, 1958).

Guey, 'Autour des *Res Gestae*' = J. Guey, 'Autour des *Res Gestae Divi Saporis*. 1. Deniers (d'or) et deniers d'or (de compte) anciens', *Syria* 38 (1961), 261–74.

Güterbock, *Byzanz und Persien* = K. Güterbock, *Byzanz und Persien in ihren diplomatisch-völkerrechtlichen Beziehungen im Zeitalter Justinians* (Berlin, 1906).

Guignoux, 'L'organisation administrative' = P. Guignoux, 'L'organisation administrative sasanide: le cas du *marzbān*', *Jerusalem Studies in Arabic and Islam* 4 (1984), 1–27.

Gutwein, *Third Palestine* = K. C. Gutwein, *Third Palestine: a regional study in Byzantine urbanisation* (Washington, D.C., 1981).

Haldon, 'Administrative Continuities' = J. F. Haldon, 'Administrative Continuities and Structural Transformations in East Roman Military Organisation ca.580–640', *ARB*, 45–54.

Haldon, *Recruitment* = J. F. Haldon, *Recruitment and Conscription in the Byzantine Army c.550–950: A Study on the Origins of the Stratiotika ktemata*, Sitzungsberichte der österreichischen Akademie der Wissenschaften, phil.-hist. Klasse 357 (Vienna, 1979).

Haldon, 'Some Aspects' = J. F. Haldon, 'Some Aspects of Byzantine Military Technology from the Sixth to the Tenth Centuries', *BMGS* 1 (1975), 11–47.

Hansen, 'The battle exhortation' = M. H. Hansen, 'The battle exhortation in ancient historiography. Fact or fiction?', *Historia* 42 (1993), 161–80.

Harmatta, 'The struggle' = J. Harmatta, 'The struggle for the possession of South Arabia between Aksum and the Sāsānians', *Studi Etiopici*, 95–106.

258

BIBLIOGRAPHY

Harvey, *Asceticism and Society* = S. A. Harvey, *Asceticism and Society in Crisis. John of Ephesus and The Lives of the Eastern Saints* (Berkeley-Los Angeles, 1990).

Harvey, 'Remembering Pain' = S. A. Harvey, 'Remembering Pain: Syriac historiography and the separation of the Churches', *Byzantion* 58 (1988), 295–308.

Haury, 'Procopiana (1)' = J. Haury, 'Procopiana' (part 1) in *Programm des Königlichen Realgymnasiums Augsburg*, 1890/1.

Haury, 'Procopiana (2)' = J. Haury, 'Procopiana' (part 2) in *Programm des Königlichen Realgymnasiums München 1892/3* (Munich, 1893).

Haury, *Zur Beurteilung* = J. Haury, *Zur Beurteilung des Geschichtsschreibers Procopius von Cäsarea* (Munich, 1896).

Haussig, 'Theophylakts Exkurs' = H. Haussig, 'Theophylakts Exkurs über die Skythischen Völker', *Byzantion* 23 (1953), 275–462.

Heather, *Goths and Romans* = P. J. Heather, *Goths and Romans, 332–489* (Oxford, 1991).

Helm, 'Untersuchungen' = R. Helm, 'Untersuchungen über den auswärtigen diplomatischen Verkehr des römischen Reiches im Zeitalter der Spätantike', *Archiv für Urkundenforschung* 12 (1932), 375–436.

Hewsen, *Ananias* = R. H. Hewsen, *The Geography of Ananias of Širak (Ašxarhac'oyc'). The Long and the Short Recensions* (Wiesbaden, 1992).

Hewsen, 'An introduction' = R. H. Hewsen, 'An introduction to Armenian historical geography', *REArm* 13 (1978–9), 77–97.

Higgins, 'International Relations' = M. J. Higgins, 'International relations at the close of the sixth century', *Catholic Historical Review* 27 (1941), 279–315.

Hoffmann, *Auszüge* = G. Hoffmann, *Auszüge aus syrischen Erzählungen von persischen Märtyrer* (Leipzig, 1880).

Hofmann, *Zur Kritik* = K. Hofmann, *Zur Kritik der byzantinischen Quellen für die Römerkriege Kobad's I* (Schweinfurt, 1877).

Holum, 'Caesarea' = K. G. Holum, 'Caesarea and the Samaritans' in R. Hohlfelder, ed., *City, Town and Countryside in the Early Byzantine Era* (New York, 1982), 65–74.

Holum, 'Pulcheria's Crusade' = K. G. Holum, 'Pulcheria's Crusade and the Ideology of Imperial Victory', *GRBS* 18 (1977), 153–72.

Holum, *Theodosian Empresses* = K. G. Holum, *Theodosian Empresses: Women and Imperial Dominion in Late Antiquity* (Berkeley-Los Angeles-London, 1982).

Honigmann, *Ostgrenze* = E. Honigmann, *Die Ostgrenze des Byzantinischen Reiches* (Brussels, 1935) (= part III of A. A. Vasiliev, *Byzance et les Arabes*).

Honigmann, 'Patristic Studies' = E. Honigmann, 'Patristic Studies', *Studi e Testi* 172 (Vatican City, 1953).

Honigmann, *Topographie* = E. Honigmann, *Historische Topographie von Nordsyrien im Altertum* (Leipzig, 1923).

Hornblower, *Greek World* = S. Hornblower, *The Greek World, 473–323 B.C.* (London, 1991).

Howard, *War* = M. Howard, *War in European History* (Oxford, 1976).

Howard-Johnston, 'Citharizon', = J. D. Howard-Johnston, 'Procopius, Roman defences north of the Taurus and the new fortress of Citharizon', *EFRE*, 203–28.

Howard-Johnston, 'Great Powers' = J. D. Howard-Johnston, 'The Great Powers in Late Antiquity: A comparison', *SRA*, 157–226.

Howard-Johnston, 'The official history' = J. D. Howard-Johnston, 'The official history of Heraclius' Persian campaigns', *RBAE*, 57–87.

Howard-Johnston, 'The siege of Constantinople' = J. D. Howard-Johnston, 'The siege of Constantinople in 626' in *Hinterland*, 131–42.

Howard-Johnston and Ryan, *Scholar* = J. D. Howard-Johnston and N. Ryan, *The Scholar and the Gypsy* (London, 1992).

Howorth, 'Sabiri' = H. Howorth, 'The Sabiri and the Saroguri', *JRAS* 24 (1892), 613–636.

Hübschmann, *Ortsnamen* = H. Hübschmann, *Die Altarmenischen Ortsnamen* (Strasbourg, 1904, repr. Amsterdam, 1969).

Huxley, 'On the Greek *martyrium*' = G. L. Huxley, 'On the Greek *martyrium* of the Negranites', *Proceedings of the Royal Irish Academy* 80 C, no.3 (1980), 41–55.

Iluk, 'The export of gold' = J. Iluk, 'The export of gold from the Roman Empire to barbarian countries from the 4th to the 6th centuries', *Münstersche Beiträge z. antiken Handelsgeschichte* IV.1 (1985), 79–102.

Isaac, 'Army' = B. Isaac, 'The Army in the Late Roman East: The Persian Wars and the Defence of the Byzantine Provinces', *SRA*, 125–55.

Isaac, *Limits* = B. Isaac, *The Limits of Empire*, revised edition (Oxford, 1992).

Isaac, 'The meaning' = B. Isaac, 'The meaning of the terms *limes* and *limitanei* in Ancient Sources', *JRS* 78 (1988), 125–47.

Jarry, 'Une prétendue invasion' = J. Jarry, 'Une prétendue invasion Perse en Égypte sous Anastase', *BIFAO* 64 (1966), 197–201.

Jeffreys, 'A lacuna' = M. Jeffreys, 'A lacuna in Theophanes' text of Malalas', *Studies in Malalas*, 268–76.

Jeffreys, 'Malalas in Greek' = E. Jeffreys, 'The transmission of Malalas' Chronicle: Malalas in Greek', *Studies in Malalas*, 245–68.

Jeffreys, 'Malalas' sources' = E. Jeffreys, 'Malalas' sources' in *Studies in Malalas*, 167–216.

Jeffreys–Scott, *Malalas*, see Mal., in sources (classical), above.

Jones, *LRE* = A. H. M. Jones, *The Later Roman Empire, 284–602*, 3 vols. (Oxford, 1964).

Jones, *Culture and Society* = C. P. Jones, *Culture and Society in Lucian* (Cambridge, Mass., 1986).

Justi, *IN* = F. Justi, *Iranisches Namenbuch* (Marburg, 1895).

Kaegi, *Conquests* = W. E. Kaegi, *Byzantium and the early Islamic conquests* (Cambridge, 1992).

Kaegi, 'Reconceptualizing' = W. E. Kaegi, 'Reconceptualizing Byzantium's Eastern Frontiers in the Seventh Century', *Shifting Frontiers*, 83–92.

Kaegi, 'Two notes on Heraclius' = W. E. Kaegi, 'Two notes on Heraclius', *REB* 37 (1979), 221–7.

Kaegi, *Unrest* = W. E. Kaegi, *Byzantine Military Unrest. An interpretation* (Amsterdam, 1981).

Kawar, 'Ghassan and Byzantium' = I. Kawar, 'Ghassan and Byzantium: A new *terminus a quo*', *Der Islam* 33 (1955), 232–55.

Kawar, 'The Arabs in the Peace Treaty' = I. Kawar, 'The Arabs in the Peace Treaty of A.D. 561', *Arabica* 3 (1956), 181–213 (= *BSO* VII).

Kawar, 'The last days of Salîh' = I. Kawar, 'The Last Days of Salîh', *Arabica* 5 (1958), 145–58.

Kazanski, 'Contribution' = M. Kazanski, 'Contribution à l'histoire de la défense de la frontière pontique au bas-empire', *TM* 11 (1991), 487–526.

Kazhdan, 'The notion' = A. Kazhdan, 'The notion of Byzantine diplomacy', *Byzantine Diplomacy*, 3–21.

Keegan, *Face of Battle* = J. Keegan, *The Face of Battle* (London, 1976).

Kelly, 'Later Roman bureaucracy' = C. Kelly, 'Later Roman bureaucracy: going through the files' in *Literacy and Power*, edd. G. Woolf and A. Bowman (Cambridge, 1994), 161–76.

Kennedy–Riley, *Desert Frontier* = D. Kennedy and D. Riley, *Rome's Desert Frontier from the air* (London, 1990).

King, 'The role of gold' = C. E. King, 'The role of gold in the later third century A.D.', *Rivista italiana di numismatica e scienze affini* 95 (1993), 439–51.

Kirchner, *Bemerkungen* = K. Kirchner, *Bemerkungen zu Prokops Darstellung der Perserkriege des Anastasios, Justin und Justinian von 502 bis 532* (Wismar, 1887).

Kister, 'The Campaign of Huluban' = M. J. Kister, 'The campaign of Hulubān — A new light on the expedition of Abraha', *Muséon* 78 (1965), 425–36 (repr. in *Studies in Jāhiliyya and Early Islam* [London, 1980], IV).

Koder, 'Climatic Change' = J. Koder, 'Climatic Change in the fifth and sixth centuries?' in *The Sixth Century. End or Beginning?*, edd. E. Jeffreys and P. Allen (Brisbane, 1996), 270–85.

Kugener, 'La compilation' = M. A. Kugener, 'La compilation historique de Pseudo-Zacharie le rhéteur', *ROC* 5 (1900), 201–4.

Labourt, *Christianisme* = J. Labourt, *Le Christianisme dans l'empire Perse sous la dynastie Sassanide* (Paris, 1904).

Lamma, 'La politica' = P. Lamma, 'La politica dell'imperatore Anastasio I', *Rivista Storica Italiana*, ser.6 vol.5 (1940), 167–91.

Lane Fox, *Pagans and Christians* = R. Lane Fox, *Pagans and Christians* (Harmondsworth, 1986).

Lang, 'Iran, Armenia and Georgia' = D. M. Lang, 'Iran, Armenia and Georgia', *CHIr* III.1, 505–36.

Lauffray, *Halabiyya* = J. Lauffray, *Halabiyya-Zenobia, place forte du limes oriental et la haute-Mésopotamie au VI⁰ siècle* (Paris, 1983).

Leclainche, 'Crises économiques' = H. Leclainche, 'Crises économiques à Édesse (494–506) d'après la chronique du pseudo-Josué le Stylite', *Pallas* 27 (1980), 89–100.

Lee, 'Embassies' = A. D. Lee, 'Embassies as evidence for the movement of military intelligence between the Roman and Sasanian Empires', *DRBE*, 455–61.

Lee, 'Evagrius' = A. D. Lee, 'Evagrius, Paul of Nisibis and the problem of loyalties in the Mid-Sixth Century', *JEH* 44 (1993), 569–85.

Lee, *Information* = A. D. Lee, *Information and Frontiers: Roman Foreign Relations in Late Antiquity* (Cambridge, 1993).

Lepper, *Trajan's Parthian War* = F. Lepper, *Trajan's Parthian War* (Oxford, 1948).

Leriche, 'Techniques' = P. Leriche, 'Techniques de guerre sassanides et romaines à Doura-Europos', *ARB*, 83–100.

Letsios, *Erythra Thalassa* = D. G. Letsios, *Βυζάντιο και Ερυθρά Θάλασσα. Σχέσεις με τη Νουβία, Αιθιοπία και Νότια Αραβία ως την Αραβική κατάκτηση* (Athens, 1988).

Letsios, 'The case of Amorkesos' = D. G. Letsios, 'The case of Amorkesos and the question of Roman *foederati* in Arabia in the Vth century' in *L'Arabie préislamique et son environnement historique et culturel*, ed. T. Fahd (Leiden, 1989), 525–38.

Liebeschuetz, 'Defences' = W. Liebeschuetz, 'The defences of Syria in the sixth century', *Studien zu den Militärgrenzen Roms II*, ed. C. B. Rüger (Cologne, 1977), 487–99.

Lieu, 'Captives' = S. N. C. Lieu, 'Captives, Refugees and Exiles: A study of cross-frontier civilian movements and contacts between Rome and Persia from Valerian to Jovian', *DRBE*, 475–505.

van Liere and Lauffray, 'Nouvelle prospection' = W. J. van Liere and J. Lauffray, 'Nouvelle prospection archéologique dans la haute Jezireh syrienne', *AnnArchSyr* 4–5 (1954–5), 129–48.

Lightfoot, *Eastern frontier* = C. Lightfoot, *The Eastern frontier of the Roman Empire with special reference to the reign of Constantius II*, D. Phil. thesis (Oxford, 1982).

Lippold, 'Hephthalitai' = A. Lippold, 'Hephthalitai', *RE* supp. XIV (1974), 127–37.

Litsas, *Choricius* = F. K. Litsas, *Choricius of Gaza: An Approach to his Work*, diss. (Chicago, 1980).

Lordkipanidse–Brakmann, 'Iberia II' = O. Lordkipanidse and H. Brakmann, 'Iberia II', *RAC* 129 (1994), 12–106.

Loundine, 'Sur les rapports' = A. G. Loundine, 'Sur les rapports entre l'Éthiopie et le Himyar du VIᵉ siècle', *Studi Etiopici*, 313–20.

Lukonin, 'Taxes and trade' = V. G. Lukonin, 'Political, social and administrative institutions: Taxes and trade', *CHIr* III.2, 681–746.

Luther, *Die syrische Chronik* = A. Luther, *Die syrische Chronik des Josua Stylites* (Berlin, 1997).

Luttwak, *Grand Strategy* = E. Luttwak, *The Grand Strategy of the Roman Empire* (London, 1976).

McCormick, *Eternal Victory* = M. McCormick, *Eternal Victory. Triumphal rulership in late antiquity, Byzantium, and the early medieval West* (Cambridge, 1986).

MacDonald, 'The seasons and transhumance' = M. C. A. MacDonald, 'The seasons and transhumance in the Safaitic Inscriptions', *JRAS* n.s. 2 (1992), 1–11.

MacDonald, 'Nomads and the Hawran' = M. C. A. MacDonald, 'Nomads and the Hawrān in the late Hellenistic and Roman period. A reassessment of the epigraphic evidence', *Syria* 70 (1993), 303–413.

MacMullen, 'How big was the Roman army?' = R. MacMullen, 'How big was the Roman army?', *Klio* 62 (1980), 451–60.

Maas, *John Lydus* = M. Maas, *John Lydus and the Roman Past: Antiquarianism and politics in the age of Justinian* (London, 1992).

Macler, 'Les apoçalypses', = F. Macler, 'Les apocalypses apocryphes de Daniel', *RHR* 33 (1896), 288–319.

Maenchen-Helfen, *Huns* = O. J. Maenchen-Helfen, *The World of the Huns* (Berkeley, 1973).

de' Maffei, 'Fortificazioni' = F. de' Maffei, 'Fortificazioni di Giustiniano sul limes orientale: monumenti e fonti', *The Seventeenth International Byzantine Congress — Major Papers* (New York, 1986), 237–78.

Magdalino, 'The history of the future' = P. Magdalino, 'The history of the future and its uses: prophecy, policy and propaganda' in *The Making of Byzantine History. Studies dedicated to D.M. Nicol*, edd. R. Beaton and C. Roueché (Aldershot, 1993), 3–34.

Mango, *Art* = C. Mango, *The Art of the Byzantine Empire, 312–1453* (Toronto, 1986).

Mango, *Byzantium* = C. Mango, *Byzantium. The Empire of the New Rome* (London, 1980).

Mango, 'Inscriptions' = C. and M. Mango, 'Inscriptions de la Mésopotamie du nord', *TM* 11 (1991), 465–71.

Mango–Bell, *Churches* = G. Bell, *The Churches and Monasteries of the Tur 'Abdin*, with an introduction and notes by M. Mundell Mango (London, 1982).

Mango–Scott, *Theophanes*, see Theoph., in sources (classical), above.

Marcus, 'The Armenian life' = R. Marcus, 'The Armenian life of Marutha of Maipherkat', *HThR* 25 (1932), 47–71.

Maricq, 'Classica et Medievalia' = A. Maricq, edd. J. Pirenne and P. Devos, 'Classica et Medievalia', *Syria* 39 (1962), 88–105.

Maricq, '*Res Gestae*' = A. Maricq, '*Res Gestae Divi Saporis*', *Syria* 35 (1958), 295–360.

Markwart, *Südarmenien* = J. Markwart, *Südarmenien und die Tigrisquellen* (Vienna, 1930).

Marquart, *Eranšahr* = J. Marquart, 'Ērānšāhr nach der Geographie des Ps. Moses Xorenacʻi', *Abhandlungen der königlichen Gesellschaft der Wissenschaften zu Göttingen, Phil.-Hist. Klasse, N.F.*, Band III, no.2 (Berlin, 1901).

Marsden, *Artillery* = E. W. Marsden, *Greek and Roman Artillery*, 2 vols. (Oxford, 1969–71).

Martin-Hisard, 'Le roi géorgien' = B. Martin-Hisard, 'Le roi géorgien Vaxtʻang Gorgasal' in B. Guillemain, ed., *Temps, Mémoire, Tradition au Moyen-Age* (Aix-en-Provence, 1983), 207–42.

Maspero, '*Foederati*' = J. Maspero, 'Φοιδεράτοι et Στρατιῶται dans l'armée byzantine au VIe siècle', *BZ* 21 (1912), 97–109.

Maspero, *Organisation* = J. Maspero, *Organisation militaire de l'Egypte byzantine* (Paris, 1912).

Matthews, *Ammianus* = J. F. Matthews, *The Roman Empire of Ammianus* (London, 1989).

Mayerson, 'A note' = P. Mayerson, 'A note on Iotabê and several other islands in the Red Sea', *BASOR* 298 (1995), 33–6.

Mayerson, *Monks, Martyrs* = P. Mayerson, *Monks, Martyrs, Soldiers and Saracens* (Jerusalem, 1994).

Mayerson, 'Saracens and Romans' = P. Mayerson, 'Saracens and Romans: Micro-macro relationships', *BASOR* 274 (1989), 71–9; repr. in *Monks, Martyrs*, no.32.

Mayerson, 'The port of Clysma' = P. Mayerson, 'The port of Clysma (Suez) in transition from Roman to Arab rule', *JNES* 55 (1996), 119–26.

Mayerson, 'The Saracens and the *limes*' = P. Mayerson, 'The Saracens and the *limes*', *BASOR* 262 (1986), 35–47; repr. in *Monks, Martyrs*, no.25.

Merten, *De bello* = E. Merten, 'De bello Persico ab Anastasio gesto', *Commentationes Philologae Ienenses* VII.2 (Leipzig, 1906).

Merriam-Webster = *Merriam-Webster's Collegiate Dictionary*, tenth edition (Springfield, Mass., 1995).

Millar, *Near East* = F. Millar, *The Roman Near East: 37 B.C. – A.D. 337*, (London and Cambridge, Mass., 1993).

Mitchell, *Anatolia* = S. Mitchell, *Anatolia. Land, Men, and Gods in Asia Minor* I, 2 vols. (Oxford, 1993).

Mitford, 'Bilotti's Excavations' = T. B. Mitford, 'Bilotti's Excavations at
    Satala', *AnatSt* 24 (1974), 221–44.
Mitford, 'Some inscriptions' = T. B. Mitford, 'Some inscriptions from the
    Cappadocian *limes*', *JRS* 64 (1974), 160–75.
Miyakawa–Kollautz, 'Abdelai' = H. Miyakawa and A. Kollautz, 'Abdelai',
    Reallexikon der Byzantinistik, ed. P. Wirth, Reihe A, Band 1, Hefte 2–3,
    88–126.
Moberg, *Book*, see sources (non-classical), above.
Moorhead, *Justinian* = J. Moorhead, *Justinian* (London, 1994).
Müller, 'Heer' = A. Müller, 'Das Heer Justinians (nach Procop und Agathias)',
    Philologus 71 (1912), 101–38.
Müller, 'Himyar' = W. W. Müller, 'Himyar', *RAC* 114–115 (1989), 303–31.
Musil, *Middle Euphrates* = A. Musil, *The Middle Euphrates. A Topographical
    Itinerary* (New York, 1927).
Napoli, 'Ultimes fortifications' = J. Napoli, 'Ultimes fortifications du *limes*',
    ARB, 67–76.
Nicholson, 'Golden Age' = O. Nicholson, 'Golden Age and the End of the
    World: Myths of Mediterranean Life from Lactantius to Joshua the Stylite'
    in *The Medieval Mediterranean: Cross-cultural contacts*, edd. M. J. Chiat
    and K. L. Reyerson (St Cloud, Minnesota, 1988), 11–18.
Nieskens, 'Vers le Zérotage' = P. J. M. Nieskens, 'Vers le Zérotage Définitif
    des Ères Préislamiques en Arabie du Sud Antique', *Arabian Studies*, 97–
    103.
Nöldeke, *Ghassanischen Fürsten* = T. Nöldeke, *Die Ghassānischen Fürsten
    aus dem Hause Gafna's* (Berlin, 1887).
Nöldeke–Bogdanov, *Iranian National Epic* = T. Nöldeke, tr. L. Bogdanov, *The
    Iranian National Epic or The Shahnamah* (Bombay, 1930).
Nöldeke, *Tabari* = T. Nöldeke, *Geschichte der Perser und Araber zur Zeit der
    Sasaniden* (Leiden, 1879, repr. 1971).
Nöldeke, 'Zwei Völker' = T. Nöldeke, 'Zwei Völker Vorderasiens', *ZDMG* 33
    (1879), 157–66.
Oikonomides, 'Silk trade' = N. Oikonomides, 'Silk trade and production in
    Byzantium from the sixth to the ninth century: the seals of kommerkiarioi',
    DOP 40 (1986), 33–53.
Olinder, *Kings of Kinda* = G. Olinder, *The Kings of Kinda of the family of Ākil
    Al-Murār* (Lund, 1927).
Oliverio, *Il decreto* = G. Oliverio, *Il decreto di Anastasio I su l'ordinamento
    politico-militare della Cirenaica* (Bergamo, 1936).
Oman, *Art of War* = Sir C. Oman, *A History of the Art of War in the Middle
    Ages*, second edition, vol.1 (London, 1924).
Palmer, *Monk and Mason* = A. Palmer, *Monk and Mason on the Tigris Frontier
    — The Early History of Tur 'Abdin* (Cambridge, 1990).

Palmer, *Seventh Century* = A. Palmer, with S. Brock and R. Hoyland, *The Seventh Century in the West-Syrian Chronicles* (Liverpool, 1993).

Palmer, 'Who wrote the chronicle of Joshua?' = A. Palmer, 'Who wrote the chronicle of Joshua the Stylite?' in *Lingua Restituta Orientalis — Festgabe für Julius Assfalg*, edd. R. Schulz and M. Görg, Ägypten und Altes Testament 20 (Wiesbaden, 1990), 273–9.

Paret, 'Note sur un passage de Malalas' = R. Paret, 'Note sur un passage de Malalas concernant les phylarques arabes', *Arabica* 5 (1958), 251–62.

Parker, 'Retrospective on the Arabian frontier' = S. T. Parker, 'Retrospective on the Arabian frontier after a decade of research', *DRBE*, 633–60.

Parker, 'Two books' = S. T. Parker, 'Two books on the eastern Roman frontier: nomads and other security threats', *JRA* 5 (1992), 467–72.

Patlagean, 'L'impôt' = E. Patlagean, 'L'impôt payé par les soldats au VIe s.' in *Armées et fiscalité dans le monde antique*, Colloques nationaux du CNRS (Paris, 1977).

Peeters, 'Sainte Sousanik' = P. Peeters, 'Sainte Sousanik, Martyre en Arméno-Géorgie', *AB* 53 (1935), 5–48, 245–307.

Pekáry, 'Le tribut' = T. Pekáry, 'Le tribut aux Perses et les finances de Philippe l'Arabe', *Syria* 38 (1961), 275–83.

Peters, 'Byzantium and the Arabs' = F. E. Peters, 'Byzantium and the Arabs of Syria', *AnnArchSyr* 27–8 (1977–8), 97–113.

Petersen, 'A Roman prefect' = H. Petersen, 'A Roman prefect in Osrhoene', *TAPA* 107 (1977), 265–82.

Pieler, 'L'aspect politique' = P. E. Pieler, 'L'aspect politique et juridique de l'adoption de Chosroès proposée par les Perses à Justin', *Revue international des droits de l'antiquité*, 3ème série, 19 (1972), 399–433.

Pigulewskaja, *Byzanz* = N. Pigulewskaja, *Byzanz auf den Wegen nach Indien* (Berlin, 1969).

Pigulewskaja, 'Theophanes' Chronographia' = N. Pigulewskaja, 'Theophanes' Chronographia and the Syrian Chronicles', *JÖBG* 16 (1967), 55–60.

Pigulewskaja, *Villes* = N. Pigulewskaja, *Les villes de l'état iranien aux époques parthe et sassanide* (Paris, 1963).

Poidebard, *Trace* = A. Poidebard, *La trace de Rome dans le désert de Syrie. Le Limes de Trajan à la Conquête Arabe*, 2 vols. (Paris, 1934).

Potter, *Prophecy and history* = D. S. Potter, *Prophecy and history in the crisis of the Roman Empire: A historical commentary on the thirteenth Sibylline Oracle* (Oxford, 1990).

Potts, *Arabian Gulf* = D. T. Potts, *The Arabian Gulf in Antiquity*, 2 vols. (Oxford, 1990).

Pugliese Carratelli, 'La Persia' = G. Pugliese Carratelli, 'La Persia dei Sasanidi nella storiografia Romana da Ammiano a Procopio', *Accademia Nazionale dei Lincei, Quaderno N. 160 – Atti del convegno internazionale sul tema 'La Persia nel medioevo'* (Rome, 1971), 597–604.

Rabello, *Giustiniano* = A. M. Rabello, *Giustiniano, Ebrei e Samaritani alla luce delle fonti storico-letterarie, ecclesiastiche e giuridiche*, vol.1 (Milan, 1987).

Ramsay, 'The speed' = W. Ramsay, 'The speed of the Roman imperial post', *JRS* 15 (1925), 60–74.

Rance, *Tactics* = P. Rance, *Tactics and Tactica in the sixth century*, Ph.D. thesis (St Andrews, 1993).

Ravegnani, *Soldati* = G. Ravegnani, *Soldati di Bisanzio in età Giustinianea* (Rome, 1988).

Rothstein, *Lahmiden* = G. Rothstein, *Die Dynastie der Lahmiden in al-Hîra – Ein Versuch zur arabisch-persischen Geschichte zur Zeit der Sasaniden* (Berlin, 1899).

Rubin, *PvK* = B. Rubin, 'Prokopios von Kaisareia'', *RE* 23.1 (1957), 273–599.

Rubin, *ZI* = B. Rubin, *Das Zeitalter Iustinians*, Band I (Berlin, 1960).

Rubin, 'Byzantium' = Z. Rubin, 'Byzantium and Southern Arabia', *EFRE*, 383–420.

Rubin, 'Dilemma' = Z. Rubin, 'The Mediterranean and the dilemma of the Roman Empire in late antiquity', *Mediterranean Historical Review* 1 (1986), 13–62.

Rubin, 'Diplomacy' = Z. Rubin, 'Diplomacy and War in the relations between Byzantium and the Sassanids in the fifth century A.D.', *DRBE*, 677–95.

Rubin, 'The Reforms' = Z. Rubin, 'The Reforms of Khusro Anūshirwān', *SRA*, 227–97.

Runciman, *Fall of Constantinople* = S. Runciman, *The Fall of Constantinople* (Cambridge, 1965).

Russell, *Zoroastrianism* = J. Russell, *Zoroastrianism in Armenia* (Cambridge, Mass., 1987).

Ryckmans, 'A Confrontation' = J. Ryckmans, 'A Confrontation of the Main Hagiographic Accounts of the Najrān Persecution', *Arabian Studies*, 113–33.

Ryckmans, *La persécution* = J. Ryckmans, *La persécution des Chrétiens himyarites au sixième siècle* (Istanbul, 1956).

Ryckmans, 'Les rapports' = J. Ryckmans, 'Les rapports de dépendance entre les récits hagiographiques relatifs à la persécution des Himyarites', *Muséon* 100 (1987), 297–305.

Sako, *L'hiérarchie* = L. Sako, *Le Rôle de l'hiérarchie syriaque orientale dans les rapports diplomatiques entre la Perse et Byzance aux Ve–VIIe siècles* (Paris, 1986).

Salles, 'Fines Indiae' = J.-F. Salles, 'Fines Indiae — Ardh el-Hind', *RBAE*, 165–87.

Sartre, *Bostra* = M. Sartre, *Bostra – des origines à l'Islam*, (Paris, 1985).

Sartre, 'Deux phylarques' = M. Sartre, 'Deux phylarques arabes dans l'Arabie byzantine', *Muséon* 106 (1993), 145–53.

Sartre, *IGLS XIII* = M. Sartre, *IGLS XIII* (Paris, 1982).

Sartre, *Trois études* = M. Sartre, *Trois études sur l'Arabie romaine et byzantine* (Brussels, 1982).

Schippmann, *Grundzüge* = K. Schippmann, *Grundzüge der Geschichte des Sasanidischen Reiches* (Darmstadt, 1990).

Scott, 'Diplomacy' = R. Scott, 'Diplomacy in the sixth century: the evidence of John Malalas', in *Byzantine Diplomacy*, 159–65.

Scott, 'Justinian's Coinage' = R. Scott, 'Justinian's Coinage and Easter Reforms and the date of the *Secret History*', *BMGS* 11 (1987), 215–221.

Scott, 'Malalas and his contemporaries' = R. Scott, 'Malalas and his contemporaries', *Studies in Malalas*, 67–85.

Segal, *Edessa* = J. B. Segal, *Edessa, 'The blessed city'* (Oxford, 1970).

Segal, 'Mesopotamian communities' = J. B. Segal, 'Mesopotamian communities from Julian to the rise of Islam', *ProcBrAc* 41 (1955), 109–39.

Seibt, 'Westgeorgien' = W. Seibt, 'Westgeorgien (Egrisi, Lazica) in frühchristlicher Zeit' in *Die Schwarzmeerküste in der Spätantike und im frühen Mittelalter*, edd. R. Pillinger, A. Pülz and H. Vetters (Vienna, 1992), 137–44.

Seyrig, 'Antiquités syriennes' = H. Seyrig, 'Antiquités syriennes', *Syria* 27 (1950), 229–52.

Shahbazi, 'Army' = A. Sh. Shahbazi, art. on 'Army: 5. The Sasanian Period', *EIr* II (1987), 496–9.

Shahîd, 'An evaluation' = I. Shahîd, 'Theodor Nöldeke's "Geschichte der Perser und Araber zur Zeit der Sasaniden": an evaluation', *International Journal of Middle East Studies* 8 (1977), 117–22.

Shahîd, *BAFIC* = I. Shahîd, *Byzantium and the Arabs in the fifth century* (Washington D.C., 1989).

Shahîd, *BASIC* I = I. Shahîd, *Byzantium and the Arabs in the sixth century*, vol.1 (Washington D.C., 1995).

Shahîd, 'Byzantino-Arabica' = I. Shahîd, 'Byzantino-Arabica: the conference of Ramla, A.D. 524', *JNES* 23 (1964), 115–31 (= *BSO* VI).

Shahîd, 'Byzantium and Kinda' = I. Shahîd, 'Byzantium and Kinda', *BZ* 53 (1960), 57–73 (= *BSO* IV).

Shahîd, 'Byzantium in southern Arabia' = I. Shahîd, 'Byzantium in Southern Arabia', *DOP* 33 (1979), 25–94 (= *BSO* IX).

Shahîd, 'Further reflections' = I. Shahîd, 'Further reflections on the Sources for the Martyrs of Najrān', *Arabian Studies*, 161–72.

Shahîd, 'Ghassanid and Umayyad Structures' = I. Shahîd, 'Ghassānid and Umayyad Structures: A case of *Byzance après Byzance*' in *La Syrie de Byzance à l'Islam. VIIe – VIIIe siècles*, edd. P. Canivet and J.-P. Rey-Coquais (Damascus, 1992), 299–307.

Shahîd, 'Procopius and Arethas' = I. Shahîd, 'Procopius and Arethas', *BZ* 50 (1957), 39–67, 362–82 (= *BSO*, I–II).

Shahîd, 'Procopius and Arethas again' = I. Shahîd, 'Procopius and Arethas again', *Byzantion* 41 (1971), 313–38.

Shahîd, 'Procopius and Kinda' = I. Shahîd, 'Procopius and Kinda', *BZ* 53 (1960), 74–8 (= *BSO*, V).

Shahîd, *RA* = I. Shahîd, *Rome and the Arabs* (Washington D.C., 1984).

Shahîd, 'The martyrs' = I. Shahîd, 'The martyrs of Najrān: further reflections', *Muséon* 103 (1990), 151–3.

Shitomi, 'De la chronologie' = Y. Shitomi, 'De la chronologie de la persécution de Našrān', *Orient* 26 (1990), 27–42.

Shitomi, 'Note' = Y. Shitomi, 'Note sur le Martyrium Arethae §20: Date de la persécution de Našrān', *Muséon* 100 (1987), 315–21.

Sinclair, *Eastern Turkey* = T. A. Sinclair, *Eastern Turkey: an architectural and archaeological survey*, 4 vols. (London, 1987–90).

Smith, 'Events' = S. Smith, 'Events in Arabia in the sixth century A.D.', *BSOAS* 16 (1954), 425–68.

Solari, 'La politica' = A. Solari, 'La politica estera orientale durante l'impero di Giustino I', *Atti della Accademia Nazionale dei Lincei – Rendiconti*, vol.3, ser.8 (1948), 350–9.

Sotiriadis, 'Zur Kritik' = G. Sotiriadis, 'Zur Kritik des Johannes von Antiochia', *Jahrbücher für Classische Philologie* supp.XVI (1888), 1–126.

Soyter, 'Glaubwürdigkeit' = G. Soyter, 'Die Glaubwürdigkeit des Geschichts-schreibers Prokopios von Kaisarea', *BZ* 44 (1951), 541–5.

Starcky–Gawlikowski, *Palmyre* = J. Starcky, rev. M. Gawlikowski, *Palmyre* (Paris, 1985).

Stein I, II = E. Stein, *Histoire du Bas-Empire*, vol.1 (Paris, 1959), vol.2, ed. J.-R. Palanque (Paris-Brussels-Amsterdam, 1949).

Synelli, *Diplomatikes Skheseis* = K. Synelli, Οι διπλωματικές σχέσεις Βυζαντίου και Περσίας έως τον στ΄ αιώνα (Athens, 1986).

Tate, 'Le problème' = G. Tate, 'Le problème de la défense et du peuplement de la steppe et du désert, dans le nord de la Syrie, entre la chute de Palmyre et le règne de Justinien', *AnnArchSyr* 42 (1996), 331–7.

Teall, 'The barbarians in Justinian's armies' = J. L. Teall, 'The barbarians in Justinian's armies', *Speculum* 40 (1965), 294–322.

Thierry, 'Monuments chrétiens' = M. Thierry, 'Monuments chrétiens inédits de Haute-Mésopotamie', *Syria* 70 (1993), 179–204.

Thomson, *Rewriting Caucasian History* = R. W. Thomson, *Rewriting Caucasian History. The Medieval Armenian Adaptation of the Georgian Chronicles. The Original Georgian Texts and The Armenian Adaptation* (Oxford, 1996).

Toumanoff, 'Armenia and Georgia' = C. Toumanoff, 'Armenia and Georgia', chapter XIV in *CMH* IV.

Toumanoff, 'Caucasia and Byzantium' = C. Toumanoff, 'Caucasia and Byzantium', *Traditio* 27 (1971), 111–58.

Toumanoff, 'Christian Caucasia' = C. Toumanoff, 'Christian Caucasia between Byzantium and Iran: new light from old sources', *Traditio* 10 (1954), 109–189.

Toumanoff, review of Stein II = C. Toumanoff, review of E. Stein, *Histoire du Bas-Empire*, vol.2, *Traditio* 7 (1949–51), 481–90.

Toumanoff, *Studies* = C. Toumanoff, *Studies in Christian Caucasian History* (Georgetown, 1963).

Treadgold, *Army* = W. Treadgold, *Byzantium and Its Army, 284–1081* (Stanford, 1995).

Trimingham, *Christianity* = J. Trimingham, *Christianity among the Arabs in Pre-islamic times* (London, 1979).

Trombley 'The decline' = F. R. Trombley, 'The Decline of the Seventh-Century Town: the Exception of Euchaita' in *Byzantine Studies in Honor of Milton V. Anastos*, ed. S. Vryonis, Byzantina kai Metabyzantina 4 (Malibu, 1985), 65–90.

Trombley, 'War and Society' = F. R. Trombley, 'War and Society in Rural Syria c.502–613 A.D.: Observations on the Epigraphy', *BMGS* (forthcoming).

Trombley–Watt, *Chonicle*, see Josh. Styl., in sources (non-classical), above.

Turtledove, 'True size' = H. Turtledove, 'The true size of a post-Justiniac army', *BS/EB* 10 (1983), 216–22.

Vasiliev, *Justin I* = A. A. Vasiliev, *Justin I: An introduction to the Epoch of Justinian the Great* (Cambridge, Mass., 1950).

Veh, *Perserkriege* = O. Veh, *Prokop – Perserkriege*, text, tr. and comm. (Munich, 1970).

Warmington, 'Objectives' = B. H. Warmington, 'Objectives and Strategy in the Persian war of Constantius II' in *Limes. Akten des XI Internationalen Limeskongresses*, ed. J. Futz (Budapest, 1977), 509–20.

Wheeler, 'Methodological Limits' = E. L. Wheeler, 'Methodological Limits and the Mirage of Roman Strategy', *Journal of Military History* 57 (1993), 7–41, 215–40.

Wheeler, 'Rethinking the Upper Euphrates frontier' = E. L. Wheeler, 'Rethinking the Upper Euphrates Frontier: where was the western border of Armenia?', *Roman Frontier Studies 1989*, edd. V. A. Maxfield and M. J. Dobson (Exeter, 1991).

Whitby, 'Arzanene' = M. Whitby, 'Arzanene in the late sixth century' in *Armies and Frontiers in Roman and Byzantine Anatolia*, ed. S. Mitchell, BAR International Series 156 (Oxford, 1983), 205–17.

Whitby, 'Dara' = M. Whitby, 'Procopius' description of Dara (*Buildings* II.1–3)', *DRBE*, 737–83.

Whitby, 'Development' = M. Whitby, 'Procopius and the development of Roman defence in Upper Mesopotamia', *DRBE*, 717–35.

Whitby, *History*, see Theoph. Sim., in sources (classical), above.

Whitby, 'Martyropolis' = M. Whitby, 'Procopius' description of Martyropolis', *Byzantinoslavica* 45 (1984), 177–82.

Whitby, *Maurice* = M. Whitby, *The Emperor Maurice and his historian: Theophylact Simocatta on Persian and Balkan warfare* (Oxford, 1988).

Whitby, 'Notes' = M. Whitby, 'Notes on some Justinianic constructions', *Byzantinisch-neugriechische Jahrbücher* 23 (1987), 89–112.

Whitby, 'Persian king' = M. Whitby, 'The Persian king at war', *RBAE*, 227–63.

Whitby, 'Recruitment' = M. Whitby, 'Recruitment in Roman Armies from Justinian to Heraclius (c.565–615)', *SRA*, 61–124.

Whitby, 'Sangarius Bridge' = M. Whitby, 'The Sangarius bridge and Procopius', *JHS* 105 (1985), 129–48.

Whitby, 'On the Omission' = Mary Whitby, 'On the Omission of a Ceremony in mid-sixth century Constantinople', *Historia* 36 (1987), 462–88.

Whitehouse–Williamson, 'Sasanian Maritime trade' = D. Whitehouse and A. Williamson, 'Sasanian Maritime trade', *Iran* 11 (1973), 29–49.

Whittaker, *Frontiers* = C. R. Whittaker, *Frontiers of the Roman Empire* (London, 1994).

Whittow, 'Rome and the Jafnids' = M. Whittow, 'Rome and the Jafnids: Writing the History of a Sixth-Century Tribal Dynasty', *JRA* 11 (1998).

Whittow, 'Ruling the late Roman city' = M. Whittow, 'Ruling the late Roman and Byzantine city: a continuous history', *Past and Present* 129 (1990), 3–29.

Widengren, 'Sources' = G. Widengren, 'Sources of Parthian and Sasanian History', *CHIr* III.2, 1261–83.

Wiessner, *Ruinenstätten* = G. Wiessner, *Nordmesopotamische Ruinenstätten* (Wiesbaden, 1980).

Winkler, 'Die Samariter' = S. Winkler, 'Die Samariter in den Jahren 529–530', *Klio* 43–5 (1965), 435–57.

Winter, *Friedensverträge* = E. Winter, *Die sāsānidisch-römischen Friedensverträge des 3 Jahrhunderts n. Chr. — ein Beitrag zum Verständnis der außenpolitischen Beziehungen zwischen den beiden Großmächten* (Frankfurt a.M., 1988).

Winter, 'Handel und Wirtschaft' = E. Winter, 'Handel und Wirtschaft in Sasanidisch-(Ost-)Römischen Verträgen und Abkommen', *Münstersche Beiträge zur Antiken Handelsgeschichte*, Bd. VI.2 (1987), 46–74.

Winter, 'On the regulation' = E. Winter, 'On the regulation of the eastern frontier of the Roman empire in 298', *EFRE*, 555–71.

Wirth, 'Anastasius, Christen und Perser' = G. Wirth, 'Anastasius, Christen und Perser', *JbAChr* 33 (1990), 81–139.

Witakowski, *Chronicle*, see Ps. Dion. II, in sources (non-classical), above.

Witakowski, 'Chronicles of Edessa' = W. Witakowski, 'Chronicles of Edessa', *Orientalia Suecana* 33–5 (1984–6), 487–98.

Witakowski, 'Malalas in Syriac' = W. Witakowski, 'The transmission of Malalas' Chronicle: Malalas in Syriac', *Studies in Malalas*, 299–310.

Witakowski, *The Syriac Chronicle* = W. Witakowski, *The Syriac Chronicle of Pseudo-Dionysius of Tel-Mahre: a study in the History of Historiography* (Uppsala, 1987).

Woodman, 'From Hannibal to Hitler' = A. J. Woodman, 'From Hannibal to Hitler: the Literature of War', *University of Leeds Review* 26 (1983), 107–24.

Wright, *Short History* = W. Wright, *A Short History of Syriac Literature* (London, 1884).

Yarshater, 'Iranian national history' = E. Yarshater, 'Iranian national history', *CHIr* III.1, 359–477.

Yarshater, 'Mazdakism' = E. Yarshater, 'Mazdakism', *CHIr* III.2, 991–1024.

Yuzbashian, 'Le Caucase' = K. Yuzbashian, 'Le Caucase et les Sassanides', *Caucaso*, 143–64.

Zaehner, 'A Zurvanite Apocalypse II' = R. C. Zaehner, 'A Zurvanite Apocalypse II', *BSOS* 10/3 (1939–42), 606–31.

Ziegler, 'Civic Coins' = R. Ziegler, 'Civic Coins and imperial campaigns', *RAE*, 119–34.

Zuckerman, 'The early Byzantine strongholds' = C. Zuckerman, 'The early Byzantine strongholds in Eastern Pontus', *TM* 11 (1991), 527–53.

Zuckerman, 'The military compendium' = C. Zuckerman, 'The military compendium of Syrianus Magister', *JÖB* 40 (1990), 209–24.

Glossary

actuarius, a military quartermaster, like the *optio* (see below). *LRE* 626.

agens in rebus, an agent of the emperor. *LRE* 578–82, *ODB* 36–7.

assessor, an adviser appointed by a high-ranking official, chiefly concerned with legal matters. *LRE* 500–01; see also p.62 n.9.

astabadh, perhaps the Persian equivalent of the Roman *magister officiorum* (on whom see below), or perhaps a variant of the title *spahbadh* (on which see below). See ch.5 n.86 and Luther, 'Die syrische Chronik', 195 n.361.

bdeashkh, the governor of a frontier province of the Persian empire. See p.176 n.22.

bucellarii, sing. *bucellarius*, élite soldiers in the service of a particular (Roman) general. *LRE* 665–7, *ODB* 316.

bucellatum, the dry baked bread served to Roman soldiers on campaign. *LRE* 628–9, 673–4.

cataphract, an armoured cavalryman on an armoured horse. *ODB* 1114.

centenarion, pl. *centenaria*, a unit of weight (100 Roman lbs.), frequently applied to gold coins. *ODB* 1121.

chiliarch, commander of a thousand men, a loose term.

City prefect, *praefectus urbi*, the official in charge of the imperial capital. *LRE* 692, *ODB* 2144.

comes, pl. *comites*, a Count, a term applied to various imperial officials and to the commander of a *numerus*. *LRE* 104–5, *ODB* 484–5.

comes excubitorum, the official in command of the excubitors (on whom see below).

comes foederatorum, the official in command of the 'federate' (allied) forces. *LRE*, 665.

comes (sacrarum) largitionum, the Count of the Sacred Largess, a high-ranking official in charge of finances. *LRE* 427–9, *ODB* 486.

comes Orientis, the Count of the East, a civilian official. *LRE* 373–4.

comes rei militaris, a military Count. *LRE* 105.

commerciarius, the fiscal official in charge of regulating trade on the frontier. *ODB* 1141.

comitatenses, the Roman field army, more mobile than the *limitanei* (on whom see below). *LRE* 608–10, *ODB* 487.

cubicularius, a palace eunuch who served 'the sacred bedchamber' of the emperor. *LRE* 567–9, *ODB* 1154.

dux, pl. *duces*, a Duke or military commander based in a particular province. *LRE* 609–10, *ODB* 659.

Eran-spahbadh, the commander in chief of the Persian army. Christensen, *L'Iran*, 107 n.3, 130.

excubitor, a member of an élite corps of 300 imperial soldiers. *LRE* 658–9.

foederati, sing. *foederatus*, technically soldiers serving in the Roman army by the terms of a treaty (*foedus*), but in fact scarcely different from *comitatenses* by the sixth century. *LRE* 663–4, *ODB* 794.

illustris, pl. *illustres*, the highest rank of senators. *LRE* 528–30, *ODB* 986–7.

kanarang, the Persian military commander in charge of Abharshahr (the north-eastern frontier of the Persian empire). Christensen, *L'Iran*, 107 n.3.

kleisoura, a mountain pass. *ODB* 1132.

limitanei, the 'frontier forces' of the Roman empire. *LRE* 608–10, *ODB* 1230.

magister militum, 'master of soldiers', a high-ranking general, in command of a large army. *LRE* 608–10, *ODB* 1266–7.

magister militum per Armeniam, the general in charge of the north-eastern frontier. *LRE* 271.

magister militum per Orientem, the general in charge of the eastern frontier.

magister militum per Thracias, the general in charge of the Balkans.

magister militum praesentalis, one of two generals stationed in the capital. *LRE* 124–5.

magister militum vacans, titular holder of the post of *magister militum*. *LRE* 535.

magister officiorum, the 'master of offices', the head of the central civil administration of the empire. *LRE* 368–9, *ODB* 1267.

marzban, the Persian title of a governor of a province. Christensen, *L'Iran*, 136–7 and see ch.3 n.44.

modius, pl. *modii*, a unit of measurement of grain or land. *ODB* 1388.

numerus, a unit of soldiers. *LRE* 659 and see ch.2 p.35.

optio, a military quartermaster. *LRE* 626–7.

patrician, a high-ranking dignity. *LRE* 528, 534, *ODB* 1600.

periodeutes, a priest responsible for tending to Christians in villages and the countryside, dependent on the city bishop. *DACL* 14.369–79.

phylarch, a commander of troops (often Arab) allied to the empire. *LRE* 611, *ODB* 1672.

praepositus (sacri cubiculi), the grand chamberlain of the palace. *LRE* 567–70, *ODB* 1709.

praetorian prefect, an important regional civil functionary. *LRE* 370–2, *ODB* 1710–11.

protector, senior soldier. *LRE* 636–40, *ODB* 1743.

quaestor (sacri palatii), a high-ranking imperial official concerned with legal matters. *LRE* 387, *ODB* 1765–6.

sacellarius, an imperial financial official, often a eunuch. *LRE* 567–8, *ODB* 1828–9.

scholae (palatinae), the corps of guards of the imperial palace. *LRE* 647–8, *ODB* 1851–2.

scholasticus, a title often applied to lawyers. *ODB* 1852.

silentiarius, a high-ranking palace official. *LRE* 571–2, *ODB* 1896.

solidus, pl. *solidi*, a gold coin referred to in Greek as the *nomisma*.

spahbadh, a Persian general. Christensen, *L'Iran*, 131.

stade, a classical unit of measurement of distance equivalent to $^1/_8$ or $^1/_7$ of a Roman mile (1480m.). *ODB* 1373, *OCD*[3] 943.

strategos, the traditional Greek word for a general. *ODB* 1964.

stratiotai, the Greek term for the Latin *comitatenses* (see above).

symmachoi, the Greek term for 'allies', who had previously been known as *foederati*. *LRE* 663–4.

tagma, pl. *tagmata*, a unit of soldiers, the Greek equivalent of a *numerus*. *ODB* 2007.

talent, a weight or unit of currency. *OCD*[3] 1621.

tribune, a term for the commander of a *numerus*. See p.35 n.109.

vir illustris, a man holding the highest dignity of the empire. *LRE* 528–30.

Chronological list of (eastern) Roman emperors (284–641)

The overlapping of the dates of some emperors is due to the existence of several (legitimate) emperors simultaneously at certain times.

Diocletian (284–305)

Galerius (305–11)

Constantine I (306–37)

Constantius II (337–61)

Julian (361–3)

Jovian (363–4)

Valens (364–78)

Theodosius I (379–95)

Arcadius (395–408)

Theodosius II (408–50)

Marcian (450–7)

Leo I (457–74)

Leo II (474)

Zeno (474–5)

Basiliscus (475–6)

Zeno again (476–91)

Anastasius I (491–518)

Justin I (518–27)

Justinian I (527–65)

Justin II (565–78)

Tiberius II (578–82)

Maurice (582–602)

Phocas (602–10)

Heraclius (610–41)

Chronological list of Sasanian kings (220s–628)

Ardashir I (224–40)

Shapur I (240–70)

Hormizd I (270–1)

Bahram I (271–4)

Bahram II (274–93)

Bahram III (293)

Narses (293–302)

Hormizd II (302–9)

Shapur II (309–79)

Ardashir II (379–83)

Shapur III (383–8)

Bahram IV (388–99)

Yazdgerd I (399–420)

Bahram V (420–38)

Yazdgerd II (438–57)

Hormizd III (457–9)

Peroz (459–84)

Balash (484–8)

Kavadh (488–96)

Zamasp (496–8)

Kavadh again (498–531)

Khusro I (531–79)

Hormizd IV (579–90)

Khusro II (590–628)

Index locorum

277

General Index

Abbreviations: n. = nephew, br. = brother, s. = son, bp = bishop, *mag. mil.* = *magister militum.*

A

Abgar, king of Edessa: 106
Abgersaton: 207, 223
Abkhazia: 125n, 128
Aborras, river: *see* Khabur
Abraha, Himyarite king: 211-3, 235, 238-40
Abraham, s. of Euphrasius: 131, 229, 236, 237n
Abrus, phylarch: 204
Abu Karib: 161n, 236n
Abu Ya'fur: 101n, 107
Achaemenids: 11
actuarii: 35
adaeratio: 36n
Addad: *see* Aidug
Adergoudounbades: 90n
Adid: 112n
Adrianople, battle of: 12, 180
Adulis: 228n, 230-1
Aegospotami, battle of: 180n
Aelas: 230, 234
'Afotho Ro"en: 99n
Africa: 34, 38n, 126, 175n, 216, 219-20
Agapius: 69n
Agathias: xiv, 33, 69
Aggel (Ingilene): 81n
Agincourt, battle of: 173, 180n
Aidug: 227, 228n, 240
Aigan: 174-5, 181
Ain-Nameh: 58, 59n
Alans, 126n, 186-7n
Albania: 92n, 122, 134n, 125, 127, 130, 141
Albanians: 45-46, 55, 125
Alexander, envoy: 165, 169n, 190-91, 213
Alexander, senator: 159n
Alexandria (Egypt): 109n, 178n
Alexandria (Syria): 107n
Alypius, *dux*: *see* Olympius
Amasea: 160
Ambar Tchai, river: 110n

Ambazuces: 129-30
Ambrus ('Amr), br. of Qays: 236
Amerdach: 207n
Amida
position on frontier: 21
inscriptions at: 71n
described: 83
Persian siege of 359: 55, 83n, 85, 86n, 88, 89n, 90-91
Persian siege of 502-3: 33-4, 40, 61, 63, 66-8, 74-5, 83-94, 119
Roman siege of 504: 74, 97-9, 110-12, 114-15, 119
mentioned 8n, 73, 75, 79n, 84-94, 96-8, 100, 107, 109-15, 118-19, 150, 151n, 158-9, 174n, 197n, 207, 209n, 210
Ammianus Marcellinus: 10n, 41, 52, 54-55, 60n, 90n, 110n, 180, 233
Ammodius: 98n, 116, 117n, 170, 171n, 176-9, 190n
Amorcesus: *see* Imru' al-Qays
'Amr, nephew of al-Mundhir: 239
'Amr ibn Matta: 69n
Anastasian War: 1, 3, 42, 61, 63-7, 73-119, 121, 129, 136, 152n, 159, 180n, 216
Anastasius, emperor
opposition to Chalcedon: 2
asked by Kavadh for money: 7
provides funds for Persians: 8n
refuses Kavadh's requests: 15-16, 18, 76-7
settles the Heruls: 31
sends an army to the East: 33, 94
limits payments to *duces*: 35n
his concern for the army: 39
rebuilding work of: 40-41, 79n
his war against the Isaurians: 50
hears of Kavadh's invasion: 78n
sends reinforcements to the east: 108
negotiates with the Persians: 115-18
builds Dara: 121n
starts reduction of Tzani: 129

284